For Liz, Richard, Katherine and Vera
– Sorry again!

European Labour Markets:
analysis and policy

Nick Adnett

Longman
London and New York

Addison Wesley Longman Limited,
Edinburgh Gate,
Harlow, Essex CM20 2JE, England
and Associated Companies throughout the world.

Published in the United States of America
by Addison Wesley Longman Publishing, New York

First published 1996

ISBN 0 582 24885–X PPR

British Library Cataloguing-in-Publication Data

A catalogue record for this book is
available from the British Library

Library of Congress Cataloging-in-Publication Data

Adnett, Nick.
  European labour markets : analysis and policy / Nick Adnett.
    p. cm.
  Includes bibliographical references and index.
  ISBN 0–582–24885–X
  1. Manpower policy—European Union countries. 2. Labor market—
European Union countries. I. Title.
HD5713.6.E85A33 1996   95–26702
331.1′094—dc20   CIP

Set by 8 in 10/12 Times New Roman

Produced through Longman Malaysia, CL

Contents

Figures

Tables

Preface

This book has been written as an applied labour economics text. It seeks to provide a comprehensive review of existing applied work in the major European labour market policy areas. It explicitly analyses these policy issues within the context of contemporary European labour market behaviour, applying both orthodox and less conventional economic analysis. It is not intended to replace mainstream textbooks in theoretical labour economics, which are largely, of necessity, slanted towards North American research and rarely provide descriptions of European labour market behaviour and existing policy. While we do develop many theoretical areas, some topics, such as certain extensions to the simple analysis of labour supply and demand, are neglected since they do not contribute to our appraisal of selected policy areas. Those chapters devoted to a specific policy issue (Chapter 4 onwards) start with a statistical description of underlying behaviour, identifying similarities and differences between European countries. This is followed by an explanation and critical appraisal of appropriate theory and associated empirical work. Guides to further reading follow the discussion of policy.

The text assumes a knowledge of introductory economics and has been designed to be accessible to professional and management students (especially HRM), though its primary target is undergraduate students. While each of the policy issues chapters is free-standing, they have been written on the assumption that the first three chapters have been read. Chapter 1 provides an overview of European labour markets, outlining developments in the structure of employment and wages, as well as identifying similarities and differences in the institutional and regulatory environments. The introductory theory chapter, Chapter 2, summarises the main traditions to be found in economic analysis of labour market behaviour, and the following chapter provides an overview of the rationale for, and role of, labour market policy.

With apologies we follow conventional usage of the term 'European', including Northern and Western Europe and the Mediterranean member states of the EU in our discussion. Our analysis does concentrate on the member states of the EU and our decision to only cite sources available in English, also causes a certain anglo-centric bias. I am sorry that these restrictions will cause some irritation, though I hope that some of the arguments and analysis will still be of interest. I use the term EC to cover data and discussion prior to the Treaty on European Union (the 'Maastricht Treaty') and similarly the EU 12 covers the succeeding period prior to the accession of Austria, Finland and Sweden. Data for Germany up to the end of 1990 refers to western Germany only.

Few arguments in this book are original and I have tried to indicate the source of particular arguments, ideas and expressions in the text; for omissions I apologise. I am particularly indebted to Rod Campbell and his staff at the much-missed Leek

Road Library at Staffordshire University for their assistance. Amongst the many colleagues whose friendship I have exploited in writing this book I would like to specially thank: Gwen Coates, Peter Davies, Yannis Georgellis, Kevin Macken, Stephen Hardy, Iraj Hashi, Steve Hurd, Richard Ledward, Helen O'Connor-Pickering, John Ramsay, Peter Reynolds, Iraj Seyf, John White and John Whittaker. Liz Adnett, Celia Egan, Anne Smith and Lisa Woodhouse provided specialist word-processing, data presentation and artistic skills, of which I am envious, and for which I am very grateful.

Nick Adnett
October 1995

1 The European labour market

In order to fulfil our objective of assessing current European labour market policies we will first investigate the nature of European labour markets. In this chapter we provide this investigation, concentrating upon important characteristics and recent trends in individual European countries. This may not seem a particularly radical approach, but it is conventional to develop first orthodox models of labour market behaviour and then assess policy in the light of those models. We prefer not to adopt the assumption that orthodox analysis provides an accurate and useful simplification of actual behaviour. Accordingly we summarise the economic analysis of labour markets in Chapter 2 and the theory of labour market policy in Chapter 3, allowing the present chapter's findings to inform our critical assessment of orthodoxy. It is not the intention to provide a detailed analysis of every European country, instead we concentrate upon key similarities and differences and upon aspects particularly important to policy considerations. We also try to identify the most important present and future policy issues, though we also discover that dramatic changes in labour market behaviour can occur in quite short periods of time.

In concentrating upon labour market behaviour we look behind some of the usual indicators of economic performance and identify causal relationships which are often neglected in more general comparisons of European economies. A common starting point for making economic comparisons of European countries is to consider income per capita, but ranking will reflect not only differences in productivity but also differences in the supply of market work per population. For example, the UK has a much lower level of labour productivity than the other northern member states; 25 per cent below the level in the Netherlands and below that of Spain in the early 1990s. However, the UK had a relatively high proportion of her population in work, with those in full-time employment supplying on average a relatively high number of hours per year to the labour market. As a consequence her per capita income in ECUs was 30 per cent higher than Spain and only around 10 per cent less than the Netherlands. Concentrating upon detailed labour market behaviour may therefore provide insights and explanations which may be hidden in more aggregate comparative studies.

In this chapter we only concentrate upon paid employment, largely ignoring non-market production in the home and, by necessity, activities in the underground/hidden economy. We organise the chapter into four areas of labour market activity. Initially we concentrate upon employment, identifying important changes in the participation rates of the population and the industrial and occupational distribution of the workforce. We also investigate the nature of flexible employment and contrast the differing forms that increased flexibility has taken in individual European countries. Secondly, we examine the pattern of wages and labour costs, concentrating upon occupational and industrial differentials, though also looking at the relative importance of different payment systems. Industrial relations is the concern of the third section, in which we trace the decline of trade union membership in many European economies and the movement in some countries towards more decentralised bargaining. In the fourth section we introduce the different national regulatory environments found in European labour markets. Here the focus is on the regulation of working conditions, wages, collective bargaining and job security. We also compare the level and composition of the expenditure of national governments on labour market policies.

The present chapter ignores detailed consideration of areas which appear as separate chapters later in this book. Hence our detailed discussion of education and training in Europe appears in Chapter 4 and the nature and extent of job search, tenure and labour mobility in Europe are examined in Chapter 5. The changing status of women in European labour markets is considered in Chapter 6 and aggregate employment growth and unemployment trends are outlined in Chapter 7. EU social policy, as opposed to national systems of regulation and intervention, is examined in Chapter 8. The present chapter's survey relies to a large extent on a few key OECD and European Commission sources and rather than repeatedly cite these, we provide a guide to statistical sources as an appendix, citing only specialist sources in the main body of the text. This survey was written in late 1995 and the appendix also indicates periodicals which can provide updates on trends in labour market behaviour and regulations.

1.1 Employment

In a market economy the ultimate source of paid employment is the demand for goods and services. It follows that the growth of employment will depend upon the difference between the growth of demand for output and the growth of the productivity of labour, that is output per worker. To prevent persistent increases in unemployment an economy needs to create additional employment at roughly the same rate as increases in its labour force. This growth of the labour force, in turn, will depend upon the growth in population of working age and changes in the participation rate. Participation may be itself dependent upon relative employment growth; increases in unemployment will tend to depress participation rates as young people prefer to defer entry and stay-on in full-time education and training and some older workers are discouraged or bought-out through earlier retirement/redundancy packages and become non-participants. Since the size of the labour force depends not only on the numbers of workers but also on the number of hours of work which they supply, we also need to analyse employment in terms of hours per job as well as number of jobs.

In the 1970s and 1980s, Europe, in common with all OECD economies, experienced a slow-down in the growth of both output and productivity. Whilst there was some variation across the EC, only Ireland escaped the slow-down with the UK economy having the weakest productivity performance over this period. Whilst in productivity growth the EC performance was superior to that of the US, between 1973 and 1990 employment in the EC grew at just 0.5 per cent per annum, less than a third of the North American rate. While Germany and Italy maintained significantly faster growth rates of employment, in Spain nearly 2 million jobs out of a work-force of 13 million in 1974 had disappeared by 1985. In the following sections we analyse in more detail the behaviour of employment in Europe in recent years. We do not directly consider the behaviour of unemployment (which is discussed in detail in Chapter 7), but a prominent characteristic of contemporary European labour markets is their high rates of unemployment and a high incidence of long-term unemployment.

1.1.1 *Participation*

In the long-run the growth of employment will primarily be driven by the rate of increase of working-age population, and thus by demographic factors such as migration, mortality and fertility rates. In the last three decades the working-age population has grown more slowly in Europe than elsewhere, averaging around half the 1.2 per cent increase found in the OECD as a whole. In the early 1990s just under two-thirds of the population aged 15 to 64 years of age in the EU 12 were economically active, a ratio 10 points lower than in the Scandinavian countries and the US. We report some of the key data on participation rates in Table 1.1, where the participation rate is total labour force divided by the working-age population (aged 15–64). The participation rate varied from 58 per cent in Italy and 59 per cent in Spain to 73 per cent in the UK and over 80 per cent in Denmark. The growth of unemployment in the EU is indicated by the fall in the proportion of the EU population of 15–64 years old who are in employment falling from around 63 per cent at the beginning of the 1970s to around 58 per cent in 1993. Over the last thirty years in the EU there has been a tendency for a decline in the participation rate of the under 25 years of age reflecting the growth of full-time schooling and training. Declining participation rates amongst older workers are also observed, especially for males; the decline has been steepest in Finland, France, the Netherlands and the UK. In Britain the proportion of males aged 50–65 in full-time employment has fallen from 71 per cent to 57 per cent since 1979. Activity rates of men of 55 and over are at or below 45 per cent in half of the EU 12 and only in Denmark and Sweden was the rate above 65 per cent. The decline in participation rates for men has been concentrated amongst the low-skilled. At the same time there has been an increase in the participation rate of women at all levels of educational attainment, especially amongst those within the prime working-age group of 25–49 years of age. It is anticipated that only this last trend is likely to continue, causing the EU labour force to grow by about a further 0.5 per cent above the 0.3 per cent growth in the working age population up to the new millennium. Whilst the role of women in European labour markets is the subject of Chapter 6.1, we note here the large differences in the relative sizes of the female labour force in different economies. For example, in the early 1990s women accounted for around 48 per cent of the work-force in Sweden, 45 per cent in the UK, but only 35 per cent in Italy.

Table 1.1 Labour force participation rates: recent trends

	Overall participation rate[1]		Female participation rate[1]		Male ages 55–64 participation rate[1]	
	1973	1994	1973	1994	1983	1994
Austria	65.1	70.0	48.5	58.9[4]	na	na
Belgium	62.2	63.9	41.3	54.1[5]	50.6	34.1[4]
Denmark	75.9	82.3	61.9	78.3[4]	67.2	65.9[4]
Finland	71.7	73.5	63.6	69.8	54.1	45.3
France	67.8	67.3	50.1	59.0[4]	53.6	42.1
Germany	69.4	69.5	50.3	61.4	63.1	51.5[4]
Greece	57.1	58.6	32.1	43.6[4]	70.8	58.7[4]
Ireland	63.5	61.2[2]	34.1	39.9[5]	78.0	64.7[4]
Italy	58.7	58.4	33.7	46.5[5]	36.8	32.9[4]
Luxembourg	64.8	61.5[2]	35.9	44.8[5]	37.8	38.4[4]
Netherlands	57.6	70.2	29.2	55.5[5]	54.2	41.8
Portugal	64.0	72.3	57.3[3]	62.2	70.4	62.5[4]
Spain	57.7[3]	58.9	32.6[3]	43.9	71.5	56.1
Sweden	75.5	76.3	62.6	74.6	77.0	74.7
UK	73.0	73.3	53.2	64.5	na	64.3[4]
Norway	68.7	76.9	50.6	71.3	80.3	71.5

na = not available.
[1] Defined as total labour force as a percentage of the working age population (15–64).
[2] 1991 figures.
[3] 1979 figures.
[4] 1993 figures.
[5] 1992 figures.
Source: OECD Employment Outlook 1995, Table J, K and B.

The combination of the increase in life expectancy at birth and the fall of fertility rates has produced an ageing population. Life expectancy at birth in the EU has risen by about 5 years for males and nearly 7 years for females since 1960. Over the same period the fertility rate, live births per 100 women aged 15 to 49 years, has fallen from 2.6 to 1.5, with only Ireland having a rate above 2. As a consequence, the share of the population aged 65 and over in Europe is now around 15 per cent and likely to increase to nearly 20 per cent by 2020 (European Commission, 1994). In terms of the work-force around 34 per cent of the EU labour force will be aged over 45 by the year 2005, with the ratio exceeding 40 per cent in Scandinavia (OECD, 1994). Johnson and Zimmermann (1993) concluded that ageing in Europe is likely to increase labour costs, reduce labour supply and increase the vintage of human capital. The potential combination of a rising proportion of retired people, falling activity rates and persistent high unemployment has caused concern about the ability of European economies to finance existing state pension schemes. Austria, France and Germany have made recent policy changes to discourage early retirement and

Belgium and Sweden are amongst countries which financially penalise early retirees (Whitting *et al.*, 1995).

1.1.2 *Working hours and working conditions*

The total labour supply in an economy depends not only on the size of the work-force but also on the number of hours supplied per worker. Sometimes concentrating upon employment alone may give a misleading picture of the behaviour of total labour input. For example, between 1983 and 1992 average hours worked per week fell by 13 per cent in the Netherlands whilst its employment growth was the fastest in the EC, reflecting a rapid growth in part-time employment. In general, countries with relatively low levels of productivity have tended to compensate by working longer hours, though as we have seen in the UK and Portugal, compensation is also through a high participation rate. While in the US the trend towards more leisure and less work ended in the early 1970s, in Europe the actual hours worked by full-time workers has tended to decline by an average of about 1 per cent per year since the end of the Second World War. Recent changes in Europe have not followed a consistent pattern however, with this trend being reversed in Ireland and the UK once structural changes are excluded. Reductions in working hours are largely the consequence of two structural changes: the shift in employment from agriculture and manufacturing to services and the growth of female employment. Almost all of the recent reductions in working hours in the EU, apart from those in the Netherlands, can be attributed to these structural changes (European Commission, 1994a).

Comparisons of average hours per worker are distorted by national differences in the importance of self-employment, part-time working and multiple-job holding. For full-time workers, the average total weekly hours worked by employees in the EU 12 in the early 1990s was just over 40 hours (Belgium had the lowest (38.0) and the UK (43.7) had the highest). Variations in hours worked in the EU are broadly consistent with the proposition that people choose to work fewer hours as income per head rises. This contrasts with our finding that participation rates rise with increases in living standards. Combining these findings it seems that employment gets more thinly spread amongst the population as modern economies grow. Unlike other European countries the UK has no tradition of regulating working hours and about 16 per cent of its employees normally work over 48 hours compared to an EU average of less than 7 per cent of employees. This helps to explain the British government's resistance to the European Commission's Working Time Directive published in 1990 which sought to restrict maximum working hours (see Box 1.1). Overall about half of males in the EU who work over 48 hours per week are in the UK, which also has the EU's highest proportion of workers who are sometimes required to work nights and who work on Saturdays.

The 1990 proposed directive also contained a statutory minimum paid annual holiday entitlement; of the EU 12 all but Italy and the UK have specified leave entitlements ranging from 25 days in Denmark, France, Luxembourg and Spain to 15 in Germany. Watson (1993) reports that about 15 per cent of full-time employees and around 60 per cent of part-time employees in the UK received 15 days paid

---

Box 1.1: The working time directive and the 'last hour' debate

The British Government's resistance to the 1990 proposed directive to limit weekly work-ing hours resurrects a famous debate between Karl Marx and Nassau Senior, the Professor of Political Economy at Oxford University, regarding the consequences of restricting hours of working. By 1836 Cotton mills in England employing children up to 18 were restricted to 12 working hours a day, with only 9 hours on Saturday. Senior wrote (though we have included Marx's punctuation!) 'the following analysis (!) will show that in a mill so worked, the whole net profit is derived *from the last hour*.' (K. Marx (1970) Volume 1, p. 224.) Senior then argued that the proposed Factory Acts before Parliament, which would reduce maximum hours by an hour a day, must eliminate all net profits and cause the clo-sure of the industry. Marx had fun ridiculing this argument with its implicit assumption of fixed productivity. No doubt Marx would also have enjoyed the British Government's argument that the European Commission's proposed maximum working hours directive would place 'crippling costs' upon employers. Modern analysts would add to Marx's cri-tique the potential for wage flexibility and more flexible patterns of working and production as ways of minimising the consequences for unit labour costs of any working hours restrictions on the 2.5 million UK workers who currently exceed the proposed limit. In Chapter 8 we review the outcome of the British Government's resistance to the pro-posed directive.

---

holiday entitlement or less. Finally, the UK has the lowest number of public holidays (8) which further increases the high relative average annual hours worked by British employees. These comparisons are our first insight into the consequences of the dif-ferent regulatory traditions in the UK and continental Europe, a difference which has been the source of much misunderstanding and controversy in EU decision-making. We return to this issue in Chapter 8.

We have so far ignored a further dimension of labour supply: effort. Little informa-tion is available on relative working conditions, especially the intensity of work, in the EU though Paoli (1992) reports the results of a survey on the work environment. The survey finds that about 30 per cent of respondents consider their health and safety at risk while at work, largely associated with exposure to noise, air pollution, handling of dangerous substances and working in painful positions. In general, employees in the southern member states and those working in agriculture, construction and trans-port industries reported the highest risks. These findings are largely in line with differences in reported accident rates, an issue we discuss in Chapter 3. Another indicator used to assess worker's satisfaction with working conditions is the rate of absenteeism. The OECD's Employment Outlook 1991 reports that nearly 22 per cent of usual hours of working were lost in Sweden due to absences, nearly 14 per cent in Denmark down to 4 per cent or below in Belgium, Germany, Ireland and Italy. Care should be taken in making international comparisons however, since the absence rate is partly determined by the type of sickness benefit scheme in operation.

1.1.3   *The pattern of employment*

Between 1961 and 1993 employment in the EU grew at an average annual rate of just 0.25 per cent, compared with a 1.8 per cent growth rate in the US. Europe's weaker employment performance can partly be attributed to much higher rates of job losses in agriculture and industry, with job losses in manufacturing occurring at twice the North American rate. Structural changes in European employment in recent years have been much analysed and we start with a consideration of sectoral changes. One of the most consistent features of economic development is the tendency for employment growth in the services sector as industrialisation proceeds. By 1992 almost as many people in the EU were employed in business services alone as were employed in agriculture. Overall, in the EU the proportion of the employed work-force in service industries increased from 53 per cent in 1980 to 63 per cent in 1993. Table 1.2 shows these changes in the composition of employment by sector for individual European countries. Within the EU, countries with the largest share of employment in the services sector tend to be the most developed economies, the service share also tends to vary inversely with the share of employment in agriculture. Germany is an exception to this pattern with its continuing large industrial employment. In the last two decades the share of employment in the service sector has been growing most rapidly in the less developed parts of the EU.

A major cause of the faster growth of employment in the service sector is the tendency for people to increase their relative expenditure on services as income per head rises. However, the faster productivity growth in manufacturing industry and agriculture also contributes to this sectoral redistribution of employment over time. Recently the growth of services employment has been exaggerated by the rapid rise of part-time workers in that sector, and the service sector's share of total hours worked, as opposed to employment, is significantly smaller especially in the Netherlands and the UK. The changes in participation discussed earlier have also affected the composition of labour demand and therefore contributed to these changes in the structure of employment. The growth of female participation in the labour force has increased the demand for catering and paid cleaning services as well as the demand for paid child-care provision.

Although the outflow of workers from industry in Europe since 1973 has been less than from agriculture before 1973, Glyn (1995) points out that the problems associated with industrial decline are more severe. Major declines in industrial employment usually cause large-scale and geographically concentrated redundancies. The jobs lost are often high-paying and filled by full-time male workers whose skills were largely industry-specific and who hold only basic educational qualifications. The expanding service sector requires different skills and patterns of working, also tending to be more evenly spatially distributed across the regions. The contraction of industrial employment has often been associated with a rise in unemployment as the new service jobs are predominantly filled by women re-entrants rather than by workers made redundant in the industrial sector.

Construction and manufacturing employment tend to be cyclically unstable, causing some problems in making national comparisons of employment patterns over

Table 1.2 Civil employment by sector as a percentage of total employment

	Agriculture		Industry		Services	
	1973	1994	1973	1994	1973	1994
Austria	16	7[1]	41	35[1]	43	58[1]
Belgium	4	3[2]	41	28[2]	55	70[2]
Denmark	10	5[1]	34	26[1]	57	68[1]
Finland	17	8	36	27	47	65
France	11	5	40	27	49	68
Germany	7	3	47	36	45	61
Greece	37	21[1]	28	24[1]	36	54[1]
Ireland	24	15[3]	32	29[3]	44	56[3]
Italy	18	7[1]	39	33[1]	42	60[1]
Luxembourg	8	3[3]	44	30[3]	48	66[3]
Netherlands	6	4[2]	37	25[2]	58	71[2]
Portugal	27	12	34	33	39	56
Spain	24	10	37	30	39	60
Sweden	7	3	37	25	56	72
UK	3	2	42	26	55	72
Norway	11	5	34	23	54	71

[1] 1993 figures.
[2] 1992 figures.
[3] 1990 figures.
Source: OECD Employment Outlook 1995, Table D.

time. At a more disaggregated level the most rapid employment growth in the decade up to 1992 has been in the 'other services' sector which includes education, health and recreational services. This sector has contributed almost half of the additional jobs created in the EU in this period, whilst a further 30 per cent of the additional jobs were in the banking, finance and insurance sector and the remainder primarily in distribution, hotels and catering. Only in Germany, Portugal and Spain was manufacturing industry a significant provider of additional employment. The proportion of the work-force employed in mechanical and electrical engineering in Germany was over 50 per cent higher than any other member state. Greece had 5 per cent of its work-force employed in textiles, clothing and footwear and Portugal, 8.5 per cent compared with an EU average of just over 2 per cent. The shares of clothing, footwear and retailing in total employment appear to be inversely related to the level of development, though in the UK the high share of retailing reflects a reliance upon part-time workers. Differences in the comparative importance of tourism cause Greece and Spain to have high shares of employment in hotels and catering, whilst the one million European domestic service employees are predominantly located in just three countries: Portugal, Spain and France. Employment shares of social services and health care are positively related to levels of development, with the shares varying from 15 per cent of the workforce in Denmark and the Netherlands to around 5 per cent in Greece and Spain. One of the unusual features of the early 1990s recession was the slowdown in the growth of the services sector in most European countries with the exception of Germany. This reflected both the particular problems faced by the financial services sector as consumers as businesses attempted to reduce their debts, and the absence of counter-cyclical employment measures in the public sector.

Current statistics do not allow differences in the occupational structure of employment between member states to be analysed in any detail. Since the early 1980s the number of workers classified as professional and technical in the EU has grown at an annual average rate of 2 per cent, whilst total employment has grown at just 1 per cent per annum, accounting for 40 per cent of the overall rise in employment. In recent recessions it has generally been the low-skill jobs which have declined, with recoveries favouring the same workers, though the early 1990s recession caused white-collar employment to decline in Finland, Sweden, Spain and the UK. In the early 1990s about 8 per cent of those in employment in the EU were legislators and managers, 11 per cent were professionals and a further 12 per cent were technicians. About 10 per cent of employed workers were in the elementary occupations, just 3 per cent were agricultural workers or fishermen, and 9 per cent plant or machine operators. Just over 15 per cent were craft workers and the rest were either clerical (13 per cent) or service workers (12 per cent). Within the EU, Italy and Spain had the lowest proportion of managerial, professional and technical workers at around 20 per cent, with France and the Netherlands having the highest (over 40 per cent).

While the decline of manufacturing and the growth of many low-paid service jobs has led to some deskilling of the work-force, there have been forces working in the opposite direction. Technological and organisational changes in manufacturing have increased the literacy and numeracy requirements across the work-force, while in the services there is an increased need for keyboard and computer skills together with an understanding of abstract principles, Box 1.2 examines these trends. An inability to objectively measure the skills requirement of a job prevents any clear conclusion concerning overall trends in the skill-intensity of employment. Data on educational qualifications would indicate a general 'upskilling' of the work-force, with a rise in the share of the work-force with upper secondary and higher education. Machin (1995) concludes that the shift towards more skilled labour was primarily driven by factors within industry and establishment factors rather than by shifts in product demand. The decrease in the relative earnings of low-skilled workers which we examine later, would also indicate that technology is biasing employment in favour of the more skilled and educated worker. An OECD study (1994) shows that during the 1980s while white-collar employment was rising as a proportion of total employment, it was the highly-skilled groups of professional, administrative and technical workers who increased their share of employment, while clerical, sales and service workers only retained theirs. The anticipated mass displacement of clerical workers by the application of information technology has yet to occur. The same study compares employment projections for the year 2000 and concludes that across-the-board increases in skill and competence levels are likely, a prediction consistent with the national forecasts reported in Heijke (1994). Employment growth is projected to be fastest for professional, technical, administrative and managerial occupations. Some low-skilled occupations may be relatively unaffected by technological change, with for example shop assistants being projected to make a large contribution to employment growth over the next decade in many European economies.

In the 1980s much attention was devoted to the critical role played by small and medium sized enterprises (SME's) in the growth of employment. In the early 1990s

Box 1.2: New technology and production management

Economies of scope

The emergence of widespread mass production in the 1940s made relatively small demands upon workers' skills, enabling the rapid absorption of workers from different sectors. With the introduction of numerically controlled machine tools, economies of scale shifted from production towards marketing and research and development, and more flexible working patterns were necessary for the exploitation of the new machinery. As Sorge and Streeck (1988) have argued economies of scope provide opportunities to escape the constraints imposed by economies of scale. Firms can move towards flexible specialisation and provide more product variety and develop quality niches in the former mass markets. Hence technology need not lead to a widespread deskilling of labour since increased product variety generates new demands for multi-skilled workers.

Lean production

Mass production traditionally implied long production runs and the maintenance of large buffer stocks to guard against absenteeism, high labour turnover and industrial disputes. Deskilled and poorly motivated workers were highly monitored by employers through supervisors and quality inspectors. With lean production techniques, buffer stocks and conventional management, control mechanisms are abandoned and working practices adjusted to directly confront organisational and motivational failures. Japanese-style horizontal co-ordination is favoured with well-qualified, multi-skilled workers co-operating to promote solutions to production constraints. Motivational issues are now paramount with internal promotion and job security being part of a process of generating mutual trust between workers and management; as a consequence responsibility for human resource management is often devolved to line managers. Employment stability is offset by greater internal flexibility, with widespread redeployment of labour. Total quality management incorporates many of the arguments of lean production, extending the process to the service sector. Quality issues are again directly confronted, with personal contact with customers becoming a key part of generating quality improvements.

Implications

Growing labour market inequality is a product of these changes but also a factor in maintaining the profitability of previous, and now less efficient, production technologies. The commitment to providing job security generates its own inflexibility problem in periods of difficult trading conditions.

about 55 per cent of those employed in the private sector in the EU worked in enterprises with less than 100 employees and almost 30 per cent in those with less than 10 employees. The southern member states tend to have a higher proportion of their employees in small firms than the northern states, Denmark apart. In Spain almost 75 per cent work in firms with less than 100 employees and over 46 per cent in those with under 10 employees, while in Germany, for example, the respective proportions are 46 per cent and 18 per cent. Small firms are more important in services and construction than in manufacturing, though again differences are found between the southern and northern member states. Whilst the shift towards services may lead to an expansion of employment in small firms, some of the US evidence which popularised the importance of SME's in job-creation has been recently reassessed. Davis *et al.* (1994) concluded that whilst smaller manufacturing firms and plants exhibit sharply higher gross rates of job creation, once their higher destruction rate is considered they do not have a higher net rate of job creation. For both new jobs and the typical existing job, they conclude that job security increases with employer size. The OECD (1994) reached broadly similar conclusions.

Most European countries experienced a large increase in the relative size of public sector employment between 1960 and 1980. The overall share of government employment was around 17 per cent in the EC in 1980, with France and the UK having over 20 per cent and Sweden over 30 per cent of employment in the public sector. The relative size of the public sector in Europe has not grown significantly since that time with the share in some countries, such as the UK, falling significantly in the last decade. If we concentrate solely upon employment in public administration and defence in the EC, then between 1979 and 1990 employment in this part of the public sector was growing at four times the rate of employment in the private sector, though peace dividends have now halted this trend. Public sector provision of subsidised social services, such as education, child care, old-age care and health care, not only shifts the production of such services out of the household but also out of the market. In a direct sense it then follows that public sector employment may be detrimental to employment and production in the private sector. When public sector financial crises require a 'down-sizing' of these services, private demand and supply may be slow to respond and overall market production and employment may fall, a process which has happened in some sectors in Scandinavia and the UK in the 1990s.

1.1.4   *Flexibility of employment*

The drive for labour market flexibility became a key policy objective in the 1980s and both the OECD *Jobs Study* (1994a) and the European Commission's *White Paper on Growth, Competitiveness, Employment* (1994b) argued the need for greater flexibility in Europe. Whilst there appears to be general agreement that increases in flexibility are necessary to increase the competitiveness of European economies, there is no such consensus about what constitutes a 'flexible' labour market. Perversely, this championing of flexibility coincided with the development of economic models of labour market behaviour, (discussed in the following chapters), which stressed the mutual benefits to workers and firms of long-term associations. A recurring theme of this book will be an examination of this contradiction. We will investigate the extent to which increases in flexibility have produced efficiency gains in European labour markets and consider whether increased flexibility has assisted or thwarted the attainment of policy-makers' other economic and social objectives.

A common element in various definitions of flexibility is the ability to adapt rapidly to changes in market conditions and technology. A common argument is that more competitive product markets, both nationally and globally, together with changes in the production processes have increased the need for new working practices. One dimension of flexibility concerns how rapidly firms adjust their labour inputs to changes in output and demand. In Britain, for example, the early 1980s recession saw employment contract slowly, with restructuring continuing through the upturn, whereas the late 1980s recession saw a much more rapid contraction of employment and, as a consequence, a fall in unemployment in the 1990s at a much earlier stage of the recovery. An important aspect of the behaviour of this *numerical flexibility* in recent years has been the rapid growth of part-time and temporary employment and the increase in self-employment, particularly that associated with the growth of sub-contracting. A second dimension of labour market flexibility concerns the match between available workers and vacancies. The growth of multi-skilled workers and the increased incidence of re-training are important aspects of this *functional flexibility*. In certain sectors a further important dimension of flexibility concerns *flexibility of working time or temporal flexibility*, with some modern production technologies and changing social habits creating additional demands for shift-working, week-end working and various forms of flexitime. These changes also give rise to *flexibility in the location of work*, with traditional home working being supplanted by teleworking, utilising computer or telecommunications equipment. Finally, employers and policy-makers may also be concerned with a final form of flexibility, that of *wage flexibility*. At the firm level this concerns matching pay to productivity and profitability and we discuss changes in payment systems later in this chapter. We have so far concentrated on flexibility at the microeconomic level and policy-makers are often more concerned with *flexibility at a macroeconomic level*. We discuss the ability of aggregate labour markets in Europe to respond to demand and supply shocks in Chapter 7.

We initially concentrate upon the issue of numerical flexibility in European labour markets. The components of numerical flexibility are illustrated for the UK in Table 1.3 which shows the employment status of the work-force in the mid-1990s. Whereas 75 per cent of the self-employed are male, 87 per cent of part-time employees are female; overall 52 per cent of women in employment were in the flexible work-force as opposed to just 38 per cent of males. The growth in the flexible work-force in the UK has been uneven, with temporary employment remaining stable and part-time and self-employment growing in importance in the last decade. There are differences between member states in the importance and behaviour over time of non-standard forms of employment (atypical workers), that is the part-time and temporary workers together with the self-employed. The European Commission (1993) reports that in the Netherlands two-thirds of the net addition to employment in the 1980s were part-time jobs and in Germany, France, Ireland and Belgium part-timers also

Table 1.3 UK employment: by status 1993 (as a percentage of those in employment)

	All	Men	Women
Traditional Workforce			
Full-time permanent employees	61.8	73.2	47.9
Flexible Workforce			
Full-time temporary employees	2.6	2.8	2.3
Part-time permanent employees	18.6	3.7	36.7
Part-time temporary employees	2.5	1.2	3.9
Full-time self-employed	10.2	15.6	3.7
Part-time self-employed	2.3	1.4	3.4
Government training schemes	1.4	1.7	1.1
Unpaid family workers	0.6	0.3	1.0

Source: Watson, (1994), Table 2.

accounted for a significant proportion of the additional jobs. Though the figures also show that in Greece part-time jobs actually decreased during this period.

In its simplest sense, part-time employment means working less than full-time hours, but since the latter varies by occupation, industry and country, operationally defining part-time work is problematic. Part-time work is also sometimes used to denote employment on inferior conditions of work, and a part-time worker in this sense may work similar hours to those of a full-time worker. Differences in conventions and practices make it problematic to make comparisons between countries and over time. Thus in the 1992 Labour Force Survey 31 per cent of female employees of industry and services in the EC interpreted their employment as part-time, with 25 per cent of all female employees working between 10 and 29 hours per week. Whilst two-thirds of women with jobs of between 30 and 34 hours a week classified themselves as in full-time employment. Meulders and Plasman (1993) and Maier (1994) provide reviews of the development of part-time working in the EU.

Figure 1.1 illustrates the growth and relative importance of part-time working in Europe. Part-time working is particularly high in the Netherlands, Scandinavia and the UK. During the 1980s, part-time working was growing particularly rapidly in Belgium and France. The number of women workers classified as part-time varies enormously in the EU, from nearly 60 per cent in the Netherlands, 44 per cent in the UK to only 8 per cent in Italy and Portugal and just 6 per cent in Greece. When different conventions in defining part-time employment are taken into consideration together with the large numbers of women in the Netherlands, Denmark and the UK who work under 10 hours per week, these differences become much smaller. In the UK nearly three-quarters of the recent growth in part-time employment can be accounted for by the changes in the industrial composition of employment discussed previously (Beatson, 1995). Only about 4 per cent of males employed in industry and services in the EU were classified as working part-time. While the growth of part-time working may indicate greater flexibility for employers it may not correspond to the wishes of the employees. Figures from the Labour Force Surveys indicate that

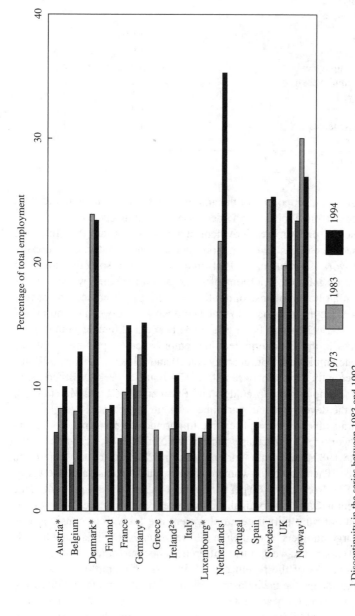

[1] Discontinuity in the series between 1983 and 1992.
[2] Ireland 1991.
* 1993 figures used for 1994.
Source: OECD Employment Outlook 1994, Table D.

Figure 1.1 Growth of part-time employment

the proportion of part-time workers who really preferred a full-time job varied from 30 per cent and over in Belgium, France, Greece, Ireland and Italy to under 10 per cent in Denmark, Luxembourg and the UK.

While in Britain the high incidence of part-time working may be a partial response to employers escaping liability for unfair dismissal, redundancy payments, maternity leave and social security contributions, in the Netherlands there are no major legal or financial inducements for employers to prefer part-time employees. Basic rates of pay do not appear to be lower for part-time workers, so their attractions to employers must lie elsewhere. For firms whose pattern of demand over the week is subject to peaks, such as in retailing, or where the task requires a limited time, such as cleaning and catering, part-time workers may be particularly attractive to employers. For other employers the attractions of employing part-time workers may be reduced overheads, an overall lengthening of business operating hours, lower unionisation rates or merely a reflection of the preferences of existing or potential employees.

Another flexible working arrangement is temporary work, that is fixed-term contracts or temporary placements by work agencies. Figure 1.2 illustrates the importance of this category in the EU in the early 1990s. Differences in definitions and regulations again cause problems in making international comparisons. In the early 1990s nearly one in three Spanish workers was on a part-time contract. This rapid rise and that in France reflected changes in legislation covering temporary workers which we discuss further in Chapter 7. Belgium, Italy and the UK seem to have the lowest proportion of employees who are in temporary jobs (around 5 per cent of the employed work-force): the first two countries having restrictions on temporary contracting (Grubb and Wells, 1993). Temporary work is more likely to be involuntary than part-time working, with over 80 per cent of temporary workers reporting that they could not find a permanent job in Greece and Spain compared with under 25 per cent in the UK. In Britain the employment of agency temporaries seems to be more closely linked to providing cover for illness, holidays and maternity leave (McGregor and Sproull, 1992). Some of the recent growth in temporary employment reflects an increased use of consultants; little is known about the extent of sub-contracting though Beatson (1995) provides some evidence of a significant increase in the 1990s.

As Figure 1.3 illustrates, the 1980s saw the reversal of the long-term trend away from self-employment in some European economies, with Italy, Portugal, the UK and Sweden (not shown) having particularly large increases in the non-farm sector. The 1990s recession in the UK, especially its persistence in the construction industry, brought this growth to a halt. Some of this growth in self-employment did not represent net employment growth but an increased use of contracting-out work as firms restructured, with production unit size contracting and the jettisoning of non-core activities. The importance of non-agricultural self-employment is greater in the southern European countries than elsewhere, reflecting the high numbers of self-employed in services and industry. In Greece the self-employed accounted for nearly 30 per cent of employment in industry and services, with Italy, Spain and Portugal having a ratio close to 20 per cent, compared with around 8 per cent in Denmark, Germany and the Netherlands. These figures exclude those involved in underground independent work, estimated at around 4 per cent of the total labour input in Italy (de Luca

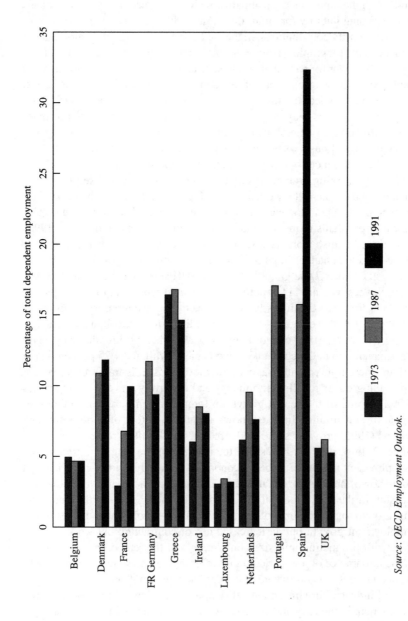

Source: OECD Employment Outlook.

Figure 1.2 Temporary employment in Europe

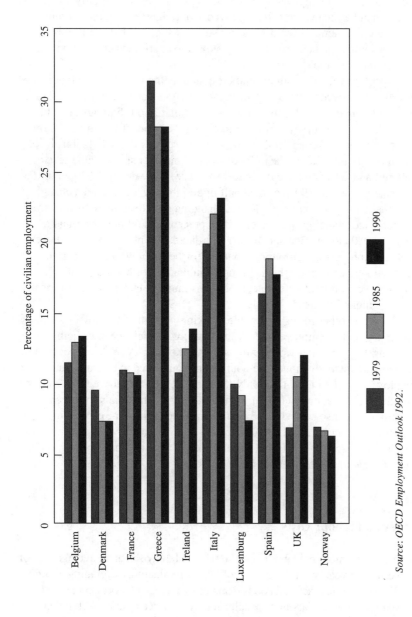

Source: OECD Employment Outlook 1992.

Figure 1.3 Self-employment in the non-agricultural sector

and Bruni, 1993). Both the Netherlands and the UK have had large inflow rates into the self-employed category in recent years, though their exit rates have also been higher. Abell *et al.* (1995) interpret the UK's experience as indicating that policies which encouraged the unemployed to become self-employed had only short-run effects. In all member states the self-employed work significantly more hours per week on average than employees. Employer surveys suggest that the provision of specialist skills dominates their use of self-employed workers, the construction industry being an extreme example.

Another aspect of a flexible labour market concerns the mobility of labour, this covers movements between employers, occupations and locations. Whilst we examine labour mobility in detail in Chapter 5 we will summarise our findings here. In the early 1990s labour force surveys indicate that about 4 per cent of workers moved annually between the 11 broad industry or services sectors (NACE 1-digit level). Inter-sector mobility is higher in the more developed member states, with the exception of Belgium and Germany, and decreases with age. More detailed figures for the UK suggest that in the mid-1990s around half of all job-moves involved a change of industry, with about 9 per cent of employees changing employer annually and about the same percentage changing occupations, both percentages falling by around a half from their late 1980s level (Beatson, 1995). Burda and Wyplosz (1994) found that job creation and job destruction only accounted for between 30 and 60 per cent of the flows of workers changing jobs in Europe. Unlike in North America temporary lay-offs are relatively unusual in Europe, though institutional factors have historically contributed to a higher incidence in Italy.

Data is lacking on other forms of flexible working, though in the UK it is known that about 12 per cent of employees work flexitime, with such schemes being more common amongst white-collar workers in larger workplaces. A further 9 per cent of employees work a system of annualised hours, commonly used in teaching, and 5 per cent of employees worked term-time only (Watson, 1994). So far we have concentrated upon the growth of non-standard working arrangements; the sectoral changes discussed earlier have also caused some decline in some of this type of working. The relative decline of agriculture and its mechanisation have generally led to a fall in the number of day-labourers and seasonal farm-workers, whilst deindustrialisation has also led to a decline in the numbers of piece-workers.

1.2   Wages and labour costs

Since the early 1970s nominal labour costs in the EU have risen at an average rate of around 11 per cent a year, with the growth of labour productivity averaging around 4 per cent and prices of manufactured goods rising at an average of 7 per cent per annum. Thus the real product wage, labour costs adjusted by the price of manufactured goods, rose in line with productivity. For the majority of the work-force the wages they receive are the single largest determinant of their living standards, whilst for employers wage costs are their single largest component of labour costs. In order to make international comparisons of wages and labour costs we need to convert to a common currency basis, whilst comparisons of living standards also require adjustment for differences in the level and structure of non-wage income, prices, taxes and benefits. Differences in the way these adjustments are made in international comparisons can be a significant source of discrepancy in the results obtained (London Economics, 1992).

1.2.1 *The structure of labour costs in Europe*

In the early 1990s average hourly earnings measured in ECUs were nearly seven times higher in Denmark than in Portugal, but we should be wary about how we interpret such huge differences. Where employers are ultimately concerned with maximising net revenue or minimising costs of a given output, the key labour market determinant of their competitiveness is their labour costs per unit of output. Firms who pay high wage rates to their workers can be competitive with low wage firms as long as productivity is high enough, or non-wage labour costs are low enough, to offset wage differences. There are some large differences in the importance of these latter costs in the EU. In Belgium, for example, bonuses and other premiums are a particularly large component of employers' costs, whilst in Denmark holiday pay and in France payments in kind are a relatively large proportion of total labour costs. However, the really large differences are in employers' statutory social security expenditure. This component accounts for over 30 per cent of Italian employers' labour costs at the end of the 1980s, just over 7 per cent in the UK and under 2 per cent in Denmark. Such huge differences are the source of the fear of 'social dumping' which we consider in Chapter 8, though as we discover later in this chapter, differences in the way in which social security systems, health care and pensions are funded are crucial for a full appreciation of the structure of employers' labour costs in the EU.

One source of comparative wage data is the series produced by the Office of Productivity and Technology, US Bureau of Labor Statistics. Their series includes all payments directly to workers together with employer contributions to fringe benefits. The high dispersion in the EU of national average hourly labour costs for production workers in manufacturing is shown in Table 1.4, with the costs of Danish workers still being four time those of Portugal. The bottom row of this table shows the relative importance of employers' social security and labour tax payments. In all countries except Denmark and the UK, the relative importance of employers' customary and statutory social welfare expenditure has been increasing since the 1970s, causing the dispersion of employers' social charges in Europe to increase over time (Adnett, 1995).

Since member states' work-force differs significantly in terms of skills, effort and the amount of capital and technology they work with, these comparisons of employers' wage and non-wage payments tell us little about the relative unit labour costs. For example, it is well known that UK labour costs per employee are relatively low yet her unit labour costs are much closer to the EU average, since UK firms have relatively low labour productivity levels (London Economics, 1992). Comparisons of productivity levels between national economies are notoriously difficult to make, reflecting additional problems concerned with differences in industrial structure and

Table 1.4 Costs of employing production workers in manufacturing in 1992

	B	DK	D	E	F	GR	IRL	I	NL	P	UK
Hourly compensation US$	22.0	20.0	25.9	13.4	16.9	6.8	13.3	19.4	20.7	5.0	14.7
Social and labour taxes as a percentage of hourly compensation	27.0	3.0	22.8	24.6	28.5	19.3	15.6	30.6	22.6	24.0	16.5

Source: Bureau of Labour Statistics; reproduced in *European Economy*, 1994, **56**, 130.

relative prices as well as the need to convert to a common currency. In Table 1.5 we report calculations by Oulton (1994) of relative unit labour costs in manufacturing, suggesting that those countries with the lowest worker hourly compensations in Table 1.4 generally have the *highest* unit labour costs. Since in general member states with low labour costs had the lowest levels of productivity, unit labour costs had less variation in the EU than labour costs. O'Mahony (1995) reports comparisons of unit labour costs for manufacturing which differ from those in Table 1.5. In particular she finds Britain and Germany had similar unit labour costs in 1992; the cause of this disagreement being differences in how output is converted to a common currency and which index of British industrial production was utilised. The European Commission (1993) reports that real unit labour costs in own currency fell in all member states in the 1980s, with the exception of the UK. Although the overall pattern has not changed much, in recent years France and Italy have achieved the most rapid fall with the Benelux countries experiencing an increase in real unit labour costs. The same report finds that comparative labour costs in engineering, textiles and clothing are in line with these aggregate trends, though in banking and insurance cost variations are much smaller, with the UK having particularly low labour costs in this sector.

1.2.2   *The structure of wages in Europe*

So far we have considered data which relate to gross wage rates and it may be argued that take-home pay (gross earnings minus personal income taxes and compulsory social security contributions but plus universal cash transfers) may be a better indicator of living standards. Such comparisons are difficult since price levels, taxation and social security systems differ markedly. However the OECD has produced comparisons for an average production worker, full-time manual in manufacturing, in industrialised countries, which are summarized in Table 1.6. These figures are converted into the equivalent purchasing power in pounds sterling. One reason why UK pay is now relatively high compared with other EU countries is its low cost of living and low levels of tax on employment. Denmark and the Netherlands can be seen to have a low ratio of take-home pay to gross earnings and the large differences in this

Table 1.5 Unit labour costs in manufacturing (UK = 100)

	1990	1992 (post £'s exit from ERM)
Belgium	97.8	na
France	101.3	114.0
Germany	107.9	128.8
Greece	115.0	na
Italy	92.5	93.2
Netherlands	93.1	112.5
Portugal	236.6	na
Spain	124.3	na

na = not available.
Source: Oulton (1994), Table 15.

Table 1.6 Average annual estimated take-home pay of production workers in manufacturing in 1993

	Single person Converted to £ Sterling	As a percentage of gross earnings	Two-child family with one earner Converted to £ Sterling	As a percentage of gross earnings
Austria	8,946	73.6	11,235	92.4
Belgium	8,644	62.8	12,104	87.9
Denmark	7,899	53.0	10,054	67.5
Finland	7,408	64.3	9,043	78.5
France	8,036	73.1	9,551	86.9
Germany	9,713	63.4	12,034	78.5
Greece	5,462	82.5	6,653	83.7
Ireland	8,571	67.7	9,991	78.9
Italy	9,400	73.5	10,566	82.6
Luxembourg	11,459	74.8	15,412	100.6
Netherlands	9,300	58.5	10,999	69.2
Portugal	4,956	82.6	5,515	91.9
Spain	8,019	81.6	8,680	88.3
Sweden	7,736	70.5	8,871	80.9
UK	10,538	74.4	11,909	84.1
Norway	9,715	71.3	22,841	86.9

Source: Employment Gazette (February 1995), Table 1, p. 51.

ratio between EU countries indicates the problems in trying to compare living standards utilising gross earnings data.

Taking the work-force as a whole we should be cautious in linking labour market income to living standards, since the sources of household income differ markedly across the EU. Overall, wage income constitutes only around half of household income in Europe, ranging from 42 per cent in Italy to 60 per cent in the UK. Transfer income accounts for a particularly large share of household income in France (27 per cent), the Netherlands (29 per cent) and Sweden (25 per cent). Property income was especially important in Germany (23 per cent) and unincorporated business profits accounted for around a quarter of household income in Italy and Spain (OECD, 1994a). There are also significant differences in employee benefits between European countries which further complicate comparisons, though as Mitchell and Rojot (1993) report health insurance is largely publicly provided and retirement pensions differences are partly moderated by the operation of public retirement programmes.

Comparisons of average earnings across countries can also give misleading impressions when distributions of earnings differ between countries. In Europe institutional differences generate significant national differences in the distribution of income for full-time workers. In the late 1980s whilst only 5 per cent of Belgian full-time workers earned less than 66 per cent of median earnings, in Ireland, Spain and the UK the percentage was around 20 per cent (OECD, 1994a). In the 1970s wage inequality and skill differentials narrowed in most economies. In the 1980s there were dramatic falls in the relative earnings of low-skilled workers in Japan, the US and UK, whilst in most of continental Europe the relative wage of low-skilled workers continued to rise. A similar pattern emerges when the behaviour of the wage premia for schooling is examined. The relative earnings of high education groups compared to low education groups in most European countries fell in the 1970s and stabilised in the 1980s, whereas in the US and UK the fall was strongly reversed in the late 1980s (Nickell and Bell, 1995). Although the hourly compensation of US production workers in the early 1990s was higher than the average European worker on a purchasing power basis, Freeman (1994) estimated that the earnings of the bottom decile of males was around 44 per cent higher in Europe than in the US. The role of minimum wage laws seems critical in an understanding of these differences. Box 1.3 explores the causes of increasing wage and/or employment inequality in more detail. Sweden has a remarkable record in reducing inequality and virtually eliminating poverty and Björklund and Freeman (1995) explore the origins of this achievement. They conclude that the Swedish population is not particularly homogenous and the source lies instead in the egalitarian distribution of employment and the operation of wage-fixing and tax and transfer systems.

Box 1.3: The causes of increasing labour market inequality

In the 1980s there were large increases in wage inequality in several developed economies. Where minimum wage laws prevented changes in wage inequality a trend of growing employment inequality was often substituted, with unskilled workers suffering a higher share of unemployment. The causes of growing labour market inequality have been much debated in recent years, Glyn (1995) provides a survey and we now summarise some possible causes. The share of less-qualified/low-skilled workers in the labour force has been declining in developed economies suggesting that supply-side factors are unlikely to be a dominant cause. Most explanations therefore concentrate upon identifying the causes of the contraction of demand for low-skilled workers.

Box 1.3: *continued*

Increased trade

The growth of world trade, together with the completion of the Uruguay round of GATT, has concentrated attention on whether globalisation has caused low-skilled jobs to be exported to less developed economies. 'Out-sourcing', where production activities are transferred to low-wage economies whilst marketing, finance, design and product development are retained in developed economies, has become an important part of popular explanations of growing inequality. Increased trade has also caused a fall in the relative price of less skill-intensive goods, further deteriorating the labour market position of low-skilled workers in Europe and North America. Controversy surrounds the strength of these effects since imports from low-wage countries have a very small share of the total market for manufactured goods in Europe and the skill-intensity of production seems to have increased across all industries in developed economies.

Technological change

Our arguments in Box 1.2 suggested that technological developments were increasing the skill–intensity of production. Improvements in communications and information processing technology were radically changing the structure of employment in favour of the more educated and skilled. Studies suggest that the share of non-manual employment has been increasing most rapidly in sectors where the introduction of new technology has been fastest.

Structural and institutional change

There are several structural and institutional changes which may have contributed to greater wage inequality. Deindustrialisation may have shifted workers into lower-paying service sector employment. Changes in unionisation rates and firm size distribution may also have been important, since studies show that unions and large companies are associated with a less dispersed wage structure.

Increased unemployment

Rather than concentrating solely on the composition of the demand for labour, reductions in the overall level of demand may be important. The upward trend in unemployment rates in Europe in recent decades may also have contributed to growing inequality in the labour market. In a recession the low-skilled will tend to be displaced by more qualified workers, especially when their relative wage rates may not decline sufficiently to maintain their competitiveness.

The 1980s saw youth wages falling relative to adult wages in most European economies, with the exception of Italy and Sweden, whilst females closed some of their earnings gap with males. Figure 1.4 illustrates the relationship between age and earnings for different categories of UK workers in 1993. For full-time non-manual workers the earnings profiles rise more steeply than for manual workers. In Chapter 4 we present the argument that this difference reflects non-manual workers' higher

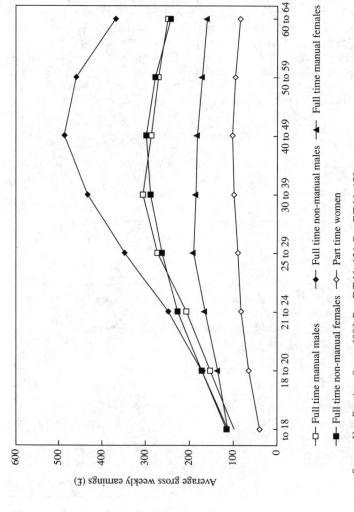

Source: New Earnings Survey 1993, Part E Table 124, Part F Table 179.

Figure 1.4 Age-earnings profiles in the UK, 1993

investments in education and training. The source of the starkly flatter profiles for females workers is examined in detail in Chapter 6. The profiles illustrated in Figure 1.4 compare the earnings of different individuals of various ages at a moment in time. They are not earnings histories for specific individuals; since earnings increase between cohorts, longitudinal data show steeper age–earnings profiles with maximum earnings for a typical worker being reached in the mid-fifties.

After allowing for differences in education and working conditions, most studies suggest that union members receive higher rates. This union premium is around 8–10 per cent in the UK in the 1980s but lower in Germany and the Netherlands, whilst the local bargaining premium in Italy is around 4 per cent for blue-collar workers and nearly double that for white-collar workers (OECD, 1994a). Overtime premiums range from 25 per cent in France to 80 per cent in Sweden (OECD, 1994). The extent of regional variations in wages seems to differ markedly in the EU, with Germany having the smallest regional differences and France the largest. In Germany, Sweden and Italy the large regional differences in unemployment in the 1980s and 1990s have not significantly altered regional wage differentials. We discuss the size and effects of this differential more fully in Chapter 5.

Conventional wisdom asserts that wage structures by industry and occupation are remarkably stable over time, but recent evidence of the growth of wage inequality suggests the need for some revisions. Gittleman and Wolff's (1993) study of inter-industry wage differentials in Europe suggested that the rank order of industries was remarkably stable over time and that there was a tendency for industry wage rankings to become more similar across countries. Their results again indicated large differences in Europe with wage dispersion across industries being eight times greater in the Netherlands in the mid-80s than in Finland. While industry–wage dispersion was falling in both these countries in the 1970s and early 1980s it was increasing in Belgium, Norway and the UK. In general, the low-wage and high-wage industries tend to be the same across countries, and studies, such as that by Lucifora (1993) for Italy, suggest the existence of large and persistent wage differentials among industries and workers of comparable skills. Marsden and Silvestre (1992) confirm the stability of relative wages between industries and report that, in general, occupational differentials in Europe seem similarly insensitive to changes in market conditions.

Evidence suggests that while the public sector is likely to employ workers who are more skilled, older and more likely to be in professional or service occupations than the economy as a whole, it does reward them differently to the private sector. Studies of the UK by Blank (1994) and Rees and Shah (1995) suggest that women in particular earn higher wages in the public sector, though males for a given set of characteristics earn less. The public/private wage differential declined rapidly in the 1980s, while the public sector wage distribution widened.

1.2.3   *Payment systems in Europe*

A central problem for any employer is that the typical labour contract specifies remuneration in terms of payment per unit of time rather than in terms of worker effort or realised output. The lack of any clear and stable relationship between wage rates per hour and unit labour costs has encouraged employers to supplement or replace time rates with various forms of incentive pay. In part this reflects some of the technological developments discussed earlier which increase the idiosyncrasy of production and the need for motivated and flexible workers. Relatively little is known about the incidence of incentive pay schemes across European countries though Marsden and Silvestre (1992) provide a short survey. Labour costs surveys also indicate that periodic bonuses and holiday pay differ significantly between member countries.

In general, in recent years traditional individual payment by results schemes, such as piece-rates, have tended to be replaced by time-based payments, while merit pay, profit-sharing and productivity bargaining have become more common ways of introducing performance-related payments. For the UK Beatson (1993) reports that about three-quarters of medium and large employers made some use of performance related payment systems in the early 1990s, with merit pay and financial participation schemes (profit-sharing and share option schemes) being the most common. About 27 per cent of British employees were receiving some form of incentive payment with 15 per cent of employees being covered by financial participation schemes and 18 per cent receiving formal appraisals. De Luca and Bruni (1993) record the growth of incentive payments in Italy, especially amongst managers, where around 40 per cent of their remuneration was individually based. Walsh (1995) reports that over a quarter of surveyed employers in Denmark, Italy, Norway and Sweden reported that individual negotiations played a role in the determination of basic pay for clerical staff, with performance related pay also becoming more important in France. The OECD (1995) study of profit-sharing suggests a rapid increase in coverage in Finland, France and the UK in the 1990s, with 5 per cent of Dutch, German and Italian employees also receiving some form of profit-sharing.

One incentive for the introduction of incentive payments in the 1980s was the effect of incomes policies, which condensed skill differentials in many European countries. In Italy, indexation in the form of the centrally negotiated *scala mobile* was a major contributor to this process. This 1975 agreement granted equal across-the-board rises according to changes in the cost of living index. Up to 80 per cent of Italian industrial employees were covered by the agreement and it accounted for the largest component of nominal wage changes in the early 1980s. Indexation was reformed in the mid-1980s and the formal indexation mechanism was abolished at the end of 1991 (de Luca and Bruni, 1993).

1.3   Industrial relations and wage fixing systems

Our investigation of the European labour market has so far ignored institutional considerations and in this section we consider the role of trade unions and the nature of the wage-fixing process. This is followed by a review of the impact of government policy and the legal system on labour market behaviour in Europe.

1.3.1 *Trade unions*

In most European countries members of different trade unions can be found in the same establishment, sometimes directly competing for membership. In France and Italy rival unions have ties to different political parties. The data in Table 1.7 provide a summary of unionisation and collective bargaining rates in European economies; trade union density or unionisation rate is defined as the number of union members as a percentage of wage and salary earners. Unionisation rates vary from over 70 per cent in Finland and Sweden to around 10 per cent in France and Spain. The collective bargaining coverage rate is the number of workers covered by collective agreements as a percentage of wage and salary earners. In Europe, coverage rates are substantially higher than unionisation rates and national differences are smaller. Scandinavian countries are an exception, having both a high unionisation and coverage rate. There are two major reasons why coverage rates are higher than unionisation rates. Collective agreements are often voluntarily extended to non-union workers by employers. Additionally, in many European countries, collective agreements are extended by statute to third parties. These national differences largely reflect institutional differences. For example, the low unionisation rates in France and Spain reflect a system where employers are legally required to bargain with unions, but collective

Table 1.7 Unionisation and collective bargaining coverage rates, 1990

	Unionisation rate[1]	Collective bargaining coverage rate[2]
Austria	46	98
Belgium	51	90
Denmark	71	na
Finland	72	95
France	10	92
Germany	33	90
Greece	34	na
Ireland	49	na
Italy	38	na
Luxembourg	49	na
Netherlands	26	71
Portugal	32	79
Spain	11	68
Sweden	83	83
UK	39	47[3]
Norway	56	75

na = not available.

[1] Unionisation rate is the number of trade union members as a percentage of wage and salary earners.

[2] Collective bargaining coverage rate refers to number of workers covered by collective agreements as a percentage of wage and salary earners. Figures are for 1990, apart from France (1985), Germany (1992) and Portugal (1991).

[3] Figure is for Great Britain.

Source: OECD Employment Outlook 1994, Chart 5.1 and Tables 5.7 and 5.8.

agreements do not discriminate in favour of union members. Therefore, this provides little incentive to join trade unions.

Most European countries have a very high collective bargaining coverage rate in the public sector, though in Austria, Portugal and Spain all or most public sector workers are governed by statutes with no formal bargaining rights and Germany has a mixed system where around 40 per cent of public employees are excluded from collective bargaining. Coverage rates are also high in manufacturing and transport, though they show no clear differences by gender and are lower in smaller firms. Union density rates have been rising in all Scandinavian countries since 1970 but there have been large falls since 1970 in France, Portugal, Spain, the Netherlands and the UK, whilst coverage rates have been more stable. In part the decline in unionisation in these countries reflects the structural changes in employment discussed earlier, with the decline of the heavily unionised manufacturing and public sectors and the growth of small firms, the service sector, atypical and female employment, though changes in the legal, political and institutional environment have often had a significant impact. For example, union recognition in Britain has fallen overall, largely because of the lack of recognition in new establishments, rather than a trend towards derecognition. Stewart (1995) finds that the decline in the union wage differential also reflected an inability of unions to establish differentials in new establishments. Collective bargaining coverage rates appear to be more stable in Europe with only the UK and the Netherlands showing a decline in the 1980s (OECD, 1994a). In the UK the decline of collective bargaining, together with the abolition of selective minimum wages (Wages Councils) means that collective pay-setting now affects the pay and conditions of less workers than it did in the 1930s. We consider the extent to which bargaining is becoming more decentralised in the following section.

A major source of trade union bargaining power is the ability to undertake collective action and a common measure of the militancy of trade unions has been the number, size and length of industrial disputes. Strikes and other labour disputes are usually a product of bargaining disagreements and therefore may be a better indicator of the degree of mutual inconsistency of the bargaining objectives of unions and employers than of militancy, be it trade union or employer. Nevertheless, international comparisons of industrial disputes are of interest, though differences in recording procedures and large year to year variability cause some problems of interpretation. Bird (1994) provides a review of these problems and the data shown in Table 1.8 is extracted from his review. Again the picture for European countries is one of variability with Greece having by far the largest number of working days lost per 1,000 employees, and Spain, Italy and Finland having high rates with Austria, France, Germany and the Netherlands having the lowest. Strike rates have been falling in most European economies since the late 1980s, with Denmark and the UK achieving the fastest reductions. Strike rates tend to vary by industry, with rates being nearly double the economy average in mining and quarrying, manufacturing, construction, transport and communications.

Table 1.8 Labour disputes: recent trends
(Working days lost per 1,000 employees in all industries and services)

	Annual Average 1984–88	Annual Average 1989–93
Austria	–	10
Belgium	50[1]	30[1]
Denmark	250	30
Finland	470	170
France	60	30
Germany	50	20
Greece	3030	4470
Ireland	370	160[1]
Italy	360	250[1]
Netherlands	10	20
Portugal	90	60
Spain	740	430
Sweden	100	70
UK	400	70
Norway	150	60

– less than 5 days lost per thousand.
[1] average based on incomplete data.
Source: D. Bird (1994) Table 1.

1.3.2   Systems of wage fixing

We have so far considered union density and the extent to which employees are covered by collective agreements, but the level at which bargaining occurs and the extent to which it is co-ordinated are also important determinants of the performance of an economy's industrial relations system. Bargaining can take many different forms ranging from single-employer bargaining between trade unions and individual firms or plants, through multi-employer bargaining, perhaps industry wide, between union federations and employer associations to the national wage agreements reached in corporatist economies between trade union confederations, central employer organisations and government. These three levels of bargaining are not mutually exclusive given multilevel bargaining and, as Walsh (1995) points out, commentators have not always agreed on how to categorise particular national systems. We discuss the relative merits of centralised and decentralised systems in Chapter 8, but for the moment our intention is merely to record the nature of bargaining in European countries and to identify any common trends over time. The study by the OECD (1994) provides a comprehensive review of the position in the early 1990s and we utilise it for much of the following discussion.

Single-employer (enterprise) and/or establishment bargaining dominates in North America and is becoming more important in the UK and France. Whilst supplementary, single-employer bargaining is also found elsewhere in the EU, sectoral and/or multi-employer bargaining still dominates, especially in Austria, Germany and the Netherlands. Some form of economy-wide bargaining has occurred in Belgium, Finland, the Netherlands, Norway, Portugal, Spain and Sweden in recent years. We examine the demise of the Swedish centralised system in Chapter 8. An important feature of the wage-fixing process is the extent to which there is any co-ordination of the bargaining outcomes. Such co-ordination may be direct (overt) in the sense that there is explicit co-ordination by the bargaining agents, or indirect (covert) where key sectors set going rates for other sectors or firms. Once again the UK increasingly follows the North American system of unco-ordinated and decentralised bargaining in the private sector, with a growing emphasis upon plant-level bargaining in which key settlements no longer dictate the going rates. In Germany, the vast majority of collective agreements are at the sectoral level, differentiated by region. Co-ordination is achieved by the strength of trade unions and employer organisations which control regional bargaining. In addition key bargains, such as the metalworking sector, set the going rate and conditions for other sectors and, in some cases, for bargaining in works councils. In 1993, in order to ease the employment consequences of the convergence of wage rates following re-unification, special 'hardship' agreements were introduced into some collective agreements allowing individual firms and their works councils to opt out of industry agreements for a short time to safeguard jobs and allow restructuring.

The OECD (1992a) reports that effective wages in Germany are on average 10 to 20 per cent higher than the rates specified in the sectoral agreements due to supplements at the firm level, and Italy and France have similarly large gaps between agreed industry rates and enterprise pay levels (Marsden, 1995). More recently there has been some decentralisation to company bargaining in Spain and Sweden and even in Austria, whose labour law in theory excludes collective bargaining at company and plant level. Following the abolition of the *scala mobile* in Italy there has been a movement towards the German collective bargaining system, with sectoral agreements determining the framework for negotiation with works councils at enterprise level. In Portugal, sectoral bargaining has been recently combined with economy-wide incomes policy agreements, though the latter have had mixed success in reducing inflation. The low wage levels in sectoral agreements have often encouraged Portuguese employers to resist company bargaining. The Swedish bargaining system has become more decentralised in recent years following the withdrawal of employers from the centralised wage bargaining in 1991. Belgium, France and Spain have tried to reintroduce tri-partite organisations to co-ordinate pay-setting and/or working conditions to maintain competitiveness, though the emphasis upon wage restraint led to a general strike in Spain. In Austria, Belgium, France and Portugal collective agreements are normally legally extendible to cover non-affiliated employees in the same sector or region. Only Norway, Sweden and the UK lack extension procedures, though Swedish unions often sign subsidiary agreements with non-affiliated employers.

Overall, as Lansbury (1995) concludes, whilst there has been some movement towards decentralised bargaining in Europe and especially in the UK, there is still a wide variety of wage-fixing systems in the EU. Walsh *et al.* (1995) report that although multinationals had standardised salary structures for senior management, they had resisted pressures for an integration and co-ordination of pay structures and bargaining systems across Europe for other workers. Increased European economic integration seems as yet to have produced little convergence of wage-fixing systems, an issue we return to in Chapter 8. Diversity also extends to terminology, with the widespread use of the concept of the social partners in continental Europe causing incomprehension to those raised on adversarial industrial relations and economic liberalism in the UK. The social partners are the main union federations and employer organisations, the latter being powerful in countries where industry or economy-wide bargaining requires individual employers to waive bargaining rights. As yet, the rise of decentralised bargaining in continental Europe has not led to a British-style move towards labour market deregulation and concerted attacks upon trade union immunities. Hence, the variety of legal and regulatory frameworks in Europe which we survey in the following section.

1.4   Regulatory frameworks

Part of recent debates concerning the advantages of flexible labour markets has concerned the desirability of reducing regulatory constraints upon employers in the labour market. We will be assessing these arguments throughout this book, in particular assessing their relationship to the European unemployment problem in Chapter 7 and to the social dumping argument in Chapter 8. In this section we merely record, rather than analyse, the extent of regulations in European labour markets in the mid-1990s, identifying key differences and trends; Ehrenberg (1994) provides a comprehensive survey of this area. Health and safety, equal opportunities and unemployment benefits are dealt with in later chapters. Here we concentrate upon employment and working conditions regulations, minimum wage laws and the legal framework governing industrial relations in European countries. In the absence of data we are unable to discuss the extent to which regulations are actually enforced, though Barnard, Clark and Lewis (1995) find evidence of an increased use of judicial mechanisms for resolving disputes in Europe. In the following sections we examine the national legislation which preceded any recently agreed EU directives.

1.4.1   *Employment and working conditions*

The large differences in European working practices which we have identified earlier are in part a consequence of differences in national regulatory regimes. In the UK there are relatively few regulations on working time or the employment of atypical workers, whilst elsewhere in the EU statutes or collective agreements or both provide workers with 'rights' regarding maximum working hours and holiday entitlements. The different philosophies underlying these regimes are discussed in Chapter 3 and debates concerning common EU regulations are analysed in Chapter 8. The extent of regulations on working-time and regulation of temporary forms of contract is summarised in Table 1.9; Grubb and Wells (1993) provide a more comprehensive survey.

Table 1.9 Regulation of employment contracts

	Legal limit on normal working week (hours)	Legal minimum annual leave (weeks)	Restrictions on employment of temporary workers
Austria	40	5	only on successive contracts
Belgium	40	4	Yes
Denmark	none	5	No
Finland	40	5	Yes
France	39	5	Yes
Germany	48	3	Yes
Greece	48	4	Yes
Ireland	48	3	No
Italy	48	none[1]	Yes
Luxembourg	40	5	
Netherlands	48	4	only on successive contracts
Portugal	48	3–4.4	Yes
Spain	40	5	Yes
Sweden	40	5.4	Yes
UK	none	none	No
Norway	40	4.2	Yes

[1] Legal right to paid leave, length not specified.
Source: OECD Jobs Study (1994a), Tables 6.6, 6.11 and 6.12.

As can be seen, only Denmark and the UK lack legislation establishing a normal or maximum number of working hours per week, while only Italy and the UK lack statutes specifying the minimum annual leave entitlements. Even though employers have recently wished to achieve greater flexibility in working time, trade unions have tried to negotiate shorter working hours, though in recent years legislation on working hours has become less restrictive with averaging hours over a one-year period now possible in Belgium, France, Germany, Italy and the Netherlands. In addition, in Austria, Belgium, France and Sweden maximum hours may be exceeded when specified in collective agreements. In Denmark, Greece, Portugal and Spain the minimum holiday entitlements are the actual entitlements for most workers, whilst in other countries collective bargaining may be used to enhance these entitlements. The employment of temporary and part-time workers gives employers the opportunity of avoiding certain obligations regarding pension and social security contributions and dismissal and severance pay procedures and entitlements. As Table 1.9 indicates, most European countries have restrictions on the employment of such workers, with Italy requiring prior authorisation by the Employment Office. In Finland, France, Germany, Greece, Italy, Norway, Portugal, Spain and Sweden, fixed-term contracts are limited to specific circumstances such as seasonal work. Where applicable, most countries have lengthened the maximum duration of fixed-term contracts, though France introduced further restrictions in 1990. In Ireland and the UK levels of social protection are lower for temporary workers. Until recently, legislation in many

European countries did not recognise the existence of part-time workers, though most countries have now adopted legislation giving these workers proportional rights in order to comply with European Law. In several countries (Belgium, France, Germany and the Netherlands), employers in large establishments are required to consult or inform employee representatives before introducing part-time workers. Britain apart, there now seems to be a general consensus in Europe that flexibility can best be realised where all employees are entitled to equivalent basic rights and protections, irrespective of employment status (Marullo, 1995).

Employment protection legislation may have three main provisions relating to notification requirements, length of notice and severance pay, and unfair dismissal provisions, including special protection for certain groups such as pregnant women and the disabled. Employment protection legislation is again more wide-ranging in southern Europe and Ireland, with Denmark, Norway and the UK having the least restrictive policies (Mosley, 1994). All member states provide some statutory protection against unfair dismissal, usually requiring a written statement of the reason for dismissal or advance consultation with employee representatives, and collective redundancies are covered under a 1975 Community directive requiring prior notification and consultation. In Denmark, France, Greece, Italy and Spain severance payments are mandatory for all but summary dismissals, whilst such payments are compulsory in Ireland and the UK for those made redundant. The extent of protection depends upon age and length of service. Only in Italy and Norway is the right to reinstatement commonly exercised. In Austria, Belgium, Denmark, Germany, Greece, Luxembourg and Italy, white-collar workers enjoy significantly higher levels of employment protection than blue-collar workers. The *European Industrial Relations Review* (1995) provides a survey of these differences in employment law by occupational status. One consequence of these differences is that average entitlement for severance pay in the Community was over 50 per cent higher for white-collar workers at the start of the 1990s. The right to contest unfair dismissal has been progressively eroded in the UK as eligibility rules were tightened. The OECD's 1994 *Employment Outlook* provides a detailed examination of recent changes with most European countries, with the exceptions of Greece and Ireland, relaxing their regulations.

The difficulty of comparing these restrictions on employers has led several researchers to develop indices of the strictness of employment protection in national labour markets, though all suffer from an inability to measure enforcement levels. In Table 1.10 we summarise some of the results surveyed in the OECD Jobs Study (1994a), concentrating upon European countries. These rankings reflect legislation at the beginning of the 1990s and ignore the major national and EU policy changes which have occurred since then. In this table low rankings indicate a low level of protection, the final column indicating that in general, employers' perceptions seem consistent with the rankings allocated. Grubb and Wells (1993) reported that these rankings help to explain the differences in the importance of atypical employment and of working hours in the EU. For example, the incidence of temporary working appears sensitive to the increase in the level of employment protection of permanent workers, and self-employment is higher and part-time working lower in countries with more restrictive regulations.

Table 1.10 Employment protection indicators

	'Strictness' ranking for regulations of dismissals[1]		Percentage of firms citing regulations for not hiring more staff
	Regular contracts	Fixed term contracts	
Austria	12.0	4.0	na
Belgium	4.0	15.0	46
Denmark	3.0	2.0	na
Finland	8.5	10.5	na
France	5.0	12.0	53
Germany	8.5	13.5	44
Greece	11.0	8.5	51
Ireland	2.0	2.0	45
Italy	13.0	13.5	62
Netherlands	6.0	5.5	58
Portugal	15.0	7.0	42
Spain	14.0	5.5	63
Sweden	10.0	8.5	na
UK	1.0	2.0	27
Norway	7.0	10.5	na

na = not available.
[1] Low ranking indicates less strict regulations.
Source: OECD Jobs Study (1994a), Tables 6.5 and 6.7.

1.4.2 *Minimum wage laws*

A major determinant of the pattern of wages in an economy is the existence and operation of minimum wage laws. In Chapter 3 we analyse the economic rationale and consequences of such regulations and in this section we merely identify the current operation of minimum wage laws in European countries. Three systems of minimum wages may be identified: statutory, collective agreements, and selective. In France, Greece, the Netherlands, Portugal and Spain minimum wages are determined by statutory instruments, with higher minimum rates established in collective agreements extendable to non-signatories by government decision. In Belgium, Germany, Spain, the 'old' EFTA countries and for most workers in Ireland, minimum wages are set by collective agreements with extension again possible. In Denmark, collective agreements again set minimum wages but extension is not possible, whilst in the UK the previous selective minimum wage system of Wages Councils, covering certain sectors including retailing, was abolished in 1993.

Comparisons between the US and continental Europe indicate that the crucial determinants of the impact of minimum wage laws on the structure of wages and employment are the level set relative to average wages, together with the frequency of adjustment and the coverage across the work-force. Gregory and Sandoval (1994) provide a survey of minimum wage laws in the EC and consider their impact upon the incidence of low pay. Freeman (1994a) provides a summary of the relative level of minimum wages across countries. The minimum wages are around 70 per cent of average earnings in Belgium, Denmark, Germany, Greece, the Netherlands, Portugal and around 60 per cent in France, Luxembourg and Spain, the US rate being only around 33 per cent of average earnings. Minimum wage laws have become more flexible in many European countries. Automatic updating mechanisms have been weakened recently, with Greece, Italy and the Netherlands abolishing indexation in the early 1990s. Similarly, Belgium, the Netherlands, Portugal and Spain now have lower minimum rates for young workers, whilst labour market programmes for youths in France pay wages below the minimum. Minimum wages are specified by industry in Portugal, whilst in Luxembourg they are differentiated by skill.

1.4.3   *Industrial relations*

In this section we concentrate upon the legal environment in which industrial relations are conducted, though we defer examination of worker participation in European countries to Chapter 8. A precondition for collective bargaining is that employers recognise trade unions, though the UK removed statutory procedures for union recognition in 1980 and some workers are prohibited from joining a trade union. In several European countries statutory provisions have been introduced to encourage collective bargaining rather than interfere with union recognition directly. For example, the 1982 'Auroux' law imposes a duty on French employers to bargain annually where there is a precedent for bargaining. Employers also face a duty to bargain in Luxembourg, Portugal, Spain and Sweden. In addition, as discussed earlier, many countries have used statutory provisions to extend collective agreements beyond the bargaining parties; the OECD Jobs Study (1994a) provides a summary of national legal provisions. Union security legislation can cover various forms of closed shops. Pre-entry closed shops require recruits to belong to a union before appointment, whilst post-entry closed-shops require workers to join a (usually specified) union after taking up employment. Only in Austria, Denmark, the Netherlands and Sweden are either type of closed shop legal. In the UK all legal protection was removed from closed shops in the 1990 Employment Act.

Legislation covering industrial disputes influences the relative effectiveness of strikes and lockouts. While all European countries accept the principle of the right to strike, the key determinant of the unions' ability to undertake successful strike action, or employers to lock out, is immunity from claims for financial damages resulting from that action. Immunities are restricted in a variety of ways in European economies. In the Netherlands and Germany strikes are only, in general, legal as a last resort. In Germany and Austria the extent of strike action must be in proportion to the objectives sought. Most countries prohibit industrial action on issues covered in an existing valid agreement, though in the UK collective agreements are not legally binding. Lockouts are banned in Greece and Portugal and in the Netherlands employers must continue to pay workers willing to work. Regulations in many countries grant immunity only when certain procedures have been followed, such as compulsory arbitration, ballots, notice periods and picketing restrictions.

The UK is unique in that since 1980 it has been willing to directly reduce the bargaining strength of individuals and unions by changing legislation covering union membership, their elections and their behaviour before and during strikes. Individuals have no right to strike and strikers can be dismissed without compensation. Immunities from civil action are given to organisers of strikes only when pre-strike ballots have conformed with statute and the industrial action covers a trade dispute.

1.5 Expenditure on labour market policies

We have so far concentrated upon regulatory frameworks rather than labour market policies. The rival philosophies underlying national labour market policies in Europe are analysed in Chapter 3 and each of the chapters thereafter is concerned with examining specific policy areas. In this section we seek to provide an overall assessment of the comparative size of government expenditure on those policies.

Initially we concentrate upon levels of social protection. In countries with a well developed government-funded social protection system, differences in funding between countries leads to differences in the structure of wages and labour costs. In the southern member states where government-funded social protection systems are less fully developed, firms have been expected to provide substitutes with their more restrictive regulatory employment framework providing direct encouragement. The compatibility of such policies with the needs of a competitive labour market, or at least a flexible one, have been much questioned in recent years.

OECD data defines social protection to include government expenditure on health, pensions, unemployment benefits and income support schemes. Total government expenditure as a percentage of GDP is shown in Table 1.11 for the years 1980 and 1990. The figures show large differences within the EU, with social protection expenditure relatively high in the Nordic countries, Benelux and France, and low in southern Europe and Ireland. There has been some convergence in the 1980s, with expenditure share rising in southern Europe and falling in Germany and the UK. Scherer (1994) provides a disaggregated analysis of these trends and in Chapter 8 we consider the debate concerning whether these differences could generate significant social dumping effects.

Another available way of comparing labour market policies concerns national expenditure on labour market programmes, data which the OECD again records. Expenditure is categorised as on active or passive policy programmes, Table 1.12 shows expenditure as a percentage of GDP. Active programmes include expenditure on public employment services, labour market training, programmes for youths in transition from school to work and subsidised employment, including those for the disabled. Passive measures include payments of benefits to the unemployed and those retiring early for labour market reasons rather than health or personal preference. Again there are huge differences between European countries with Denmark's share of GDP devoted to labour market programmes being over five times greater than that of Greece. In recent years only Ireland, the Netherlands and the UK have devoted a

Table 1.11 Government expenditure on social protection as a percentage of GDP

	1980	1990
Austria	23.4	24.5
Belgium	25.4	25.2
Denmark	26.0	27.8
Finland	21.4	27.1
France	23.9	26.5
Germany	25.4	23.5
Greece	13.4	20.9[1]
Ireland	20.6	19.7
Italy	19.8	24.5
Luxembourg	26.0	27.3
Netherlands	27.2	28.8
Portugal	13.6	15.3
Spain	16.8	19.3
Sweden	32.4	33.1
UK	21.3	22.3
Norway	21.4	33.1

[1] Figure is for 1989.
Source: OECD Employment Outlook, 1994, Table 4.7.

reduced share of GDP, though the increase in other countries, especially in the Nordic countries, has partly been due to increased expenditure on passive measures as unemployment increased. Only in a few countries, (Germany, Ireland, Italy and the Netherlands) has the share spent on active measures increased significantly. The European Commission (1993) has concluded that member countries with more restrictive employment legislation tend to devote more government expenditure to employment adjustment programmes. We consider these differences in more detail in Chapter 7 where we also assess the effectiveness of the active programmes.

1.6   Privatisation and competitive tendering in the public sector

The political philosophy which has generated labour market deregulation in some European labour markets has produced even greater adjustments in goods and services markets, where policies of privatisation and compulsory competitive tendering in the rump of the public sector have been pursued. These latter policies have generated a decline in the share of workers employed in the public sector in several European countries, but they were predominantly introduced to promote significant productivity gains and radically change conditions of employment. In much of Europe these policies are too recent to assess, but in the UK there are now sufficient studies to reach some broad conclusions. Haskel and Szymanski (1992) conclude that privatisa-

Table 1.12 Expenditure on labour market policies, 1994[1]

								as a % of GDP							
	A	B	DK	D	E	F	FI	GR	IRL	I	L	NL	P	SW	UK
Active measures															
Public employment services & admin	0.13	0.21	0.11	0.24	0.11	0.15	0.17	0.07	0.14	0.08	0.04	0.20	0.13	0.27	0.24
Labour market training	0.11	0.27	0.47	0.42	0.15	0.44	0.47	0.16	0.48	0.02	0.04	0.18	0.33	0.80	0.16
Youth measures	0.01	na	0.34	0.06	0.09	0.28	0.13	0.04	0.43	0.80	0.09	0.11	0.27	0.26	0.14
Subsidized employment	0.04	0.62	0.43	0.34	0.18	0.26	0.78	0.08	0.28	–	0.02	0.13	0.07	0.81	0.02
Measures for the disabled	0.06	0.15	0.46	0.26	0.01	0.08	0.15	0.01	0.14	–	0.05	0.59	0.05	0.82	0.03
Passive measures															
Unemployment compensation	1.42	2.34	3.78	2.03	3.11	1.72	4.56	0.81	2.81	0.62	0.35	2.61	1.00	2.46	1.59
Early retirement for labour market reasons	0.13	0.73	1.41	0.49	–	0.38	0.46	–	–	0.26	0.53	–	0.14	0.02	–
Total expenditure on active and passive measures	1.90	4.33	7.00	3.84	3.64	3.31	6.73	1.20	4.27	1.77	1.12	3.82	1.98	5.44	2.18
Ratio of passive to active expenditure	4.4	2.4	2.9	1.9	5.9	1.7	3.0	2.1	1.9	1.0	3.7	2.2	1.3	0.8	2.7

na = not available

[1] Countries listed in the following order: Austria, Belgium, Denmark, Germany, Spain, France, Finland, Greece, Ireland, Italy, Luxembourg, the Netherlands, Portugal, Sweden, UK. Belgium, France, Luxembourg, and the Netherlands 1993, Italy 1992 and Ireland and Luxembourg 1991. Greece some data 1993 other 1992.
Source: OECD Employment Outlook, 1995, Table T.

tion has led to large-scale labour shedding and whilst the overall effects on wages are uncertain, wage inequality seems to have increased. Parker and Martin (1995) conclude that privatisation has had a mixed effect upon labour productivity, with most concerns achieving significant improvements in the run-up to privatisation, but these improvements were not always sustained. The attempts to imitate the market in those activities remaining in the public sector through compulsory competitive tendering, covered work to the annual value of around £2.4 billion at the end of 1994. The Audit Commission (1995) summarises some of the findings of investigations. Their most dramatic example is the 40 per cent fall in the net cost of refuse collection since 1980/81, with two-thirds of this reduction occurring before the introduction of legislation requiring competitive tendering. In part this reduction reflects reduced quality of service, with front-gate rather than back-door collection, and technological changes such as the introduction of large capacity collection trucks. However, there appears to have been a significant reduction in labour costs, the product of inferior working conditions, and this has provoked a new confrontation between EC law and British government policies which we investigate in Box 8.2.

1.7 Concluding comments

1.7.1 *What is the labour market for?*

In this chapter we have concentrated upon describing key elements of labour market behaviour rather than assessing that behaviour. It is sometimes difficult whilst making comparisons not to imply that certain outcomes are more favourable than others and we need briefly to address this issue before our study progresses further. There is nothing intrinsically beneficial in an economy providing a high level of employment or more flexible working patterns. Most paid employment in a market economy reflects workers producing parts of goods and services to be consumed by others. Motivation for seeking work for most labour market participants is primarily to earn income in order to consume goods and services they themselves do not produce. The more home production that takes place in an economy, the lower the need for market employment for a given material living standard. Similarly, the lower the relative price of goods and services to labour, the lower the necessary input of market labour for the achievement of a given material standard of living. It follows that we cannot simply judge the success of a labour market in terms of employment creation.

In assessing labour market performance the quality of the jobs created is important. Whilst this may be obvious in respect to occupational health and safety, there are other important dimensions. To the extent that individuals wish to minimise the physical and psychological demands of employment then, the intensity of work, its certainty and its distribution over time are important. An expansion of temporary employment or growth of shift and weekend working may reduce perceived living standards, if achieved at the expense of more traditional patterns of working without compensating increases in anticipated lifetime earnings. Similarly, productivity improvements need not increase social welfare if they entail reductions in the quality of the working environment or merely switch costs from employers to workers or tax-payers.

It follows that it is much easier to comment on the nature of labour market trends or policy initiatives, than it is to assess whether a particular trend or policy is beneficial or harmful. Trade-offs are usually inevitable in any changing environment and social science provides few means of assessing outcomes when losses and gains are allocated to different groups in society.

1.7.2 *Some important trends*

Whilst Box 1.4 provides a stark summary of some recent trends in European labour markets, in this section we briefly summarise the significance of these trends. One important finding which we restate now and examine in the following section is the diversity of labour market behaviour in Europe. This diversity is much greater than we would expect from differences in the structure of production and reflects the importance of historical and institutional influences, especially those concerned with the regulatory environment and the system of wage-fixing.

A common underlying consequence or cause of the trends identified in Box 1.4 is the increase in competitiveness within European labour markets. In part this reflects increased international trade and economic integration but it is also the consequence of reduced discrimination and unionisation. Even in the service sector, technological developments are increasing international trade and policies of privatisation and compulsory tendering are striking at the core activities of the public sector.

Several of the trends we have identified have consequences far wider than the labour market. The ageing of European labour forces and the more even spreading of employment across the population require radical restructuring of taxation and

---

Box 1.4: European labour markets: ten stylised trends

* National labour market behaviour in Europe is diverse!
* The labour force is ageing
* Employment is being spread more thinly amongst the population
  Growth of non-standard employment
  Decline in participation rates of older male workers
* Deindustrialisation is continuing
* Gender gaps in labour market status are being reduced
* Demand for unskilled labour is falling
* Unemployment is high and unevenly distributed
* Labour market inequality is increasing
* Collective bargaining is becoming more fragmented
* Labour markets are becoming (slightly) less regulated

National and EU labour market policies have not fully adjusted to these trends!

social welfare systems, restructuring which may modify the social forces which initially generated those trends. The inability of European labour markets to prevent increasing inequality also generates a need to consider more carefully the interaction between labour market policy and the tax and benefit system.

The contribution which the internationalisation of production and company structures and increased European integration has made to these trends is an issue which we raise in Chapter 8, where we also discuss the process of economic convergence and its interaction with labour market behaviour.

1.7.3 *Some important differences*

We have repeatedly stressed the diversity of labour market behaviour in Europe and it is now time to try to examine these differences more systematically. We will concentrate upon three differences in labour market behaviour, those between: Europe and North America; southern and northern member states, and between the UK and the rest of the EU.

Compared with Europe, North America has a superior record in job creation, but not in productivity growth, and has experienced a huge growth in wage inequality since the end of the 1970s. While Europe lacks the levels of flexibility of employment and wages achieved in North America, it has managed to provide greater job security and industrial democracy for its work-force. The more developed social welfare systems of Europe also mean that the economic well-being of Europeans is far less dependent upon their labour markets earnings than in North America. As Freeman (1994) explains, in part these differences reflect differences in preferences, but they also are the result of differences in the rules and institutions which determine labour market outcomes.

The differences between the southern and northern member states are, in part, the result of differences in the level of economic development, the differences in the sectoral distribution of employment being an example. In part, the apparently lower level of enforced social protection in southern member states is also a product of lower living standards. Indeed, when we consider aspects of employment which are not dependent on the level of development or climate, the homogeneity of the southern member states disappears. (Consider their diverse composition of non-standard employment and the differences in female participation rates.)

While the differences between southern and northern member states have been the source of some divisions in the EU, particularly over agricultural and regional policies, the differences between the UK and the rest of the EU have pervaded all EU social policy debates. Since these debates represent a significant part of this book it is worthwhile examining the uniqueness of the UK labour market. It is tempting to stress the contribution which the reforms of successive Conservative governments have made to this difference. Regulations have been eased, trade unions weakened and encouragement given to part-time and self-employment and a widening of wage dispersion. While all of these changes have moved the UK closer to the American rather than the European pattern, the antecedents of the differences lie much earlier in the retention of a legal system which relied on individual and collective bargaining rather than legally enforceable rights. Opt-outs from EU social policies notwithstanding, it is important not to over stress the uniqueness of the UK. At the macro level the behaviour of unemployment and real wages in the UK has followed the European rather than American pattern, whilst differences in the structure of labour costs have more to do with funding decisions rather than philosophical differences in the appropriate role of Governments and the legal system. Regardless of short-term opt-outs, British employers, workers and firms face the same technological, organisational and institutional changes as elsewhere in Europe and the pressures of increased competition may tend to produce similar outcomes. We return to this proposition at the end of this book.

Guide to statistical and updating sources

As emphasized in the Preface a major limitation of this book is that it cites only English language sources, in addition it does not attempt to provide a review of sources of national labour market data. The Preface also lists conventions which we follow in the presentation of data in this book. McDonald and Dearden (1994) and Artis and Lee (1994) provide excellent general introductions to the European Union.

The *OECD Jobs Study: evidence and explanations* (1994a) provides two volumes of detailed description and assessment of national labour market behaviour covering developments up to 1993. This study not only allows similarities and differences within Europe to be examined but also allows comparisons to be made with North America and Japan. The European Commission's annual report, *Employment in Europe*, provides a summary of labour market developments in the EU, as well as providing analysis of topical issues. The annexe to *Employment in Europe 1995* provides a particularly helpful introduction to labour market trends within the EU. The *Employment Observatory* published by the European Commission provides regular updates of employment policies and trends in the EU. The OECD's annual *Employment Outlook* provides a similar service for the developed economies and allows European developments to be compared with those elsewhere in the world economy.

The OECD's *Quarterly Labour Force Statistics* provides compatible data for many of the key labour market statistics of member countries, whilst the ILO publishes a mammoth *Yearbook of Labour Statistics* covering around 200 countries. *European Economy* and *Social Europe* provide many key background papers broadly reflecting the Commission's priorities, if not their actions. Blanpain (1994) provides a comprehensive encyclopaedia of international labour law and industrial relations, whilst the *European Industrial Relations Review* provides a monthly update of EU and national developments in this area. *Labour Market Trends* (previously the *Employment Gazette*) is increasing its coverage of European issues, presenting comparisons consistent with current British government bargaining positions.

The National Bureau of Economic Research's project *Working Under Different Rules* in combination with European researchers has produced five books in a University of Chicago Press Comparative Labor Market Series. The main findings of these stimulating works have been summarised in Freeman (1994), and this provides a good starting point for those wishing to investigate the consequences of differences in labour market behaviour. Ehrenberg (1994) provides an excellent alternative source. Finally, Anderton and Mayhew (1994) provide an alternative, brief anglo-centric comparison of European labour markets aimed at readers with intermediate level economic analysis.

2   Labour market economics

At the heart of most disputes about labour market policy lie disagreements about how labour markets react to changes in the economic environment. Since Adam Smith the dominant approach to the analysis of labour market behaviour has been to examine the interaction of labour supply and demand within a competitive framework. As we explain in the following chapter, it is this analysis which provides the rationale for minimal government regulation of labour markets. In this chapter, we examine how this neoclassical approach has developed in recent years. We also introduce some of the diverse models which have sought to replace this approach in the analysis of labour markets.

In essence the neoclassical approach treats the labour market as comparable to any goods market, applying the tools of marginal analysis to participants' behaviour. Neoclassical analysis was initially developed at the turn of the twentieth century to interpret labour market behaviour in economies in which the work-force was overwhelmingly male, poorly educated and predominantly employed in small manufacturing establishments. The evolution of modern neoclassical analysis from this base is the initial task of this chapter. This text does not seek to provide a comprehensive review of theory and for those requiring a more detailed review of the economic theory of labour market behaviour a guide to further reading concludes this chapter.

2.1   The basic neoclassical model

Consider a world of individual decision-makers where potential workers are motivated by a desire to maximise utility and firms by a desire to maximise profits. Initially also assume that the labour market approximates to an auction market, in which these decision-makers are price-takers in the sense that they cannot by their own actions influence the outcome of the interaction of market forces. A uniform wage prevails in such a market if we maintain the assumptions of completely (perfectly) competitive labour and goods markets. Assume also that the labour market is characterised by large numbers of small independent firms wishing to hire labour, and unorganised workers seeking to find employment. Workers and jobs are homogeneous, so that firms view all applicants as having the same productivity characteristics and workers view all job offers as identical in non-wage characteristics. All job offers and acceptances are for a single, infinitely divisible time period and there are no barriers to mobility in the market. Finally, firms and workers have perfect information about existing conditions in the labour market.

In this framework, firms wish to hire labour because they wish to generate profits from additional production. Workers are incapable of producing for themselves all of the goods which they wish to consume, and in a capitalist and monetary economy seek employment to earn wages which enables them to increase their total utility by purchasing goods and services they do not produce. Let us now consider how the labour market would operate in such an economy during the short-run: a period of time when firms operate with given technology and fixed quantities of plant and machinery.

2.1.1   *The demand for labour*

Consider the demand for labour of an individual firm in the short run. In this time period there can be no substitution between factors of production and thus there is a direct relationship between the desired production and employment levels. Given that the firm has a fixed quantity of machinery and plant in the short run, as the firm hires additional inputs of labour output will tend to rise, but not proportionally. As more and more labour is employed, workers become capital-starved, having to share their machines with more fellow workers. Once machines are being operated by the designed number of operatives at the optimal capacity, further hiring of labour is likely to lead to the extra workers having a smaller impact on production levels than previous recruits. If we define the marginal physical product of labour as the additional units of output produced by the employment of an extra unit of labour, then the argument implies that the marginal physical product of labour must eventually fall as labour input rises. This relationship is called the Law of Diminishing Returns. (Firm's output will generally rise as employment increases, but at a decreasing rate.)

Given this relationship between employment and output, what determines how much labour the firm will wish to try to hire? The firm is motivated by the desire to increase profits and its desired employment level should correspond to that level which maximises profits from the sale of production. Consider a firm which is already producing profitably, it has to decide whether its current production and employment levels are optimal; that is whether they are consistent with profit maximisation. It can solve this problem by considering whether it should employ an extra unit of labour. In perfect competition the firm is a price-taker in both the product market and labour market. It can therefore calculate the value of the marginal physical product of the extra unit of labour as being the product of the price it is taking for its good and the marginal physical product of labour. If this total exceeds the money wage it must pay to attract the additional unit of labour, its profits will rise by an expansion of employment. Where the monetary value of the marginal physical product of labour falls short of the going money wage rate then it can increase profits by reducing the input of labour. The optimal input of labour will therefore be when the value of the marginal physical product of labour is equal to the going wage rate. The firm will have applied the profit maximising rule of equating marginal revenue with marginal cost. It follows, other factors remaining unchanged, that a higher money wage rate must lead to a reduction in the desired level of employment given diminishing marginal physical productivity. An alternative specification of the equi-marginal rule is that the firm should equate the marginal physical product of labour with the ratio of the price of labour to the price it is taking for its product, that is the real wage it is paying. Once again, as the marginal physical product falls as the firm hires additional labour, it will only wish to hire more if the real wage is also falling. This argument therefore explains why the demand curve for labour is downward sloping with respect to the real wage.

Consider how we can use this demand curve for labour to analyse the consequences of the decline in the demand for unskilled labour which we identified in the previous chapter. Figure 2.1 shows a downward sloping demand curve for unskilled labour, with n^d_{70s} representing the demand curve in the 1970s. Let us assume that the real wage of unskilled workers in the 1970s was W_{70s} and their employment level was n_{70s}, this means that point A represents the employers' chosen combination of real wage and employment. For reasons which we discussed in Box 1.3, the demand for unskilled labour appears to have fallen and we represent the new relationship between demand and real wages as curve n^d_{90s}, that is at every real wage employers now wish to employ fewer unskilled workers. What are the consequences of this change? Figure 2.1 allows us to illustrate the possibilities. In the US where wage flexibility is high, this shift in demand predominantly lowered the real wage of unskilled workers. We can represent this by a movement from A to B with real wage falling to W_{us} in the 1990s. In Europe with minimum wage laws and other institutional factors restricting wage flexibility, the contraction of demand predominantly reduced employment opportunities for less-skilled workers. In terms of Fig. 2.1, in Europe the movement was from A to C with employment of unskilled workers declining to n_{eu}. In Chapter

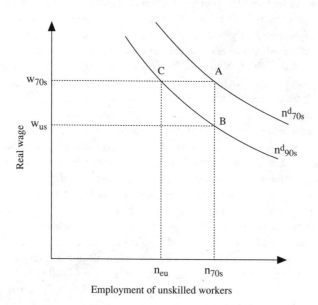

Figure 2.1 The decline in demand for unskilled labour

7 we provide a more sophisticated analysis of the consequences of the shift in demand, but this example illustrates the way in which our neoclassical analysis may be used to interpret the consequences of changes in the employment environment.

In extending our analysis to the long run we have been assuming that firms can now alter their production techniques as technology changes. In addition production techniques will also respond to changes in relative factor prices. This indicates that the demand for labour becomes more sensitive to the level of real wages in the long run, the demand curve becoming flatter. The sensitivity of the demand for labour with respect to real wages is called the wage-elasticity of the demand for labour. The elasticity of demand for labour for a given change in the wage rate will depend upon:

1. How sensitive the demand for the firm's product is to changes in price. The more elastic is the demand for the product the more elastic is the firm's demand for labour.
2. The ease of substitution of capital for labour. The greater the ability to substitute capital for labour, the greater the elasticity of demand for labour.
3. The importance of labour costs in total production costs. If labour costs are a small proportion of total costs, the effects of higher wages on total costs and therefore sales and employment will be small.
4. The elasticity of supply of substitute factors of production. The more inelastic are the supply of other factors the more inelastic is the demand for labour.

If we aggregate this analysis, to the industry or economy level, then we can no longer maintain the assumption that product price remains unchanged as firms adjust to different wage rates. However, if we maintain the assumption that the final level of demand is independent of the wage rate, then we can conclude that, as the scale of aggregation increases, the elasticity of demand for labour will tend to increase. As employment in an industry rises in the short run, now both the marginal product of labour and the price of the product fall. This makes demand more elastic for a given change in the wage rate, or in other words, the demand for labour curve becomes flatter at the industry level.

Contrary to the beliefs of some early exponents of this theory, since the value of the marginal product of a worker depends upon how much capital they have to work with, wage levels in accordance with marginal productivity have no normative implications. Marginal productivity theory cannot resolve the issue of what constitutes a 'fair' wage; Box 2.3 returns to this issue. The neoclassical marginal productivity theory already outlined is purely a theory of profit-maximising firms' desired demand for labour. In a competitive market economy firms are constrained in their labour market behaviour by the freedom of workers to reject undesired job offers. It follows that our analysis of the demand for labour tells us little about the behaviour of employment and wages in the economy unless we combine it with a theory of labour supply.

2.1.2   *The supply of labour*

Before we can summarise the neoclassical theory of labour supply we need to make one clarification and one modification to our earlier discussion. We have so far been reluctant to specify the units of measurement for the demand and supply of labour. At this stage we wish to follow the approach of Chapter 1 and treat the quantity of labour as a two-dimensional variable: the quantity of workers and the hours worked per worker. Neoclassical analysis has only recently acknowledged the effort dimension of labour supply and we consider this modification later. Any analysis must therefore examine both the participation rates of the population and hours supplied per participant. The modification we need to make is to the earlier statement that neoclassical labour market analysis is concerned with individual decision-making. Such analysis is particularly inappropriate when we discuss the supply of labour where decisions are typically taken by households. A simple assumption is to view household, not personal, utility maximisation as the goal of rational labour market participants.

The neoclassical model assumes that participants are free to vary their hours of work. In deciding the appropriate supply of labour the household has to decide the optimal combination of market work and non-market activities. Market work generates income which enables the household to purchase goods and services, but utility is also obtained from leisure and the home production of non-marketed goods and services. The opportunity cost of market work is therefore the foregone leisure and home production. The optimal supply of labour will be that which maximises utility subject to the constraint of an exogenously determined wage rate.

Unfortunately for the purposes of testing, this model gives us an ambiguous response of labour supply to changes in the real wage rate. A change in the real wage rate represents a change in the relative price of work and non-market activities, and as such must generate both substitution and income effects. Any rise in the wage rate increases the opportunity cost of leisure and home production and will generate a substitution of income-generating time for the more expensive non-market activities, that is less labour will be supplied to the market. However, the rise in the wage rate has altered the household's income from its existing supply of market labour and the previous income level can now be earned with a lower supply of labour. If, for example, the household has already achieved their target income then the income effect of a rise in the real wage rate would be to reduce their market labour supply. The net impact of the wage rise therefore depends upon the relative size of the substitution and income effects, and labour supply may rise or fall as a consequence. For the multi-person household the analysis is even more complex with, for example, a rise in one member's wage rate causing changes in both the quantity and composition of the household's labour supply. It is not therefore clear whether the labour supply curve with respect to real wages has a positive slope. Conventionally and without any obvious justification, neoclassical economics proceeds by assuming that over the relevant wage range the substitution effect dominates during the short run, giving us an upward sloping supply curve of labour.

2.1.3 *The interaction of labour demand and supply*

The basic neoclassical model of labour market behaviour merely combines the analysis of labour demand and labour supply outlined earlier. Box 2.1 illustrates how this

Box 2.1: Classifying the causes of the rise in female participation

A common feature of European labour markets in recent decades has been the rise in female participation rates; according to our model we should be able to classify the causes into demand and supply factors.

Increased demand for female workers

Changes in the structure of production in European economies have favoured sectors which traditionally have been major employers of female workers, the service sector and in particular education, health and retailing. The replacement of electro-mechanical production techniques by electronic ones has also altered the types of skills required in the production industries, favouring qualities other than physical strength. Changes in patterns of demand for goods and services, in some countries assisted by the operation of employment protection legislation and the taxation and social welfare systems, have favoured employers' use of part-time working, again favouring female employment.

Increased supply of female workers

According to our model any factors which raise female labour market wage rates will induce a substitution effect away from home production. In recent decades the increased education and training undertaken by females has raised their earning power, whilst equal opportunities policies have also contributed to a rise in female wage rates. Note that a rise in female relative wages due to reduced discrimination should *reduce* the demand for female workers, though as we note in Chapter 6 there is little evidence of such feedbacks. Factors which increase productivity in home production may also cause increased labour supply. Increased technology in the home, such as increased use of freezers, microwaves, tumbler dryers, etc., allows time to be redirected from home to market production. Changes in fertility rates and marital instability also have contributed to the increase in supply as have changes in social norms and attitudes regarding motherhood and marriage.

approach can be used to classify the possible causes of the increased female participation rates identified in Chapter 1.

Consider a single labour market where individual firms' and households' decisions have been aggregated to generate market demand and supply curves for labour; such a market is shown in Fig. 2.2. The assumptions of perfect competition, particularly homogeneity of workers and jobs, allow most of the potential problems of aggregation to be avoided at this stage.

Assume initially that the prevailing real wage level is w_1, at this wage firms in aggregate wish to hire n_1 units of labour whilst households in total wish to supply a greater quantity, n_2. Therefore at a wage of w_1 the market is experiencing an excess supply of labour. The adjustment mechanism in this model is that those workers without jobs or underemployed, that is $n_2 - n_1$, offer themselves to firms at lower wages. This downward movement in wages has two effects: households withdraw marginal

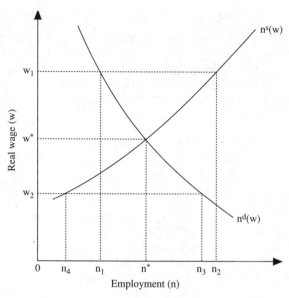

Figure 2.2 A perfectly competitive labour market

units of labour from the market and firms are stimulated to increase employment. The latter effect arises from the lower wages enabling firms to lower their output prices, this stimulates domestic and international demand, especially in markets with price elastic demand or labour-intensive production. Given the assumptions of the model, the downwards movement of wages will eventually be sufficient to restore the market to equilibrium, where employers' and households' plans can both be fulfilled, that is at w^* and n^*. Now consider the alternative case of disequilibrium, at wage rate w_2. At this wage rate employers plan to hire n_3 units of labour whilst households only wish to supply n_4. In this case the market has an excess of demand for labour, $n_3 - n_4$. Here the model argues that profit-maximising firms in their desire to fulfil production plans will bid up wages. Rising real wages will encourage households to supply more labour and also discourage firms from some of their expansion plans, once again pushing the market towards equilibrium. This neoclassical description of labour market interaction has managed to avoid an explanation of how wages change in a world where all participants are price-takers and the dynamics of the adjustment mechanism remains unclear.

2.2 Extensions to the basic neoclassical model

If we now apply this model to the economy as a whole, whilst retaining our assumption that labour is homogeneous, wage flexibility necessitates that markets clear at the same wage rate. The mobility of labour between markets ensures that wage differentials are competed away, with temporarily high or low wages producing a movement of workers and firms. This basic neoclassical model of the labour market produces allocative efficiency: profit-maximising firms and utility-maximising households acting purely on the basis of their own interests produce outcomes where additional societal wealth is produced at minimum cost. The neoclassical model is broadly compatible with what sociologists term the middle-class work ethic, which consists of three main propositions. Firstly, work is equated with employment, non-market work being neglected. Secondly, the unequal distribution of income is justified by explaining rewards as reflecting contributions to societal wealth. Thirdly, it argues that work involves making a career, and people are supposed to find self-fulfilment through their work. Opportunities for advancement are available for all, a harmony of interests between employers and employees is assumed and disutilities of employment apart from lost leisure are largely ignored. This set of beliefs may not be relevant for major groups in society such as temporary, part-time and unskilled workers, mothers and ethnic minorities. Whilst radical and non-competitive critiques are considered later, we initially review refinements within the dominant neoclassical approach. The development of neoclassical labour economics has been the result of a gradual realisation that many real-world labour market characteristics are inconsistent with the perfectly competitive model. In order to develop these refinements we gradually relax some of the restrictive assumptions of our basic model.

2.2.1   *Heterogeneity of workers and jobs*

Once we relax the assumptions of homogeneous workers and jobs, wage differentials will persist in the long run. Workers now have different preferences regarding conditions, responsibilities and regularity of work, and utility maximisation is no longer synonymous with income maximisation. Workers maximise the sum of monetary and non-monetary returns from employment, attributing a monetary value to the characteristics of employment such as level of safety and incidence of weekend working. Even with all workers having the same productivity characteristics, it is the 'net advantages' of employment which are equalised by competition, not wage rates. Workers, however, do not have the same productivity characteristics and the main explanation of wage differentials in the neoclassical approach is in terms of differences in education, training and experience.

Workers can invest in costly, productivity-augmenting activities and so gain increased future labour market income as a return on their increased human capital. Such investment decisions are treated akin to fixed and financial investment decisions, and competition ensures that in the long run rates of return on investments of equal risk are equalised. Wage differentials in the long run will therefore reflect the costs of acquiring the required skill and experience to enter the market, as well as different rates of time preference and attitudes to risk taking. Implicit in this human capital explanation of wage differentials is the view that productivity is worker, not job, determined and that labour market opportunities are unaffected by characteristics of workers unrelated to productivity, such as gender and race. Where firms have unique production processes then training will have to be firm-financed. Such firm-specific training encourages the adoption of employment practices which reduce labour turnover and therefore lower training costs.

51

In the short run any shortages of skills in an expanding market should cause an increase in the relative wage in that market. The rate of return from investment in that skill is now higher and that should induce an increase of labour supply to that market. This adjustment mechanism is not instantaneous and disequilibrium wage differentials may persist for long periods. Human capital theory is more fully examined in Chapter 4, together with competing theories which reject the notion that education enhances earnings through directly augmenting worker productivity.

Modern neoclassical analysis can therefore accommodate certain aspects of real-world heterogeneity. The labour market now consists of a collection of perfect sub-markets, classified by occupation and location, in each of which a single wage rate prevails and within which employees are perfectly mobile. There are fundamental theoretical problems introduced by factor heterogeneity, particularly concerned with whether factors can be aggregated and marginal products identified, but we ignore these issues and consider other refinements to our basic model.

2.2.2 *Monopsony and organised labour*

The basic neoclassical model outlined above assumes that firms faced perfectly competitive product and labour markets. If the assumption of perfectly competitive product markets is initially relaxed, the market now consists of firms with downward-sloping demand curves for their products. As they hire more labour to increase output they not only face diminishing marginal productivity but also a lower price per unit for their product. The main consequence of this change is that wage and employment levels will be lower with the introduction of imperfectly competitive product markets, assuming that the rate of innovation is independent of market structure.

Alternatively, by introducing a dominant employer in a particular labour market we can consider the behaviour of monopsonistic labour markets. When a monopsonist wishes to hire more labour, since they face the market's upward-sloping supply curve for labour, the firm has to offer a higher wage to induce additional supply of labour. Compared to a perfectly competitive market, employment and wage levels will again be lower in equilibrium.

More problematic to neoclassical theory is how to model a market where labour is organised. Trade unions operating within the framework so far discussed, must face a downward sloping demand curve for their members' labour supply. It follows that unions must face a trade-off between wage and employment levels. Early attempts to integrate trade unions into the neoclassical approach relied upon treating unions as being equivalent to monopolists in product markets. Models of bilateral monopoly were developed but had the fundamental weaknesses that they provided no justification for their specific assumptions regarding the union's wage-employment preference or explanation for the prevalence of collective bargaining. The efficient bargain model attempts to rectify these objections by allowing unions and firms to bargain about wage rates and employment. As relative strength determines outcomes there is no unique relationship between employment and wage levels. However, outside Japan unions rarely seem to bargain directly about employment. To explain such behaviour it appears that we have to move away from the notion of unions as monopolists and consider union bargaining behaviour as reflecting the interests of the majority of their members. These models of trade union behaviour are discussed in Chapter 7 in the context of explaining the behaviour of unemployment in Europe.

2.2.3 *Imperfect and costly information*

The competitive model of labour market behaviour relies upon labour mobility to adjust wages to market-clearing levels. Typically the model views supply-side forces as dominating the adjustment mechanism: workers move from low-paying to higher-paying firms so equalising wage rates in a market. For this adjustment mechanism to operate speedily workers and firms must be aware of labour market conditions. Where workers and jobs are not identical, information is not fully and freely available and search will be a basic feature of the market. Markets will therefore take time to adjust to environmental changes, and in the short run imperfect information gives all firms an element of monopsony power. Mobility of labour no longer instantaneously eliminates disequilibrium wage differentials. Neoclassical search theory tames some of these problems of imperfect information by the application of the standard tools of constrained maximisation decision-making. Facing costly search, decision-makers on both sides of the labour market adopt optimal strategies where the costs and benefits of further search are equalised at the margin. Such analysis can be utilised to explain the existence of inter-firm wage differentials within local labour markets. Market clearing is no longer instantaneous and persisting inter-firm differentials may reflect different solutions to optimal recruitment strategy. To an extent, wage costs and search costs are substitutes for a firm, and firms can pay lower wage rates if they search more intensively.

In such an environment firms wishing to fill a vacancy no longer hire the first applicant and workers no longer accept the first job offer. The existence of unfilled vacancies and unemployed workers is now consistent with efficient labour market behaviour, since firms and workers invest in productive search prior to job-matching. Job-matching theory is more closely examined in Chapter 5 where we consider the extent of mobility in European labour markets. If workers and firms have different attitudes to risk-taking it is possible that they can find mutually beneficial solutions to coping with uncertainty in the labour market. The implicit contract theories introduced in Section 2.4.1 have developed from this proposition.

2.2.4 *Costly turnover and job-changing*

In our basic neoclassical model developed at the start of this chapter, labour mobility is assumed costless to firms and workers. This does not conform with real world experience, firms do not view labour turnover benignly nor do workers view involuntary redundancy with indifference. The reasons for the model's failure to explain this feature of labour markets is that so far we have equated firm's costs and worker's benefits with the prevailing wage rate. For firms the critical variable is labour costs per unit of output, not wage costs per unit of labour. There are fixed costs of employing labour as well as the variable wage costs. These fixed costs, in part, consist of turnover costs, such as firm-specific training and recruitment costs. To replace existing employees is expensive to firms because of the hiring costs and the lower productivity of new workers during training. Where these costs are significant firms will adopt personnel policies which attempt to minimise turnover. For these firms, compulsory redundancies are avoided where possible, instead when they wish to shed labour they initially rely on natural wastage. In temporary downturns firms with significant fixed costs will tend to hoard labour, especially skilled labour. This widespread behaviour explains why output will decline faster than employment in recessions and why labour productivity tends to be higher in economic upturns. Severe and lengthy recessions make labour hoarding prohibitively expensive and 'shake-outs' of labour can then occur across all categories of firms and occupations.

Where turnover costs are high, employers will pursue policies designed to reduce voluntary quits, for example, wage and non-wage benefits may be based upon seniority, such as holiday and sick pay entitlement. The personnel policies which firms introduce to encourage and reward worker loyalty generate rents for their employees. These rents mean that workers can be earning higher wages than their labour could command elsewhere in the market. However, the benefits which workers receive from employment are not purely financial; socialisation produces consumption benefits. The level of psychological gratification obtained at work reflects social interaction and status and a stable work environment will generate higher levels of gratification for its members. Involuntary separation requires costly search by workers as well as by firms, and the non-wage characteristics of job offers cannot easily be discovered. Risk-averting workers and cost-minimising firms are therefore likely to produce low mobility in those sections of the labour market, where the fixed costs of employing labour are high. Implicit in the contracts between workers and firms in these sectors will be employee tenure rights.

2.2.5 *Contemporary neoclassical labour economics*

In these sections we have tried to summarise the 'central core' of the neoclassical approach to labour market behaviour. In its basic form this model has a coherence and elegance unapproached by its predecessors and competitors. The major refinements made to the basic model have now been summarised and this approach can now reconcile many of the features of contemporary European labour markets which we identified in the previous chapter. Changing patterns of participation, employment structure and wage differentials can be explained in terms of shifts in demand and supply forces in the labour market. However, the popularity of any analysis should in principle be a reflection of its empirical performance rather than analytical elegance or consistency with widely held philosophical or political beliefs. On this basis, modern neoclassical analysis is still supply dominated, too often ignoring intra-firm decision-making and assuming that production is the outcome of a purely technical relationship between inputs. Its reliance upon a representative firm in analysing labour market behaviour also seems at odds with our discovery that job creation and job destruction appear to co-exist within well-defined labour markets. However, competitive analysis is not monolithic, indeed it is so malleable and robust that it is difficult to find testable propositions unique to the approach or to identify its distinctiveness. The uniqueness of neoclassical theory appears to rest on the belief that marginal analysis applied to individual decision-making in competitive markets can explain real-world labour market behaviour. The remainder of this chapter largely considers analysis which seeks to replace traditional theory rather than refine it.

Box 2.2: Beauty in the labour market

Beauty is not amongst the list of the determinants of labour market earnings acknowledged by conventional theory. An American study by Hamermesh and Biddle (1994) suggests that there is significant labour market discrimination in favour of good-looking partici-pants and against the plain-looking. In their study they used interviewer's ratings of respondents' physical appearance, concluding that the penalty for appearing plain-look-ing was of the order of 5–10 per cent of the earnings of those rated as average-looking; the beauty premium being slightly smaller. These results held for both males and females, with plain-rated women having lower participation rates and marrying men with lower human capital. Whilst there was a tendency for better-looking workers to work in occupa-tions where beauty may be more productive, beauty seemed to earn a premium in all occupations. The extent of 'lookism' discrimination in Europe remains to be investigated.

2.3 Alternative approaches to understanding the labour market

At this moment of time there is no obvious successor to the competitive analysis of the labour market already summarised. The potential successors are a very diverse group and there is no agreement as to how these approaches should be categorised or sub-divided, indeed the same analysis and insights can be described as post-Keynesian, New-Keynesian, radical or institutional according to the prejudices of individual authors. What these approaches share is the view that the neoclassical model is relevant to only certain sectors of the labour market and even within these sectors it ignores key forces in determining labour market behaviour, such as power and social relationships, custom and fairness. The purported weakness of market forces in most sectors of the labour market leads these approaches to emphasise the importance of internal, firm-specific factors in wage and employment determination and to view persisting unemployment as a normal feature of unregulated labour mar-kets. In the following sections we outline the major variants of the non-competitive approach.

2.3.1 *Labour market segmentation theory*

Prior to the neoclassical model being formally developed, John Stuart Mill writing in the middle of the last century, introduced the concept of non-competing groups. He argued that to treat the labour market as competitive was erroneous and would generate false policy pronouncements. This century the apparent failure of policies based on conventional theory to improve the position of the low paid, led to a resurgence of interest in segmented labour market theory. Dickens and Lang (1992) identified the two key elements of this approach as:

1. The labour market consists of distinct segments within which wages and employment are determined by idiosyncratic rules and processes.
2. In at least some segments of the labour market jobs are rationed and workers queue for jobs in these sectors.

Segmented labour market models have always suffered from their inability to define operationally these 'distinct segments', a problem compounded by the popularity of the simplest variant of this approach, the Dual Labour Market model associated with Doeringer and Piore. In their approach, the auction or open labour markets of the simple competitive model are only found in labour-intensive, low technology firms and industries. Here employment is often irregular, offering little training and few promotion prospects. These 'bad' jobs are collectively termed the secondary labour market. Elsewhere there are substantial barriers to labour mobility. In the 'good' jobs, or primary sector, firms operate a structured internal labour market, largely independent of competitive forces in the wider market. In this sector firms offer training opportunities and create career labour markets with promotion prospects for their workers. Labour relations tend to be formalised, with set procedures legitimising existing wage structures and working practices. The primary labour market does not clear, it is characterised by an excess supply of labour but the prevalence of wage rigidity leads to non-price rationing, with workers queuing to enter this sector.

Internal labour markets take two main forms: firm internal labour markets and occupational internal labour markets. Firm internal labour markets are operated by 'good' employers who recruit predominantly at the lowest grades, the higher grades being filled internally, often on the basis of seniority. The firm's presumption is that hired workers will be given tenure and progress up the job ladder, hence the screening process for recruits is extensive and applicants with characteristics similar to existing employees are likely to be favoured. According to the segmented labour market approach 'good' jobs make 'good' workers, not vice versa. Wages in jobs are therefore set by the technology-constrained productivity, not by the productivity potential of the particular employee or external market conditions. Written agreements will specify wage rates for different jobs rather than employees and specify firing and redundancy procedures. Firms attaching wages to jobs not people have developed the term 'company wage policy'. This proposition becomes particularly important when we discuss education and training in Chapter 4 and labour market discrimination in Chapter 6. Firms who operate internal labour markets are reluctant to adjust wages when faced with specific labour shortages or changed product market conditions. This reluctance stems from the disruption which would be caused to established wage differentials and relativities. They fear that this disruption would produce disenchanted employees and turnover would increase. Instead adjustment takes place through overtime, shift-working or short-time working according to established rules. Where demand is particularly unstable, firms in the primary sector may sub-contract out these activities.

Occupational internal labour markets transcend particular employers. Movement of workers between firms follows established rules unique to that occupation, professions such as medicine and law illustrate this behaviour. Occupational licensing and entry requirements are controlled by a professional body such as the British Medical Association which also specifies a procedure for promotion. Membership of the professional association almost guarantees employment, since entrance is restricted. Withdrawal of membership is only countenanced when specific rules have been violated. In certain periods and countries craft workers have managed to maintain an occupational internal labour market.

The composition and form of labour market segments will change over time. The retail trade presents a good example. Originally the department store was commonly a locally-based family firm with an internal labour market, which recruited school-leavers as full-time sales assistants and provided a job ladder to those management posts not filled by the family. Since the 1960s nationally-based chain-stores have replaced these stores and changed the nature of the labour market. The greater firm size has created a need for professional managers and extended internal labour markets have been developed for this section of employees. At the same time electronic cash tills, pre-packaging and self-service have de-skilled sales jobs. Firms have replaced many full-time employees by unskilled part-time or casual workers, who work the tills or fill the shelves at peak sales times only. Differences in monitoring costs and procedures means that in some countries cash till operators have retained a relatively high status (as in North America), whereas in other European countries anti-fraud and theft policies rely upon direct detection. Different and changing environments will cause employment structures to differ both within firms' sub-markets and over time; primary labour market firms being neither monolithic nor sacrosanct.

The Dual Labour Market model is often linked to sociological models of the Dual Economy developed by Averitt (1968) and the distinction between core and periphery firms. Core firms are successful ones who have established some monopoly power and tend to have a high return on capital and employ capital-intensive production methods. Core firms will tend to offer primary employment, but low skilled tasks, such as cleaning and security, may be contracted out. On the other hand peripheral firms tend to employ few managerial and technical workers, offering predominantly unskilled employment in labour-intensive production activities. Some industries tend to be dominated by core firms, such as pharmaceuticals and durable goods manufacturing, whilst others are dominated by peripheral firms, for example agriculture, textiles and hotel and catering.

The original work on internal labour markets focused on behaviour in blue-collar, male and unionised employment in manufacturing and Baker and Holmstrom (1995) question how appropriate this model remains given the changed nature of employment we examined in the previous chapter. Their studies suggest that internal labour market models cannot be easily applied to white-collar employment, recruitment is limited to a few ports of entry and wage variation within job levels is much greater than implied by the rigid wage structures suggested by the earlier work.

The various segmentation models stress the important role played by firm-specific technology and idiosyncratic products in generating structured internal labour markets. Whilst structured internal labour markets have been fully integrated into human resource management analysis, labour economics until recently has not been so enthusiastic. Some modern neoclassical economists are now utilising information economics and contract theory to analyse behaviour in internal labour markets and we discuss later the extent to which the two approaches have converged.

2.3.2 *Insider-outsider model*

The most popular form of the segmentation approach at the present time is the insider-outsider model originally developed by Lindbeck and Snower (1989). This approach argues that the existing workers in a firm, insiders, can expropriate rents from their employers since they are costly to replace. Hence outsiders, the unemployed and entrants, are disenfranchised in the wage-fixing process. Since outsiders' productivity is lower than that of existing employees, even trying to price themselves into work by under-cutting insiders may not be effective. Insider-power may also be maintained by the threat of non-co-operation since if insiders refuse to co-operate they can reduce the productivity of new recruits still further below that of existing workers. Insider-power may form the basis of trade union bargaining power and has been a popular explanation for the collapse of simple relationships between inflation and unemployment and the persisting high rates of European unemployment. We consider this model in more detail in Chapter 7.

2.3.3 *Employer-employee relationships*

Segmented labour market theory has also been linked with approaches which concentrate upon the impact of industrial relations on labour market behaviour. Orthodox theory pays little attention to the importance of industrial relations in the labour market. It assumes that the production of goods and services is purely the consequence of a technological relationship between labour input and output. Hours of work are assumed to have a unique productivity for a given worker in a given job: the motivation of the worker is treated as irrelevant to the outcome and conflicts of interest between workers and employers are ignored. An alternative approach is to adopt Leibenstein's suggestion that, rather than operating on their production function, firms inevitably suffer from inefficiencies and their task is to minimise this X-inefficiency. Employers and workers can usually agree on an appropriate wage per hour worked but it is difficult to specify an agreed outlay of employee effort per hour worked. In Marxian terms there is a distinction between labour and labour-power; firms hire and workers lease only the human potential to work. Accordingly, there is a basic conflict of interest between employers and employees: the former wish to maximise effort supplied per hour of work, workers to minimise it. Unlike capital, firms are restricted in the way they can use labour, by health and safety legislation for example, and monitoring worker-performance is costly and imperfect. It follows that employers have an incentive to generate a spirit of co-operation. To an extent supervisors and quality inspectors can monitor workers' effort and limit shirking, but employers need to get workers' co-operation if they are to achieve maximum potential profits. Though in other market conditions and where monitoring costs are low firms may seek to widen divisions amongst their work-force, reducing worker solidarity and their bargaining power, by rigid grading structures and discriminatory hiring and promotion practices.

2.3.4 *Radical labour economics*

These arguments can generate both competitive models of internal labour markets to be discussed later, and radical models of labour market behaviour originally developed from Marx's analysis of capitalist economies. Marx emphasised the unequal exchange between capitalists and workers resulting from the former's monopoly ownership of the means of production. This inequality is sustained and enhanced by the capitalists' dominance of political power and their ability to utilise institutions, especially the legal system, to disguise, consolidate and extend the exploitation of workers. Radical economists see discrimination and unemployment as part of this process, by which capital regulates workers in order to sustain the existing economic and political system; Rebitzer (1993) provides a summary of the contribution which radical political economy has made to the analysis of labour markets.

The emphasis in radical economics on the importance of institutions in consolidating employer ascendancy is shared by institutional economists and the French Regulation school. According to these approaches schooling is designed to generate attitudes and expectations in workers conducive to the existing work environment. De-skilling of the work-force may also be part of the process which employers instigate to control workers. Radical writers such as Braverman (1974) explained how 'Taylorism' was designed to reduce industrial strife by substituting scientific, and therefore 'fair', rules for worker remuneration. 'Taylorism', and in particular the use of time and motion studies, is interpreted as another example of policies designed to increase management control of the work-force and reduce worker bargaining power. The combination of this scientific management approach with mass production is often labelled 'Fordism' and resulted in the de-skilling of many production processes and extreme division of labour. Fordism was a system of work organisation based upon large-scale production units specialising in long-production runs utilising large amounts of dedicated capital equipment. Workers were sub-divided into particular operations which required little training and only maintenance and retooling of production for different products required high levels of skill. The end of the post-war boom saw a relative stagnation in most Western economies and a crisis of confidence in the ability of the existing mode of accumulation to generate desired rates of profit and growth. From the radical viewpoint, the recent adoption of flexible production discussed in Box 1.2, is merely a further stage in the development of capitalism: a stage where collective bargaining is de-centralised and labour supply further fragmented.

Radical economists interpret labour market segmentation as the consequence of cross-sectional differences in these labour control mechanisms. In primary labour markets the establishment of social norms may be important in creating a culture of reciprocity and fairness which makes workers willing to work hard. The argument that productivity is not purely technologically determined has been a fertile area in recent years and we now turn to a consideration of alternative approaches to the determinants of productivity.

2.3.5   *Fairness, habits and social factors*

Akerlof (1982) attempts to integrate some of the work of sociologists and Marxists. In his model concentrating on team production, workers have sentiment for their fellow workers and cannot be treated individually by their employer. In such an environment the determinants of workers' effort will be the norm of the work group and employers and workers may participate in a process involving reciprocal 'gifts'. Workers exchange their gift, effort in excess of minimum standards, for that of employers, wages above external market levels. Wages and effort are therefore mutually reciprocal gifts. To integrate this model with the segmented labour market approach, Akerlof suggests that primary labour markets are those where the gift components of the labour input and wage levels are sizeable. Secondary labour markets in contrast are where the wage level reflects market-clearing requirements.

Such an approach questions a fundamental assumption of neoclassical wage theory, that of individual utility maximisation. An associated approach is to question the competitive model's assumption that workers' utility is based upon their own wage and hours of work. As discussed in Box 2.3, fairness seems to be an important determinant of real world wage-fixing, a view shared by psychologists and sociologists who also emphasise relative deprivation, envy and jealousy as motivating factors. Workers' perception of fairness does not seem to be defined by the outcomes of market forces as in the neoclassical framework, but by comparisons with appropriate reference groups. In reality, bargaining rarely centres upon disagreements about the movements of demand and supply but on the appropriate reference group for comparative purposes. Fairness enters the bargaining process at the bequest of existing employees, which indicates that the relative wage must enter into workers' utility functions. Clark and Oswald (1993) analysed a sample of British workers and found that their reported levels of well-being were almost uncorrelated with absolute income, whereas measures of relative income were significantly and positively correlated with happiness at work. The apparent importance of relative pay in motivating workers ties in with our earlier discussion of how firms use job evaluation techniques to legitimise their wage structure and avoid disputes about differentials and relativities. Downwards wage rigidity may be a further reflection of how the reference wage may become associated with the current real wage, and wage reductions are hence seen as 'unfair' and are therefore strongly resisted by workers. Interestingly, Bewley (1995) reports that employers seem much more willing to cut the pay of new hires when the work-force is composed of temporary, part-time or agency workers. Since such workers often have little contact with each other and do not expect a permanent relationship with their employer, internal pay comparisons are not as important as in more traditional working patterns.

These explanations are not fully convincing since in a capitalist economy equality of treatment is usually argued to produce large disincentive effects. Lazear (1989) provides an efficiency interpretation for a stable and compressed wage structure.

Box 2.3: The importance of a 'fair wage'

'To sum up, I find the pattern of industry wages difficult to understand unless we assume that firms pay attention to equity in setting wages, an assumption that only an economist would find controversial.'
Thaler (1989) p. 191.

The earliest economists tended to equate the value of a commodity or resource with the morally right price or the 'just' price. In stable societies the just price tended to be equal to the customary price and represented a socially acceptable scale of values. The idea of a just price or wage disappeared from economics with the dominance of neoclassical analysis, in which the 'fair' price or wage is the equilibrium price produced by the interaction of supply and demand. Only with the analysis of long-term employment relationships has the importance of 'fairness' re-emerged in analysis of labour market behaviour. This time in the context of producing co-operative behaviour and avoiding the threat which opportunistic bargaining poses for the stability of labour market relationships. 'A fair day's wage for a fair day's work' can now represent an efficient strategy for generating the mutual benefits from long-term employment relationships between workers and firms. Altering wage levels and structures in the face of changing market conditions is generally not perceived as fair, and accordingly is not widely observed in internal labour markets.

Solow (1990) utilised a similar argument to explain why unemployed workers were rarely observed to undercut the wages of employed workers. According to Solow, the social norm against wage cutting is the product of an environment where individually attractive behaviour which is socially destructive becomes socially unacceptable. Accordingly, it may be rational for the unemployed to await re-employment at the existing wage rather than turn the labour market into a 'free for all' where wages are permanently bid down.

Where wages are differentiated by relative performance, workers can benefit from a poor performance by their fellow workers. This creates incentives for individual workers to reduce their co-operation with fellow workers or even to sabotage colleagues' efforts at work. The more unequal the treatment the greater the disincentives to co-operate, hence to avoid these effects, production technologies that require co-operation in the work-force should be characterised by compressed wage structures. Alternative explanations for compressed wage structures relying on monitoring costs of worker output and tastes for relative status have also been advanced. In the former the need is to prevent workers inflating output, in the latter to compensate the low-achievers, whilst high-achievers are partly compensated by their superior performance.

This discussion exposes another area often neglected by the neoclassical analysis of worker behaviour: the importance of past choices on current utility. Becker (1992) has summarised modified neoclassical models where habits, addictions and traditions may be important determinants of preferences. These approaches may be particularly important for a fuller understanding of labour market behaviour. The stability of wage structures and employment relationships which we discovered in Chapter 1 may be more easily reconciled with models of worker behaviour where past decisions have a strong influence on present preferences and choices.

It may have been noticeable over the last few pages how sociological factors have become increasingly prominent in our discussions. It is helpful to try to distinguish the particular approach of sociologists and how their work has influenced contemporary labour economics; Barron and Hannan (1994) provide a more comprehensive assessment. Sociologists emphasise that preferences and behaviour need to be analysed within a social context and that as social and institutional frameworks change so too will labour market behaviour. In their explanations of differences in labour market outcomes sociologists turn to arguments based upon structural constraints on the demand side rather than to the differences in human capital investments and tastes preferred in the neoclassical approach. Stereotypes employed to simplify the collation of labour market information may be self-reinforcing, whilst access to social networks may explain unequal returns to similar labour market characteristics and the importance of initial job allocations in determining lifetime earnings. A feature of the most recent work within the neoclassical framework is the possibility of multiple equilibria, causing problems in identifying, *ex ante*, the consequence of shocks. Social, cultural and psychological forces appear particularly important to explaining resistance to change and the perpetuation of behaviour in the labour market which appears inconsistent with the more rigid competitive approaches to labour market behaviour.

2.4 Competitive and non-competitive models of the labour market

In some ways many of the arguments developed in the previous section are reminiscent of the neoclassical approach with imperfect information, heterogeneous workers and fixed costs of employing labour. All of these refinements lead to the conclusion that firms view turnover as costly, that wage costs are a poor proxy for unit labour costs and that wages may be slow to reflect changes in market conditions. The possibility that through incentive or selection effects labour productivity depends upon wage and not vice versa, repeals the Law of Single Price that competition ensures that identical factors receive identical rewards. At present many of the non-competitive approaches lack the elegance and coherence of orthodox theory, raising questions about what additional insights are gained by rejecting the competitive approach. Perhaps this is the wrong question to be asking at this time. There are two main reasons for this suggestion; firstly, competitive and non-competitive approaches are not wholly incompatible. In certain areas such as internal labour markets (discussed in section 2.4.1), they provide complementary explanations with each approach borrowing insights from the other. Secondly, both approaches are at present so amorphous that almost any labour market behaviour appears consistent with at least some part of each paradigm. The wider use of terms such as 'segmentation', 'duality', 'insider-outsider' and 'internal labour markets' has not been accompanied by agreement on their origins or even about their meaning.

2.4.1 *Competitive theories of internal labour markets*

As part of our initial discussion of neoclassical analysis we noted that the existence of firm-specific skills would tend to generate long-term relationships between workers and firms. Personnel policies which firms adopt to minimise labour turnover isolate their workers from the external market conditions and therefore create internal labour markets. The emphasis upon the behaviour of internal labour markets is therefore not unique to the segmented labour market approach and can be consistent with competitive models of labour market activity. In addition to the human capital model, Siebert and Addison (1991) identify four other reasons why internal labour markets may be efficient, cost-minimising responses to labour market conditions: transaction costs; efficiency wages; deferred compensation; and risk insurance. We briefly introduce these arguments here.

In Williamson *et al.*'s (1975) transactions cost model, contracts between employers and employees are necessarily incomplete: it being too expensive to write and enforce contracts specifying all potential eventualities. Since workers possess firm-specific skills opportunistic bargaining needs to be prevented, that is workers or firms should not be able to exploit short-term market conditions to grab bargaining concessions. If they were to pursue an opportunistic strategy their behaviour would threaten the sustainability of long-term, mutually beneficial agreements. This need to maintain co-operative behaviour, even in the face of unforeseen circumstances, leads to internal labour markets being developed. Rules and procedures are developed which legitimise the status quo and prevent opportunistic bargaining. For example, job evaluation and work study methods are adopted to gauge 'fair', that is acceptable, relativities which are maintained in the face of changes in market conditions. Firms implement a single unified pay structure, where wage rates are specified by job, not by individual workers. Labour management is therefore bureaucratised, elaborate rules and job criteria are specified to fragment the work-force and encourage individual worker commitment and loyalty. Recognition of trade unions and/or the empowerment of work councils may be complementary to this process.

The transaction costs model is an application of agency theory, a solution to the problem of how principals ensure that their agents adopt behaviour consistent with the principals' objectives. Efficiency wage theory represents another application of this approach, concentrating on how employers (principals) ensure that workers (agents) supply acceptable levels of effort when contracts typically only specify the time duration of the labour supply. In the 'shirking' variant of this approach, employers who face high monitoring costs use their wage structure to coerce workers into acceptable behaviour. Paying a wage above the external market 'going' wage raises the workers' opportunity costs of being fired, since any re-employment outside their current job would be on inferior conditions. In this case internal labour markets are an efficient response to high monitoring costs. We will discuss this and the other versions of the efficiency wage argument when we discuss wage rigidity and unemployment in Chapter 7.

Deferred payments may be yet another solution to this agency problem. Paying entrants a wage below their initial productivity whilst rewarding experienced workers at a rate in excess of their productivity, may represent an effort-motivating/turnover-reducing wage contract. However, workers need to have confidence that firms will not renege on this agreement and sack them once their wages exceed their productivity. Once again, internal labour markets may produce a framework conducive to the creation of mutual trust and co-operation and again provide a solution to this agency problem.

If workers are risk-averse and firms risk-neutral then there is potential for employers to provide workers with implicit insurance against income volatility. These mutually beneficial arrangements need to be protected from the dangers of opportunistic bargaining discussed earlier. Workers may be tempted to quit when external wages are above the insured level and firms to sack workers when recessions cause the value of workers' productivity to fall below the insured wage level. Asymmetric information exacerbates this problem and reputation effects may be inadequate to eradicate cheating. Once again internal labour markets may again consolidate the long-term relationships between employers and workers.

Box 2.4: The new economics of personnel

Traditionally the design of personnel policies has been within the realm of industrial psychologists and sociologists, economists having little to contribute to issues such as how to motivate workers. Recently renewed interest in the economics of organisations has spilled over into human resource issues, we illustrate this approach with two examples.

Designing piece rates

Worker-effort is rarely directly measurable. The basic piece-rate system is as follows:

$$Pay = s + rQ$$

where output (Q) is measured in terms of profit. Lazear (1993) shows that if workers are risk neutral then s should be allowed to adjust to its market clearing rate and $r = 1$. Making $r < 1$ means that workers would supply too little effort, since if they only received 50p for each £1 of profit created they will quit at some point where extra effort is still profitable in both private and social terms. Alternatively $r > 1$ causes workers to provide above the socially optimal level of effort. Since firms have to earn profits this argument implies that s is a charge which workers 'pay' for the right to work in this job, and hence worker's remuneration is Q-s. The attraction of this type of contract is that in comparison with normal contracts, where remuneration is $s_1 + rQ$ where $r < 1$ and $s_1 < s$, the right workers are attracted to the job. The greater the workers' output the more attractive the former contract and the higher the quality of recruits.

Where profitability is volatile and workers risk-averse, the firms may be forced into a pay scheme where $s > 0$ and $r < 1$. This insures workers against some of the wage volatility but produces the moral hazard problem that, as shown, with $r < 1$ too little effort is supplied. Firms offering a high s will also tend to suffer an adverse selection problem since the most risk-averse, lowest productivity workers are attracted by this type of contract. Given forward looking-behaviour and asymmetric information concerning worker effort, piece rate contracts need to be long-term, otherwise workers may supply too little effort for fear that employers exploit the revealed information to reduce unit wage costs.

Box 2.4: *continued*

Mandatory retirement

Conventional analysis suggests that workers get paid wages related to their current productivity. This argument seems unable to explain the widespread practice in Europe of requiring workers to retire on reaching a specified wage. Where output cannot be regularly monitored, Lazear (1979) argued that an upwards sloping age-earnings payments system would act to motivate workers. Young workers, although paid less than they are worth, are motivated by future earnings in excess of their worth and their 'investment' makes them keen to avoid dismissal. Older workers continue to supply effort to ensure the continuation of their high earnings. The payment of wages in excess of productivity to older workers can explain the prevalence of compulsory retirement at a pre-determined age, since otherwise workers would extend their working life above the optimal time.

2.4.2   *Contrasts and common themes*

Within the neoclassical approach there is such an enormous range of opinions and theories, that the label neoclassical appears no longer to be useful, as a means of specifying a particular belief or approach. A better dichotomy for our consideration of labour market policy in this study is between competitive and non-competitive models of the labour market. Whilst any simple division is somewhat arbitrary, and to an extent produces 'straw men', our dichotomy will illuminate many of the key differences in contemporary debates.

The competitive approach can be summarised as follows: the emphasis is on labour markets responding to market forces. Whilst the auction market is recognised as an over-simplification, wages do move to equilibrium levels and do produce market-clearing adjustments in labour supply. Though there is some rigidity in absolute and relative wage levels in the very short-run, for policy purposes labour markets can be viewed as flexible-price markets. The long-run movement towards equalising wage-differentials means that any persisting differentials, after adjustment for the non-pecuniary aspects of the employment, reflect differences in employee productivity, due to uneven investments in education, training and experience. Given the quantity and variety of sub-labour markets, information is costly, and firms and workers search prior to job-matching causing unemployment and unfilled vacancies.

The non-competitive approach pays much more attention to custom and practice in the labour market and adopts a bargaining approach to pay determination. Collective rather than individual decision-making is dominant, with individual workers facing many restrictions and constraints on their behaviour. Enterprise-specific rents are often paid to workers, and this together with their individual bargaining power leads to highly stable work groups in many sectors of the labour market. These stable groups develop norms concerning the fairness of work effort and distribution of those rents. It is social cohesion, rather than efficiency, which underlies the development of relative wage rigidity and seniority-determined pay scales in internal labour markets.

Firms in many sectors of the economy have structured their labour markets in order to produce motivated and loyal employees. This primary sector consists of career labour markets where there is long-term tenure. Firms are reluctant to change wage structures when labour and product market conditions alter, and any adjustment is slow and largely through previously determined rules for changes in working patterns. Wage increases are a result of a bargaining process and tend to be applied across the board. The size of wage increases reflects the firm-specific factors such as financial performance, rather than just the external market forces which drive wage changes in the competitive model. Education and training can assist workers' acceptance into internal labour markets but luck is important, with wages reflecting the job's, not worker's, characteristics. Under-employment and unemployment are partly a consequence of this quantity-adjustment, rather than price-adjustment in the labour market, with unemployment being unequally shared by the work-force. Much greater emphasis is placed on the determinants of labour demand in this approach, with employers usually being the dominant decision-makers in the hiring process. Since the productivity characteristics of the worker no longer determine their present employment, and X-inefficiency is always present, employment levels no longer indicate efficiency in the economy. Efficiency is no longer an absolute concept and can only be assessed once a social welfare function has been specified.

Whilst competitive forces may dominate the secondary labour market they are not completely absent from the primary sector. Primary labour markets need to attract entrants and firms in this segment face competition in the product market. These forces may be weak in the short run but cannot be ignored in the long run. The sharp dichotomy between 'good' and 'bad' jobs in the dual labour market model appears too simple, and the distribution of the quality of jobs is more likely to be multi-modal rather than bi-modal. The recent emphasis upon the social foundations of internal labour markets, as opposed to human capital, price incentives and technical efficiency foundations, has begun to produce additional insights into labour market behaviour.

Critically these two approaches are not really substitutes for each other since they incorporate over-lapping concepts and analysis and labour market behaviour consistent with both approaches can be observed in the economy. Indeed, Box 2.4 indicates how insights from both approaches have generated a new, economic approach to personnel policies. The important question concerns the relative importance, location and permanence of these two types of behaviour. We consider this question in our detailed discussion of specific policy issues in the following chapters. First of all we take a general look at the implications this analysis has for the role of government in regulating labour market behaviour.

2.4.3 *Conclusions*

Our summary of the development of economic theories of labour market behaviour followed our review of recent developments in European labour markets in Chapter 1. In the previous chapter we traced the expansion of the flexible labour market in recent years, whereas in this chapter we have seen how much recent theoretical work has been devoted to explaining the benefits of long-term employment relationships between workers and firms. This apparent inconsistency can be partially resolved by our earlier finding that for most workers in employment long tenure is the norm, suggesting that increased flexibility is, in part, increasing segmentation (see Section 5.1.2). Chapter 1 also stressed the diversity of European labour market behaviour and dissimilarities between European and North American labour markets. This finding suggests that the models of labour market behaviour discussed earlier may not travel well. In particular, there remains a fear that the dominance of American labour economists has led to the development of orthodox models which may be inappropriate for our analysis of European labour market policies.

Guide to further reading

This text does not purport to provide a comprehensive theoretical guide to labour economics, there are many texts which can provide this facility. Sapsford and Tzannatos (1993) provide a well-organised, traditional summary of orthodox labour economics. This book also provides a summary of empirical findings and is accessible to students without mathematical or econometric skills. Smith (1994) is a more recent text but pays little attention to recent developments in both the labour market and labour economic theory. Polachek and Siebert (1993) is less comprehensive than the earlier texts but more than compensates with a theoretical rigour and commitment to the neoclassical approach which complements the heterodox approach of the following chapters. Elliott (1991) still impresses as a comprehensive and rigorous review of mainstream labour economics, whilst the forthcoming text by Bosworth *et al.* will provide a graduate level treatment of mainstream theory. Ulman (1992) and Lazear (1991) provide accessible introductions to recent work in the economics of human resource management. Marsden (1986) explores the importance of customs and social norms in the labour market and Glyn and Miliband (1994) consider the interaction between inequality and efficiency in the labour market. Booth (1995) provides an excellent introduction to the economic analysis of trade union behaviour.

3 Labour market policy: an introduction

Before we examine specific areas of labour market policy we should first try to discover whether there are any general principles which should underlie government intervention in the labour market. Indeed, a prior question concerns whether governments should intervene in labour markets at all. Since government policies consume resources in their design, implementation and operation, the onus is on their proponents to establish their net benefits. In the simplest neoclassical model the free, unrestricted operation of market forces should produce optimal results. In such an environment a legal framework establishing freedom of contract and property rights would appear to be sufficient government involvement to ensure the efficient operation of *laissez-faire*. Since Adam Smith economists have recognised the fragility of market forces and have, almost without exception, echoed his support of government intervention to police markets to ensure the survival of competitive market forces. More controversial have been policies designed to correct supposed imperfections and failures in the operation of those market forces.

In contemporary neoclassical analysis the presumption that competition promotes efficiency still dominates policy design, since inefficient practices and institutional arrangements are speedily displaced from markets by competitive forces. From this viewpoint policy requirements are predominantly microeconomic, correcting market failures or adjusting for their consequences. Fear of government failure replacing market failure has provided a further reason for minimal intervention. Within this framework, unemployment above that resulting from imperfect information is seen as primarily reflecting the imperfections produced by trade unions and the system of unemployment compensation. Similarly, poverty is the result of low investments in human capital, reflecting failures in the capital market and/or discriminatory practices in the labour market, though the latter is continually being undermined by competitive forces.

Non-competitive theoretical frameworks question the efficiency of unregulated markets and provide a rationale for more widespread government intervention in the labour market. Competition cannot be relied upon to produce optimal levels and distributions of employment and income, indeed in the absence of intervention labour markets are likely to produce rising inequality of employment, incomes or conceivably both. Inefficient human resource management policies may persist in depressing productivity levels, since firms can temporarily sustain competitiveness through lower wage and non-wage costs or governments allow continual devaluations to restore competitiveness. The non-competitive approach is also more likely to countenance interventionist policy to produce structural and environmental changes in the

68

market, often at the macroeconomic level. Causes of unemployment now encompass macroeconomic shocks, with the self-correcting mechanism of real wage adjustments being ineffective in all but the longest time period. Discrimination may now be interpreted as the consequence of a disfavoured group's inability to gain access to 'good' jobs. Poverty may be due to an inadequate aggregate supply of 'good' jobs or impediments to entry into the labour market.

These sets of beliefs are an example of the fundamental confrontation between two views of appropriate economic policy, where one policy is generally limited to the protection and creation of competitive markets, whilst the other advocates widespread government intervention into markets. Originally this confrontation reflected a disagreement about whether markets are price or quantity-adjusting in the short and medium term. More recently it has also come to reflect disagreements about whether government failure is more costly than market failure.

In the first part of this chapter we develop the case for a *laissez-faire* approach to labour markets, this is followed by an examination of the possible sources of market failure in the labour market. Whether such failures constitute a rationale for government intervention will depend upon the extent of government failure and the next section assesses the nature of such failures in European labour markets The example of health and safety at work is used to provide an illustration of how the presence of market imperfections may provide a rationale for government regulation, even within a competitive environment. This is followed by a general consideration of the nature and types of government intervention in the labour market. We then turn to discuss policy at the multi-national level, addressing the issue of subsidiarity and its importance for designing policy in the EU. The penultimate section illustrates many of the chapter's main points by considering the case for the introduction or retention of a statutory national minimum wage. The chapter concludes with an initial assessment of the relative merits of different types of labour market policy, providing a starting point for our following discussions of specific policy areas.

3.1 Neoclassical theory and the case for *laissez-faire*

As we explained in the previous chapter, neoclassical theory analyses the behaviour of rational individual utility-maximisers in competitive markets. In its modern form the approach treats the decision-makers as forward-looking, continually making model-consistent expectations to inform their decision-making over time. In a perfectly competitive environment since decision-makers know their own interests best and are assumed to be rational in exercising choice, they consistently make optimal choices. It follows that these decision-makers will also generate socially optimal outcomes in the absence of market failures and in the absence of government induced constraints and distortions. It follows that a policy of *laissez-faire* promotes resource efficiency, and efficient utilisation of society's resources is maintained over time by the competitive process eliminating inefficient and irrational decision-takers.

A supportive legal framework is still necessary for socially optimal outcomes to be sustained even in an environment where governments are otherwise essentially passive. Specifically in the labour market, as long as workers have freedom of contract then they have freedom to choose between alternative job opportunities and will choose that employment contract which maximises their expected utility. The legal framework also ensures that contracts are honoured or, in the case of default, that appropriate compensation is available. The freedom of employers and workers not to renew contracts provides a market discipline on decision-makers, ensuring that remuneration reflects workers' potential earnings elsewhere in the market place. Once this legal framework has been developed the government's only role is to sustain competition by requiring, for example, any monopsonist or trade union still tolerated to desist from exploiting their market power.

3.2 Market failure

The previous summary of the analysis underlying the policy of *laissez-faire* assumed the simplest, perfectly competitive, variant of neoclassical analysis. If we now add the refinements to that approach which we developed in the previous chapter, we can not only develop more sophisticated arguments for *laissez-faire* but also develop a case for an interventionist approach to labour market policy. We initially concentrate upon four possible sources of market failure: asymmetric information; externalities; market power and missing or incomplete markets. The existence of market failures implies that unregulated markets may no longer generate socially efficient solutions.

3.2.1 *Market failures*

Our arguments for *laissez-faire* developed earlier required full information flows to inform decision-making in the labour market. In practice, the existence of heterogeneous workers and jobs makes information flows highly complex. The costs of acquiring and updating the information necessary for decision-making may become exorbitant and lead to the use of infrequently updated stereotypes which distort decision-making, perhaps causing discrimination to be perpetuated. In many situations information is available asymmetrically in the labour market. Firms, for example, may find it expensive to discover the true characteristics of applicants and job-seekers the full characteristics of job-offers, these difficulties may cause off-the-job search to be inefficient. Another example is that existing employees may be unable to get information from their employers about job security, information which is necessary for their taking of investment decisions regarding human capital and search. Firms may hide difficult trading conditions from their work-force in order to prevent job search and quits amongst their most valuable workers. In many markets the presence of asymmetric information may not pose problems since the need to acquire and preserve reputations as a good employer or worker will lead to contracts being honoured and accurate information being purveyed. However, reputational effects may be less effective in markets characterised by small firms and mobile workers, in these circumstances firms and workers may indulge in misinformation activities for short-term benefits.

The presence of externalities in the labour market may distort the relationship between individual maximising behaviour and social welfare. Firms considering the closure of branches are unlikely to internalise the costs to local workers or to the government in the form of lost tax revenue and increased benefit payments. Similarly, unemployed job-seekers considering accepting an offer of employment fail to internalise the costs to the firm and government of rejecting their offer. Where firms or workers are prepared to internalise these costs 'free riders' who do not make the sacrifice may nevertheless share in the resulting benefits. Governments may have particular advantages in the collection and dissemination of labour market information, given that such information may be a joint-product of their other activities such as tax collection. Though, as we shall see, in order to fulfil this role they need to acquire a credible reputation for accuracy and consistency. The failure to fully internalise externalities into private decision-making means that the unregulated labour market may no longer produce socially-optimal outcomes.

A third potential source of market failure can arise where product market monopolies, trade union or labour market monopsonist cause the relationship between productivity, real wages and employment to be distorted. Such distortions are likely to cause resource efficiency problems in an unregulated economy. In practice, the presence of technology which is idiosyncratic to a particular firm causes much on-the-job training to be non-transferable to other employers. Such training makes labour turnover costly and implies that virtually all firms and employed workers possess an element of market power. In such an environment labour mobility will be restricted and normal competitive forces may fail to generate a wage structure which clears the labour market. Similar distortions to wage and employment structures can result from trade union or monopolists' actions.

In addition to the imperfections already discussed the absence of whole markets for goods, services or resources may distort the operation of demand and supply. For example, the inability of workers to realise the value of their human capital in the same way in which they can sell their financial assets distorts their investment decisions. This illiquidity of human capital may, in the absence of intervention, cause too little education and training to occur for a given distribution of returns and time preference. Similarly, the inability to obtain full insurance against redundancy or failure to obtain promotion may distort inter-firm mobility in the labour market. This inability is partly the result of moral hazard problems which result when insured workers change their behaviour as a consequence of them not facing the full costs of any adverse consequences. In our example, workers with redundancy or no-promotion insurance may be more likely to shirk or be caught shirking, unless premiums are risk-rated and/or claims are subject to excesses or lengthy investigations.

These individual sources of market failure are not mutually exclusive and they may interact to cause widespread market failure: consider the case of unemployment insurance. If individuals who become unemployed have failed to insure themselves against unemployment risk there are likely to be negative externalities resulting. Either the government will support their subsistence and therefore impose a burden on tax-payers, or if it refuses to support them, poverty, disease, crime and political and social unrest are likely to result if spells of unemployment are lengthy. Requiring individuals to take out compulsory unemployment insurance would be likely to generate moral hazard problems in the form of reduced incentives to retain employment or to find it once unemployed. If unemployment insurance was voluntary and premiums were not risk-rated then individuals with a low risk of unemployment would find the premiums unattractive and prefer self-insurance. As a consequence those groups with a high unemployment risk, such as the young and unskilled, would face prohibitively high insurance premiums. Such adverse selection problems has led, in practice, to many European governments having to utilise significant resources to monitor compliance with their compulsory insurance legislation.

3.2.2   *Incomplete employment contracts*

Reliance on a legal framework to enhance and formalise the operation of market forces generates additional sources of failure. Labour market contracts are unlike those found in goods markets in that they tend to be incomplete, having implicit terms and conditions. This is a consequence of the employment of labour in any particular job tending to be 'idiosyncratic', in that it has dimensions other than duration which cannot be easily quantified or communicated, such as attentiveness and creativeness. Since these dimensions are not specified in the contract between employers and employees they cannot be legally enforced and agency problems result.

   As we discussed in the previous chapter, an agency problem arises in the labour market when a principal, the manager in our context, employs an agent, the worker, to produce output. The manager has to design policies which ensure that the worker behaves in a manner consistent with the manager's interests rather than their own. Specifically, since the labour contract typically specifies an agreed wage per period of time, the employer has to design monitoring and incentive schemes to encourage workers to supply acceptable levels of effort and the other dimensions of work. Such incentive mechanisms may be piece rate systems of pay or internal promotions and they may lead to the development of internal labour markets as discussed in the previous chapter. The rules governing behaviour in these internal labour markets may distort the operation of market forces or may themselves be a reflection of the operation of those forces. These alternative possibilities have very different policy implications, the former viewing internal labour markets as a vehicle for perpetuating rigidities and discrimination and therefore requiring regulation. While the latter interpretation views internal labour markets as solving the problems caused for *laissez-faire* by incompletely specified labour contracts, asymmetric information and long-term relationships between workers and firms.

3.2.3   *Aggregate market failure*

Our list of imperfections has so far been constructed from a static, microeconomic viewpoint. Proponents of the Keynesian tradition would argue that competitive labour markets are prone to co-ordination problems resulting in widespread market failures and persisting aggregate unemployment. In practice firms and workers agree to specify money wages in their contracts, though our analysis argued that workers were motivated by real wages and firms by unit labour costs. Agreeing contractual terms is therefore an expensive process, and both firms and workers lack the information necessary to convert money wages into their preferred terms. One consequence is that contracts are only revised at discrete intervals, usually annually in Europe, causing any adjustment to unforeseen changes in market conditions to be achieved through employment, rather than wage adjustment. We develop these arguments more fully in Chapter 7, but the key Keynesian point has now been made, competitive market forces cannot maintain optimal aggregate levels of employment in the face of widespread contractionary shocks.

More recently, 'new' growth theory has added concerns about the ability of unregulated labour markets to produce optimal growth performance in an economy. In these models growth performance depends crucially upon the rate of technical progress. Not all of the research and development benefits of having a trained and educated work-force will be internalised into private decision-making. In which case without government intervention growth may be lower than that achieved in economies with more interventionist regimes.

3.2.4 *Equity*

We have so far concentrated upon whether unregulated labour markets will produce socially efficient outcomes. Others may question whether the outcomes of unregulated competitive labour markets are consistent with the social justice objectives of a society. The different definitions of social justice, or equity, preclude any simple answer to this question; Barr (1993) provides a thorough introduction to this topic. We merely conclude that unregulated labour markets ignore equity considerations and that inequalities of outcome may not promote efficiency, an issue we return to in our discussion of discrimination in Chapter 6.

3.2.5 *Implications*

Taken together these arguments suggest that in practice labour markets are far removed from the perfectly competitive ones assumed in our previous section. The public interest theory argues that as a consequence governments should act to correct these failures in the operation of the labour market. The theory implies that governments can be relied upon to respond to a public demand for the correction of inefficient outcomes. The theory does not require an extension of regulations since alternative policy responses are possible, for example, taxation and subsidies could be used to offset distortions in wage structures. Alternatively, where incomplete property rights pose problems the legal framework can be revised to encourage the internalisation of externalities, for example in the case of asymmetric information concerning job security by establishing a right for workers to have full access to job security information. However, the recognition that labour markets may fail to automatically produce socially efficient outcomes does not by itself indicate that government interference of any form can produce superior outcomes.

3.3   Government failure

Modern arguments for reducing government regulation and strengthening market forces recognise the potential for market failures, but stress that government interference may reduce efficiency still further. At the simplest level, if additional government expenditure is incurred as a result of any labour market intervention then the necessary imposition of taxes to fund that expenditure will generally reduce efficiency. Taxes are likely to distort key relative prices, such as those between work and leisure or between the rate of return on human capital and financial capital. These price distortions cause labour market behaviour to deviate from that consistent with producing socially efficient outcomes, they discourage market work and therefore lead to too little specialisation or cause a growth in the tax-free underground economy. Similarly, government regulations by prohibiting certain working conditions, reduce an individual's freedom of choice and therefore may prevent the signing of mutually beneficial contracts between workers and firms. Enforcement of these regulations must again absorb resources which could be used directly for wealth creation.

Information imperfections may also create government failure as public choice theory has emphasised. The overwhelming desire of governments to be re-elected induces two sorts of problems, Firstly, 'short-termism' where governments are biased against policies where the net social welfare gains are unlikely to be recognised by those voting in the next election. For example, policies which require additional short-term expenditure to produce long-term benefits, such as improving the match between schooling, training and labour market employment, may be unattractive to governments facing re-election. Secondly, governments will be prejudiced in favour of policies which whilst reducing social welfare may produce concentrated benefits and widely diffused costs, costs which may not be perceived by those affected. In such a case, such as subsidies for the purchase of shares in newly privatised industries, although this subsidy may reduce social welfare, it may increase government popularity. At the same time many areas that require intervention, such as improving information flows in the labour market, may be neglected by governments since the benefits are widely distributed and thus have little attraction to a government chasing electoral success. Thus, government intervention is not a costless corrective device and in addition governments cannot be relied on to intervene in a way which will increase social welfare, intervening to correct market distortions may therefore be counter-productive.

Recently time-inconsistency arguments have been utilised to extend these criticisms of government intervention. The time-inconsistency argument is that government policy initiatives designed to promote certain behaviour may be discontinued once that behaviour has been generated. Since decision-makers cannot be repeatedly fooled by such government behaviour, the initiative will tend not to have the intended favourable effects even in the short-run. For example, consider the offer of generous long-term subsidies to firms creating employment in a local labour market following a large plant closure. Would-be takers of this subsidy may deduce that once they have taken advantage of the subsidy and re-located in this labour market, the resulting fall in unemployment means that governments will target other policy objectives. Governments will now wish to find revenue savings to finance new initiatives and be tempted to renege on previous subsidy agreements. In this case unless the government can develop a reputation for pursuing consistent policies over time, policy initiatives will be ignored by forward-looking decision-makers.

The economic theory of regulation provides an alternative interpretation of the sources of government failure. In the analysis of Peltzman (1976) regulation is treated like any other good. Regulation confers benefits on certain labour market participants by providing subsidies or restricting competition: examples are government subsidies for recruiting the long-term unemployed or requiring firms to pay minimum wage rates or licensing certain occupational groups. In a static framework these policies redistribute wealth towards particular groups, and those groups try to retain or extend the regulations by political or financial support to politicians favouring these regulations. The economic theory of regulation can therefore explain both the introduction and retention of inefficient regulations in the labour market.

Since both free markets and governments are likely to produce inefficient outcomes the desirability of *laissez-faire* or intervention will depend upon a comparison of the relative inefficiency of the two. The resolution of this comparison will depend upon comparative advantage. Snower (1993) stresses that government is a unique economic organisation in four major respects. Firstly, governments can require universal membership of any scheme which in principle implies that problems of free riding and asymmetric information can be avoided. For example, they can avoid adverse selection problems by imposing a universal and uniform unemployment insurance system. Secondly, governments have special powers of compulsion which allow them to tax and penalise those evading tax. These same powers mean that governments may face too few incentives to use their powers efficiently, especially in a changing environment. Additionally, as we have noted, the ability of governments to redistribute income and wealth leads to the creation of pressure groups to further group interests and this again diverts resources from wealth creation. Thirdly, governments have a multiplicity of objectives which means in principle they can implement policies which favour the public interest rather than just profits or individual utility. One consequence of this multiplicity of objectives is that citizens have much difficulty in assessing accurately government performance, since governments have an incentive to emphasise any individual target that they are achieving and neglecting those where they are unsuccessful. Finally, governments have restricted powers to make future governments maintain existing policies and agreements. The sovereignty of each specific government has the advantage of making governments responsive to changes in the public interest. However, the inability of governments to make credible long-term contracts worsens the time-inconsistency problems raised earlier.

Where governments seek to reassure citizens against their abuse of power by employing a non-political civil service, then additional dangers of a self-perpetuating bureaucracy are created. If civil servants cannot be fired, rents are created for these workers as well as administrative inertia. Since productivity is often difficult to measure in the public sector, such policies create major problems for human resource managers trying to produce an employment environment conducive to the efficient provision of public services. Hence, the introduction of compulsory competitive tendering in the public sector discussed in Chapter 1.

Our list of the advantages and disadvantages which the government possesses as an economic organisation indicates that there can be no presumption that government intervention will always be harmful or beneficial. Once this is recognised then the only way forwards is to try to develop some general principles and then apply them carefully case by policy case. For many of those at the forefront of the deregulation movement in the last two decades, there was a fundamental belief that governments facing elections in the short-term could not be relied upon to make appropriate policy responses to medium and long-run problems. If this belief is coupled with a further belief, that taxes to finance labour market policies themselves generate large distortions on the supply of working hours and demand for human capital investments, then the modern argument for *laissez-faire* emerges. We return to a consideration of this viewpoint and the nature of the general principles in the design of labour market policy at the end of this chapter.

3.4   Case study: occupational health and safety

In this section we utilise the case of occupational health and safety to illustrate some of the arguments about the nature and extent of market and government failure. Initially we identify the extent of industrial accidents and occupational illness using data for the British labour market. Statistics collected as part of the 1990 British Labour Force Survey indicate that about 1.6 million industrial accidents occurred in the previous twelve months, one for every fourteen workers. The Health and Safety Executive, the regulatory agency in the UK, estimated that industrial accidents and work-related ill-health had a total cost to the UK economy of up to 3 per cent of GDP (Davies and Teasdale, 1994). Comparisons suggest that the UK has a relatively low accident rate compared to other EU economies (Health and Safety Executive, 1991), but differences in definitions and especially reporting rates makes comparisons of accident rates across countries problematic. Accident rates are typically 50 per cent higher in manufacturing and 300 per cent greater in construction than the average for the economy as a whole. Data on work-related illnesses is even less reliable than that for accidents, but the 1990 Labour Force Survey found that around 10 per cent of workers claimed to have had an illness in the previous year which had been caused or made worse by work.

Whilst industrial accidents may appear to be inevitable joint-products of the production of goods and services, in aggregate their incidence will be dependent upon the behaviour of firms and workers. At any moment of time reducing accident rates is costly, requiring modifications to machinery or work practices. It follows that we can talk about a socially optimal level of industrial accidents; this is where accident prevention has been pursued up to the point where the marginal cost to society of reducing accident rates further is equal to the marginal benefits to society of increased safety. According to the competitive model developed in Chapter 2, actual wages are the sum of two components: a payment for labour services and worker characteristics and a payment reflecting job attributes. Since accident risk generates disutility for workers they require additional payments to compensate for working in risky environments. Freedom of contract ensures that workers will only accept job offers if they are satisfied that they are being adequately rewarded for all of the characteristics of that employment, including accident risk. It follows that firms deciding on their profit-maximising level of workplace safety will trade-off increased expenditure on accident risk reduction against the lower wages they can pay their workers in a safer workplace. Firms therefore will minimise the wage and safety costs of a given level of output, equating the marginal expenditure on safety with the marginal benefit of reduced wage payments. In a perfectly competitive environment such firm behaviour will generate a level of accident risk which minimises total accident and accident prevention costs.

The automatic generation of an optimal level of industrial accidents in the analysis summarised above has been used by Siebert (1991) amongst others, to argue that government regulation of occupational safety is likely to be undesirable. Any safety regulations which alter firms' behaviour must cause increases in safety levels which reduce social welfare. They prevent workers earning risk premiums in dangerous jobs which they would otherwise be willing to accept. The same argument can be used against government regulations on maximum working hours and holiday leave, indeed such regulations on adult female workers were abolished in the UK on the grounds that they were discriminatory and restricted women's ability to compete against male workers. Public choice theory interprets the willingness of large companies and trade unions to accept enhanced safety regulations as reflecting the tendency of such regulations to force small, often non-union, companies to adopt more expensive production technologies and therefore reduce their ability to compete. We can also apply this *laissez-faire* argument at a global level: the observation that the fatality rate in manufacturing in Pakistan is over twenty times that in the UK can be interpreted as indicating the lower wage premiums for risk-taking in the Pakistan labour market. Hence requiring multinational companies to adopt similar accident prevention policies in different national labour markets would cause a distortion in international trade, and further lower the standard of living of workers in low-income economies.

In practice all developed economies regulate occupational safety, indeed it was one area of EU employment policy where the British Government was willing to accept majority voting. This preference for a non-market solution reflects a belief that there are significant imperfections in the market for occupational safety. Problems of imperfect information in the markets for workplace accidents have commonly been advanced as a rationale for intervention. If errors in workers' estimation of the risk of accidents are randomly distributed across the work-force, then it follows that the marginal worker in any particular job will underestimate risk and accident rates will exceed the socially optimal level. However, in a competitive labour market it is difficult to see how these errors could persist unless accidents are so rare that actual probabilities cannot be calculated on the job. Otherwise, since labour turnover is expensive for most firms then a high drop-out rate amongst entrants, as they learn of the 'true' accident rate, is likely to act as a sufficient deterrent to firms who would otherwise try to disguise accident risk in order to prevent paying appropriate wage differentials. Reputation inertia may be a more convincing explanation of informational imperfections. Since reputations are slow to change firms who invest in accident reducing expenditure do not immediately get the benefits of paying reduced wage premiums, hence they under-invest in this type of expenditure.

Even where workers and firms have accurate information of accident risk, irrational behaviour may lead to sub-optimal levels of safety. Failure to voluntarily wear seat belts or install smoke alarms is symptomatic of a tendency to underestimate true probabilities when the event has a very low probability. In most jobs accident risk is very low and therefore may be ignored by workers, in which case accident prevention expenditure will be based upon employers' costs only. Where the risk of accidents is high an alternative market failure is possible. Workers can gain utility once they have agreed to accept a wage premium for a dangerous job by convincing themselves that the accident risk is lower than the true rate. This process of cognitive dissonance leads to an excess accident rate since workers take too few precautions, but the benefits of believing the job is safer compensate workers for their losses caused by the higher accident rate.

Accident rates are often highest in activities requiring group production, and failure to internalise the accident costs of fellow workers may be an important cause of workers taking inadequate accident precautions. In most economies *ex post* compensation for industrial accidents is available via litigation and/or social insurance or workers' compensation. Since the 1969 Employment Liability Compulsory Insurance Act all British employers have been required to take out employer's liability insurance. Compulsory insurance for employers and voluntary insurance for workers again raises issues of adverse selection and moral hazard as well as introducing failures in the legal market due to the difficulty of proving liability and/or negligence. Even where liability is assigned by the courts bankruptcy may prevent damages being received by the successful claimant. A compulsory system of social insurance for industrial accidents and disease, whilst avoiding the problem of assigning fault, suffers from its failure to act as a deterrent to accidents, unless insurance premiums can be risk-rated.

In all of this discussion we have so far ignored the existence of externalities in the form of accident costs not borne by firms and/or workers involved. In many European countries hospital costs are not fully borne by participants and, given the operation of the tax and benefit system, the costs of lost output and disability benefits are also not borne exclusively by those firms and workers directly involved in the original employment contract. Externalities therefore also prevent individual firms and workers from negotiating socially optimal levels of occupational health and safety.

This discussion indicates that even in a competitive environment without large scale unemployment there are many reasons why accident rates may diverge from the socially optimal level. Such a possibility does not establish the desirability of health and safety regulations, since a regulatory agency requires resources which have opportunity costs and the agency may not set regulation and enforcement policies at optimal levels. It may still be preferable to rely upon compensating wage differentials to determine occupational safety levels, utilising tort liability to constrain firms' moral hazard. Alternatively property rights to a safe working environment may be invested in workers and firms have to pay all the costs of accidents. Coase (1960) showed that in a perfectly competitive environment these alternative environments will produce the same outcome as voluntary agreements produce socially optimal outcomes even in the presence of externalities. The Coase theorem assumes that income effects are small and the transaction costs of establishing the agreements negligible; neither of these assumptions may be appropriate in the case we are discussing. A further problem with an interventionist approach is that there is always a danger that a regulatory agency, which has to work closely with employers, may be 'captured' by these employers and merely represent their interests. In this situation, *laissez-faire* may still be preferable and institutions could be reformed to more fully internalise externalities, perhaps by extending property rights.

Our occupational health and safety example has helped to highlight how the general arguments surrounding the introduction or extension of labour market policies can be applied to a specific policy area. We now proceed to classify those policies and consider appropriate rules for the enforcement of those policies.

3.5   Types of labour market policy

We have already examined the different traditions of labour market policy in Europe in Chapter 1 and we further examine their development in Chapter 8. In this section we distinguish types of policy. Labour market policy regimes can be classified in three categories:

1. *laissez-faire*
2. supportive policy
3. active policy

Within Europe these individual policy regimes tend to be identified with specific legal frameworks. In the UK and Ireland the largely *laissez-faire* policy stance is associated with an *Anglo-Irish system* of legal regulation, where the state plays a limited role and in which neither the individual nor the collective labour relationship is subject to extensive legal regulation. Elsewhere in Europe, supportive and active labour market policy regimes are normally associated with the *Roman-Germanic system* of legal regulation. Here, the state has a central and active role in industrial relations, with the state guaranteeing a core of fundamental rights and freedoms for workers. Barnard *et al.* (1995) examine European systems of legal regulation of industrial relations in more detail.

As we have seen the *laissez-faire* approach starts from a presumption that competitive markets are a better judge of desirable actions than government. Most forms of interventionist policies are rejected and appropriate policies are restricted to repairing breakdowns in those competitive forces, for example eliminating insider power in the labour market. Policies which encourage product market competition and capital mobility will be effective in this case, since the rents appropriated by insiders are bid away. In terms of our case study above, firms and workers would be allowed to freely bargain over wage premiums for accident risk without government intervention. Once property rights have been allocated voluntary agreements will generate socially optimal levels of safety.

We illustrate the *laissez-faire* policy regime by considering the case of 'employment at will' policies where both employers and employees have the right to terminate an employment relationship at any time. This doctrine prevails for most workers in most US states unlike in Europe where, as we summarised in Chapter 1, legislation prohibits unfair dismissal for certain groups of workers. Ehrenberg (1989) explains how *laissez-faire* economists would argue that the 'employment at will' doctrine is fair, since either party can terminate the contract of employment. Workers can quit if they receive better employment offers and firms can fire workers if they believe their productivity is too low for the wage agreed. If workers have transferable skills then workers suffer no permanent loss from being fired. Such contracts are likely to be efficient since they are self-enforcing and have low monitoring costs: employers and workers who renege on agreed behaviour face the contract being terminated. Reputation effects prevent firms from unjustly firing workers, since such actions would dissuade new workers from accepting job offers and existing workers may quit in anticipation of similar treatment. Where skills are firm-specific then firms would have even less incentive to unjustly fire workers since turnover is expensive and similar arguments hold for firms with structured internal labour markets. Given the benefits of employment-at-will contracts then the courts should only provide compensation for short-term losses incurred by workers who have been fired unjustly.

Supportive policies also rely upon the superiority of market forces but recognise the existence of imperfections. Markets once again need assistance but now policy actions not only include those which allocate and enforce property rights but also cover areas where improved economic performance justifies supplanting market forces. For example, regulatory provision for minimum standards may help reduce the cost of information gathering and reduce the potential for abuse of asymmetric information advantages. This policy makes labour markets more transparent and therefore enables relative wages to be a more efficient signalling mechanism. Similarly, a government agency may be countenanced to improve accident risk information, investigating accidents to establish causes and therefore assisting workers to interpret the adequacy of the wage premium offered. Insurance market imperfections could be addressed and passive policies such as the payments of injury benefits may be introduced. Such policies should also internalise any externalities, since by raising the cost of accidents to participants more efficient levels of preventative behaviour will be generated. The ultimate incidence of these particular types of policies needs addressing; if labour supply is inelastic then the burden of labour market regulations will eventually fall on workers in the form of lower wages. Thus, even well-designed policies which promote labour market efficiency may result in lower wages for the least mobile segments, often the lowest paid, of the work-force, whilst employers and higher wage workers benefit by lower taxes.

If labour market imperfections are significant then the employment-at-will contracts discussed earlier are unlikely to be socially optimal. Within this policy regime more interventionist policies will be sanctioned. Houseman (1990) examines these arguments. If firms have dominant bargaining power and worker opportunities are limited, then firms may not be effectively constrained in unfairly dismissing workers by reputational costs. In this scenario unfairly dismissed workers may suffer from undeserved reputational costs, facing permanent losses of income if they lose entitlement to unemployment benefits or are 'blacked' by alternative employers. In this case supportive policies options include imposing a tax on unjust dismissals, thereby increasing employers' turnover costs. Most European countries employ these types of policies in the form of increased severance pay for workers whose dismissal has been found to be unjust.

The active policy regime encompasses a much more substantial role for government policy in the labour market. Market judgements are now suspect and market failures widespread, in this situation regulatory agencies should provide financial inducements to change behaviour in the labour market. Proscribing certain behaviour or even as a last resort replacing the market with government sponsored activities may also now be countenanced as a means of improving efficiency or equity in the labour market. Public intervention, such as safety standards, minimum wages and employment subsidies, is a second best response to the market power of employers and the inability of markets to clear through wage and price adjustment. In our employment protection example, governments may now wish to give workers more extensive property rights to their employment. For example, in some European countries unjustly dismissed workers have the right to reinstatement and employers no longer have the right to terminate employment at will. The extension of property rights to workers may promote efficiency given time-consistency problems. In the case of firm-specific training, new employees may be reluctant to undergo this type of training if they fear that employers may renege on agreements to reward them adequately once trained. Where the training is related to the specific requirements of a firm then the worker has no credible quit threat to enforce the agreement. In this case job protection legislation may reassure workers that they cannot be exploited and encourage the mutually beneficial accumulation of non-transferable skills. We discuss training market imperfections in more detail in the next chapter.

In our health and safety case study we have already discussed some of the problems of the market providing *ex ante* incentives to produce optimal accident rates. In this situation advocates of a passive or supportive policy stance would usually favour an 'incentive regulation' approach, relying on fiscal or legal devices. Relying on taxes and property rights is often difficult in the labour market; imposing a tax on firms responsible for causing accidents or selling firms permits for an agreed level of accidents requires information which is unlikely to be available to the authorities. The effectiveness of tort liability in providing *ex post* compensation is undermined by the difficulties of proving contributory negligence. In the UK firms' insurance premiums against successful legal action by employees is only 0.3% of payroll, a tenth of the US rate, reflecting both the low probability of successful claims and the low damages awarded by the British courts. This may explain the popularity of regulations, which although inflexible and often slow to change do have the benefits of generating new risk information and curtailing 'free rider' problems.

Where a regulatory agency has been established it remains to be considered how that agency should operate. Where, on the basis of internal costs and benefits, it is profitable for a firm to comply with health and safety or equal opportunities legislation the agency is redundant apart from its education and information role. If an employer's internal costs and benefits induce non-compliance then the agency has to raise the costs of non-compliance by an effective threat of fines or damages to a firm's reputation. The agency can increase these costs on firms either by increasing the likelihood of detection or the probability of prosecution or the size of the fine. In practice, in Britain the Health and Safety Executive favours a policy of negotiated compliance and rarely prosecutes. The average fine imposed by the courts where prosecution is successful is low in Britain, even in the face of repeated non-compliance. Fenn and Veljanovski (1988) have argued that such behaviour may be optimal for a budget constrained agency operating with the constraints of fixed fines. The agency's opportunity cost of prosecution is a reduction in detection rates, for the Health and Safety Executive a prosecution costs on average 5 inspector days whilst a visit takes a single day. Mookerherjee and Png (1992) argue that where the monitoring of compliance is necessarily incomplete or very expensive then the agency should only monitor small accidents and levy experience-rated fines. Large offences should always be investigated and punished, where appropriate, with the heaviest fines.

We will reconsider many of these issues in more detail when we consider specific policy issues in the following chapters. However, we have so far failed to consider an important dimension of the policy decision: at what level should policy be decided? Over the last fifteen years, disagreements about the appropriate answer to this question have proved especially divisive in the EU. It is to this issue of 'subsidiarity' that we now turn.

3.6 Subsidiarity and EU labour market policy

The debate concerning 'subsidiarity' concerns the appropriate balance of powers between the institutions of the European Union and those of its individual member states. In other words it is about the 'F' word. Should the EU become a federal institution? Article 3(b) of the Treaty on European Union, commonly known as the Maastricht Treaty, articulates the concept of subsidiarity. The concept is that the EU institutions should only make policy which cannot be appropriately made at the national level. For our purposes we are concerned with the extent to which subsidiarity should be applied to labour market policy, that is, whether social Europe should be superseded by a decentralisation of policies to national governments in line with the principle of subsidiarity. More generally, subsidiarity also raises the issue of the extent to which labour market policy should be made at local and regional levels. In this section we wish to limit ourselves to general arguments leaving specific policy issues concerning migration policy to Chapter 5 and those concerning the development of EU social policy to Chapter 8.

The EU has evolved centralised policy-making powers in certain areas, in particular the Single European Act formalised the role of the EU in regional policy, with the amount of expenditure rising rapidly since 1989. In 1993 the total EU expenditure on regional development was 14 billion ECU with Greece, Portugal and Ireland obtaining assistance equivalent to at least 3% of their GDP. The Treaty of Rome originally established the Social Fund to encourage employment, specifically by raising the employability of the young and the long term unemployed through education and training. The Treaty of Rome also gave the Community competence for policies towards migrant workers and the training of handicapped workers. The Single European Act has now generated new responsibilities, primarily in the areas of social dialogue and health and safety at work.

The rationale for the centralisation of some labour market policies may initially appear straight forward. Retaining sovereignty at the individual national level would tend to generate protective policies in individual member countries designed to distort EU trade patterns. In general, national policy spillovers need co-ordinating in the EU and only centralised policy-making provides a credible mechanism for that co-ordination. Further, if preferences differ at national and regional levels then it is possible to develop a centralised system which contains regional variations. However, centralisation may reduce the quality of information available to policy-makers and may make those policy-makers less responsive to the interests of individual citizens. The latter follows because the more centralised is decision-making the less effective is the movement of taxpayers as a device for promoting efficient and responsive government and the smaller the incentive for individuals to vote, thus 'government failure' becomes more likely. This loss in the accountability of decision-makers may also make 'regulatory capture' more likely, the situation where the regulator comes to represent the interests of those they are supposed to be regulating.

The centralisation-decentralisation debate really centres around the benefits of increased co-ordination against the costs of reduced accountability. However, in practice any actual assessment of appropriate policy jurisdiction needs to recognise that we are operating in the real world within second-best systems. Desirable changes may sometimes make matters worse if they interact with existing distortions. Thus, for example, adoption of a centralised Social Fund for the training of unemployed youths may weaken the policing of those schemes for fraud, since although member countries are required to police the schemes, they have to repay any amounts recovered to the EU budget. It follows that national governments now have fewer financial incentives to ensure that expenditure is properly targeted. In practice therefore, trying to apply the principle of subsidiarity provides no magic rule for the division of policy responsibilities between the different layers of government.

The success of the EU in increasing intra-union trade and mobility of resources creates additional problems for policy-makers, since policy spillovers increase between member states. In the labour market this increase in competition takes the form of increasing the wage elasticity of demand for labour within member countries, whilst increased mobility increases the elasticity of labour supply. Such changes increase the attractiveness of 'beggar-thy-neighbour' unilateral policies, for example, suppose one member state introduces lower social welfare contributions for domestic employers. Since increased European economic integration has increased the elasticity of demand for labour, such policies can increase domestic employment in part because resident firms increase their share of EU markets. The resulting displacement of foreign producers, causes an export of unemployment from the country which introduced the subsidy to the other member states. Such policies are likely to invoke retaliation and therefore have the potential for causing a competitive deregulation of labour markets within the EU. This sort of process raises the prospects of social dumping as economic integration increases, an issue we consider in Chapter 8.

3.7   Case study: minimum wage laws

Many of the topics discussed earlier will reappear throughout the remaining chapters of this book. However, it may be helpful to try to summarise the arguments of the last two chapters in terms of a case study. We have chosen the arguments for a statutory national minimum wage, an important issue given calls for more flexible European labour markets. As we reported in Chapter 1, most EU countries have either a statutory minimum wage or mimic such a policy by collective bargaining at the national or sectoral level. We also noted that in comparison with the US, minimum wages in Europe are at a much higher level with respect to the median wage, and are adjusted much more frequently. This prevalence of minimum wages will be unexpected to those who have read the previous chapter and understood the neoclassical arguments concerning the behaviour of competitive labour markets. We now discuss the theoretical analysis of minimum wages and review recent empirical studies of their effects.

Within a neoclassical theoretical perspective the employment consequences of minimum wage laws will depend upon the size of the minimum wage and the elasticity of demand for labour. In Figure 3.1 we replicate the basic model of Chapter 2.1; here any effective minimum wage, that is above w^*, must reduce employment. In this diagram a minimum wage of w_{min} causes employment to fall from n^* to n_1 and since the higher wage stimulates labour supply unemployment rises by more than the fall in employment, in our case unemployment rises by $(n_2 - n_1)$. The contraction of employment in this static analysis represents two effects generated by the higher real wage: a substitution effect towards more capital-intensive or overseas production and a wealth effect caused by the higher product prices reducing real demand in the economy. Applying the rules determining the elasticity of demand for labour developed in the previous chapter, job losses should therefore be greatest where: there are a large number of low-paid workers; product markets are the most competitive; low-wage labour is easy to replace with capital and/or high wage labour and where low-wage labour contributes a high proportion of total costs. We would therefore expect job

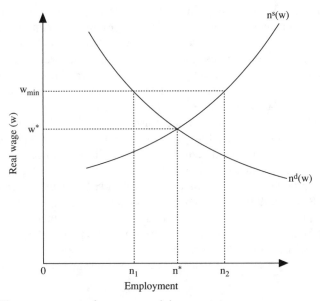

Figure 3.1 The consequences of a statutory minimum wage

losses to be greatest in industries such as textiles and amongst the young and unskilled workers. Conventional theory therefore seems to suggest that equity arguments for minimum wages are misplaced, since such policies reduce wage inequality only at the cost of increasing employment inequality. In addition, arguments relating to the reduction of poverty also seem misplaced given that changing working patterns, increased marital instability and higher unemployment have further weakened the correlation between low wage rates and low household income.

Interestingly, the British government in justifying legislation introduced in 1993 to abolish selective minimum wages used the very arguments developed in the previous paragraph. Dickens *et al.* (1993) examined these arguments and found little evidence that British wage controls had lowered employment in the sectors covered. They argued that there was a significant link between workers covered by the Wages Councils and low family income and argued that the growth of wage inequality in Britain, which we discussed in Chapter 1, had created a new rationale for minimum wage laws. Whilst there are few empirical studies of the introduction or abolition of minimum wages, there are many of the consequences of changes in the minimum rates. If minimum wages are designed to discriminate between regions, industrial sectors and worker experience they appear to cause little unemployment, as Fitoussi (1994) found for France. Indeed several recent US studies, Card and Krueger (1995) for example, find a positive relationship between small changes in the minimum wage and employment changes in their studies, results which Machin and Manning (1994) replicated for changes in the selective minimum wages in the UK. Van Soest (1994) does find evidence consistent with the standard model in his study of the effects of Dutch minimum wage rates for young workers, while Koutsogeorgopoulou (1994) finds little evidence of negative employment effects for Greece.

These empirical findings have stimulated new theoretical work which rejects the basic neoclassical model of labour market behaviour utilised in Figure 3.1. In a more sophisticated competitive framework the observed behaviour could be explained by reduced non-wage benefits or less job security as minimum wage rates are raised. Similarly, higher wage rates may induce firms to adopt internal labour markets, reducing turnover and monitoring costs. Monopsony models have been used to explain the observed positive relationship between employment and wages, most recently where inertia and other frictions cause individual firms to have at least short-run monopsony power (Dickens *et al.* 1994). For those starting from a non-competitive perspective the above empirical results pose few problems. Since the relationship between wages and productivity is the reverse of neoclassical theory, higher wages here can generate better jobs and higher productivity. Employing such a dynamic framework, Boyer (1993) has argued that by raising the relative price of unskilled labour, minimum wages force employers to raise both the skill intensity of production and capital-labour ratios. Both of these responses increase productivity growth, whilst by encouraging firms to shift production into the more sophisticated segments of product ranges, they also assist economies to achieve sustained increases in competitiveness.

3.8   General principles of labour market policy

The diversity of behaviour in European labour markets means that policy changes can easily lead to unintended, sometimes perverse outcomes. In this section we try to identify some general principles which should guide the design and implementation of labour market policy.

A starting principle in designing effective labour market policies is to recognise the importance of credibility. Any policy which is designed to have more than a very short-run effect needs to have credibility if it is to produce sustained modifications to labour market behaviour. Decision-makers in the labour market need to be convinced that the policy will be maintained over their planning period if they are to take the policy into account. Frequent changes in regulations or financial incentives are likely to produce changes in the timing of private decisions, but may not produce quantitative changes in behaviour over time.

Policy makers have not always taken notice of the theory of the second best in designing labour market policy. This theory suggests that if there are imperfections in the labour market, then a policy which may have been first-best in a highly competitive labour market will not necessarily improve labour market efficiency. Indeed in certain situations such policies could even cause a deterioration in market performance. For example, encouraging pay flexibility and increased motivation by providing tax incentives for share ownership schemes may increase the potential for insider-dealing and significantly distort the operation of equity markets.

Policy designers need also to acknowledge the potential for government failure. The limitations of European governments' attempts to tackle poverty provide a salutary lesson. The poor are a small and politically inactive group in most European economies, hence rather than concentrate social welfare expenditures on the poor, governments tended to allow or facilitate the capture of this expenditure by the middle classes. The composition of government expenditure on housing, higher education and child benefits illustrates this point in many European countries. Once the middle classes have captured this expenditure then governments find it politically difficult to cut this expenditure. They tend therefore to target those areas of the social welfare system which still support the poor, such as health care and unemployment and welfare benefits.

A key advantage of government which is often neglected by policy makers is their access to information. Some of the failures of the capital market to allow the unemployed to smooth their consumption over time or to finance human capital investments reflect the problems which financial institutions have in tracking people and ensuring repayment. Government's access to the tax and benefit system provides much lower monitoring costs and therefore generates a comparative advantage in areas such as providing loan guarantees for the unemployed, students and trainees (Snower, 1993).

Policy should be aimed at increasing output rather than just re-allocating it. As we can see in Table 1.12, most European governments spend much more on offsetting some of the income losses of the unemployed than they do in trying to restore their labour market income. Passive policies such as paying unemployment benefits may actually discourage the poorest groups from seeking work or encourage them to enter the low-wage hidden economy. Active policies which promote higher employment levels, such as wage subsidies, can raise output reducing rather than increasing the tax burdens.

We have now completed our introduction to labour market policy in Europe. In these first three chapters we have initially described the key characteristics of European labour markets and discovered similarities and differences important to our later studies. In Chapter 2 our survey of the economic analysis of labour markets explained the nature of the neoclassical model and provided a critical assessment of its present status and that of its competitors. Finally, we have introduced alternative perspectives concerning the role of governments in European labour markets. Our task is now to combine these elements in a detailed study of the main areas of labour market policy.

Guide to further reading

The theory of labour market policy has not been well developed in the literature and much of the content of this chapter has been developed from the theory of industrial policy and regulatory control. Veljanovski (1991) provides an accessible introduction to the latter literature with Mayhew (1994) serving as political balance. Barr (1993) provides a comprehensive introduction to social welfare policy and Chapters 5 and 6 of Centre for Economic Policy Research (1995) contain a careful introduction to the economics of labour market regulation. A challenging introduction to the issue of subsidiarity in the EU is contained in the study by the Centre for Economic Policy Research (1993), and Eichenberger (1994) provides a review of the debate and makes the economic case for Federalism. Card and Krueger (1995) and Bazen (1994) contain a more thorough examination of recent international experience with minimum wage laws.

4   Education and training

Our discussion starts with an examination of some of the key characteristics of education and training in European countries, concentrating in particular on the differences in the organisation of the school-to-work transition. Conventional competitive analysis is then considered, the human capital approach emphasizes adjustment on the supply of labour side of the market, with technology usually assumed to be fairly fixed. In this approach it is predominantly the supply, not demand of labour, which responds to changes in relative wages; evidence concerning the adjustment mechanisms is then considered and the policy implications of this approach are outlined. The rival screening hypothesis is then developed. It suggests an alternative relationship between education and productivity and predicts that increasing workers' potential productivity may not directly improve employment prospects, unless entrance into structured internal labour markets can be gained. Potential market failures in schooling and training markets are then assessed as a way of introducing our discussion of recent educational and training policy. The chapter ends with a critical study of the present role of the state in both on and off-the-job training in Europe, with a particular emphasis upon British attempts to close her training gap with other European countries.

The long-running debate about the importance of education and training in determining the relative performance of national economies has been given new impetus by the emergence of endogenous growth theory. The central role of schooling, training and research and development in this new growth theory has again focused attention on this area of labour market policy. This attention is similar to that produced by the early growth accounting studies of Denison, who in the 1950s and early 1960s discovered large 'residuals', that is economic growth not due to inputs of homogeneous factors of production. These results were often interpreted as showing education to be a major determinant of economic growth, and the economics of education became an established branch of economics. This development was reflected by western governments being much more proactive in issues related to the quality of their work-force. In the 1960s the persistence of widespread skill shortages in cyclical upturns was interpreted as indicating the failure of private sector training and there were widespread reforms of state educational and training systems as a consequence. Many of these western countries became disillusioned with these activist policies in the late 1970s, causing a retreat towards a more voluntarist or passive approach to on-the-job training. However, the relative success of the German, Japanese and Swedish economies has maintained interest in reforming educational and training systems. Most recently changes in the composition of demand for labour, the rise in European unemployment and the growth of labour market inequality have together given extra prominence to educational and training systems as determinants of labour market performance.

Economic theory may aid an understanding of these education and training policies debates, but it is important to stress the limitations of conventional theory in this area. The dominant human capital theory emphasises that education and training increase worker productivity, and through that channel earning-power in the labour market. The consumption benefits of education are often neglected, as are the potential social and political positive externalities associated with having an educated population. Conventional economic theory is directed at a narrower issue: the quality of the match between the knowledge and skills of the supply and demand for labour. Even as a theory of the link between education and earnings, human capital theory has been attacked by economists extending the segmented labour market approach.

4.1   Current patterns of education and training

One way of comparing the output of different educational systems is to consider the educational attainment of the population. The data in Table 4.1 provides an indication of the composition of the stock of human capital in European countries in the early 1990s. These figures are taken from the OECD; Labour Force Survey data tend to produce a higher post-compulsory education figure for France and significantly lower rates for the UK. The European Commission (1993) provides a detailed comparison of these two sources. Once again we note the large differences between the southern and northern member states, in the former only around a quarter of the population have attained at least upper secondary education. However, the educational structure is changing rapidly, in the southern member states the proportion attaining upper secondary education is between three to six times higher amongst those aged 25 to 33 than amongst the 55 to 64 age group. Overall, convergence is slow, with the differences in educational attainment in the EU being only slightly reduced if the labour force aged 25 to 34 is taken rather than the work-force as a whole.

While Table 4.1 provides an indication of the stocks of human capital, the rapidly changing educational structure suggests that we should concentrate upon flows, that is the current position of educational provision. We provide a range of indicators in Table 4.2, though the differences in education and training systems between European countries make any simple comparison of statistics problematic. Expenditure as a proportion of GDP is highest in the Nordic countries with their school-based system and lowest in Germany, where the dual system means that the apprenticeship system is responsible for the generation of vocational skills. Expenditure per student data suggests that Ireland and Spain have particularly low funding, though in general the higher income countries tend to spend more per student. Differences in starting ages and the duration of the various categories of education complicate comparisons of participation rates. Early childhood and primary participation rates for three year olds vary from just 1 per cent in Ireland and 11 per cent in Greece to 37 per cent in

Table 4.1 Educational attainment of the population, 1992

	Percentage of the population (aged 25–64 years of age) that has attained a specific highest level of education			
	Early childhood, primary and lower secondary	Upper secondary	Non-university tertiary	University education
Austria	32	61		7
Belgium	55	25	11	9
Denmark	41	40	6	13
Finland	39	43	8	10
France	48	36	6	10
Germany	18	60	10	12
Greece[1]	66	21	3	10
Ireland	58	25	9	8
Italy	72	22		6
Netherlands	42	37		21
Portugal[1]	86	7	2	5
Spain	77	10	3	10
Sweden[1]	30	46	12	12
UK	32	49	8	11
Norway	21	54	13	12

[1] Figures are for 1991.
Figures for Luxembourg not available.
Source: OECD *Education at a Glance* (1995a) Table C01.

Denmark, Spain and the UK and nearly 100 per cent in Belgium and France. Participation rates in tertiary education are also distorted by the tendency in Denmark, Germany and the Netherlands for students who have completed upper secondary education to stay on at school and pursue additional qualifications. Participation rates for 17 year olds in full-time education in the early 1990s varied from around 60 per cent in Spain and the UK to 90 per cent in Germany and the Netherlands. Participation rates for 17 year olds have risen fastest in the Nordic countries and those lacking a strong apprenticeship tradition, such as France, Ireland and Spain. High European levels of unemployment have contributed to this trend, while in Belgium compulsory schooling was extended to 18 in the mid-1980s and in the UK increased access to higher education has provided a powerful incentive for young people to stay in full-time schooling. The productivity of the schooling system will also be dependent upon non-completion rates; Italy appears to have a particular problem in this area with de Luca and Bruni (1993) reporting drop-out rates above 10 per cent in the compulsory school curriculum and 30 per cent in higher secondary schools.

The final column of Table 4.2 contains a proxy for tertiary education participation rates. The tertiary new entry index is the number of new full-time entrants per 100

Table 4.2 Indicators of educational provision, 1992

	Total public expenditure on primary and secondary education as a percentage of GDP	Expenditure per student for public secondary education $	New entrants to tertiary education per 100 persons in starting age group
Austria	3.7	6,420	34.1
Belgium	3.4	6,470	52.6
Denmark	4.5	4,940	52.8
Finland	5.0	4,820	na
France	3.8	5,870	48.0
Germany	2.6	4,260	49.0
Greece	na	na	29.3
Ireland	3.7	2,770	39.9
Italy	3.4	4,700	41.7
Netherlands	3.3	3,310[2]	40.1[3]
Spain	3.3	3,140	43.3[3]
Sweden	5.1	6,050	52.0
UK	4.1	4,390	36.9
Norway	5.0[1]	6,200	38.0

na = not available.
Figures for Luxembourg and Portugal not available.
[1] Direct public expenditure for educational institutions only.
[2] Public and government–dependent private.
[3] University only.
Source: OECD *Education at a Glance* (1995a) Tables F01, F03 and P05.

individuals in the population at the most common starting age for tertiary education. Whilst for most countries participation rates in tertiary education are highest for 18 to 21 year olds, in Denmark and Finland the rates are higher for 22 to 25 year olds and Austria, France, Germany, the Netherlands and Norway have high participation rates amongst the 22–29 age group. Participation rates are not the same as graduation rates and in Italy drop-out rates in the 1980s have been around 70 per cent. In 1992 about 40 per cent of Finnish and German graduates were in architecture, science and engineering compared with around 32 per cent in the UK and just 20 per cent in Italy and Spain. Changes in the structure of education can occur rapidly, over the period 1960–1990 the number of graduating higher education students in Britain increased fivefold during a period when the workforce grew by only about 10 per cent.

Participation in job-related continuing education and training again appears to be high in the Nordic countries and is heavily concentrated amongst the younger age groups and those with high educational attainment. Concentrating upon educational achievements, about two-thirds of the non-graduate Swiss and German work-force had vocational qualifications, but only 40 per cent of the French and 25 per cent of the British work-force had intermediate vocational qualifications. Britain appears to have a particularly low proportion of its work-force with craft qualifications, with apprenticeship numbers again declining rapidly after 1992. Auer (1994) and the European Commission (1995a) provide comparisons of training undertaken by employees based upon Labour Force Survey data. The survey indicates that about 15 per cent of employees aged 25 and over had undertaken training in the previous four weeks in the Netherlands and Denmark, whereas in France, Portugal, Italy, Spain and Greece the proportion was around 3 per cent or less. In general, training is more likely amongst the well-qualified and amongst workers in larger firms. The limited data available on the training expenditure of the private sector again suggests large differences in Europe, with French companies spending around 3.6 per cent of their wage bill, Sweden 2.7 per cent, UK 2.4 per cent , Germany 2 per cent and Spain 1.7 per cent (CBI, 1991).

Lynch (1994) divides training systems into two broad categories: work-based systems and all other systems including: school-based, individual choice and government led-systems. Amongst the former systems she includes apprenticeships (Germany and Denmark), company-provided and low labour turnover (Japan) and employer training tax (Australia and France). Amongst the 'other' category Norway has a school-based youth training programme and Canada and the USA rely upon individual autonomy with few nationally recognised vocational qualifications. The workplace system links formal training programmes with employment and most of the countries with this system have high rates of training. Countries following a work-based system have to solve the problem of how to encourage providers to supply training in transferable skills. Validation of skills and abilities acquired through certification together with low apprenticeship relative wages is the German solution to this problem, whilst in Japan low labour turnover has in the past provided employers with sufficient incentive. International comparisons of training and tenure undertaken by the OECD (1993) suggest that when new recruits are excluded, formal training paid for by employers tends to rise with tenure. On the basis of data available Japan and Finland appear to be much greater providers of training for experienced employees than the Netherlands and Norway.

In Box 4.1 we provide a more detailed outline of the British, French and German schooling and training systems. Whilst the German system is a dual one, there are opportunities to transfer between academic and vocational education. Its success is reflected in the very high proportion of young people who obtain a nationally recognised qualification, only about 6 per cent leave school without any qualification. Compulsory schooling lasts from the ages of 5 to 16 in Britain, a year longer than in France and two years longer than in Japan and most German Länder, though in practice British children have on average less full-time education, since fewer British children attend pre-school institutions and a smaller proportion stay in full-time education after the age of 16. Green and Steedman (1993) provide a detailed comparison of these three countries' educational systems, together with those of Japan and the US. The British system tends to produce a narrower curriculum than in France and Germany where children have to show attainment in a wider range of subjects if they are to matriculate. Recent changes in the organisation of post-compulsory schooling in Britain have produced a threefold differentiation which is similar to the general, technical and vocational pathways of the French system, though uniquely Britain is

Box 4.1: Three national education and training systems

	ENGLAND AND WALES	FRANCE	GERMANY
Schooling	National Curriculum and national assessment centrally planned and compulsory for all schools funded publicly. Non-selective compulsory education, but mixed ability teaching rare in secondary education. Highly specialised post–15. Low participation in post–16 education. Target of 60 per cent of young people to achieve 2 A level passes or NVQ equivalent by 2000. Small private sector specialising in gaining entrance to the most prestigious universities.	National Curriculum and national assessment centrally planned. 96 per cent of 3 year olds in school. Non-selective compulsory schooling. Selection at upper secondary level to general, technical or vocational schools. Target of 80 per cent of young people studying at Baccalaureat level by 2000. Streaming from age 13/14, grade repeating common. Large private sector (17 per cent of those in compulsory education), often religious foundations, and not concentrating upon the wealthy or most able pupils.	Lander system with Federal co-ordination and standard length of schooling, types of schools and qualifications. Part-time schooling obligatory till 18. Most secondary schools selective: Gymnasium (28 per cent of age group) offer academic schooling with specialist provision to university level, Realschulen (29 per cent) offer general schooling and Hauptschulen (38 per cent) provide a general education for the less academic. Each has their own leaving certificate and provides progression routes for successful pupils. Great variety of vocational education institutions. Small private sector.
Post-compulsory education and training	Mixed system: academic, broad vocational and narrow vocational (occupational). Rapid expansion of higher education in the last decade. National certification of vocational qualifications. Government-funded initial training largely covers the least qualified segment of school-leavers. Apprenticeship system in long-term decline.	Predominantly education-led and school-based. Single Baccalaureat system of qualifications for academic and vocational fields promotes transfer and access to higher education. All vocational courses have a substantial element of general education. Apprenticeship system (10 per cent of cohort) partly funded by tax on employers.	Dual system provides apprenticeship training for 70 per cent of young people who join at ages 15–19. Individual apprenticeship contracts with firms of 2–4 year, three days a week work-based training and remaining time in Berufschule studying general education and theoretical aspect of their occupation, 90 per cent obtain their certificates of vocational competence.

developing vocational qualifications which are competency based. Initial work-based education is part-funded by employers in Germany and France and in both of these countries trade unions and works councils are more heavily involved in the organisation and monitoring of initial training than is currently the case in Britain. We consider the relative merits of these systems in the following sections, but first we develop analysis appropriate to this assessment.

4.2 Economic theory and education and training

4.2.1 *Human capital theory*

Human capital theory makes no fundamental distinction between education and training: individuals, or more recently households, are concerned with maximising lifetime income and it is assumed that each level of education and training is uniquely related to an earnings stream. This latter relationship reflects causal relationships from education to skills, between skills and marginal productivity, and finally from productivity to earnings. The latter link is the marginal productivity theory of labour demand introduced in Chapter 2. Human capital theory interacts with this theory to provide an explanation of wage differentials. The decision-taker is viewed as following conventional investment appraisal methods. The student or worker compares the benefits of further investment in education and training with the costs. The benefits are expected higher future labour market income, while the costs are of two forms: the direct costs of undertaking the education or training course and the indirect opportunity costs of foregone earnings whilst studying. These benefits and costs extend over time and the individual will have to compare the present value of the expected benefits with the present value of the expected costs. The rational investor in human capital will therefore invest up to that level of education and training where marginal benefits just exceed marginal costs. In equilibrium, the rate of return on this marginal investment should just equal the rate of return on fixed investments of comparable risk and uncertainty.

To model the investment strategy of a wealth-maximising individual, consider the decision of whether to undertake an additional year of schooling or training. Let C be the cost of undertaking the extra year, in most cases consisting largely of foregone earnings. This has to be compared to the anticipated benefits of higher labour market earnings. Let the present value of these returns be R, then:

$$R = \sum_{t=1}^{N} k_t (1+i)^{-t} \qquad [4.1]$$

where k_t = expected extra annual earnings in the tth year;
    i = market rate of return on investments of comparable risk and uncertainty;
    N = length of remaining working life.

If R > C then the net present value of the investment is positive and the individual should invest in the extra human capital. An alternative formulation is to calculate the internal rate of return, r, which equates the R and C of the marginal investment, here:

$$C = \sum_{t=1}^{N} k_t (1+r)^{-t} \qquad [4.2]$$

The individual should invest as long as r > i. Investment in human capital formation is therefore encouraged by both low costs of undertaking education and training (C), and market rate of return (i), and high expected additional earnings (k) and a longer time-span over which to earn them (N). The human capital theory of life cycle accumulation can explain the observed concavity of the age-earnings profile. During the formal schooling period individuals specialise in the accumulation of human capital as the returns are high due to the length of future employment, N, and opportunity costs of foregone earnings, C, are low or even approach zero where there are legal constraints on child labour. Post-compulsory schooling investments are more costly and as retirement approaches N falls and the shorter pay-off period makes most investments unprofitable and the stock of human capital, and with it earning capacity, falls as depreciation dominates. This depreciation will take the form of out-dated knowledge and skills which have been displaced by new technical processes and products.

It is usual to assume that the marginal rate of return to human capital investments declines as the quantity of human capital acquired by the individual increases. One supportive argument is that an individual may have a fixed capacity to benefit from human capital and therefore diminishing marginal return to ability applies. This assumption leads to individuals having a negatively sloped demand for human capital investments; r falls as investments increase. On the supply side where funds to finance investments are obtained by borrowing or selling assets, extra funds are only likely to be available to individuals at a higher rate of interest, and the supply curve of funds for investment in human capital will be positively sloped. The supply and demand for investment in human capital are illustrated in Figure 4.1.

As we have seen wealth maximisation requires that the individual invests in all schooling and training that yields a rate of return (r) greater than the rate of interest (i). In Figure 4.1 this optimal level of investment is represented by I* where r = i. Factors making it easier to finance investments in human capital such as subsidised loans for students, shift the supply curve to the right and raise I* and lower the equilibrium rate of return. If capital markets are imperfect then internal sources of finance will be cheaper than market sources, it follows that our analysis predicts that, other things being equal, the rich will tend to invest in a higher level of investment in human capital than the poor. Factors which raise the rate of return such as increased wage differentials for educated workers or the provision of cheaper training facilities, shift the demand curve to the right and raise both I* and r*.

Let us consider how to apply this analysis to a competitive economy where government and unions have no influence on the supply of education and training resources.

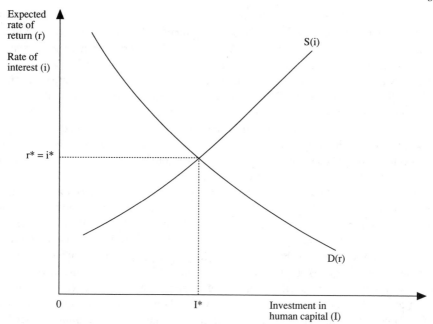

Figure 4.1 Investment in human capital

Consider the consequence of the rise in demand for professional workers identified in Chapter 1. The emergence of skill shortages causes a rise in the relative earnings of workers with these skills and therefore raises the rate of return for those training to enter these occupations. If we now view Figure 4.1 as the demand and supply curves for investment in education and training for this particular occupation, say for lawyers, then the demand curve has shifted outwards. The higher rate of return induces a higher inflow to legal training and the shortage is gradually eliminated by newly qualified workers. This adjustment process also gradually eliminates the excess returns to the human capital investments enjoyed by qualified lawyers. Accordingly, in the long run in a competitive economy differences in earnings across individuals should be related to differences in education and training investments, with equilibrium wage differentials just compensating for these differences.

Tests of these predictions of the simple human capital approach, suggest that interpersonal differences in human capital investments appear to be capable of explaining substantial proportions of actual income variability. As yet we have ignored the impact of differences in ability in our analysis; linking earnings to schooling may be ignoring the powerful influence of ability on both the quantity of human capital investments and labour market earnings. We consider this argument in Section 4.2.3 where the need to relax some of the other implicit assumptions of this approach is considered. In particular the simple model assumes perfect knowledge and a perfect capital market; imperfections will in practice prevent people of the same ability achieving the same educational level. Human capital investments are not homogeneous and quality as well as quantity measurements of investments are required to refine the model. Dispersions in the rates of return on investments will also be caused by differing non-pecuniary returns from employment and these may be linked to educational attainment. In addition the model ignores other sources of income variations such as scarcity of natural abilities, nepotism, discrimination and luck, which lead to people with the same educational attainments receiving different compensations. While the model can be modified to include many of these refinements its central proposition remains that the human capital element dominates earnings differentials. Its usefulness rests upon the empirical issue of whether workers can and do respond to the signals of relative wages when making their supply decisions in the labour market. Do occupational labour markets actually adjust through future and present workers making educational and training decisions on the basis of wage differentials?

A further assumption of the model so far developed is that individuals pay their own education and training costs. Becker (1975) argued that the relationship between human capital investments and earnings would be distorted where these investment costs were partially borne by firms. Investment in human capital has one major difference from investment in physical capital: the property rights of the enhanced human capital reside in the worker regardless of the source of the finance for that investment. Outside a slave or feudal society, freedom of contract ensures that workers retain their right to sell their labour to any employer with whom they can negotiate mutually favourable terms. Becker analyses the question of who pays for training in such an environment and in answering it makes an important distinction between general and specific training. General or transferable skill training enhances workers' productivity both within their present firm and in other firms and accordingly has a market value. The increase in potential earnings which such training produces, irrespective of employer, provides the worker with a direct incentive to invest. It follows that workers will pay the costs of general training undertaken voluntarily, usually by working for a wage lower than the value of their output. This outlay reflects their expectation that such investment will be profitable. The observed low pay of many trainee accountants, football apprentices and junior doctors is consistent with investment in general training.

We illustrate this argument in Figure 4.2, where the length of the training period is t_0. During this period actual productivity of the worker falls to MP_t and there are direct costs of training equal to d, paid by workers in the case of general training. Since the workers' pre-training productivity was MP_0 this represents the wage offered prior to training and therefore $(MP_0 - MP_t)$ is the wage loss during training and $[(MP_0 - MP_t) + d]$ represents the total costs of training per period to the worker, and is represented by the shaded area in Figure 4.2. Workers who are investing in general training will therefore only be offered a wage of w_t during their training period. However, at the end of period t_0 the trained worker's productivity rises to MP_x and the worker will be offered a wage w_x equal to the higher productivity generated by the acquisition of the transferable skill. Thus $(w_x - MP_0)$ is the skill premium which represents the flow of returns on the investment in general training. The size of this premium in the long run will be positively related to the length of the training period, t_0, and the training costs incurred including earnings foregone, $[(MP_0 - MP_t) + d]$. As in the simple human capital approach, the adjustment

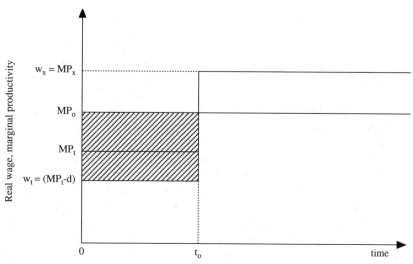

Figure 4.2 General training

mechanism to changes in labour market conditions is a change in relative wage rates. Firms facing transferable skill bottlenecks raise the relative wage of that occupation, thereby increasing the anticipated rate of return from investment in that general training and inducing workers to undertake the training necessary to enter the occupation.

Some training, Becker argued, has no outside market value. Learning the organisational structure of a particular firm or its stores procedure would not increase the value of the worker to other employers. The worker, therefore, has no incentive to forgo current earnings to undertake this specific or non-transferable skill training. Accordingly, firms pay all of the costs of this type of training, induction courses for example. The firm must decide itself on the optimal level of specific training, investing in such training until its rate of return is equal to the rates of return on other investment opportunities of comparable risk and uncertainty. The adjustment mechanism to any imbalance is more direct in this case and requiring only information internal to the firm, though implementing their optimal investment policy for specific training is made more complex since the ownership of the training belongs to the worker. A critical input into the investment decision will be the expected turnover of labour, since the present value of the returns from training will depend upon the post-training tenure of the worker. As we argued in Chapter 2, quits and other involuntary terminations of trained employees represent foregone returns to the firm on their investments in specific training and they will want to reduce such investment 'losses' by increasing worker loyalty. One mechanism may be to share the benefits of specific training with employees and, accordingly, the costs. Therefore employers will encourage workers undertaking specific training to accept wages below their potential earnings elsewhere by promising higher wage levels after completion. Workers' post-training wages will be above their earning capacity with alternative employers, and this rent will promote low turnover. The armed forces are an example of employers

99

providing specific training; they often require entrants to sign contracts for a minimum specified period, applying penalties to those wishing to leave before their contract expires. In addition they try to market the highly specific training required of servicemen as having a high general component, by for example, suggesting preferred treatment by civilian employers, again as a way of sharing costs and reducing turnover.

The case of specific training is illustrated in Figure 4.3, where t_0 is again the length of the training period and MP_0 is the pre-training productivity of the worker. In a competitive labour market MP_0 determines the wage offer and in the case of specific training financed wholly by firms, this would be the wage paid before, during and after the training. The post-training productivity is again MP_x but since the training is in firm-specific skills, the post-training wage offer remains at MP_0. However, if the firm only pays this wage, which is equal to that offered by other firms, they run the risk of workers quitting and they lose the returns on their training investment. Hence they will try to strike a deal with their workers, by which during training a wage below MP_0 is paid, while completion of training results in a wage above MP_0. Alternatively, Hashimoto (1981) explains the sharing of training costs and benefits as a consequence of transaction costs associated with identifying MP_x and alternative potential earnings. In either case workers who share training costs and benefits have to trust that firms will not renege on the deal once training has been undertaken. Their fear of opportunistic bargaining by employers may lead to the creation of internal labour markets as discussed in Chapter 2 and provide an efficiency rationale for the introduction of job protection legislation as discussed in Chapter 3.

In both of the above cases the adjustment mechanism to changes in labour market conditions is not instantaneous and short-term skill shortages will emerge. 'Poaching', the bidding away of workers from the firms who trained them, is here viewed benignly since it has no effect on the quantity of training. Poaching can only occur with general training since specific training does not make the workers more attractive to other employers. Since the Becker model asserts that general training is costless to firms, poaching cannot dissuade firms from providing training. Advocates of the competitive approach thus prefer to view poaching as part of the normal mobility of labour necessary to adjust to changes in the product and labour markets. This argument relies on a very rigorous distinction between general and specific training which we question later.

4.2.2 *Policy implications of the human capital model*

Supporters of the human capital approach view educational and training markets as potentially efficient; it follows that market forces should be strengthened and then allowed to operate with minimal government interference. If social benefits and informational externalities can be internalised, and imperfect capital markets compensated for, say by the provision of educational vouchers and provision of manpower forecasts of labour demand, then the supply of educational places can also be left to be decided by market forces. Similar policy conclusions hold in the training market, if we assume that any imperfections in the training market are largely independent

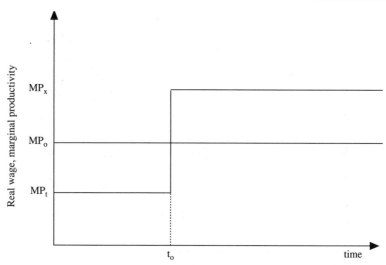

Figure 4.3 Specific training

of firms' behaviour and are correctable by institutional reform. If firms, in general, can be relied upon to generate the socially desirable level of specific training and respond to workers' demand for general training, then it follows that there is no rationale, at least on economic grounds, for long-term government supervision or any direct training provision.

Consider how we can utilise this approach to analyse the appropriate policy response to the changes in the composition of the demand for labour identified in Chapter 1. In the short-run the relative decline in the demand for unskilled labour (increase in the demand for more educated labour) has increased the premium earned by educated workers and hence the returns to larger investments in education. Figure 4.4 illustrates this situation in terms of our earlier diagrammatic representation of the basic model. The change in the pattern of demand will pivot the demand curve anti-clockwise, from D_0 to D_1, since the increased wage inequality causes lower returns for small investments and higher returns for larger investments in education and training. The normal response of optimal decision-makers to this change will be to increase their investment from I_n to I_1 and we automatically move to a more educated and skilled work-force. Let us now consider the situation faced by workers with low education, those who previously invested only I_u compared to the original optimal investment of I_n. This low investment of these workers may be a reflection of their attitude to risk-taking or their inability to finance desired investments, the latter due perhaps to the unwillingness of capital markets to lend on the basis of human rather than physical assets. As we have noted, the normal workers' response to this change in demand will be to increase investment up to I_1 where S_0 and D_1 intersect, widening the gap in human capital stocks between the less educated and the norm for the work-force.

Although the less educated initially received a higher marginal rate of return on

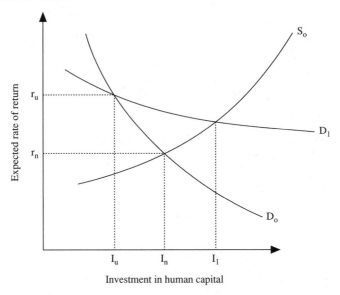

Figure 4.4 Policy responses to increased labour market inequality

their additional investments, $r_u > r_n$, the change in demand has reduced this differential. If we wish to counter the tendency towards greater labour market inequality, one solution is to provide subsidised education and training for this group of workers, implicitly shifting them back on to S_o, thereby removing a constraint on their investments in education and training. A successful policy initiative along these lines would reduce the supply of less-educated workers and increase the supply of more educated and therefore help to reverse the pressures towards greater wage inequality in the labour market. Notice that this argument implies that the less educated face the same labour market rewards for investing in education and training as the rest of the workforce.

An earlier illustration of this type of policy package was the adoption by many western economies in the 1960s of educational and training programmes for anti-poverty purposes. At that time it was common to interpret poverty as being the consequence of low labour market earnings and to view the appropriate response as an increase in those earnings. According to the human capital theory a major cause of low earnings is low investment in education and training. The alphabet of programmes which constituted President Johnson's War on Poverty in the US during the mid-1960s had as their philosophical base the arguments illustrated in Figure 4.4. Help towards doing without help, was the message underlying these policies, the apparent failure of which led to a radical reassessment of human capital theory. If the cause of poverty lies in the inability of blacks or other groups to gain access to good jobs regardless of their human capital, then policy needs to be directed at the demand side of the labour market, not the supply, an argument we return to in our discussion of labour market discrimination in Chapter 6.

In order to further assess these policy prescriptions of human capital theory we need to consider its empirical performance and whether there are alternative models of schooling and training decisions which are consistent with empirical results in this area. We also need to identify more systematically the potential sources of schooling and training market failures before the adequacy of the competitive approach can be assessed. These are the tasks for the next few pages of this chapter.

4.2.3   *Human capital theory: empirical work*

There are two stages to the human capital explanation of earnings differentials: accumulated human capital determines worker productivity and the latter determines relative wages. Initially empirical studies did not separate these two relationships and instead directly tested the impact of education and training on earnings levels. The early emphasis was on the performance of earnings equations of the type first popularised by Mincer (1962). Following Mincer's derivation, a typical human capital based earnings function looks as follows:

$$\ln Y = a + \beta S + \phi e + \gamma e^2 + \sum_{t=1}^{N} \theta_i\, D_i + u \qquad [4.3]$$

where $\ln Y$ = the natural log of some earnings measure;
  S   = the number of years of schooling;
  e   = years of experience, a proxy for post-school investments;
  e^2 = included to proxy the depreciation of human capital
  D_i = vector of dummy variables to allow for personal characteristics such as health, sex, location and union membership.
  u is the error term.

The influence of e and e^2 are expected to give the function the parabolic shape with respect to age discussed earlier. If it is assumed that the rate of return is independent of the number of years of schooling then β is an estimate of the rate of return on schooling, ϕ generates an estimate of the rate of return from on-the-job training only when the fraction of working time devoted to training is known. Siebert's (1985) survey of estimates for the private rate of return indicated a range around 10 per cent, a rate both above the returns on physical investments and the market rate of interest. There seems to be a particularly large return to completing upper secondary schooling. Historically, studies adopting this approach suggest widespread international under-investment at all levels of education (Psacharopoulos, 1985), and declining rates of return by level of education and across levels of national income. Though the survey by Alsalam and Conley in OECD (1995b) indicates that the rate of return on long-duration tertiary education exceeds that for upper secondary education in most European countries, with Denmark, the Netherlands and Switzerland being exceptions. Using General Household Survey Data for 1985–8 Bennett *et al.* (1992) estimated expected private returns to post-16 qualifications in Britain. Their results indicated an average rate of return to 'A' levels of almost 10 per cent for females and 6 per cent for males. For those entering higher education the returns were again higher than those available on long-term financial assets at around 7 per cent for males and 6 per cent for females. Of interest for our later discussion was their finding that the estimated rates of return varied greatly between social classes. Some of the returns to education take the form of increased access to formal training and a lower probability of lengthy unemployment spells, though Kettunen (1994) found that at the highest levels additional education reduces the probability of re-employment of unemployed Finnish workers and the relationship is weak in Greece, Italy and Spain (OECD, 1994a).

Specification problems abound with the Mincer approach, allowances need to be made for ability, the interaction between education and experience and missing quality adjustments to jobs and schooling. Returns to schooling appear greater if adjustment is made for the quality of jobs, some of the returns to education apparently being taken in the form of better working conditions and more stable employment. Ability poses a much greater problem for the Mincer approach, since ability will tend to be related both to level of schooling and observed wages, hence utilisation of simple least squares estimation methods are likely to produce biased results (Blackburn and Neumark, 1993). If heredity or environmental factors affect the ability of individuals to benefit from education then these 'family' influences are difficult to separate from human capital ones. In terms of Figure 4.1, the supply curve for members of more 'able' families lies to the right of those for other families, since they have a greater chance of success in any schooling. However, this group also face a demand curve which lies to the right of that shown, since the more able are more attractive to employers, and they therefore invest more and get higher rates of return.

There have been three broad approaches to deal with this issue of unobserved ability. Use of ability proxies such as IQ test scores is currently viewed as inferior to experimental approaches estimating rates of return on education of twins or of those entering compulsory schooling at a different age. The study of returns to schooling within families allows comparisons of workers who have similar genetic and family background and avoids some of the problem of imperfect measurements of ability. Most recent studies suggest very large returns to schooling, with Ashenfelter and Krueger (1994) reporting that the better educated American twin may earn on average up to 14% more for each extra year of schooling. Harmon and Walker (1993) illustrate the third approach in their examination of the consequences of the raising of the school leaving age from 15 to 16 in England and Wales in the mid-1970s. They conclude that for males the effect of additional compulsory education was significantly less than the effect of additional elective schooling. This result taken together with the associated loss of experience suggested that the net effect of the change may have been to produce a negative net return for this cohort.

Since experimental data are rare in economics, estimations of earnings functions are always likely to face sample selection problems. An alternative approach to testing the human capital approach to schooling is to consider whether the demand for education is responsive to economic forces and whether structural and other environmental changes have the predicted impact. Freeman's 1986 survey finds that the demand for higher education appears sensitive to wage incentives and to tuition costs. Pissarides in two associated studies (1981, 1982) found some evidence that the staying-on rate at school was sensitive to economic incentives, though the relationship was weak for girls and he ignored social factors important in decision-taking. While the positive unemployment effect upon school staying-on rates has been confirmed by Bennett *et al.* (1992), their results for females were inconsistent with the human capital model. Despite the expected returns to 'A' levels being higher, less than 11 per cent of their female sample studied for this qualification, whilst 27 per cent opted for vocational qualifications which generated lower returns than alternative academic qualifications. Rice (1987) estimated a model of investment in post-compulsory education which did allow the socio-economic background of the family to influence investment decisions. Family background, a factor not stressed in the human capital model, was found to be an important independent determinant of participation in both her study and that of Micklewright (1989). Attempts to directly test whether family background influences the accuracy of labour market information have been scarce, but low ability and working class pupils appear to have a poorer awareness of the economic returns from educational investments. Makepeace (1994) finds evidence for the UK that occupational choices are affected by lifetime earnings, though supply elasticities are relatively small and substantial subsidies would be required to make significant changes in the training decisions of young males.

Studies of the returns to training received by individual workers suffer from most of the problems discussed, but in addition they have to consider how to divide up training costs between firms and workers before the rates of return can be estimated. Studies indicate that, as with education, part of the returns to training are in the form of an increased probability of being employed, and a reduction in the duration of any unemployment spell. Chapman (1993) and Lynch (1994a) provide surveys of available studies and they conclude that training has a positive impact upon a person's wage, though the impact appears to differ widely for different types of training and different groups of workers. In general, employer-provided training in their current job generates greater earnings growth for workers than government or school-based training. Greenhalgh and Stewart (1987) found that full-time vocational training yields significant returns in the UK in terms of advances in occupational status, though the marginal benefit declines to zero after four weeks of training. Booth (1993) found that training in their current job generated significant returns for her sample of graduates, though only males received a positive return on training in previous jobs. Lynch (1992) finds that young American workers received higher wages as a return for undertaking training, though in the case of on-the-job training this only applies to that provided by their current employer, indicating that much on-the-job training is firm-specific. Groot and Mekkelholt (1995) find very high rates of return to male Dutch workers from on-the-job training, over 80 per cent for those with the highest education level, suggesting widespread under-investing.

Little is known about the returns to firms from training investments, though Alba-Ramirez (1994) reports a positive training effect on labour productivity for Spanish firms. Studies of the determinants of training produce results generally compatible with the human capital approach. Blundell *et al.* (1994) summarise the evidence as follows. The probability of undertaking training decreases with age and with tenure, while industries with growing or changing technology tend to provide more training.

Males have better access to training than females, as do the more highly educated and those with higher status occupations, whilst minority groups, part-timers and those working in smaller firms have a lower probability of receiving training. International studies such as that by the OECD (1993) indicate a positive relationship between tenure and skill training in an industry. Though Elias (1994) finds that the expected negative effect of employer-provided training on turnover was only confirmed for female workers. We return to some of these findings later in this chapter and in our discussion of discrimination in Chapter 6.

The education and training studies summarised have produced results broadly consistent with the human capital approach. A problem with all of these studies is that they fail to identify the individual components of the model. By directly considering the relation between education and earnings they fail to address the nature of the causal link between the two variables. This is a particularly important issue when we come to consider policy issues. To equate the apparent private profitability of most educational investments with social profitability it is necessary to establish how the accumulation of human capital enhances earnings. With human capital theory the higher earnings of educated and trained workers reflect higher output and therefore both private and social benefits stem from such investments. If instead education largely acts as a signalling device to employers about the employability of applicants, then private returns are a poor proxy for social returns and human capital theory is fundamentally flawed. A further problem follows from our analysis of structured internal labour markets in Chapter 2. Here wage and salaries do not adjust readily to changes in the balance of supply and demand in labour markets. Internal labour markets may prevent the required signals being sent to human capital investors, in which case human capital theory as developed above is not a helpful explanation of supply decisions in European labour markets. We now turn to an assessment of alternative approaches.

4.2.4 *Alternative approaches to education and training: screening hypothesis*

In Chapter 2 the segmented labour market approach to labour market behaviour was outlined. The main conclusions of this approach are that firms design internal employment policies largely independent of external competitive forces. These policies will be characterised by internal job-ladders and wage-rates specified by job, rather than by individual worker. How does this model explain the role and determinants of education and training? On-the-job training will be concentrated in the primary labour market and the strength of these internal labour markets make all such training essentially firm-specific. Given the anticipated long-term attachment between workers and firms the distinction between general and specific training is in practice redundant. Any on-the-job training, even in a transferable skill, will have a content unique to the firm such as work organisation, or a particular machine or product specification. Firms are therefore not indifferent between current employees and applicants from the external labour market with supposedly the same transferable skill. The former have higher productivity due to their firm-specific knowledge and are of known and acceptable quality and reliability. The quantity of on-the-job training will be determined by the firm, and it will be insensitive to the demand for training amongst workers. Any short-ages of labour will not be countered by wage changes, that would distort existing agreed relativities; instead firms will initially respond by flexible employment strate-gies such as restructuring existing work schedules and subcontracting.

Within this environment, gaining entry into the primary labour market is the crucial determinant of worker access to training opportunities. In part, such access reflects luck but education and pre-entry training have the function of assisting access to good jobs. Recruitment occurs by firms choosing between applicants to fill positions usu-ally at the bottom of the job-ladder. The observed high 'wastage' of skilled workers to promotion is here interpreted as a consequence of the dominance of internal labour markets. It is not workers' short-term productivity which employers are interested in, since all recruits require firm-specific training and are offered, implicitly, long-term contracts. Here the emphasis is upon employers' hiring policy and firms choosing between applicants on the basis of their 'employability' and 'trainability'. Employers cannot directly discern these characteristics and therefore applicants need to signal these qualities.

The 'screening' hypothesis develops from this framework and argues that formal education can perform the signalling role. High quality applicants may find it prof-itable to invest in acquiring a characteristic which signals their qualities to employers. A good signal will be one which lower quality applicants will have difficulty in achieving due to inability or cost. Educational qualifications meet such requirements and high quality applicants will have to invest in relatively large amounts of education in order to generate an effective signal to employers. Thus, employers exercise 'sta-tistical discrimination' on the basis of educational attainment, it being too expensive to identify atypical members of a given group and 'employable' members of a lower educational achievement group therefore suffer discrimination. Employers take edu-cational credentials as proxies for the qualities which they require; this lack of concern with the specific knowledge of applicants explains the poor match observable between specific educational qualifications and actual occupational profiles. A fur-ther advantage of education as a screen is that it is legal for employers to discriminate on this basis, whilst the use of other stereotypes, such as race or sex, is not. Moreover, discrimination on the basis of educational attainment is also at present socially accept-able. All elements of society seem to view educational achievement as reflecting individual effort and accept their 'fairness' as criteria for recruitment. Its use therefore promotes good working relations and avoids conflicts which threaten to constrain pro-ductivity growth.

This screening view of the role and effects of education and training in the labour market is often linked with radical arguments about the objectives of formal education in a capitalist economy. Bowles and Gintis (1976) argue that most jobs require non-cognitive personality characteristics such as: concentration, compliance, industry, punctuality and co-operation. These characteristics rather than cognitive knowledge dictate productivity for the bulk of the labour force. Radicals argue that it is the role of compulsory schooling to generate these valued behavioural characteristics in future workers. The emphasis which schools place upon discipline is just one example of their proposition that the social relations within schools in capitalist economies reflect the realities of the social division of labour in the economy at large. If employers care more about how school-leavers behave than about what they know, then the traditional argument for off-the-job vocational education for the majority of the population dissolves.

The term 'screening hypothesis' has also been used to describe the view of education as a non-competitive barrier to entry rather than as a signal. Here education is a means of transmitting privilege and maintaining inequality over time. Employers discriminate on the basis of education, education being a proxy for preferred characteristics, such as class or race, which are unrelated to potential productivity. This is a more radical version of our earlier argument that since employers cannot identify individual potential productivity they require a low-cost screen. In this variant firms are not trying to identify potential productivity but to sustain class or racial inequality. Implicit is the argument that productivity and profitability are almost independent of worker qualities, otherwise competition would progressively eliminate firms exhibiting such discriminatory behaviour. Credentialism has sometimes been used to categorise this approach, but both this term and screening are ambiguously used in the literature.

There are some similarities between the screening hypothesis and the human capital approach. Both view the benefits of education as being higher lifetime earnings and generate similar determinants of the individual's optimal investment strategy. Statistical discrimination and internal labour markets can explain why educated workers on average earn more, although their potential labour market productivity remains unaffected by their investments. It is when the social, as opposed to private returns, to education are considered that the crucial difference of the approaches becomes clear. The screening approach identifies the benefits to society from education in terms of the quality of the signal it provides to employers about the pre-existing characteristics of applicants. The socially optimum level of education thus depends upon the relative cost and effectiveness of this signal and the output gains from a better allocation of workers between jobs. These gains are illustrated by Akerlof's analogy of jobs as dam sites (1981). A dam which is too small for a particular site permanently under utilises that site, similarly employers must fill vacancies with the best available workers if they are to produce efficiently. The screening approach rejects any general application of manpower planning, outside a few professional labour markets. Generally the required characteristics which education should promote are universal to employment and therefore the educational system cannot be a source of labour market bottlenecks. The emphasis on vocational education in current policies to reduce youth unemployment and promote higher growth paths is, according to this view, misplaced. Economic growth has deskilled many jobs and technical innovations like calculators and word processing have reduced the importance of traditional numerate and literate skills in the majority of labour markets. Required manual and cognitive skills are best acquired on-the-job where firms can impart their particular requirements. It should by now be clear that radically different policy implications follow from these alternative approaches to schooling and training.

Whether the established link between education and earnings reflects the influence of education on productivity, recruitment probabilities or discrimination has yet to be empirically established. There are severe problems in finding tests which distinguish between these views and relatively few empirical studies are available; Weiss (1995) provides a survey. A British study, Shah (1985) found evidence supporting the screening hypothesis by examining earnings differentials between employed and self-employed, where education should have little impact upon earnings, and screened and non-screened employment. Kroch and Sjoblom (1994) include both absolute and relative measures of education in their earnings functions, arguing that if education is a screen then it is the relative position in their cohort which should generate the signal. Although their US data does not generate unambiguous results, they conclude that the results give more support to the human capital model. The continuing uncertainty concerning the relative explanatory power of these two approaches creates an associated uncertainty about the relationship between the private rate of return and social rate of return. This latter uncertainty makes it difficult to reach any firm conclusions in our discussion of educational and training policy issues.

4.2.5 *Human capital theory: an assessment*

Human capital theory currently dominates the way economists view educational and training issues. This dominance reflects the theoretical ascendancy of neoclassical analysis and the balance of the empirical results of studies utilising Mincer-type earnings functions. This dominance is threatened, Lazear (1979,1983) for example, has raised problems with the human capital interpretation of the positive relationship between tenure and wages. Seniority-based pay according to human capital theory is a reflection of the positive relationship between tenure and productivity, itself the result of previous firm-specific on-the-job training. According to this theory the observed rise in earnings with tenure also reflects the negative relationship between training and tenure, experienced workers are paying less training costs and therefore their earnings are higher than those of recent recruits. However, these arguments imply that for long-tenure workers their productivity must lie above their wage, since firms must also be getting a return on their share of the investment in firm-specific training. Hutchens (1989) concludes that empirical studies find that although relative earnings increase with tenure, within a given grade of employment relative performance does not. Moreover, in the European labour market we commonly observe compulsory retirement and actuarially unfair pensions, the latter being pension schemes which are designed to induce early retirement. If wages were really below productivity then firms would not seek to retire workers and forgo additional returns on their previous investments. Hence the popularity of non-human capital interpretations of tenure-related wages such as those based on deferred payments or uncertain post-training outcomes. Deferred payments are payments rewarding good behaviour and owe their origins to the costs of accurately monitoring worker behaviour discussed in Chapters 2 and 3. Implicit contracts which specify such payments break the link between current remuneration and current productivity. Workers are paid below their productivity when they join a firm and this investment is returned as payments in excess of productivity in later years. The threat of losing these payments above productivity, ensures that workers with tenure provide acceptable workplace behaviour. In the Carmichael (1983) version of this approach it is the uncertainty of post-training productivity and external earnings which creates an incentive for workers and firms to adopt tenure-related pay scales.

The debate concerning the origins of tenure-related pay does not yet threaten the ascendancy of the human capital model but it does raise additional questions about the model's explanation of the link between earnings and schooling and training investments. These are questions which again concern the adequacy of the evidence linking human capital investments to increases in workplace productivity.

4.3 The rationale for government intervention

4.3.1 *Schooling*

Human capital theory asserts that rational individual decision-makers operating within perfectly competitive capital, product and labour markets should make optimal schooling investments. As we noted in Section 4.2.2, in this framework there appears to be no reason why government should want to interfere with these investment decisions or itself become a monopoly provider of schooling. A rationale for government intervention must lie in the importance of market failures discussed in Chapter 3. Capital market failure could arise if financial institutions were less willing to lend on human capital rather than physical capital investments, preventing arbitrage from equating expected, risk-adjusted, rates of returns on different assets. The illiquidity and non-transferability of human capital makes such lending more risky for financial institutions and therefore creates such an imperfection, also providing an equity argument for government intervention. The beneficial political, social and economic externalities produced by an educated population have, since Adam Smith, convinced most economists that education is a merit good which governments should subsidise and require all citizens to make minimum investments in. Recently growth models have been developed which presuppose that the stock of knowledge has a positive external effect on the production of goods. Language and computer software, for example, make knowledge a public good and mean that a competitive market economy would always under-invest in education and training. These endogenous growth models provide a further rationale for public subsidies of schooling and we discuss these models in the following section.

The difficulty of consumers distinguishing and monitoring the quality of education offered in a private market has been a major factor in causing government regulation and/or government provision of schooling in most economies. This justification can be challenged from a public choice perspective, since as the beneficial externalities of education have as yet to be quantified, organised interests such as teachers can mislead disorganised and ignorant tax-payers into both an over-expansion of education and a toleration of low teaching standards in state schools. Since such groups resist attempts to measure performance and increase parental choice, greater competitive pressures than can be provided in a public education system may be required to recapture educational provision from these reactionary pressure groups. Proposals for increased national testing and publication of school league tables follow from this type of analysis, as do those advocating the introduction of education vouchers to mimic the process of consumer sovereignty in the public educational system. A critical assessment of these policy prescriptions lies outside the boundaries of labour market policy though they will impinge on our discussion of training policy.

Recognition of the importance of externalities requires a distinction to be made between social and private benefits and costs. Society should favour individual investments in education and training as long as social benefits exceed social costs. Where individuals are under-investing in education and training and marginal social benefits therefore exceed marginal social costs, governments should intervene to ensure efficient levels of investment. Since these social benefits and costs are spread over time, society will have to discount according to its preference for present consumption over future consumption. This is measured by the social rate of time preference and it is often proxied by the rate of interest on long-term government bonds. The social rate of time preference is usually assumed to be lower than individuals' rates of time preference as the government is less myopic than individuals and more concerned with the needs of future generations. Though where governments are subjected to regular elections it is not so obvious that they will be more far-sighted than the electorate.

While the appropriate measure of social costs is foregone output plus the resource costs of the education or training, a problem concerns the specification and measurement of social benefits. Leaving aside for the moment the true nature of the private benefits, any calculation of social benefits of education and training requires calculations of the size of the externalities produced. Few estimates of these have been produced; Haveman and Wolfe (1984) review these externalities, from the impact on the quality of leisure and non-market work, through effects on health and fertility to social cohesion, crime reduction and consumer and search efficiency. In addition there are the potential contributions to economic growth from greater mobility, elimination of skill bottlenecks and technological and organisational improvements. The inability to measure these externalities has precluded any systematic use of social cost-benefit studies, though the 1986 British White Paper on higher education utilising relative wages and allowing for the direct costs of teaching, estimated the social rate of return to be around 8 per cent, about equal to the test discount rate though double the long-term yield on financial assets. Given these problems with cost-benefit analysis, educational policy has been much more influenced by studies purporting to quantify the major contribution made by education and training to economic growth.

4.3.2 *Schooling and economic growth*

In the 1960s attempts to estimate the sources of growth popularised the belief that education was a major source of growth. Studies using this approach produced estimates of education's share in output growth ranging from 3 to 27 per cent (Englander and Gurney, 1994). The inability to define and measure skills and competencies led to the adoption of arbitrary rules of thumb in growth accounting studies. With the increasing sophistication of empirical research in economics this approach seemed unwarranted and their popularity has since waned. An alternative approach to determining the allocation of resources to education, also popular at this time, held that there were fixed input coefficients for education groups of workers specific to each industry, hence shortages of a particular level of educated workers could constrain growth. Accurate manpower forecasts could therefore identify labour bottlenecks and educational needs and provide a manpower planning approach to the allocation of schooling resources. This approach depended critically upon a low elasticity of substitution between different levels of educated labour and between educated labour and capital. Freeman (1986) reported elasticities between more and less educated labour of between 1.0 and 2.0, suggesting that elasticity was sufficiently high to make the manpower planning approach to the allocation of educational provision too rigid.

An alternative indication of the macroeconomic effects of education is provided by Englander and Gurney (1994) whose results from Mincer-type earnings functions suggest that each year of additional schooling increases private earnings by between 5 and 10 per cent. If these annual returns reflect net increases in productivity then the additional two and a half years of schooling of average OECD citizens since 1960 would have raised productivity levels by about 12–25 per cent. If this is averaged over the last thirty years then such an increase in schooling would have raised annual productivity growth in the OECD by between 0.4–0.7 per cent. Ahlroth *et al.* (1994) utilise a similar approach in their estimation of the output of the Swedish education sector, producing output estimates much greater than those generated utilising input measures.

Following the work of Romer (1990), endogenous growth theory has provided explanations of differences in growth performances compatible with orthodox economic analysis. In his approach private investments in human capital can generate positive growth externalities as a more knowledgeable work-force increases the probability of successful innovation. In their turn, higher rates of successful innovation induce greater expenditure on research and development thereby stimulating faster productivity growth. In Grossman and Helpman's 1991 model, international trade causes economies with a highly skilled work-force to specialise in skill-intensive production where their faster rate of innovation and the faster rate of growth for their products enables them to sustain a higher growth rate. Empirical support for such analyses appears far from overwhelming, though Fagerberg's 1994 survey of cross-country growth studies shows that educational measures, such as the share of an age group in secondary education and literacy rates, are positively related to relative growth performance. However, when both education and investment measures are included the effect of both variables diminishes, investments in education and physical capital being positively correlated.

Most of the commonly employed proxies for education such as literacy and percentage of cohort enrolled in schools do not vary significantly between developed economies and therefore less is known about the role of education in explaining growth differences in developed economies. The high correlation found between educational attainment and the level and growth of productivity in international cross-sectional studies raises issues of causality. As Englander and Gurney (1994) argue, whilst basic scholastic skills are necessary for the successful use of modern technology, the incremental value of additional schooling is less clear in OECD countries and probably depends upon the type and quality of that education. The statistics compiled by Barro and Lee (1993) indicate that since, as discussed in Chapter 1, technology is favouring educated/skilled labour and thereby tending to cause a worldwide increase in the return to education, even less developed countries who have closed some of the education gap with industrialised countries have found that the income gap has widened. In Chapter 1 we noted that the same technological changes had tended to increase wage inequality within developed economies.

4.3.3 *Training market failures*

American studies indicate that returns to company-provided training are high, with productivity increases of the order of 16 per cent (Lynch, 1994). These findings raise the question of why the training market cannot be relied upon to generate optimal levels of training. Most of the imperfections we identified in the schooling market are also likely to be present in the training market. For example, under-investment in general training (transferable skill) may occur if workers cannot finance desired training due to imperfections in the capital market. Greenhalgh and Mavrotas (1994) implicate individual financial constraints in their finding that low income groups in the UK had little access to employer-based training. In addition, collective bargaining may compress the wage structure and therefore prevent workers financing such training through accepting lower wages. The growth of the importance of small firms in the economy may create further problems for a market-based approach to training provision. Smaller firms may have higher training costs per employee than larger firms, since their fixed costs of training are more thinly spread. Studies of training provision in Britain by Booth (1991) and Green (1993) confirm the hypothesis that larger establishments do more training, predominantly due to their greater provision of on-the-job training. Training may also be constrained because workers are more risk-averse than firms and unstable employment coupled with last-in first-out (LIFO) firing practices may distort investment between general and specific training. Any losses from failed training investments fall directly upon workers themselves, whereas firms have limited liability and any losses are borne by shareholders whose portfolios of assets are already diversified. A further imperfection in the training market may arise because firms and workers adopt too short a time horizon for training decisions, perhaps because of the absence of a futures market in labour services or turnover uncertainty (Booth and Zoega, 1995). One final source of imbalance may be that institutional forces prevent the flexibility of relative wages necessary to signal market changes to investors in human capital. Trade union bargaining behaviour and the creation of internal labour markets are here seen as potentially major impediments to the workings of the market for general training since inflexible wage structures are generated. Those competitive economists who are prepared to argue that costly turnover induces firms to share the costs of specific training, develop this argument further. They argue that trade unions have 'artificially' increased apprentice wages above market-clearing levels, reducing the profitability and hence the supply of general training by firms.

The 'poaching' of skilled workers by non-training firms is ruled out as a market failure by Becker's analysis; general training imposes no costs on firms whilst specific training is by definition unattractive to alternative employers. This argument relies upon a rigid distinction between general and specific training which seems inappropriate for real world training. Where firms have labour market power, they may be able to obtain some of the returns to an investment in training, even when that training is in transferable skills. In this situation, as Stevens (1994) points out, since other firms can benefit from the investment there is an externality which may cause under-investment. In practice most training has elements of both transferable and non-transferable skill development and therefore is likely to be jointly-financed. Katz and Ziderman (1990) reach a similar conclusion, arguing that information asymmetry means that potential recruiters of workers do not possess full information on the extent and type of on-the-job training undertaken by workers. Certification of training can assist in reducing information costs of recruiting firms but perversely this will reduce the benefits of firms training rather than poaching. A similar argument has been developed by Stevens (1994a) who argued that the expenses associated with recruiting skilled workers may introduce a specific element into what would otherwise be general training. She uses her model to explain the decline of engineering apprenticeship in Britain in the 1980s. With the growth of labour market inequality and flexible working patterns a further poaching argument is of importance. Workers in the secondary labour market who have few firm-specific skills may in imperfectly competitive labour markets be unattractive to train since they are associated with a relatively large poaching externality. That is, a relatively large proportion of the benefits of training are available to potential 'poachers' who can bid the workers away from employers who provide training. Hence the social benefits of such training exceed the private benefits to trainees and training firms, providing a further rationale for government intervention.

Snower (1995) has further developed the above arguments, concluding that training market failures can cause economies to get stuck in low-skill equilibriums. If firms are imperfectly informed about the availability of skilled workers and workers have incomplete knowledge of skilled employment opportunities, then Becker's categorisation of training is inappropriate. Here training that is potentially beneficial to all firms is not fully general, since some firms are unaware of the availability of these trained workers. Similarly the training is not specific since the information is available to more than one employer. In this situation the free market will be unlikely to provide sufficient training opportunities. Workers when making training decisions ignore in their calculations the benefits to firms of an increased ability to fill skill vacancies, what Snower calls the 'training supply externality'. In addition, when they create new skilled vacancies, firms increase the probability of a skilled worker finding appropriate employment and hence increase the workers' returns to training, what Snower calls the 'vacancy supply externality'. These externalities can interact to produce a 'low-skill equilibrium' since the former implies that when 'good jobs' are scarce workers are under-compensated for acquiring skills and the latter, that where skilled workers are scarce firms are under-rewarded for creating skilled jobs. In Snower's model there are multiple equilibria and different industries and economies facing similar market conditions may adjust in very different ways. Different European economies facing similar market conditions may therefore not converge on the same productivity growth rate. Specifically, for economies caught in a low-skill equilibrium even high wage differentials may prevent significant supply responses, since skilled vacancies are scarce.

These arguments suggest that training markets left to themselves are unlikely to generate socially optimal levels of training in the current European employment environment. In the absence of major government failures this conclusion suggests that government intervention to influence the quantity and quality of skill acquisitions is desirable. In principle to stimulate the quantity of training, either a training subsidy could be provided to workers or a skilled employment subsidy to firms. If we consider their respective merits in a model such as Snower's, where the general/specific training dichotomy is rejected, then the latter is superior. Both subsidies encourage more workers to train, but for an economy or a sector in a low-skill equilibrium an employer subsidy is more effective at stimulating the supply of skilled jobs and therefore inducing a movement towards a high-skill equilibrium. At the same time, providing access to on-the-job training for unemployed workers can also be beneficial since the enfranchisement of outsiders will assist in the reduction of insider-power and help to improve labour market performance (Lindbeck and Snower, 1989).

4.4 Policy issues

4.4.1 *Schooling and the labour market*

Our discussion so far should indicate how far economists are from offering firm guidelines for educational and training policy. Given that economic objectives may not dominate such decision-making, this is in part inevitable and even desirable. However, training and education policies have been changed on the basis of perceived economic advantages and it should be stressed how little evidence exists to support many common beliefs in this area. Beliefs about the supremacy of vocational over more academic schooling, and of work-based training schemes over school-based ones, are not backed by any systematic empirical evidence. Similarly the encouragement of a rapid expansion of higher education, such as the policy pursued in Britain in the 1980s, lacks adequate empirical support. Indeed the conclusion of much of the recent work is that contrary to recent policy emphasis in Europe the fundamental determinants of the effectiveness of a nation's schooling and training system may lie in the earliest stages of compulsory schooling.

Conventional economic approaches to education and training rely on individuals making informed investment decisions. Such analysis requires schoolchildren to make career decisions on the basis of information about their own abilities, tastes and opportunities. Vocational guidance would therefore appear to be a crucial determinant of efficient decision-making in this area. Studies of vocational guidance in Europe (Jarvis, 1994) indicate that in Germany, the Netherlands and Switzerland careers guidance begins much earlier than in Britain and is taught by careers specialists in separate, specialised lessons. In addition, work experience in most European countries begins at an age of fourteen at the latest, a year earlier than in Britain, and lasts for up to three weeks. In France the *alternance* and the *baccalaureat professionnel* have been developed, alternating learning periods at school and work. Sweden and Finland have opted for an integrated cycle of upper-secondary education offering broad vocational qualifications, grouped into a small number of tracks with increased emphasis upon general education and work experience. The relative neglect of vocational guidance and work experience in the British educational system is symptomatic of its failure to facilitate an easy school to work transition for those not pursuing post-compulsory schooling. In addition, the results of Bennett *et al.* (1992) suggest also that the expected private returns from higher education for working-class young people are particularly high and the low take-up of such education of this group may also reflect informational problems.

The sectors where the rate of job creation has been most rapid in Europe, banking, insurance and business services, health and education, are also the sectors where the average level of educational attainment is highest. While the sectors where employment decline has been the most severe are also sectors where educational requirements are at their lowest (European Commission, 1993), forecasts collected in Heijke (1994) suggest that these trends are likely to continue in European labour markets. The increased importance of education in contemporary labour markets which we also identified in Chapter 1, has concentrated attention on whether schooling factors can explain the relative performance of European economies. Much of this research is of the case study variety and in Britain important work has been carried out at the National Institute for Economic and Social Research (Prais, 1993 and Green and Steedman, 1993), though this type of research rarely produces hard evidence in favour of particular systems or policy initiatives. In their comparison of educational provision and attainment in Germany, France, Japan, USA and Britain, Green and Steedman (1993) conclude that the English system produces a long tail of low achievers. International comparisons of schoolchildren's mathematical competency suggest that British children not only have a lower average competency than most other European children but that there is a much higher variability of competence in Britain. Researchers have been unable to statistically identify particular characteristics of an educational system which influence national educational attainment. School organisation, class size and educational expenditure seem to have little explanatory power and the IAEP report (1992) that only the time spent studying by children is systematically correlated with relative mathematical competency. Thus it appears that a host of factors determine the performance of a particular educational system rather than any particular form of organisation or resource level. Green and Steedman (1993) argue that countries which achieve high standards of education such as France, Germany and Japan do share a common 'learning culture' where parents and teachers have high aspirations for their children and where the educational system provides motivation for learners of all abilities. This is reinforced by society and the labour market rewarding those who do well in education. In such systems high expectations are formalised into norms and uniform practices and regular assessment, with grade-repeating for those failing to achieve the norm established for their particular stream. Prais (1993) concludes that the variability of British educational achievement may be due to the tendency to teach classes in England in small groups. In other EU countries whole class teaching is more common and this may enable pupils of average and below average ability to make better progress. Whole class teaching requires students to begin at about the same level of attainment and thus requires some streaming. On the other hand, mixed ability teaching may provide more opportunity for the less able and reflect an appropriate response to the challenge posed by increasing labour market inequality.

Concern about educational attainment standards in Britain led to the introduction of a National Curriculum, but no formal target has been set for reducing the variability of educational achievement and the publication of simple league tables of school performance may exacerbate this problem. As Britton (1995) commented, prescribing in great detail what should be taught does not ensure that pupils obtain a grounding in the basic skills of literacy and numeracy necessary for further vocational training. Our outline of the pattern of schooling and training in Section 4.1 indicates that Britain has an especially low proportion of its work-force with intermediate level vocational qualifications and it is in this area that policy has been the most discussed in recent years. The launch of a new all-embracing national system of vocational qualifications in Britain reflected a desire to link more closely the sectors of education and training and promote the transferability and portability of qualifications. This innovation was in part a response to the supposed success of the German and Dutch educational systems, where their high standards in mathematics and widespread vocational education generates a high level of skill in their work-force and a resulting high level of productivity (Mason *et al.* 1992). The lack of well-trained craft workers tends to have knock-on effects; Steedman *et al.* (1991) found that graduate engineers were often performing tasks in Britain which elsewhere in Europe would be performed by qualified craftsmen. The formation in Britain in 1986 of the National Council of Vocational Qualifications was designed to reform and standardise the fragmented system of vocational education and training. By making the system more understandable to employers and potential trainees it was hoped to promote an expansion of high quality and transferable vocational education and training. The introduction of National Vocational Qualifications in 1992, utilising testing of competencies of specific tasks at five levels required the co-operation of over 300 different awarding bodies and led to the creation of about 160 industrial lead bodies responsible for setting occupational standards for different industrial sectors. Whilst increasing the information content of qualifications is beneficial, Prais (1993) has argued that the reduction of the role of written exams, external examiners and college-based general education at the lower levels of qualifications has led to the creation of very narrow qualifications which reduce their marketability. Hence they fail to address what the National Institute views as the main British problem: a deficiency of basic transferable skills. Such skills are necessary to produce a flexible workforce capable of adjusting to changing demands of technology and these skills include: communication, presentation, numerical and keyboard. The introduction of General National Vocational Qualifications (GNVQs) has reduced the strength of this criticism since these basic transferable skills form the compulsory core skills components of these courses.

In recent years European governments have encouraged participation in their various youth training programmes by a combination of guaranteed placements and financial incentives. In Britain trainees receive a training allowance significantly higher than the Child Benefit paid to parents of children who remain in full-time education. Whitfield and Wilson (1991) examined the potential distortionary effect of this allowance and found that the growth of youth training schemes had significantly reduced school staying-on rates. The low staying-on rate of children from working-class families appears inconsistent with the expected rates of return available to this group reported earlier in our chapter. However, if discount rates are higher for this group due to time preferences or capital market constraints then those with the highest discount rates will tend to enter occupations with high entrance wages and low schooling requirements and training allowances further distort this choice. Low staying-on rates may also reflect the previous bias in favour of academic routes to higher education and the introduction of GNVQs and their acceptance as an entry qualification into higher education may correct this bias.

Workers entering the European labour market in the 1990s with few educational qualifications are especially disadvantaged, reflecting the shift away from unskilled employment. The rise in the minimum threshold of educational attainment falls first and heaviest on the entrants with the lowest level of qualifications, and completion of upper secondary education or a vocational training programme appear to generate persisting advantages in the labour market treatment. Early school-leavers suffer above average unemployment rates and are substantially less likely to receive enterprise-based training, further lowering their lifetime relative earnings. The dual systems in Austria, Germany, the Netherlands and Switzerland have managed to maintain high participation rates by the development of alternative pathways for education and training. Targeting those at risk of low educational attainment early in their schooling can also increase participation rates. In Germany policies have concentrated support measures on disadvantaged young people, providing supporting programmes for those on vocational training, while in France and the Netherlands targeting is on geographical areas and schools with large numbers of at-risk students. In addition, the growth of pre-compulsory schooling has also been supported for its effects in reducing educational failure and early school-leaving.

This concentration on the failures at the bottom end of the educational and training markets also reflects our earlier concern that economies may get stuck in a low-skill equilibrium. Soskice (1993) argued that the key skills desired by employers in a service and client dominated economy were social, organisational, problem-solving and computing ones. His arguments were supported by results from the Employment in Britain Survey of 1992, which indicated a large increase in employers' demand for these types of skills. Soskice argues that the recent expansion of higher education in Britain provides a hiring pool of such skills which enables firms to follow an American-style path towards a high-skill equilibrium. Higher education here serves as general education, developing the desired social and communicative skills and teaching a high degree of self-organisation and self-discipline amongst students. However, reliance on the growth of higher education offers no solution to the problem of how to raise productivity of the lowest third of the ability range, who in the US have suffered such a dramatic fall in their relative and absolute living standards.

The issue of who pays for schooling has emerged most noticeably in the context of higher education. The rapid expansion of British higher education in the 1980s and early 1990s was encouraged by the British Government who calculated that the private rates of return to graduates were as high as 27 per cent. These estimates were used to justify the shifting of a higher proportion of the costs of higher education onto students. Bennet *et al.* (1992) estimated much lower returns and concluded that a further shifting of the costs onto students may reduce demand for higher education. The government also tried to install more market incentives in the funding of higher educational institutions. Institutions were made more reliant on fees and research income as a way of giving consumers more power and introducing more competition between institutions. Student loans were introduced which have, according to Barr (1993a), released no public expenditure in the medium term to finance the expansion but have harmed access. In Sweden, and most of the rest of Europe, institutions are funded via tax revenues rather than fees; a student loan system introduced in the 1960s which resulted in a high level of student indebtedness was replaced by increased tax-funded student support and income contingent repayments. However, a solely tax-funded higher education system will tend to be small. As a society wishes to develop a larger system an inflow of private funding is required if the unit of resource is not to be lowered to a level where the quality of the system declines rapidly. The function of a well-designed student loan system would therefore appear to be to bring in private funds to finance expansion whilst not deterring access.

4.4.2 *The school to work transition*

One way of illustrating the labour market problems facing young people is to consider their relative unemployment rate. In the early 1990s the unemployment rate amongst teenagers was six times the adult rates in Italy and four times greater in Norway, only in Germany and the UK was the rate less than double the adult rate. The relatively low teenage unemployment rate in Germany has been attributed to the success of the dual system and we now consider the key differences in national training systems in Europe, concentrating in this section on the school-to-work transition.

Within these national systems there are a variety of institutional and policy features designed to stimulate private sector on-the-job training by ensuring that training firms receive appropriate returns on their investments. In Japan, tenure is very heavily rewarded compared to other economies and this provides a disincentive for worker-quits, whilst high social costs dissuade would-be poachers from 'cherry-picking' the best trained workers (Mincer and Higuichi, 1988). The German dual system of apprenticeship training with its tripartite determination of strategy and training content and joint investment by workers and firms, produces a system which ensures a nationally recognised certification of skills for the two-thirds of all young people who become apprentices. As Steedman (1993) explains this ensures a high general training content without reducing the relevance of training to providers and high completion rates. This provision of high quality training encourages trainees to finance their training through low wages and loans from their employers, whilst government finances the vocational schools (Oulton and Steedman, 1994). Moral suasion is used to protect firms from large scale poaching and firms that contribute to the costs of training appear to be willing to do so in order to ensure access to the most able of those seeking apprenticeships. In 1991 Steedman (1993) reports that 69 per cent of those who had completed an apprenticeship between two and four years earlier, were still working for their original training firm, though Winkelmann (1994) finds much lower rates of retention.

In the Netherlands, a similar training system operates. Training funds administered by unions and employers are available to support training in small and medium-sized companies. The Dutch system combines workplace and school-based training linked to employment in a firm. Groot *et al.* (1994) report large wage gains from firm-provided training and in an earlier work estimated returns to firms from this type of training of between 11 and 20 per cent. In Nordic countries training market failures have been met directly by government training. In Norway this took the form of school-based vocational training and in Sweden, government training programmes. In general, school-based vocational training seems to generate low returns to the individual trainees. Elias *et al.* (1994) find such results for short, school-based and course-based vocational training in Norway. They attribute this result to the de-coupling of such training from the demand for skilled workers, their preference being for a firm-based system. Government training programmes may overcome the funding problems associated with private training but at a cost of efficiency. Such training may be poorly related to employer needs or alternatively may risk exploitation by firms who wish to shift their training costs onto tax-payers.

A key issue concerns the financing of the work-related training of entrants; in Austria, Denmark and Germany apprentice pay is relatively low, a third-year apprentice earning about 30–40 per cent of a skilled worker's wage. In addition in Austria and Germany the government pays for the schools which the apprentices attend, and in Denmark employers are reimbursed for the wages paid to apprentices through a fund financed by a levy on private sector employers. While low or subsidised training costs may make the provision of initial training attractive to employers, we have seen that the content and standards of training are also important factors in determining participation. Most apprentice based systems therefore have mechanisms for quality control, with certification to ensure the transferability of the training provided.

Recent British experience is of particular interest to our discussions of the relative merits of alternative initial training systems. In the 1980s the British government decided to replace the declining apprenticeship-based initial training system with one based upon a government-led youth training program. Whereas about half of British school-leavers went directly into employment at the end of the 1970s, the proportion is now less than a tenth. Initially this growth of government activity was targeted at reducing youth unemployment and was coupled with exempting young workers from Britain's selective minimum wage regulations. More recently, reflecting the results of international comparisons already discussed, the policy has been aimed at improving the quality of initial training. Surprisingly the British government appears to have chosen to opt for a French pattern, in which higher education provides for the top 25 per cent of the attainment range, the next 50 per cent pursue a variety of full-time GNVQ courses and a youth training programme covers the remaining 25 per cent of young people.

Since the introduction of the Youth Training Scheme (YTS) in Britain in 1983 all eligible school-leavers have been guaranteed a place on a training scheme; a guarantee which was followed by the withdrawal of unemployment benefits to the under 18's in 1988. While trainee employment prospects are influenced by academic qualifications and local unemployment rates, recent studies indicate serious deficiencies in the YTS. Dolton *et al.* (1994, 1994a) report that YTS participation lowered the probability of employment for males and their results suggested that participants earned lower wages after completion of their training. These results were interpreted as indicating that participation in YTS may send a negative signal of ability to potential employers. Green *et al.* (1994) conclude that compared with those continuing full-time education or entering employment without training, YTS trainees experienced lower wages even three years after graduation. The explanation provided for these unfavourable results and the high drop-out rates on the scheme have been linked to the low level of school attainment of the trainees and the lack of tripartite co-operation to ensure well-targeted and high-quality training provision. Responsibility for this training now rests with local, employer-led Training and Enterprise Councils (TECs) in England and Wales and Local Enterprise Companies (LECs) in Scotland, and funding for training providers is now linked to the success rate of their trainees in achieving NVQ awards. This is consistent with the conclusions of Blanchflower and Lynch (1994) that a system of nationally recognised qualifications appears to generate higher returns to initial training. One consequence of the linking of TEC funding of youth and employment trainees to NVQs has been to increase the usage of these qualifications by firms. By 1993 about 6 per cent of British firms were using NVQs and Occupational Standards and a further 22 per cent expressed an interest in using them (Callender and Toye, 1994). However in some occupations this linking of payment to NVQ achievements has had the effect of denying entry to those with weak academic backgrounds or lowering competence standards (Steedman and Hawkins, 1994). In some occupations, such as those in the building trades, the introduction of NVQs has led to a decline in mathematical elements and increased the gap between British and European initial training standards. Under the present scheme trainees are no longer entitled to off-the-job training, and training could take place entirely within a company. The diversity of providers and their recruitment methods makes any simple assessment of the effectiveness of the current British initial training system very difficult. There is some evidence that the Training Credits Scheme, where trainees have vouchers to 'spend' on training, is attracting a slightly broader range of the cohort and, with the link to NVQ qualifications, making employers more aware of the merits of such training. The tendency for employer-based initial training in the Training Credits Scheme to become very narrow and firm-specific, needs to be addressed if the scheme is really to promote a more flexible work-force.

4.4.3 *Government and skill shortages*

Our discussion in Chapter 1 identified the large and rapid changes in the structure of employment which have occurred in European labour markets in recent years. Technological progress and changes in expenditure and competitiveness render jobs, skills and some occupations obsolete over time. Educational and training systems which only provide for entrants cannot respond adequately to such pressures, since entrants only account for around 2–3 per cent of the labour force. The need to update or convert existing skills and competencies requires a system providing training throughout the work-force. Persistent skill shortages, perceived 'poor' quality and the cyclical instability of the quantity of training provision in the private sector have together encouraged several European governments to intervene in the training market. The effectiveness of these policies will be considered later, but it is first necessary to consider what constitutes a skill shortage.

To the neoclassical labour economist a labour shortage means the existence in a well defined market of *ex ante* excess demand at the current relative wage. The anticipated adjustment mechanism is through changes in that relative wage. However, studies in the UK by Bosworth (1993) and Haskel and Martin (1993) indicate that such behaviour is rare with shortages being only weakly related to wages and conditions of work. More important determinants of the incidence of shortages were local supply-side factors such as unemployment rates and educational qualifications of the local work-force. Surveys of firms suggest that they view a labour shortage as occurring when they have difficulty in recruiting and retaining staff at their offered wage and working conditions. Their actual adjustment to any shortage tends to be by overtime working, sub-contracting, improving non-pecuniary benefits and substituting less skilled workers, behaviour that is more consistent with the segmented view of the labour market.

Overall between 1979 and 1991 an average of about 5 per cent of EU firms reported being unable to hire as many skilled workers as they wished (Haskel and Martin, 1993). Whereas an average of 4 per cent of French firms and 5 per cent of German firms reported such skill shortages, amongst UK firms the average was 14 per cent even though this period included a particularly severe recession in the UK. Nevertheless, skill shortages appear to be strongly pro-cyclical in Britain; an observation consistent with our earlier finding that local supply-side factors are important in determining the incidence of skill shortages. The CBI Quarterly Industrial Trends Survey found less than 5 per cent of British manufacturing firms reporting skill shortages in the early 1980s with almost 33 per cent reporting such shortages before the last recession in 1989. This survey asks firms whether they expect output to be constrained over the next quarter by skill shortages and is currently the most widely used measure of skill shortages in the UK. In the UK skill shortages tend to differ greatly between industries (Haskel and Martin, 1992), with electrical engineering suffering particularly severe shortages in recent years, and small firms appear to be more prone to shortages, a finding consistent with our earlier discovery that larger firms do proportionately more training.

The difficulty in defining and identifying skill shortages becomes even greater when the screening hypothesis is raised: do shortages reflect a lack of specific job-related skills or in reality do they often reflect a shortage of social skills amongst applicants? The study by Oliver and Turton (1982) emphasizes a key consequence of structured labour markets: managers have often adopted a behavioural concept of skill. In their survey managers seemed to operate on a basis that skill refers to trainability and socially acceptable behaviour. Although technical skills and work experience were important in the hiring of skilled workers, skill shortages were often a reflection of shortages of certain types of temperament and social characteristics, rather than shortages of specific levels of cognitive and manual dexterity amongst applicants. They concluded that it was often 'good blokes' which firms could not recruit, rather than electrical fitters or other trades. Skill shortages of this type are not solvable by market forces or training policy and have implications for labour market discrimination discussed in Chapter 6.

Deficiencies in the supply of skilled labour appear to be important in explaining international differences in the level and growth of labour productivity. The studies conducted by the National Institute for Economic and Social Research include comparisons of plants in different countries using similar machines. A study of matched engineering plants in the UK and Germany found output per worker nearly two-thirds higher in Germany, a difference attributed to the lower level of skills in the workforce, especially amongst foremen and maintenance workers. Breakdowns of machinery were much more common in Britain with maintenance workers more often employed in a 'fire-fighting' capacity rather than in the routine maintenance role of their German counterparts. The higher level of training amongst machine operatives in Germany also led to them often cleaning their own machines and being aware of machine malfunctions earlier than would occur in Britain. Faster introduction of new technology in the Dutch engineering industry has been attributed by Mason and van Ark (1994) to the greater provision of full-time vocational education and training in the Netherlands than in Britain. Although British engineering firms devoted more funding to initial and continuing training than their Dutch counterparts, this was not sufficient to eliminate the skill gap. A comparison of biscuit production in France, Germany, the Netherlands and the UK found that although output per worker was not particularly low in the UK, concentration on low quality products caused the UK to have the lowest value-added per worker. Higher quality output implied more sophisticated baking processes and packaging and smaller production-batches all of which required a more skilled work-force. Similar comparisons in the clothing industry suggested that whereas British producers were more likely to concentrate upon long production runs of standard items, German producers were more efficient at producing specialised shorter runs of higher market value products, enabling them to respond more effectively to individual customer requirements. Given the trend towards flexible specialisation identified in Chapter 1, it is significant to find that the superiority of German producers in these areas is a product of their training system.

At a more aggregated level Haskel and Martin (1992) report that their analysis of UK manufacturing industries in the mid to late 1980s indicated that skill shortages significantly reduced productivity growth. If training underinvestment is widespread, the loss of competitiveness will cause external competitors to gain markets, and domestic firms move 'down market' in world trading terms. Training deficiencies in this case lead to the adoption of techniques and products which have low training needs, a view consistent with the findings of Webster (1993) that Britain's comparative advantage in the mid-1980s had made it a net importer of goods intensive in skilled and semi-skilled manual labour. Oulton (1995) also finds some evidence that the UK's skill deficiencies influenced manufacturing trade performance. Skill shortages are also a determinant of the unemployment rate which governments can sustain over time and may curb economic recoveries at a relatively low level of capacity utilisation, contributing to output instability and worsening the stop-go cycle. Such effects may permanently reduce the growth rate of an economy. We return to these issues in Chapters 7 and 8.

We have argued that skill shortages may be costly to an economy and may not be removable by merely refining the interaction of market forces. Before we concentrate upon government's role in improving the performance of the training market we should consider alternative policy responses. If skill shortages differ between regions then a reallocation of firms to low skill-shortage regions will improve market efficiency as may more flexible hiring and working practices. We consider both of these possibilities in the following chapter, however, in the long run policies are required which increase the supply of skilled labour and it is towards a consideration of these policies that we now turn.

4.4.4   *Government and on-the-job training*

We have argued that the presence of training externalities, imperfections in information and in capital and insurance markets and the tendency of firms to cut training outlays for short-run cost savings all contribute to inefficient training provision. The belief that private sector training is deficient has encouraged a number of European governments to introduce policies designed to improve training market efficiency.

Britain, France and Sweden are among countries which at various times have imposed measures requiring all firms to spend specified ratios on training or pay an equivalent amount of tax. In Britain the 1964 Industrial Training Act was an early attempt to produce such changes as well as to confront the inequity of training provision generated by poaching. The Industrial Training Boards established by that Act operated a levy-grant system, levying on a payroll basis. A 1980 review publicised widespread employer hostility to the Industrial Training Boards; while managers often acknowledged that the boards had improved the profile and standards of training, they resented the bureaucracy and the 'paper' training promoted by the system. There is no evidence that the Act had any significant long-term impact on the quantity of training, though given the emphasis on training for a firm's own, rather than the industry's long-term needs this may not be surprising. In the early 1980s British government policy returned to a 'voluntarist' approach and when employers were faced with the prospect of financing the full costs of the training boards two-thirds were quickly abolished and responsibility for determining the socially optimal level of training again returned to the market. In France, employers have faced a training tax since 1971. This tax was increased to 1.5 per cent of the total wage bill in 1993. It is collected from all firms employing 10 or more workers who cannot document training expenditure equal to their tax liability. Verdier (1994) reports the large quantitative increase in training which has resulted, with training expenditure as a proportion of the gross wage bill doubling between 1972 and 1989, though quality has not always increased proportionately and training has become more concentrated amongst the more highly qualified. Australia introduced a similar tax in 1990, whilst Belgium, Greece and Ireland raise a levy on the wage and salary bill to fund unemployment support schemes and/or general training. This type of policy may provide insufficient incentives for firms in skill-intensive sectors to increase training whilst those in low-skill-intensive sectors may have no incentive to increase the quality of their training. Overall, existing evidence suggests that such policies may do little to increase training opportunities for unskilled workers or for workers in small firms.

An alternative policy has been to provide tax credits for training, but again, such policies are often poorly targeted, and may not stimulate training where it is most needed. In Britain the government has also introduced subsidised loans for workers wishing to undertake off-the-job training. The Career Development Loan was directly targeted at compensating for capital market failures and has been predominantly used to finance tuition fees. Almost all of the risks associated with the uncertainty of post-training employment are still carried by the trainees, though pilots are being undertaken to see whether take-up increases when those risks are reduced by the extension of repayment holidays for the unemployed.

A more fundamental policy response concerns institutional reform aimed at reducing the cyclical instability of training. Although firms rarely apply investment appraisal techniques to training expenditure, in recessions the illiquidity of training investments causes them to respond on cash-flow considerations rather than on long-term profitability. In contrast with their treatment of expenditure on physical investment expenditure, firms treat training as an operating cost and since these costs are wholly included in the period in which they occur they become vulnerable when profitability is low. The OECD (1994a) points out that changing accounting conventions to capitalise training costs, and to treat as assets the knowledge and competencies generated by further training, would distinguish training costs from other operating costs and provide a clearer justification for training and turnover-reducing expenditure.

4.4.5 *Government direct training schemes*

Rather than government attempting to improve private sector training provision, direct training schemes involve the government providing training opportunities itself. The government may provide training facilities to further a variety of objectives: promote economic growth; relieve poverty or reduce registered unemployment. There have been a large number of studies, especially American, which attempt to measure the effectiveness of this 'merit good' training. The absence of data on social and political benefits, leads to the benefits being treated in most studies as largely output gains. Traditionally it has been argued that the social benefits are likely to exceed private benefits because of the net effect of externalities. The replacement effect is likely to reduce the output opportunity costs of the training, as there will be direct or indirect substitution of the trainee's labour by previously unemployed labour. Complementary effects will raise the benefits of training above those to the trainee if they eliminate a labour bottleneck and so cause an increase in the employment of auxiliary and ancillary workers. Competitive markets should internalise some of these benefits in the post-training earnings of trainees. The displacement effect will partially offset these positive externalities as trainees will displace some existing or potential employees, especially when placed outside their training occupation. To the extent that the training acts as a screen, social benefits will again be lower than the private benefits.

Surveys of studies of national training programmes by Björklund (1991,1994) discovered that programmes tended to work best for the least experienced and most disadvantaged groups, women and less educated groups tending to get the highest benefits. The OECD (1993) concluded that programmes which were broadly targeted and where all unemployed workers were entitled to a training place tended to have low or zero impact. This result held for German and Dutch programmes, though Swedish and Norwegian studies found that employment prospects and earnings improved for those completing their courses. Raaum *et al.* (1995) in their study of the Norwegian vocational training scheme for unemployed adults found no employment effects on average, but positive effects emerged for training which provided qualifications. Few studies of subsidies for training of employed adults have been undertaken but results for Canada have suggested large deadweight effects, though a Danish programme offering short courses to largely unskilled workers produced significant wage and employment stability effects. Disenchantment with government provision of training has caused Finland, Sweden and the UK to make independent the bodies established to provide labour market training. These bodies, such as the Labour Market Training Board in Sweden and the TECs in England have also been encouraged to purchase training from private providers and to strengthen their links with smaller enterprises. The latter priority is based upon our earlier finding that further training provision is lower in this sector.

The basis of EU action on further training lies in the Treaty of Rome's requirement that the Commission develop a common vocational policy. The Treaty also established the European Social Fund (ESF) to promote the reemployment of unemployed workers. The Single European Act (1986) and the Treaty on European Union (1992) augmented this area of policy to explicitly target regional disparities in labour market outcomes. Addison and Siebert (1994) provide a review of these mechanisms and initiatives. We discuss the regional dimensions of these programmes in the following chapter and the issue of convergence is addressed in Chapter 8. While much EU assistance has been through the provision of funding for national systems of training, the Commission has been trying to increase the share of funds allocated to its own initiatives which have sought to aid the convergence of national systems and increase their transnational dimensions. For example, LEONARDO (introduced in 1995) funds networks for the exchange of trainees, data and best practice and also promotes the development of language skills.

EU policies which encourage the standardisation of qualifications and exchange of information are likely to improve the private and social returns to training. However, their emphasis on subsidising national training programmes increases the problem of displacement effects, where national governments merely replace their own funding with that of the EU. The requirement that member states must match EU funds has not provided an effective policing mechanism and additionality remains a key concern with EU level policy. As Addison and Siebert (1994) explain this strengthens the Commission's argument that EU funding should be targeted at EU initiatives rather than directly supporting existing national training systems.

4.5 Conclusions

The emergence of human capital theory and early growth accounting studies led to a burst of policy initiatives in the 1960s and early 1970s. Gradual recognition of the practical limitations of educational and training policies in influencing growth, poverty and discrimination has been combined with fundamental theoretical questioning of the whole human capital foundations. Nevertheless, in many European countries there have been rapid changes in schooling and training policies in recent years. Our previous discussion indicates education and training policies need to be jointly determined and mutually consistent. Without the development of core mathematical and communication skills across all segments of schoolchildren, any training system will have to divert resources to ensure this development. In addition, an educational system which is designed primarily for the benefit of the most able and provides financial incentives to pursue academic rather than vocational education, is unlikely to be compatible with the adoption of a German-style apprenticeship system for a sizeable proportion of each cohort.

To design appropriate schooling policies requires an appreciation of the benefits and costs of education, yet at present we have no indications of the size of the externalities produced by different systems. It may be the case that a more selective and streamed system of schooling would raise overall potential labour market production, but the personal and social divisiveness of such policies may prevent such gains from occurring or cause unacceptable increases in inequality when combined with the technological and structural changes occurring in the labour market. In our discussions we have identified reducing early school-leaving as a priority area. European experience suggests that this requires the provision of diversity in the content, teaching and learning methods available in upper secondary education. For those countries with high rates of early school leaving the OECD (1994) concludes that an improvement in the quality of vocational and technical studies is required together with the adoption of policies designed to prevent educational 'failure' at early stages of schooling.

The need to ensure compatibility between a nation's education and training system has become more important with recent trends in technology and increased international competition. The growth of international trade and the increase in the rate of technology transfer have not only altered the composition of the demand for labour but have also increased the intensity of competition in product markets. Countries caught in a low-skill trap are therefore likely to find that a low-wage strategy for retaining international competitiveness is unable to sustain employment opportunities, especially amongst the less-skilled. Another consequence of these trends is an increased need for updating of skills and competencies amongst the workforce. However, the ageing of European labour forces together with increased employment flexibility creates a problem of how a lifetime vocational learning system will be funded. Many workers will have to take personal responsibility for acquiring and financing this training. It follows that removing the problems faced by atypical workers in gaining access to capital markets is likely to become an important area for future policy. With the increased skill intensity of many production processes and products and the increased costs of acquiring and developing appropriate skills, the government faces difficulty in encouraging employers to increase their training efforts. This implies a greater government commitment to developing the external training market, especially that part targeted at older workers (Lindley, 1994).

Simple prescriptions for training policy were often based upon the distinction between general and specific training. Certainty regarding the exclusivity of this categorisation has now disappeared. In the US the government relies upon firms to generate investments in skill formation and training consistent with the needs of their own internal labour markets. For insiders such a system may provide high lifetime training opportunities, but this approach leads to very narrow, firm-specific training without any common standards of attainment. It seems that there are a variety of alternative training systems which can work effectively, but that in the absence of Japanese-style firm-worker relationships, it seems likely that the German model of intermediate skill training is the most appropriate for European economies. It is in this particular area of skills development that unregulated market forces generate insufficient incentives for firms and workers to invest in optimal levels of transferable skill training and where technological and other forces threaten to impoverish workers. Governments must therefore help to establish and support a system which provides and certifies high-quality training, both off and on-the-job, for labour market entrants.

In the British context this may require the sort of proposal outlined by Layard (1992), where all off-the-job vocational education and training is free of tuition costs and where all young people under 19 are only employed on a traineeship basis. These trainees would receive rates of pay linked to adult rates and there would be an obligation on employers to release young workers for off-the-job training for at least one day a week as in Germany. A key element of a successful school-to-work transition seems to be the creation of a partnership between the formal education system, employers and the young people covering issues of co-financing investments, curriculum content and certification. Quality assurance of such training is critical if 'paper' training is to be avoided and an effective national system requires accredited training with external assessment and a content reflecting the specific occupational needs of each trainee. Where training standards are high and the content includes a general education element, youths are likely to find such training attractive and may be induced to increase efforts at school to obtain the best training placements. If government is financing the provision of off-the-job vocational education and training then employers and trainees must meet the cost of on-the-job training. This implies youth-adult wage rates comparable to those in Germany. Where countries are trying to move towards a German-style dual system there is a danger of relying wholly on employer-dominated training bodies to supervise the emerging system. If the problem is one of a 'low-skill' equilibrium, firms may have too few incentives to break with existing behaviour, in particular the temptation may be to reduce the transferable element of the training provided. In this case all that may happen is that firms 'capture' much of the government expenditure diverted to training.

So far our assessment has largely focused on intermediate level skill for entrants, but training market failures are also likely in the provision of more firm-specific, higher level skills. If skilled workers are fully employed whereas some less-skilled workers are unemployed, then training-up the less-skilled workers is likely to be socially profitable. Any resulting reduced wage pressure in skilled labour markets may produce additional dynamic benefits as employers are encouraged to create more skilled jobs.

Guide to further reading

Bottani (1995) provides a helpful introduction to the intricacies of utilising the data on educational inputs and outputs across countries contained in the OECD's *Education at a Glance* (1995a). A good place to begin a study of theory in this area is Sapsford and Tzannatos (1993), Weiss (1995) providing a complementary study of the signalling critique. The chapter by Alsalam and Conley in OECD (1995b) provides a good introduction to empirical analysis of rates of return on human capital. Bosworth and Simpson (1995) provide a general introduction to training policy, whilst McNabb and Whitfield (1994) introduce training market failures which are further examined in Booth and Snower (forthcoming). Dolton (1993) provides a useful introduction to the economics of youth training, paying particular attention to Britain. Chapter 7 of the OECD's *Job Study: Evidence and Explanations* (1994a) contains an excellent review of the relationship between workers' skills and competencies and labour market performance.

5   Job matching: search and migration in the labour market

The job-matching process plays a crucial role in the competitive analysis of labour market behaviour. It is worker and employer search and the resulting mobility of workers and jobs which ensures that compensating wage differentials are paid, and appropriate equalising adjustments made to market shocks. Whilst models of labour market search now play a less prominent role in explanations of the determinants of the stock of unemployment, two other developments have maintained the importance of job-matching theory in recent years. Firstly, as we found in Chapter 2, the structure of employment in European economies is changing: increased labour market flexibility has made employment less stable and secure and job-changing more frequent. Secondly, European economic integration and the EU's tentative movement towards monetary union has increased the importance of labour mobility as an adjustment mechanism. Increased economic integration should increase the speed of convergence of per capita national output levels, partly through increased labour mobility. We leave a fuller treatment of this adjustment mechanism to Chapter 8, though our examination of migration and regional economic convergence later in this chapter will assist that discussion.

The productivity of the total labour force and thus the standard of living in any economy, will, in part, depend upon the speed and quality of the job matching process. Time which workers spend searching for suitable vacancies represents time not spent producing. Unfilled vacancies which reflect employers' search for suitable workers may similarly represent lost output. The quality as well as the speed of the hiring process is also important; to maximise output and maintain incentives for human capital investments employers must make efficient use of workers' productive potential. Substantial mismatch in the labour market may also produce wage pressure at relatively early stages of cyclical upturns and therefore reduce the long-run growth of capital and output. In this chapter we discuss the way in which workers and firms search in the labour market and then consider the appropriate role of government in facilitating search. We largely neglect the implications of search and migration for the behaviour of the stock of unemployment, these aspects are included in Chapter 7. Instead we concentrate upon the reasons why most developed economies have a state-financed placing agency and how such agencies should operate to promote efficient and equitable hiring practices. In the first part of this chapter we are implicitly concerned with job-matching within a local labour market. In the second part we concentrate upon inter-regional and international job-matching; producing an assessment of geographical mismatch to complement the previous chapter's discussion of occupational mismatch. Our main interest in this latter section is to assess the role of policies to encourage migration as a means of reducing spatial differences in employment opportunities and in the level of per capita output.

In the first part of the chapter we initially consider the current nature and extent of job search in European economies. Conventional neoclassical search theory is then examined and some of its limitations are exposed. A discussion of how employers actually recruit leads to the derivation of the job-matching function. The rationale for state employment agencies is then considered and their current operation reviewed. In this chapter we only discuss the job-broking role of these agencies, considering their benefit administration role in Chapter 7. We conclude the first part of this chapter with a consideration of the appropriate role for governments in the job matching process.

5.1 Patterns of job search

5.1.1 *Origins*

In isolated communities with low mobility, nepotism and direct personal relationships may dominate the matching of employers with workers, but in modern developed societies the bulk of the matching will be between parties who have no prior knowledge of each other. Workers will wish to discover the pecuniary and non-pecuniary rewards of each available wage offer, whereas employers will wish to learn the potential productivity of applicants in their workplace environment as well as the wage levels offered by other employers. Initially, following the work of Stigler in the early 1960s, the orthodox view was that workers search firms until they find an acceptable wage offer. Implicitly employers were initially conceived as taking a fairly passive role in this search process; once they fixed a wage level they hired those applicants of acceptable quality who were prepared to accept employment offers until they had no further vacancies. More recently these job search models have been augmented by job matching approaches which attempt to model the interaction between employers and workers in the labour market.

The competitive model also implies that workers and firms are always looking to make better 'deals' in the labour market. Workers are always hoping to find higher paid jobs and firms hope they can recruit at lower wages. This continual searching is also the consequence of certain labour market information only being obtained after a match is made. Workers only discover the social environment of the workplace and the realities of the supervisory and promotion structure after working in the firm. Similarly, employers only accurately discover many of the worker's personal characteristics after hiring. Search theory was initially developed to understand the anticipated high turnover in the labour market. It suggests that search is not concentrated in entrants and re-entrants but is exhibited by all participants in the labour market. The accuracy and appropriateness of this view has been recently challenged and we later survey this dispute.

The traditional economic arguments for a public employment service (PES) have been in terms of improving the speed and quality of job-matchings. In some European economies the PES dates back to the beginning of the twentieth century, initially concentrating upon helping the search of unemployed workers. Improving labour mobility, the quality of the work-force and assisting manpower planning were also stressed in the early years of the employment service. The emergence of inflation as the major post-war macro-economic constraint on economic growth and employment expansion led to a new emphasis upon the need to reduce 'frictional' unemployment, and the evolution of search theory provided a theoretical frame-work for the analysis of such unemployment. Search theory also provided a new rationale for a state placing agency: a centralised employment service could inter-nalise some of the externalities of private search. Before we outline and assess search theory and discuss the role of employment agencies we need to summarise what we know about the actual search behaviour of firms and workers in European labour markets.

5.1.2   *The extent of job mobility and search in Europe*

In most European economies available data on the search-hiring process is incom-plete and of poor quality. For example, few countries collect regular data on the amount and type of on-the-job search, that is search by workers already in employ-ment. The 1992 Labour Force survey allowed for the first time comparisons across the EU on the extent of job-changing. Overall around 17 per cent of those in work in the EU had not been in their present job a year earlier, in Spain the figure was 28 per cent and in Greece and Italy under 13 per cent. More detailed figures are reported for Britain, which appears to have above average mobility. In the mid 1990s the British Labour Force Survey indicated that around 88 per cent of employees had been in the same occupation with the same employer for at least twelve months. In the previous year, about 9 per cent had changed employers, of which slightly more than half remained in the same industrial division, and about the same proportion had changed occupation. Beatson (1995) reports that job mobility is pro-cyclical, and changes in employment vary significantly with age, 95 per cent of the over 50s who remained in employment neither changed occupation nor employer compared with only 75 per cent of 16–19 year olds. Only about 5 per cent of employed workers engage in job search, though the proportion is three times higher for those who had recent experi-ence of unemployment.

International evidence on tenure suggests large differences between economies. It should be no surprise that Japan and the United States represent the extremes, but large differences are found in Europe. In Italy, 52 per cent of all employed people reported in 1992 that they had never had any other employment, and 49 per cent reported that they had been in their job for at least ten years, a percentage even higher than in Japan (OECD, 1995). As Table 5.1 indicates, the Netherlands has a distribu-tion of tenure similar to that of the United States, whilst France and Germany have a profile much closer to that of Japan. Spain has a high proportion of workers with tenure of less than a year, reflecting the importance of fixed-term contracts, whilst Norway has a high proportion of workers with a tenure of between 5 and 20 years.

The average tenure figures are for workers currently in employment and therefore represent uncompleted tenure. If on average we are sampling workers half way through their tenure, then completed tenure would be roughly double the average figures shown. Women's current tenure is usually a lot lower than that of men, though the same national patterns emerge with France having the highest average female tenure and the Netherlands the lowest. Some of the reasons for these differences will be considered in our discussion of discrimination in Chapter 6. Interpretation of the tenure figures in Table 5.1 is made difficult by the impact of demographic factors and by the different position of economies in their business cycle. The former problem reflects the tendency for tenure to increase with age. Average tenure in Europe seems to have been falling since the mid-1980s, though there is little sign that increased flexibility has dramatically altered tenure for the average worker.

We have so far concentrated upon the experience of the average worker, and since job-changing appears to be highly concentrated in the labour market we cannot easily identify increasing instability for a minority of the work-force. Gregg and Wadsworth (1995) provide a detailed analysis of tenure and labour turnover for Britain since the mid-1970s. They find that whilst tenure and security have changed only slightly for the majority, entry positions for those not in full-time employment have become increasingly unstable and low paid. Median uncompleted job tenure for male workers was 6.4 years in 1993, a fall of 1.5 years since 1975. Job-changing is unevenly distributed within the working population, being high amongst those with short tenure, the young, the less-skilled and those in part-time employment. Gregg and Wadsworth conclude that the British labour market can increasingly be categorised into primary and secondary sectors, with secondary sector employment becoming more risky and concentrating employment inequality amongst certain groups in the work-force.

If we are concerned about information flows in the current European labour market then it may be important to concentrate upon job turnover rather than labour turnover. *Job creation* is the sum of new jobs in new or expanding establishments, while *job destruction* is the total job losses in closing and contracting establishments. *Net employment change* is the difference between job creation and job destruction, while *gross job turnover* is the sum of job creation and destruction. Evidence summarised in Burda and Wyplosz (1994) for Belgium, France, Germany, Italy and the US indicates that job creation and job destruction only account for somewhere between 30 and 60 per cent of worker flows. Table 5.2 provides a comparison of average annual job gains and losses as a percentage of total employment for selected European economies covering periods from the mid-1980s to the early 1990s. Job turnover rates varied from nearly 30 per cent in Denmark to under 17 per cent in Germany. Each year about 1 in 5 jobs changes on average. The range for annual rates of job gains is slightly greater than that for job losses and higher job gain rates tend to be associated with high loss rates and vice versa. The main source of increases in employment was the expansion of existing establishments, suggesting the importance of cyclical conditions. Surprisingly, most turnover occurs within industries rather than between them. At any moment of time job creation and job destruction coexist within narrowly defined sectors, suggesting that individual firms either react differently to the same environment or face different shocks or a combination of

Table 5.1 Patterns of tenure, 1991

	Austria[a]	Finland	France	Germany[c]	Netherlands	Norway[d]	Spain[f]	Switzerland	United Kingdom	United States	Japan[e]
Current tenure (%)											
Total	100.0	100.0	100.0	100.0	100.0	100.0	100.0	100.0	100.0	100.0	100.0
Under 1 year	13.8	11.9	15.7	12.8	24.0	14.9[e]	23.9	17.6	18.6	28.8	9.8
1 and under 2 years		12.8	10.7	10.3	15.5	11.0[e]	7.7	11.7	12.4	11.6	16.1
2 and under 5 years	15.2[b]	24.5	15.6	17.9	22.9	18.0[e]	14.8	20.7	23.9	21.3	11.5
Under 5 years		49.2	42.0	41.0	62.4	43.9[c]	46.4	49.9	54.8	61.7	37.4
5 and under 10 years	32.6[b]	16.7	16.2	17.8	11.4	19.7	14.0	16.8	16.1	11.7	19.7
10 and under 20 years	36.7[b]	21.4	25.6	24.5	15.2	24.1	21.3	18.8	19.3	17.8	23.6
20 years and over		12.8	15.8	16.7	11.0	12.3	18.4	13.8	9.6	8.8	19.3
Unknown	1.7	–	0.4	–	–	–	–	0.8	0.1	–	–
Average tenure (years)											
All persons	–	9.0	10.1	10.4	7.0	9.4	9.8	8.8	7.9	6.7	10.9
Men	–	9.4	10.6	12.1	8.6	10.2	10.6	10.4	9.2	7.5	12.5
Women	–	8.5	9.6	8.0	4.3	8.4	8.2	6.6	6.3	5.9	7.3

[a] 1988.
[b] 1 and under 3 years, 3 and under 10 years, and 10 years and over.
[c] 1990.
[d] 1989.
[e] Under 21 months, 21 and 33 months, 33 and 57 months and under 57 months.
[f] 1992.

Source: OECD *Employment Outlook* (1993), Table 4.1.

Table 5.2 Job gains and job losses in firms (average annual rates as a percentage of total employment)

	Finland		France		Germany		Italy[a]		Sweden		United Kingdom[a]	
	1986–89	1989–91	1984–89	1989–92	1983–89	1989–90	1984–89	1989–92	1985–89	1989–92	1985–89	1989–91
Gross job gains	**11.1**	**9.3**	**13.9**	**13.7**	**8.7**	**10.2**	**12.7**	**11.8**	**16.1**	**12.6**	**9.1**	**8.0**
Openings	4.4	3.1	7.3	6.9	2.4	2.8	4.1	3.6	7.3	5.6	3.1	1.9
Expansions	6.7	6.2	6.6	6.8	6.4	7.4	8.6	8.2	8.8	7.0	6.0	6.1
Gross job losses	**10.3**	**14.5**	**12.8**	**13.9**	**7.7**	**6.6**	**10.5**	**11.9**	**13.2**	**16.1**	**6.7**	**6.4**
Closures	3.3	3.4	6.9	7.1	2.0	1.8	3.6	4.0	5.2	4.9	4.2	3.4
Contractions	7.0	11.1	5.9	6.8	5.7	4.8	7.0	7.9	8.1	11.3	2.5	3.0
Net employment change	**0.8**	**−5.2**	**1.2**	**−0.2**	**1.1**	**3.6**	**2.2**	**−0.1**	**2.9**	**−3.5**	**2.4**	**1.6**
Net entry (openings less closures)	1.0	−0.3	0.5	−0.2	0.4	1.0	0.6	−0.4	2.1	0.8	−1.1	−1.5
Net expansion (expansions less contractions)	−0.2	−4.9	0.7	−0.1	0.6	2.6	1.6	0.3	0.8	−4.2	3.5	3.1
Job turnover	**21.4**	**23.9**	**26.7**	**27.6**	**16.4**	**16.8**	**23.3**	**23.7**	**29.4**	**28.7**	**15.8**	**14.4**
Base period employment (thousands)	1,308	1,329	12,778	13,594	16,350	17,400	8,381	9,347	2,306	2,588	16,744	15,835

[a] Data refers to firms.
Source: OECD Employment Outlook (1994), Table 3.4.

135

these possibilities. Additionally, worker heterogeneity may cause firms to hire and dismiss different workers throughout the cycle, though in Germany and Italy job turnover appears to be uncorrelated with cycles (CEPR, 1995). The European Commission (1994a) provides some evidence that suggests that countries with low labour turnover may compensate through higher rates of job turnover, a more flexible internal labour market substituting for a less flexible external one. Klette and Mathiassen (1995) find that the highly regulated Norwegian labour market exhibits a similar degree of job creation and job reallocation as less regulated economies such as the US. In summary, there is a complex pattern of labour and job turnover in modern labour markets, suggesting that information necessary for designing efficient search strategies is expensive to obtain, collate and analyse.

Information on the behaviour of vacancies in European labour markets is again relatively scarce. Most countries rely upon data collected by employment offices, though the Netherlands has a regular vacancy survey. In many situations the incentives for employers to register vacancies at the employment service is low, and this registration rate will be sensitive to the economic cycle. In some countries (the Netherlands again for example), collective bargaining agreements may require employers to notify their vacancies to the public employment service (PES), in others there is a legal requirement on employers to notify the PES of vacancies. Muysken (1994) provides a comparison of registration rates for five European economies suggesting that the rate at the beginning of the 1990s varied from about 70 per cent in Sweden, where use of the PES is compulsory, to 35 per cent in Germany, the Netherlands and the United Kingdom and about 25 per cent in Austria. Muysken concludes that corrected vacancy rates have shown a similar pattern since 1960 in these five countries, although from 1970 their unemployment experience diverged. Average vacancy duration has fallen in all of these countries over the period, with duration at the start of the 1990s varying from around 2 months in Austria and the Netherlands to about one month in Sweden and the UK.

Results from Labour Force Surveys reported in Table 5.3 indicate the diversity of job search patterns in Europe. The PES plays a less central role in the search process of unemployed workers in Greece and Portugal and informal job search seems particularly important in Spain and private employment agencies in the UK. In the UK about 70 per cent of the unemployed, 30 per cent of employed job-seekers and 50 per cent of employers use the Jobcentre network as part of their search activities. In Italy Employment Offices are used by over 90 per cent of the unemployed and about half of employed job-seekers, accounting for about 28 per cent of total hirings (de Luca and Bruni, 1993). The pattern of job search in the UK seems to differ markedly between male and female and employed and unemployed searchers. Over the last decade unemployed workers in the UK have made much greater use of private agencies and direct contacts with employers, whilst employed workers have become less likely to use Jobcentres. Private agencies in the UK have increased their importance to all job seekers in recent years, but especially amongst males. The importance of the PES may differ significantly between regions, in Italy for instance, the PES overall accounts for about 28 per cent of hirings, but only 19 per cent in the relatively prosperous north (de Luca and Bruni, 1993).

Table 5.3 Methods of job search among the unemployed
(Percentages of unemployed seeking paid employment – excludes unemployed seeking self-employment)

	Belgium	Denmark	France	Germany	Greece	Ireland	Italy	Netherlands	Portugal	Spain	United Kingdom
Only registered at exchange	**12.3**	–	**17.3**	**47.4**	–	**5.6**	**41.5**	**1.3**	**7.6**	–	**1.4**
Both registered and other method	**76.8**	**90.4**	**70.7**	**38.8**	**14.9**	**66.7**	**50.6**	**61.7**	**40.0**	**92.1**	**62.4**
Private employment office	11.5	17.8	14.2	7.8	–	15.7	1.3	16.3	–	0.5	24.2
Direct contact with employers	25.4	39.7	18.5	4.8	7.1	14.3	13.5	3.0	10.3	–	5.4
Through the press	27.7	30.5	26.4	22.7	3.7	26.3	1.0	30.6	2.8	17.0	24.8
Asked friends, relatives etc.	7.0	1.8	7.4	1.8	2.5	10.2	6.3	2.1	12.9	32.8	6.5
Other methods	5.2	0.0	4.2	1.7	1.2	0.0	28.5	9.7	13.4	41.8	1.5
Only another method	**10.9**	**9.6**	**11.9**	**13.8**	**84.7**	**27.7**	**7.9**	**37.0**	**52.4**	**7.8**	**36.2**
Private employment office	1.3	–	1.5	3.8	–	4.4	–	5.6	–	–	8.1
Direct contact with employers	3.2	4.1	3.9	1.7	33.5	5.3	3.2	4.1	11.4	–	3.1
Through the press	4.1	4.7	3.9	6.2	20.9	12.9	0.2	20.9	4.2	2.1	19.5
Asked friends, relatives etc.	1.5	–	2.0	1.1	24.0	4.9	1.4	4.0	21.2	5.0	3.6
Other methods	–	–	0.7	1.1	6.2	–	2.9	2.4	15.4	0.7	1.8

Source: Office of the European Communities, *Labour Force Survey Results 1991*, (1993), Table 79.

5.2 Neoclassical models of job search

5.2.1 *The basic model of worker search*

Acquiring market information is costly. In goods markets sellers can take advantage of the resulting information imperfections by charging higher prices to the less knowledgeable consumers. Stigler in the 1960s applied this logic to the labour market, explaining that one consequence of costly search was wage dispersion. Firms find it expensive to identify the potential productivity of applicants, whilst workers find it costly to calculate their potential earnings in alternative employment. These information gaps can cause wage differentials to emerge and persist between workers with seemingly identical job and personal characteristics. Another consequence of information gaps may be unemployment, and the early popularity of search theory was due to interest in explaining the movements in unemployment as inflation changed. The re-emergence of economic analyses of business cycles and growth with their emphasis upon sectoral shifts in the economy has led to a new role for search theory.

The starting point for modern theories of job search is the proposition that with imperfect information about labour market opportunities it is irrational for workers to accept the first job offer. Given that wage variability exists, workers enhance the probability of discovering a better job offer by prolonging the search. Search is a productive activity, an investment in accumulating knowledge which allows an optimal job acceptance policy to be formulated and implemented. In order to develop the basic model we will consider the behaviour of an individual unemployed worker. Typically this searcher will have some information concerning labour market conditions but will not know the wage that will be offered, if any, by any specific firm. Additional search in such a situation holds the promise of identifying a higher wage offer but such a strategy incurs additional search costs. The tools of investment theory which we developed in the previous chapter can now be applied to the determination of an optimal search strategy. The solution can either be framed in terms of an optimal length of search or a sequential stopping rule, where search ceases when a wage offer exceeds or equals a pre-specified level, termed the reservation wage. Later theorists have concluded that a fixed sample rule is generally inferior to the reservation wage strategy and we now concentrate on this latter approach. Prior to search the individual chooses a reservation wage which maximises the expected benefits from search. If the observed wage offer falls below the reservation wage the offer is rejected and search continues. The first offer of employment at or above the reservation wage is accepted.

If we are to apply the neoclassical tools of equi-marginal analysis to the identification of the optimal search strategy, the marginal benefits and costs of this search need to be identified. The benefits of search are higher expected lifetime earnings. As workers are searching a given distribution of wage offers, the higher their reservation wage the longer the expected duration of their search and the higher their expected post-search income. For a given normal distribution of wage offers, the increase in the expected wage from raising the reservation wage will decline as the reservation wage increases. The marginal benefit of choosing a higher reservation wage therefore eventually falls, as illustrated in Figure 5.1, both because the chances of locating an offer above the reservation wage decline and because the expected longer search causes a depreciation of human capital and reduces the time period over which the higher wages are earned. A higher reservation wage also implies a higher level of expected search costs, both the opportunity costs of lost income, home production and leisure (minus any benefits payable to searchers) and direct search costs, such as travel costs. The marginal search costs may initially fall due to economies of scale in job-search, reflecting geographical factors and indivisibilities such as suits and haircuts! However, as the most likely firms are searched first, together with other low search-cost firms such as those in the locality of the searcher, marginal costs are likely to eventually rise as assumed in Figure 5.1. The optimal reservation wage will be the wage which just equates the marginal benefits and marginal costs arising from any small change in the minimum wage required to cease search. It is the wage which maximizes the expected returns from search. At R*, the optimal reservation wage, the marginal benefit from a small rise in that wage, higher expected income over the duration of the job, is equal to the marginal costs, largely foregone earnings for the anticipated extra period of search.

Initially much of the literature in this field was concerned with uncovering the properties of this optimal reservation wage (Pissarides, 1985). The general conclusions about the nature of the underlying trade-off between discovering higher wage offers and enduring longer search were as follows. Given a finite time horizon and a finite number of searching opportunities and assuming that searching workers cannot recall previous wage offers which they rejected, the reservation wage is likely to fall with the duration of search. Alternative explanations for this tendency include non-random search, wealth constraints and diminishing marginal utility of leisure.

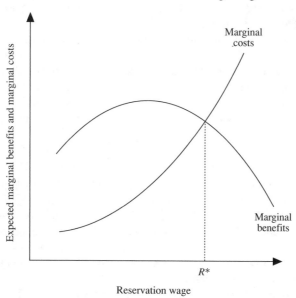

Figure 5.1 Determination of the optimal reservation wage

An increase in some or all wage offers will shift the marginal benefit curve to the right and therefore raise the optimal reservation wage. Any lowering of search costs will shift the marginal cost curve to the right and therefore increase the reservation wage and extend the anticipated period of search. For example, unemployment benefits paid to those conducting active search will lower the opportunity costs of off-the-job search, raising their reservation wages and lengthening the duration of their unemployment spell, an issue we investigate in Chapter 7. Workers with the shortest time horizon, such as those close to retirement, will tend to have the lowest search activity and reservation wage, since they calculate the stream of higher post-search incomes over fewer years and their marginal benefits curves are therefore below those of other workers. The almost infinite variations one can make to the assumptions of this approach, such as attitude to risk-taking, rate of time preference and knowledge about distribution of wage-offers, has led to an explosion of literature in this area in the last twenty years.

The original search models outlined had a major weakness in that they treated work and search as mutually exclusive alternatives and as a consequence concentrated upon the behaviour of unemployed searchers. Rational behaviour requires all employees to conduct regular search in order to assess their current employment contract and prepare for wage negotiations. The problem to be solved by workers is to attain a maximising combination of income, home production, leisure and search. Workers have to choose the intensity of search as well as its duration; they can combine work and search by adopting less time-intensive on-the-job search. The choice of the method of search will depend upon the relative costs and effectiveness of different intensities of search at uncovering job offers. We follow Polachek and Siebert (1993) in providing a simple illustration of this choice, utilising Figure 5.2. Inputs to the search process are search intensity (measured, for example, in employers contacted per week) and the duration of search. The budget line I_0D_0 shows a certain total search budget made up of search time and search intensity costs. The cost of search time we have already identified as the opportunity costs of lost earnings, home production and leisure, minus any benefits payable to searchers. The cost of search intensity is the cost per employer contact, and these transaction costs will include travel and communication costs. If we proxy home production and leisure costs by the potential wage rate then the total search budget (TC) is:

$$TC = (w - b)D + cI \qquad [5.1]$$

where w is the weekly wage, b weekly income when not working, D is the duration of search in weeks, c is the cost of contacting an employer and I is the number of employers contacted. The slope of the budget line is therefore (w − b)/c. These inputs generate an output of job offers, O_1, O_2 and O_3 show a progressively higher level of job offers; the shape of these isoquants will reflect the relative marginal productivity of search time and search intensity in producing job offers. Given the relative costs and productivity shown in Figure 5.2 then the cheapest way of identifying O_2 job offers is I* intensity and D* duration.

Now if governments reduce the costs of contacting employers, c, by, say, Job Clubs which provide free telephone and fax facilities and free travel to interviews, then the

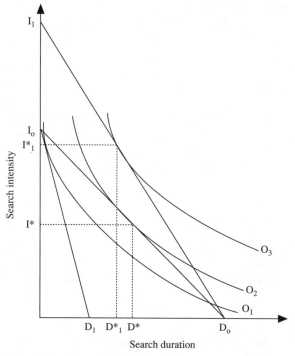

Figure 5.2 The choice of intensity and duration of search

budget line shifts to, say, I_1D_0 and the new equilibrium shows more intensity, $I*_1$, a lower duration, $D*_1$, and a higher level of job offers, O_2. Alternatively, assume that unemployment benefits are reduced, shifting the budget line to, say, I_0D_1, again increasing the intensity of search and reducing the duration, but now reducing the offers received to O_1, and therefore worsening the job match. The effect of a change in the relative cost of duration and intensity will depend upon substitution and wealth effects and these results are not general, with the exception of the increase in offers. In a recession the isoquant curves move outwards, since a higher budget is required to produce the same number of offers. If in a recession employers take the length of uncompleted search as a proxy for the quality of the applicant and are more likely to screen out those with a long duration, then the isoquants become flatter, favouring a more intense strategy of search for any given search budget.

This last argument should have raised some concern, since we know that unemployment duration tends to increase during a recession. Indeed we are now confronted with a fundamental criticism of the theory of worker search: as a model of labour supply it only models workers' reactions to job offers. Not only is such analysis partial, it ignores the total number of workers and employers involved in the search process. The effectiveness of any individual search method will depend upon the number of vacancies available and the number of competing searchers. Models of worker search have nothing to say about the likelihood of workers receiving job-offers or about involuntary quits, such as lay-offs and sackings. In short they ignore

141

the demand-side of the labour market. Barron *et al.* (1985) were among the first to point out that the traditional search model which stressed searching workers receiving job offers and accepting or rejecting them via reference to a reservation wage, was an inaccurate description of actual labour market practices. Most vacancies are filled by a single job-offer: it is the employer who chooses from a pool of searching workers not the other way around. Only in the tightest labour market will a significant number of workers be able to choose between competing job offers. The reservation wage models of employee search therefore need supplementing by models which examine the determinants of employer search. When we reconsider job-matching in this manner, it is the employer's perception of the characteristics of applicants which becomes crucial in all but the tightest labour markets, not the applicants' search intensity or reservation wage.

5.2.2 *Employer search behaviour and the job matching function*

If individual job-searchers have different reservation wages, firms can raise the probability of applicants accepting their job offer by raising the wage offered. Firms therefore can substitute between length of search and wage levels offered for any given quality of applicant. When heterogeneous workers are introduced into the analysis firms have a choice of adjusting not only search and wage costs and acceptable worker-quality but also monitoring actual performance on the job. Different solutions to this choice will be a cause of wage variability within clearly defined labour markets. Since searchers will be aware of the search policy adopted by firms, those with fuller search strategies must compensate applicants for the reduced probability of a wage offer by raising the general level of wages offered. Firms' choice of search method will be influenced by similar forces to those discussed for worker choice. For example, in periods of high unemployment firms may not utilise employment agencies since informal and direct methods provide adequate supplies of applicants. Franz and Smolney (1993) find evidence of such behaviour by German firms and van Ours (1994) by Dutch ones. While it may be tempting to treat worker and employer search symmetrically, studies indicate that for most vacancies firms' search is non-sequential. Van Ours and Ridder (1993) concluded that employers fill most vacancies from a pool of applicants chosen soon after the vacancy is publicised. Most vacancies exist because it takes time to select a suitable applicant, not because there are no suitable applicants. Accordingly, they argue that vacancy duration should be interpreted as a selection rather than a search period.

Where individual decision-makers on both sides of the labour market are pursuing optimal search strategies then the rate at which they receive offers is determined by a matching function. The matching function relates the number of potential matches to the number of active searchers on each side of the labour market. Following work by Diamond (1982), aggregate matching functions have become popular in examining flows in the labour market, particularly those determining the duration of unemployment. Such models, rather than assuming that all separations are induced by a desire to search, often assume that separations are the result of job destruction. Indeed, Blanchard and Diamond (1992) regard the search of unemployed workers as being more appropriately termed 'waiting'. Pissarides (1990) develops a general model of the aggregate matching function which we now summarise. The flow of new jobs formed at any moment of time will depend upon the stock of workers looking for a new job and the stock of firms looking for workers. If we assume that all unemployed workers are looking for a job, then the number of new jobs formed (M) is:

$$M = M(U, V, Z) \qquad M_1, M_2, M_3 > 0 \qquad [5.2]$$

where U is the number of unemployed workers, V is the number of vacancies and Z is a vector of other variables which influence the ease with which unemployed workers are matched with vacancies. Empirical work for the UK and US suggests constant returns in U and V (Layard *et al.*, 1991). The number of employed job seekers can be included as part of the Z; Burgess (1993) finds that their inclusion improves the matching functions ability to explain the outflow from unemployment in Britain. His results suggest that as hirings rise, more of the employed workers search and as a consequence unemployed searchers are 'crowded-out' of the new jobs. Another component of Z will be the search intensity of firms and workers, and also Layard *et al.* (1991) explore the importance of the composition of unemployment with increases in the proportion of the long-term unemployed depressing the number of matches.

In the matching function approach firms now play as important a role as workers. Within a competitive equilibrium framework job separations now occur because they are in the best interests of workers and firms, given the presence of adverse shocks. Separations occur because the private returns from a job fall below some reservation level, a level chosen by firms and workers on the basis of alternative returns. In such a framework the distinction between voluntary quits and layoffs is no longer critical. This approach is consistent with our earlier discovery that within industrial sectors job destruction and creation mutually coexist throughout the cycle, suggesting the importance of job-specific shocks and worker heterogeneity.

Burda and Wyplosz (1994) estimate matching functions for France, Germany, Spain and the United Kingdom. Their results were supportive of the existence of a matching function, with an estimated elasticity of matches (including exits from the labour force) with respect to unemployment of between 0.5 and 0.7. With the exception of Spain, their results indicate rapid labour market adjustment. Lindeboom *et al.* (1994) utilise a matching function to investigate search in the Netherlands. Rather than using aggregate time series data to estimate a single matching function, they divide the labour market into sub-markets according to job type and search method used, and estimate a matching function for each. Their results indicate differences in the effectiveness of different search methods, with employed workers having a greater probability of success than unemployed workers. Advertisements and informal search methods are effective at matching employed workers and vacancies, whilst the employment service and informal search are effective for matching unemployed workers and vacancies.

Various refinements can be made to the matching function approach. Coles (1994) argues that the simple function is misspecified since job seekers do not search randomly. A quarter of the vacancies posted in Jobcentres are filled on their first day, and the probability of the vacancy being filled falls to a tenth of that rate on succeeding days. Coles argues that a better description of the matching process may be that the stock of unemployed workers is matching the flow of new vacancies, as they have already sampled the 'old' vacancies. Similarly, the stock of vacancies is matching the flow of new job seekers. The existence of a stable matching function does not itself favour any particular approach to analysing labour market behaviour, since as Hosios (1990) has argued, it is consistent with a variety of analysis. The lack of suitable data means that few applications of this approach are available at the micro level. Holzer (1994) using US data found that there was substantial variation in vacancy rates across firms, occupations, industries, regions and over the business cycle. Unionised and/or large firms had lower vacancy rates as did firms in high unemployment areas.

5.2.3   *The rationale for government intervention*

Search and job matching analysis was often utilised by economists who had a presumption that unregulated market forces generally produced an efficient job-matching system; workers and firms could be relied upon to design efficient search strategies. Within the confines of search theoretic models there appear two justifications for a public employment service (PES), one relying on public good arguments and the other on externalities. Firstly, governments can reduce the cost of search for workers by supplying information on outstanding vacancies, allowing workers to sample more firms per period of search and therefore raising the efficiency of a given search budget. Such intervention may be justified on efficiency grounds if workers are myopic or if vacancy information has the characteristics of a public good. The national collection, collation and dissemination of vacancy information is comparable to a natural monopoly, and one which the government's role in data collection and unemployment benefits gives it a comparative advantage to fill. Salop (1973) and Barron and Gilley (1981) have developed models where indirect search via a PES leads to fewer contacts made with employers but a higher chance of locating an acceptable job offer per period of search. Here, rather than the reservation wage being influenced, it is the duration of unemployment which is reduced and their empirical results supported this conclusion.

Pissarides (1984) and Lockwood (1986) provided arguments for government intervention in the job matching process based upon the second justification, search externalities. These externalities are ignored by agents deciding to enter a market, accept a match or search more intensely. By altering their behaviour firms or workers alter the matching probabilities of other searchers. For example, the more firms advertise their vacancies the easier it is for workers to target their search. Generally, one agent's trading costs can be reduced if agents on the other side of the market devote more resources to their search. Similarly, acceptance of a job offer by an optimising decision-maker saves the other party further search costs, but these costs are not internalised by the acceptor. In normal situations wages do not internalise these externalities and as a consequence Pissarides shows that the steady state equilibrium unemployment rate generated by the search process is likely to be above the socially efficient level. Private employment agencies could internalise some of these externalities and speed up the matching process, but if their market share remains small few searchers will utilise their services. In such situations the agencies may not survive since the value of other searchers registering remains small given there is a low probability of making a successful match through the agency, and its operating costs may not be met from fee income. Coles (1994) provides a formal analysis of the operation of such agencies and the case for public funding.

Trade externalities associated with congestion and thin markets provide a further source of job-matching market failure. If an employer is looking for a worker with very special features, it is more likely to find her or him in a large market rather than a small one. Hence the potential benefits of a PES providing initial information on market possibilities, though the reasons for favouring a public rather than private agency are less clear in this case. Lockwood also drops the assumption of firm and worker homogeneity and argues that further kinds of inefficiency can be generated in the search process. Highly skilled workers or high-productivity firms will cause low-skilled workers and low-productivity firms to have a low probability of acceptance in the matching process. For example, unemployed workers may receive no job offers even when they are the only applicant. Firms may make no offer to poorly matched or low quality applicants anticipating that current output losses will be offset by the increased production of future, better-matched employees. This market solution may represent in equilibrium a lower acceptance probability for these disadvantaged agents than is socially desirable. Unemployment hysteresis may be the result of this process, an argument we return to in Chapter 7.

Although a PES may limit the duplication of costly search and otherwise improve the efficiency of search, its role in reducing unemployment is ambiguous according to search theory, since its presence may reduce the variety or intensity of search. Indeed, in the 1980s during times of rising unemployment both the UK and the US governments cut resources available to the placing service. There is some theoretical support for such views in that search intensity of the unemployed may have fallen in some European countries and this is considered later. Pissarides (1979) provided a different rationale. He assumed full registration of unemployed workers with employment offices and partial notification of vacancies, concluding that policies to encourage search outside registered vacancies increased labour market efficiency. Keeley and Robins (1985) also argued that the use of the PES results in the reduction of total resources devoted to private search, probably produced an inefficient allocation of search resources by the unemployed. Both of these papers ignore any divergence of social costs and benefits from private ones in the job search process. Moreover given that all jobs and searchers are identical in Pissarides's model it is difficult to explain incomplete registration of vacancies where the public employment service makes no charge for its services. Partial registration requires that the internal costs of informing the agency exceed the total costs of private advertising and it is difficult to explain this difference unless the speed of filling vacancies differs significantly between recruitment methods. Alternatively, the attractions of relying upon private agencies may reflect a desire to perpetuate discrimination or to sustain other abusive employment practices.

5.2.4   *Non-competitive approaches*

Although job matching analysis illuminates some important issues for policy it sometimes obscures the importance of informal search methods in modern labour markets. The availability of effective low-intensity and low-search time methods, such as business associates, friends and newspapers has been used to explain the dominance of on-the-job search in the labour market. Lindeboom *et al.* (1994) summarise German studies as finding that the informal search channel was the most productive for workers, while Roper (1988) found that employer's informal search was the most successful method as measured by vacancy duration. These findings have been taken by some commentators to imply that there are aspects of the job-matching process which are not adequately addressed in conventional theory.

Some recent studies try to estimate the extent of ignorance in the labour market. Their results suggest some further problems with job search models. If people earn less than would be expected, given their education and experience, then this may reflect a lack of information regarding their worth in current market conditions. Polachek and Hofler (1991) found that white male workers had wages 31 per cent below their potential on average and black males 44 per cent. The measures of ignorance were lower for college graduates and union members. Polachek and Yoon (1987) found that employers pay more for labour than they would if well informed; again the figures suggested an overpayment of around 40 per cent. While there are acknowledged data problems in the control of quality measures in these studies, their findings do suggest the possible limitations of adopting an equilibrium search approach.

The evidence of widespread use of informal methods of recruitment and our earlier discovery of long tenure for the majority of employees is interpreted by the non-competitive approach as reflecting the importance of internal labour markets. The importance of both firm-specific skills and worker morale encourages firms to adopt employment policies that limit turnover. Only in markets where technical skills are important, such as certain professional markets, and where turnover is not expensive, as in secondary labour markets and for young workers, will we experience high mobility and extensive job search. The long-term relationship which primary-sector employers anticipate with recruits, leads them to adopt an extensive searching, screening and hiring process. Although existing employees should maintain job-search to ensure that their employers are paying them their rent, some will sub-contract this duty to trade unions and others will have confidence that their employers can be trusted to reflect changes in the external labour market. According to this approach, on-the-job search may be much less widespread than anticipated by search theory, an argument consistent with the data from the British Labour Force Survey already reported.

Another consequence of structured internal labour markets is that since firms will concentrate on retaining their best workers, job-changers have a disproportionate number of less able workers. This produces adverse selection or the 'lemon' phenomenon in the labour market, employers may be reluctant to hire job-changers and the consequential reduction of wages and opportunities for occupational advancement in the 'second-hand' market dissuades mobility. This process strengthens the internal labour market and produces a very different world to that described and analysed by search theory earlier. Barriers to labour mobility created by adverse selection, trap workers in unsuitable or disliked jobs. Typically job changes and off-the-job search will be highly concentrated in the secondary labour market, since established workers in the primary sector rarely change employer or become unemployed. In recessions however workers are displaced from good jobs and the characteristics and aspirations of unemployed workers become more diverse.

The observed popularity of recruiting non-skilled manual workers through existing employees gives rise to what has been termed the extended internal labour market (EILM). Surveys of employer recruitment strategies, such as Way (1984), suggest that the use of the EILM as a recruitment channel reflects both managerial and worker self-interest. For many managers the EILM represents a low-cost screening device, particularly conducive to recruiting a stable work-force. Relying on present employees to act as recruiting agents is likely to ensure a supply of applicants with the required social skills to minimise workplace frictions. Such social skills are otherwise very difficult for firms to identify prior to employment. Jenkins (1984) reports that many managers often proxy the applicants' quality by that of the employee who introduces them, much like in a private club. Others, again like a club, expect that the employee who recommends the applicant will act as an unpaid trainer and supervisor, reducing the firm's unit labour costs. For still other employers the EILM is favoured for the community it produces, the 'family firm' ethos, or for the industrial relations environment with which it is associated, though the built-in solidarity of the work-force can lead to bitter and lengthy industrial disputes when mutual confidence between employers and employees is lost.

The advantage for employees of recruitment via the EILM seems to be the improvement in social relationships at work. Combining the social networks of family and friends with those of work improves the work environment, whilst securing the appointment of friends gives additional status in the community. For searchers an additional advantage which the EILM produces is the greater certainty about pecuniary returns, availability of overtime, operation of payment systems and the workplace environment. The EILM thus improves the quality and lowers the cost of information. It also reduces the costs of job changing, because entrants already have contacts in the workplace who can ease their entry into the new social networks.

Where social stability is low, such as in new towns, or in periods or regions of low unemployment, then the EILM is unlikely to be the dominant recruitment channel. Similarly in higher skilled employment where technical skills are more important than social skills, more formal methods of recruitment will be the main mechanism for obtaining new workers. In periods of high unemployment firms already using informal recruitment channels can rely on the EILM for all their manpower requirements. The low mobility of their work-force in such labour market conditions appears to induce firms to conclude that such practices are efficient. Other firms, who face severe product market and or financial constraints, try to reduce recruitment expenses by substituting informal channels of recruitment for more expensive formal ones.

5.3 Policy issues

5.3.1 *Regulating search behaviour*

Where many firms recruit through informal channels 'cold-calling' may be inefficient and this may make it very difficult to define, and therefore measure, 'active' search or the intensity of search in the labour market, an issue to which we return in Chapter 7. The importance of the EILM also gives a new insight into the role of a state employment service. It has been argued that the social and economic roles of the service may conflict. Maximising placements and penetration rate may lead to the service no longer giving special treatment to 'hard to place' unemployed job-searchers. In an economy where internal labour markets have developed, such 'disadvantaged' workers can neither price themselves nor search themselves into employment. Adverse selection and non-wage labour costs cause firms to screen out even unemployed applicants who offer to work for less than their existing employees. Their use of the EILM for recruitment may both be a reflection of insider-power and be a contributory factor to the concentration of unemployment experience amongst certain groups.

Those unemployed searchers without access to the social networks of the employed workers will be disadvantaged in the job-matching process, and therefore over-represented in the stock of unemployment. Employers' use of the EILM makes 'who you know' rather than 'what you know' important for successful search. The inability of certain groups to gain the labour market information available through informal channels makes them particularly reliant upon the PES in their search process. Predominant amongst those discriminated against by recruitment through the EILM will be entrants and re-entrants whose social circle will include fewer employed workers. Labour market discrimination will be cumulative since racial and religious minorities will again have fewer employed workers in their numbers. Holzer (1987) found that up to 90 per cent of the difference in employment probabilities between white and black youths in the US could be explained by differences in the use and effectiveness of informal search methods. A desire by employers to pursue discriminatory hiring practices whilst avoiding anti-discriminatory legislative constraints may be a further cause for the initial adoption of informal recruitment channels. In non-discriminating firms use of the EILM may still lead to a high concentration of racial or religious minorities amongst their work-force. These groups' exclusion from large parts of the labour market contributes to their high unemployment rate, and to the declining probability of leaving unemployment as duration increases, issues which are explored further in the following chapter. The process outlined is unlikely to produce efficient job matching since potential productivity may be unrelated to the social networks of employment. If such discrimination is inefficient then the case can be made for regulation to require firms to advertise vacancies.

5.3.2 *Public employment services*

In this chapter we are concentrating upon the job-matching role of the PES, though in recent years the registration of job-seekers and the placing of workers into subsidised employment and training programmes has absorbed more of their resources. In many European countries the PES has become an essential part of the implementation of active labour market policies which we considered in Chapter 1. Table 1.12 contained data both on the size of these programmes in the EU and expenditure on public employment services and administration. Unfortunately for our purposes, this data includes the costs of administering unemployment benefit agencies and this can account for up to two-thirds of the total expenditure in this category. The figures for Denmark, Finland and the Netherlands exclude administration costs of unemployment benefits since non-governmental funding is involved in these countries. Another indicator of the capacity of the public employment service (PES) to perform their tasks is the number of unemployed per staff member. The OECD Jobs Study (1994a) found large differences in the EU, Spain having a ratio at least seven times greater than that of Sweden in 1992. The actual demands upon PES staff of these caseloads will also depend upon the stock of unfilled vacancies, the notification rate of these vacancies to the PES and the technology to support job matching. Table 5.4 brings together some recent data on PES workload and market share. The data suggest no simple relationship between workload and the PES share of hires, which is not surprising given the differences in the role and legal restrictions in these countries. PES hiring share is relatively high in Italy and the UK, countries with very different workload indicators, the Italian PES having at this time a legal monopoly of placements and the 31 per cent share was via a rank-order system, outlined later, now abolished.

The variety of institutional and legal frameworks within which the PES operates has been explored by the OECD (1993a, 1995). In Spain employers are legally required to notify all vacancies to the PES and are prohibited from using other recruitment methods until three days after notification. The Spanish PES also has the responsibility to register all written employment contracts. This responsibility together with work associated with the payment of benefits restricts PES staff time

Table 5.4 Indicators of PES workload and market share

	Number of unemployed per staff member in employment offices 1992	Monthly placement per staff member[3]	Placements as a percentage of all hires[3]
Denmark	134[1]	3	10
Finland	136	2	17
Italy	370[2]	7	31
Norway	56	2	11
Spain	350	3	20
United Kingdom	82	4	30

[1] 1993 data.
[2] Registered job searchers.
[3] Denmark 1993 figures, Finland 1994, Italy 1990, other countries 1988 estimates.
Sources: OECD: *Jobs Study: Evidence and Explanations*, Table 6.16.
OECD: *The Public Employment Service in Japan, Norway, Spain and the UK*, 1993, Table 6.
OECD: *Employment Outlook 1995*, Table 3.2.

available for placement work. Compulsory vacancy notification is also the rule in the Nordic countries, though the legislation is rarely enforced and the growth of flexible employment has created a demand for private agencies specialising in the provision of temporary workers.

Data for North America and Europe suggest that job seekers who use the PES have longer spells of search unemployment than those reporting other methods of search. Antolin (1994) reports that Spaniards registered with the PES are less mobile and that the PES may have contributed to a decline in job search. The belief that PESs may be inefficient at matching workers and jobs is consistent with the observation that employers frequently justify their low notification rate of vacancies to the PES by citing the low ability and motivation of applicants submitted by the PES (van Ours, 1994). Thomas (1994) utilises a model of systematic search to reconsider the relationship between use of the PES and duration of search of UK male unemployed workers in the late 1980s. He concludes that the positive relationship between PES use and duration of search may reflect unemployed workers switching to using the PES as their search duration increases, rather than any PES inefficiency. Indeed, among those with unemployment spells below six months, individuals who find work via the Jobcentre have shorter spells than other searchers.

The contribution which the PES can make to the efficiency of the job matching process will be dependent upon the manner in which it operates as an intermediary between employers and searchers. Where it merely displays notified vacancies and operates a passive, self-service system such as in Italy, it imposes additional screening costs upon employers and lengthens the duration of vacancies and hence increases the stock of both vacancies and unemployment. Such a passive role may encourage, as in Italy, private forms of intermediation even without legal foundations. In Denmark the total number of vacancies registered nearly doubled between 1988 and 1994, partly due to a 'fully-open' system of reproducing advertisements from newspapers but also increased use of a 'semi-open' system where applicants are screened by the PES before being sent for interviews with the employer. Barron and Mellor (1982) provide a formal model to analyse why employers do not automatically notify vacancies to state employment agencies. Their reasoning is that firms do not view applicants arising from employment offices as perfect substitutes for applicants from alternative recruitment channels. Where payment of unemployment benefits is linked to evidence of active search, firms who register vacancies decrease the likelihood that applicants will actually accept any wage offer. Thus for some firms the increased likelihood of searchers contacting the firm is more than offset by the costs associated with the increase in the number of non-serious applicants. Non-registering firms are likely to be those with high interview costs, typically those employing higher skilled workers or providing substantial firm-specific training to recruits. Barron and Mellor's model includes heterogeneous workers with qualifications indicating productive potential. Employers derive a reservation index of qualifications, and workers are retained if monitoring confirms that their productivity exceeds wages. The higher the interviewing costs and the higher the reservation index of qualifications the more likely that the job will not be notified to the PES. This analysis is consistent with the PES in Britain having a higher notification rate amongst the less-skilled and low-paying vacancies. As a consequence Gregg and Wadsworth (1994) find that the greatest beneficial impact of Jobcentre use is amongst the less skilled and long-term unemployed. Björklund (1994) reports the results of Swedish experiments which suggest that more intensive provision of employment services for the unemployed may increase their employment stability and earnings.

Van Ours (1994) analyses the relative effectiveness of different types of vacancy matching undertaken by the Dutch public employment office. The Dutch service uses a classification of four types of assistance: self-selection, conditional self-selection, administrative matching and selective matching. Self-selection implies that information on job seekers and vacancies is recorded in files available to both employers and searchers. Conditional self-selection covers the provision of information by telephone or files to job-seekers. Interested searchers who are deemed suitable are provided with the employer's particulars. Administrative matching is where the PES provides a more active role in notifying job-seekers and/or employers of potentially suitable matches. Finally, selective matching is where in addition to the previous assistance the PES screens potentially suitable job-seekers prior to applicants being forwarded to the employers. Van Ours uses a matching function with constant returns to scale to analyse the efficiency of these different systems. The results indicate that use of administrative and selective matching reduces the duration of the vacancy, whether such benefits exceed the additional costs of a more active PES role is not investigated.

A fundamental aim in providing a free public employment service has always been to assist unemployed searchers and with the PES also usually administering unemployment benefits this has normally encouraged the 'down-market' bias in the placement role discovered earlier. Giving priority to assisting the job search of unemployed workers, produces a danger that employers will complain about the quality of applicants referred and be less willing to notify vacancies to the PES. Recognition of this potential vicious circle led to the introduction of Jobcentres in Britain which aimed at increasing market share by attracting more employed searchers and improving employers' image of the service. Although this policy achieved some success, the early 1980s saw more emphasis on reducing the average costs of placements and, after 1986, on targeting the placement of the long-term unemployed in employment or on various employment and training schemes. The average cost of a placement fell by over 40 per cent in real terms between 1981/2 and 1986/7; the main reason for this fall was that about two-thirds of placements were made via the self-service system, though the elimination of occupational guidance and centralisation of other specialist services also contributed to reduced costs. Reforms also led to a reduction in matching and screening of applicants responding to notified vacancies. Overall this change of emphasis reproduced the vicious circle, with a decline in the use of Jobcentres by employed workers and reduced vacancy flows, the former being partly reversed as labour market conditions worsened in 1990.

Reorganisations have also taken place recently in Belgium, Germany, Austria, Finland, France, Ireland and Sweden, largely as a consequence of the growth of unemployment. In the first two countries special temporary agencies have been established for the unemployed. These have been modelled on the Dutch START agencies which have targeted the long-term unemployed and other difficult-to-place searchers with some success (European Commission, 1995a). Elsewhere the emphasis has been upon placement, counselling and job club initiatives targeted at the long-term unemployed. We consider these in Chapter 7.

Overall it appears that only around half of vacancies in Europe are publicly announced. Although increases in the penetration rate of employment service may enhance the efficiency of worker search, the reliance on recruitment through informal methods makes such increases difficult within a system of voluntary registration. In Spain employers have been required to notify job vacancies to the PES by law and there are social security incentives for them to do so. In Italy and Norway the PES also have a virtual monopoly on employment services, though in Austria, Denmark and Finland restrictions on private employment agencies were abolished in the 1990s and in the UK private employment agencies are increasing their market share as we noted earlier. Italy provides an example of a system where regulation has been taken too far and as a consequence circumventive innovation has occurred. The legal monopoly of the PES over placements has not prevented the growth of temporary work agencies violating social security, tax and labour standards. Each Italian worker has a personal workbook which shows their employment history and all labour movements must be registered with the PES. Until recently only relatives of owners, apprentices and top management were allowed to be hired without prior notification to the PES. Up until 1991 Local Employment Commissions produced a priority list of unemployed job-seekers who were ranked on the basis of number of dependants, duration etc. and employers were required to make half of their hirings in accordance with these lists. Quota and list systems still remain, requiring firms in theory to have 15 per cent of their work-force with 'protected' status and 12 per cent of hires from the long-term unemployed. However, the OECD (1995) reports that although employers are required to make annual declarations to the Labour Inspectorate, quotas are not binding in reality and hiring practices have been changed to avoid recruiting from lists. The obligation on Italian employers to notify all vacancies to the PES was abolished in 1995 and replaced by a requirement to notify only after hiring.

The central problem faced by a PES is how to maintain both a high market share and prioritise search assistance to the unemployed and those entering the labour market. Compulsory notification of vacancies to the PES would entice more employed job-seekers to utilise the service and help to solve perceived quality problems of applicants submitted. The main arguments against compulsory vacancy notification which governments have advanced are that it would distort vacancy data, prevent the development of specialist matching-agencies and prejudice employers' good relations with the employment service. Given the widely acknowledged weakness of vacancy data as an indicator it is difficult to take the first argument seriously and the second mainly applies to firms not using the service. Although compulsory vacancy notification may promote efficient and equitable search in the labour market there is likely to be employer resistance to such policies. Any politically feasible system has to allow firms to recruit through their favoured channel, and European experience suggests that employers often continue to screen out PES applicants even when they have to register vacancies. One way of retaining both a high market share and a bias towards assisting the search of unemployed workers is to link compulsory vacancy notification with a wage subsidy for unemployed workers, a policy which we assess in Chapter 7.

5.4 Assessment

Changes in the structure and composition of employment in Europe have increased the complexity of search in the labour market, while the (slight) increase in the instability of employment for the typical worker has also increased the importance of the search process. We have identified a number of causes of inefficiency in the job-matching process in European economies, which in principle a PES could address. One remaining problem concerns the role of private employment agencies. Whilst they may help to improve job-matching efficiency if they concentrate on particular specialised labour markets where the PES may lack expertise, they may segment the market for information and increase search costs in 'thicker' labour markets. In addition, the benefits which they offer employers in terms of greater screening of applicants could be duplicated by the PES without the risk of reinforcing inaccurate employer stereotypes and perpetuating discrimination. The worry remains that the tendency towards increased segmentation in European labour markets identified earlier, may be assisted by the expansion of private employment agencies. This issue is linked to another main policy problem which we have considered; the balance which the PES must maintain between market share and favouring unemployed searchers and entrants. The growth of active labour market policies has helped to supplement the search assistance which the PES can provide for these groups and we have provided examples of strategies which may help to improve the trade-off between the competing job-broking objectives.

5.5 Geographical mobility: theory and evidence

5.5.1 *Introduction*

We have so far implicitly assumed that search and job-matchings are taking place within a local labour market. Persisting high levels of unemployment in Europe together with increased economic integration have generated renewed consideration of whether migration or regional policies could improve or supplant other adjustment mechanisms in the labour market. Efficiency losses can result if a potential match between an unemployed worker and unfilled vacancy is prevented by spatial factors or if these factors cause the quality of that match to differ between regions such that workers in some regions are consistently under-employed. These losses provide a rationale for policy initiatives targeted at assisting geographical mobility of workers and jobs.

The simplest forms of competitive models of the labour market expect regional unemployment differentials to be temporary, since resulting wage differentials should produce labour market adjustments. First, surplus workers compete down wages in high-unemployment regions which enables resident firms to gain a higher share of markets at the expense of firms in high-wage, low-unemployment regions. Second, high regional wage rates in low unemployment regions induce an inflow of migrant or commuting workers seeking higher rewards for their labour and an outflow of 'foot-loose' firms seeking cheaper labour. Standard neoclassical theory anticipates that the potential migrant, worker or firm, will compare the net present value of the higher returns from moving to another area with the costs of moving. In practice labour mobility within a regional, national or international context will reflect the extent of marker failures, such as substantial re-location costs or government restrictions, which distort the adjustment mechanism and cause persistent regional differentials in unemployment and wages. In the following sections we do not attempt to duplicate available summaries and assessments of regional policy in the EU, such as in Artis and Lee (1994) and the collection of papers in Volume 11(2) of the *Oxford Review of Economic Policy*. Instead we concentrate upon migration issues leaving a more focused discussion of mismatch unemployment to Chapter 7. Initially we briefly examine the nature and persistence of regional differences in the EU and the extent of migration. We then discuss the determinants of that migration and introduce the important debate on the extent and speed of regional convergence in the EU. A discussion of the rationale for government intervention in this area precedes our consideration of national and EU policies to encourage greater locational mobility of workers and jobs.

5.5.2 *Evidence on migration in the EU*

To assess the significance of current rates of migration it is necessary to indicate the extent of national and regional economic inequality in the EU. Comparisons of national and regional economic performance are often made by using Gross Domestic Product per head and unemployment rates. As we saw in Chapter 1, national differences in GDP per head in the EU are large, with Greece and Portugal having a level less than half that of France, Germany and Sweden. These large international differences are replicated when we consider intra-national differences in GDP per head within the EU. In Belgium, France, Italy and Germany GDP per capita is nearly twice as high in the richest region as in the poorest region (Collier, 1994). Similarly, large differences are found in regional unemployment rates, Italy providing the extreme case where unemployment rates can be over five times greater in Sicily than in Lombardy. In general, these differences tend to persist over time in Europe, in contrast to Australia and the USA where regional unemployment rates are not correlated across recent periods (Layard *et al.*, 1991).

Given these large differences in national and regional economic conditions in the EU it is of interest to discover the extent of geographical mobility of workers. Most commentators conclude that the flows of workers between member states of the EU are surprisingly low and have been falling since the 1970s. Recent estimates suggest only about 300,000 a year or 0.1 per cent of total population (European Commission,

1993). Ireland is a notable exception to this overall picture, with Irish workers moving abroad effectively reducing her labour force by around 1 per cent a year in the early 1990s. Apart from Belgium and Luxembourg, no member country in 1991 had more than 3 per cent of their population of working age who were nationals from other EC countries. One note of caution needs to be made: most of the migration data available measure net flows in the EU and as such may be compatible with much larger gross flows in both directions. Labour Force Survey data indicate that males and younger people are more likely to move between member countries, with 70 per cent of the total movements being to Germany and the United Kingdom.

Internal migration rates differ markedly between European countries with about 4 per cent of the Swedish population changing their region of residence annually compared to around 1 per cent of the population in France, Germany, Italy and the United Kingdom. A problem with such simple comparisons of migration rates is that the geographic units of analysis may not be comparable. The high mobility rates in Sweden and Norway are in part a consequence of these countries measuring flows between a large number of relatively small areas and mile-for-mile mobility differences in Europe are much smaller. Internal migration rates fell during the 1970s and early 1980s in most European countries (OECD, 1994a), for example, Bentolila and Blanchard (1990) note how inter-regional labour mobility fell in Spain as her overall unemployment rose. Eichengreen (1993) estimated that the migration rate was about three times greater, and the elasticity of migration with respect to wage differentials about five times greater, in the US than in Britain or Italy. In Britain the Labour Force Survey indicates that overall about 11 per cent of people in employment change their address annually, of these about 85 per cent do not involve a change of region. The same source indicates that changes of region were more likely amongst the unemployed, the young, the highly qualified and those changing employers (Department of Employment, 1991).

5.5.3 *Migration decision-making*

We should be wary of any simplistic interpretation of this data since labour may be less mobile within European countries because there is less incentive to move. To analyse migration, reflecting actual or potential job-matching, within a neoclassical framework we need to utilise search and human capital theory developed earlier. The former argues that workers continually search for better job-offers or at least continually consider whether such search could be expected to yield net returns. This implies that workers accumulate knowledge of employment opportunities both within and outside their present local labour market. In comparing the net present value of offers outside with those within, workers should adjust for differences in commuting costs and the costs of having to move from the present market. Given that returns and costs vary between workers depending upon their personal and family characteristics the neoclassical model predicts differences in migration rates dependent upon these characteristics. For example, we can explain the observed negative relationship between age and migration, since for older workers any benefits of higher post-move earnings are discounted over fewer years. Other major determinants of the migration rate would be the costs of acquiring labour market information outside the local labour market, availability of higher wage offers and the costs of moving, largely associated with housing and resettlement costs.

Information costs for many workers are likely to rise steeply outside their local labour markets. Earlier the importance of informal informational networks in the labour market, especially for relatively unskilled and part-time employment, was established. These channels are unlikely to provide reliable information outside the local labour market and searchers have to rely on more formal and costly search methods. The observed higher mobility of technical and professional workers may in part reflect the dominance of more formal methods in job-matching in these labour markets. Information on job opportunities in such markets is either acquired on-the-job or job advertising is structured nationally in trade journals. High income workers may also avoid some of the capital and housing market imperfections which cause migration costs to be prohibitive for some lower income groups.

Whilst some of these predictions, such as age and educational qualifications, are consistent with our earlier summary of the nature of migration in Europe, empirical work has yet to confirm the importance of the central adjustment mechanism. Surveys of firms' locational decision-making, summarised in Armstrong and Taylor (1993), indicate that wage differentials are not a dominant determinant of location and that firms do not simply search for the most profitable locations for their plant and offices. Recent research has also questioned the conventional view of migration in Britain, namely that it made a minor, positive contribution to the equalisation of regional unemployment rates. This view reflected the observed net aggregate migration from depressed regions, Pissarides and Wadsworth (1989) confirmed that individual out-flow data presented a similar pattern in net terms. However, more disaggregated analysis by Hughes and McCormick (1994) of the British Labour Force Survey for the mid 1980s provided a different picture of migration. They concluded that, in net terms, manual labour is not migrating from the high unemployment regions: the observed small net migration from these regions is occurring amongst non-manual workers. Since regional unemployment differentials predominantly arise from the manual labour market, migration is unlikely to correct regional imbalances in the absence of relative wage adjustments.

The neoclassical theory of equalising net advantages suggests that regional differentials in labour market pressures and cost of living should generate a complementary adjustment mechanism featuring changes in regional wage rates. Labour-scarce regions should bid away workers from high unemployment regions by establishing a pay differential. Although earnings differ between regions Blackaby and Manning (1990) point out that part of this differential in Britain reflects differences in the characteristics of the regional work-force and hence overstates the potential returns from migration. Eichengreen (1993) reports that immigration within Britain responds positively to changes in relative wages, though the same model performs poorly for Italian regions and the estimated wage elasticity is much lower. Blanchflower and Oswald (1994) found that after controlling for workers' personal characteristics and regional fixed effects, there was an inverse relationship between the level of pay and the local unemployment rate in Britain over the period 1973 to 1990. One interpretation of this 'wage curve' is that it reflects costly migration and differences in the non-pecuniary attractiveness of regions. Hughes and McCormick (1994) in their study using data disaggregated by occupation, found that relative regional wage rates had the expected effect on both the decision to leave a region and the choice of destination.

This discussion indicates that the adjustment mechanisms of regional labour markets are far removed from those suggested by simple competitive models of the labour market. At best labour migration seems to be a slow and uncertain contributor to the elimination of regional imbalance within national economies. The poor performance of the simple competitive model reflects the importance of imperfections in markets caused by imperfect and costly information and institutional constraints upon their operation. When we acknowledge the existence of cultural, social and language barriers to international migration in the EU we should no longer be surprised by the size of current migration we have discovered. The contributions of trade and capital mobility to the elimination of regional imbalances have also been questioned in recent studies and this raises an important question of whether regional economies in Europe tend to converge in terms of their economic performance.

5.5.4   *Regional convergence in the EU*

The dominant model of economic growth is the neoclassical model developed in the 1950s; in essence the model formalises the adjustment mechanisms of a competitive economy we have already outlined. Its assumptions of competitive factor markets, diminishing returns to capital and costless transfer of technology taken together imply a global convergence of the level of GDP per worker. According to this model regions with initially low capital, and therefore low labour productivity, will have a high marginal productivity of capital and therefore high profit rates. The differing relative price of factors in high and low income regions generates a movement of capital and labour which produces convergence of per capita output. Barro and Sala-i-Martin (1991) were the first to provide a test of this proposition. They found evidence that the income per capita gap between rich and poor states in the US closed at about 2 per cent per annum. Labour migration played a relatively small part in this process, the main adjustment coming through migration of capital and the growth of high productivity employment in low income states as agriculture declined. Remarkably they also found a similar rate of convergence within individual European economies. Button and Pentecost (1993) and Armstrong (1994) reached similar conclusions, though convergence in the EU appears to be more rapid in periods of high demand and to have slowed down or been halted in recent years. The slight overall regional convergence which seems to have occurred in the 1980s appears to be due to convergence between the peripheral countries and the EU12, a feature which de la Dehesa and Krugman (1992) largely attribute to capital inflows in those peripheral countries. Dignan (1995) points out that in contrast within-country regional relativities in Europe have tended to diverge on average.

The tentative conclusion that slow convergence of regional economic performance in Europe seems to be the post-war norm is an important finding. Fears that greater

European integration would inevitably lead to cumulatively-widening regional disparities seem to be, so far, unfounded. However, the increase in European economic integration and world trade have increased the speed of structural change. It seems clear from the above discussion that market forces are, at best, very slow to produce the structural adjustment necessary to produce the full benefits of a more competitive European and world order. Regional policies therefore represent a potentially helpful response to these needs and we now discus their rationale.

5.6 Migration: policy issues

5.6.1 *Rationale for government intervention*

The extent and persistence of regional economic disparities in the EU are a source of social and political pressures for regional policies at the national and European level. The economic case for such policies rests upon the proposition that the marker failures which underlie the persistence of these disparities cause inefficiency. This inefficiency is reflected in excessive unemployment and inflationary pressures and a sub-optimal use of the economic infrastructure.

The unemployment argument for regional policy will be more fully considered in Chapter 7. It rests on the proposition that a reduction in regional inequalities will reduce mismatch and hence improve the speed and quality of job-matching in the economy. Such changes should reduce the overall level of unemployment and raise productivity levels. For a given rate of unemployment this change will also tend to reduce inflation, as the better balance between labour demand and supply eliminates some inflationary bottlenecks. This enables the economy to sustain cyclical upturns longer and should again raise overall average productivity levels. Finally, the reduction of regional economic inequalities may reduce overall congestion and pollution costs. The immobility of social overhead capital such as roads, airports and housing leads to their over-utilisation in rapidly expanding regions and relative over-capacity in declining ones.

In practice, EU regional policy has been significantly strengthened in recent years, though individual member countries differ greatly in their national policies and the resources which they allocate to them. As always the subsidiarity question arises: at what level should regional policy be designed and funded? The fact that European economic integration has itself been a significant cause of regional economic disparities does not by itself indicate that the appropriate response is for an EU regional policy. Instead, the arguments in favour of a role for the EU centre around the benefits of cohesion, co-ordination and the avoidance of unfair competition. Firstly, the European Commission has always been motivated by a desire to maintain social cohesion, a concept which seems to entail the maintenance of popular political support for the EU. The Commission's persistent fear seems to be that the structural changes required by increased economic integration may increase 'europhobia'. Secondly, the importance of the inter-relationships between member countries implies that the benefits we ascribed to national economies of a reduction in regional economic inequality also apply at the EU level. Accordingly, regional policy at a national level may be undermined unless it is co-ordinated across the EU. Agriculture and energy may be the obvious examples where the trade policy of the EU as a whole is the dominant determinant of the potential effectiveness of national policy in these sectors. Finally, the severity of regional imbalance differs between member countries, and is generally worse in those countries which have the least resources to fund regional policy, Greece and Ireland for example. Where individual member countries can use their own regional policies to bid for inwards investment, poor countries would lose out and regional imbalance worsens in the EU as a whole. If the relatively rich member countries wish to discourage increased migration within the EU there may be further mutual benefits from an EU policy aimed at reducing the incentives for workers to migrate from the poorer countries.

While these arguments suggest that regional policy should be at the EU level there are rival arguments which suggest that national level policies may be more appropriate. Financial transfers from rich to poor member countries are unlikely to be sufficient by themselves to fund regional policy, and domestic transfers require national political consensus. A uniform approach to regional inequality is unlikely to be efficient given that the nature of those problems differs between, say, Greece and Belgium. Over-centralisation is also likely to stifle innovation and reduce accountability. This suggests that whilst the EU has a fund-raising and co-ordinating role, member states should have the major role in financing, prioritising, and implementing regional policy.

Present EU regional policy originated from the 1989 reforms of the three structural funds: the European Regional Development Fund (ERDF), European Social Fund (ESF) and the European Agricultural Guidance and Guarantee Fund (EAGGF). These reforms set common objectives for these funds which included the development of backward regions, predominantly Ireland and the Mediterranean South, and regions in industrial or agricultural decline. EU financial assistance to the disadvantaged regions doubled in real terms between 1988 and 1993, at the same time the reforms concentrated these funds on regions deemed most in need. Previously up to 80 per cent of EU regional expenditure had been on infrastructure; the new policies gave a greater emphasis to supporting productive investment, particularly in smaller enterprises. This new emphasis also involved greater co-ordination with national regional policies, the new partnership being based upon the expectation that member states will provide complementary funding, the additionality criteria.

We have yet to identify the particular types of regional policy available. In the following section we concentrate upon the area of most relevance to our overall concern in this book: policies to assist migration.

5.6.2 *Policies to encourage geographical mobility of workers*

There are relatively few examples in Europe of large scale policies to promote labour mobility. In part this reflects the unimportance of migration in the adjustment process discovered earlier. More recently it is also a recognition of the overall depressed nature of the European labour markets and the consequential collapse of a rationale for a large scale labour-transfer policy.

In order to consider a move, workers need to acquire information not only on specific vacancies but on the general labour and housing market conditions in other locations. Such search costs are generally fixed and, as we have already argued, may preclude inter-regional search by unemployed or low wage workers. Given that the searcher has located and been offered a suitable job-offer acceptance requires that the expected net present value of additional earnings exceed the costs of re-location. The latter are usually interpreted as largely concerned with costs in the housing market, though some evidence also suggests that unsuccessful migration is often the result of psychic costs associated with an inability to adjust to changed social customs and norms. Housing market imperfections and government housing policies may have contributed to low migration rates in Europe, especially for manual workers in Britain. Housing subsidies to manual workers in the UK have traditionally taken the form of low rental public sector housing; administrative arrangements for allocation have often in practice discouraged regional movements. Whereas housing subsidies to non-manual workers are more likely to be through tax breaks to owner-occupiers which are transferable across regions.

The review by Charney (1993) suggests that policies have generally had little impact upon migration in Europe. In Britain policies to subsidise migration originated in the inter-war years, though post-war regional policies concentrated upon the movement of jobs rather than workers. The most important scheme was the Employment Transfer Scheme which provided assistance with removal costs to enable unemployed workers with poor local job prospects to accept job offers in other local labour markets. These policies create large displacement effects in a depressed national economy as unfilled vacancies disappear in even the prosperous regions. Reflecting this problem the schemes were reduced in scale and stringent regulations attempted to target the schemes on vacancies which were hard to fill. The British government showed more concern with countering imperfections in the housing market than with subsidising directly relocation costs for workers. The National Mobility Scheme was introduced in 1981 to allow easier movement for council tenants between local housing authorities and policies were adopted to de-control private rented accommodation.

The removal of all remaining statutory obstacles to labour mobility in the EU under the Single Market Initiative raised the issue of immigration from outside the EU. Two traditions exist within the EU. Germany has favoured a system of rotation where immigration is short-term and consists, predominantly, of the economically active. In contrast, in Britain and Sweden permanent immigration has been the norm, a consequence of which has been to adopt very restrictive eligibility requirements. Assessed in terms of the removal of mismatches the latter policy is likely to be inferior. The decline and ageing of Europe's labour force, the elimination of internal border checks and the potential of large inflows from Central and Eastern Europe have recently raised the profile of immigration issues in the EU. Zimmermann (1995) concludes that past immigration has been beneficial to European labour markets and calls for a unified policy of selective labour immigration.

5.6.3   *Regional policy*

This earlier discussion suggests that there are severe problems in generating sufficient migration to make a noticeable impact on regional mismatch. Any increase in migration would tend to widen other regional disparities and in particular raise congestion and social capital costs. In the post-war period such arguments led to a growth of regional policies aimed at moving employment opportunities, largely manufacturing, into depressed regions. A wide range of policies has been tried in Europe: tax incentives, employment subsidies, investment grants and location controls. EU policy has traditionally concentrated upon subsidies for investment in infrastructure whilst national policy has been more impressed by the advantages of direct incentives for inward investment. In the northern member states the dominant trend since the 1980s has been a decline in real expenditure on regional policy, a narrower range of incentives have been offered with grants replacing tax allowances and other incentives. Incentives have also been applied more selectively and in smaller target areas. In the UK and Denmark disillusionment with the impact of the constantly changing policy measures has led to their displacement by national policies targeted on unemployment and to make wage rates more reflective of local market conditions. The prospect that increased integration in the EU as a result of the Single European Market programme would create increased disparities between the core and peripheral regions prompted a major reassessment of EU regional policy. The Commission has placed greater emphasis upon human capital and technology in the poorest regions and real expenditure on Structural Fund spending doubled between 1988 and 1993. These priorities are consistent with the findings of de la Fuente and Vives (1994) that equalisation of schooling levels and effective stocks of public capital would reduce the dispersion of regional incomes in Spain by around one-third, in the long-run.

Evaluation of regional policy typically involves either econometric or survey techniques. In 1990 the European Commission conducted a cross-country study in which they consulted firms about the importance of regional incentives in determining competitiveness. Even where regional policy was deemed to have a positive influence, that influence was ranked relatively low compared to other determinants of competitiveness. Econometric studies rarely provide the means to properly evaluate policy, though Dignan (1995) concludes that regional policy has been particularly effective at encouraging footloose new investment projects to assisted areas, often generating a higher birth-rate of local firms. Whether these benefits exceed the costs is the key criterion of the efficiency of regional policy and few studies are available to provide answers to this question. This largely reflects the diversity of regional policies and the problems of identifying the net employment effects of those policies. As we noted in the previous chapter any subsidy will tend to produce secondary effects, such as displacement of non-subsidised employment.

Apart from the time consistency critique there have been a number of consistent criticisms of regional policy across Europe. Locational controls have been widely used in Britain and France to constrain private sector developments in the prosperous regions, but these controls have not always benefited the least prosperous regions. Whilst the financial incentives to relocate or concentrate new developments in the disadvantaged regions, policies favoured by Italy and the Netherlands, have often produced 'branch plant' problems or proved very expensive in terms of net jobs created. Branch plants are usually externally controlled and often have few intra-regional linkages to generate positive spillover effects on the local economy. They are also often technologically unsophisticated, creating largely unskilled employment linked to assembly and distribution. The popularity at various times, of creating growth centres and concentrating assistance on small firms has tended, respectively, to exacerbate intra-regional problems and create low technology and low-skill production.

5.7 Assessment

Whilst the EU has made great efforts to remove restrictions on the mobility of workers between member states in recent years, cross-border migration remains small and intra-national mobility of labour seems to have been in decline in Europe since the early 1970s. While the inequality of regional economic development in Europe generates some labour market inefficiency, there is little evidence that increased labour migration would be an effective response to this problem. There is some evidence that migration is more sensitive to relative wages than to relative unemployment and this may be important for governments to note when they design minimum wage and employment subsidy policies. The earlier discussion suggests that any policy to encourage migration through greater relative wage flexibility should target manual workers. However, increased migration cannot be a major part of the solution to regional imbalance, not least because it is the young, more skilled and more enterprising who move, leaving behind a still more disadvantaged region. In contrast, policies which are effective at reducing the national unemployment rate, particularly of the long-term unemployed, are likely to promote regional convergence. Similarly, the sort of policies which we discussed in the previous chapter to stimulate increases in the stock of skilled labour, if they were biased towards the disadvantaged regions would again be likely to promote more balanced regional growth and thereby generate advantages for the whole European economy.

Guide to further reading

Sapsford and Tzannatos (1993) provide a helpful introduction to job-search theory while Polachek and Siebert (1993) and Bosworth *et al.* (forthcoming) provide more rigorous treatments. Bendick (1989) raises some critical issues about the operation of a PES albeit in a US context. Eichengreen (1993a) provides an introduction to the importance of labour mobility in the context of European economic integration. Begg (1995) provides a useful introduction to labour migration in the EU whilst Dignan (1995) provides a review of EU regional policy. Johnson and O'Keeffe (1994) trace the recent development of EU law establishing the free movement of workers.

6   Discrimination

Under the heading of Social Policy, Article 119 of the Treaty of Rome lays down the principle that men and women should receive equal pay for equal work. The origin of this policy appears to have been the fear that the employment of 'cheap' women workers may distort competition between member states. More generally concern with labour market discrimination may reflect governments' pursuit of both the efficiency and equity objectives of an economic system. Labour market discrimination will cause resource misallocation, reducing the speed and quality of job-matching in an economy and causing output losses. On an equity basis, it can be argued that large persisting inequalities in opportunity represent a fundamental contradiction for any nation which believes in the economic and political virtues of a competitive economy. The burst of anti-discrimination legislation in Western economies in the decade following the enactment of the 1964 Civil Rights Acts in the US, was largely a reflection of this latter concern. Since the late 1970s the re-emergence of *laissez-faire* policies in the guise of deregulation has led to pressures in several countries to weaken anti-discriminatory legislation.

Only relatively recently have economists made systematic attempts to analyse the causes and effects of discrimination in the labour market. As we shall see current economic analysis is more suited to assessing the consequences of anti-discriminatory legislation than it is to identifying the origins of discriminatory behaviour. Largely studies have been concerned with sex and racial discrimination, though age, health, sexual behaviour, physical appearance and national origin may also stimulate discriminatory behaviour in the labour market. Although the earliest economic models of discrimination were of racial discrimination, the models and analyses adopted by economists are usually assumed to be equally applicable to other types of discrimination without significant adjustment.

In this chapter we concentrate upon discrimination by gender in European labour markets. Whilst the terms gender discrimination and sex discrimination are sometimes used interchangeably in the literature, the former term encapsulates in addition to *biological* differences, the *socially constructed* differences between men and women. Since labour market behaviour is influenced by perceived differences between the sexes, often reflecting norms regarding socially appropriate roles, we prefer to concentrate upon gender discrimination in our discussion. Our general neglect of racial and religious discrimination reflects the paucity of European studies in these areas. In this chapter we start by expanding our statistical examination of women in the labour market introduced in Chapter 1. We then examine the forces which are likely to change the economic status of women in European labour markets in the future. This is followed by an explanation of how the gender wage gap has been conventionally partitioned into discriminatory and non-discriminatory components and we note the problems associated with such divisions. This enables us to identify why defining, and therefore measuring, labour market discrimination is so difficult. After introducing the classification of different types of labour market discrimination, we review contemporary economic theories of discrimination. The present unsatisfactory nature of the economic approach is then established and the advantages of a more general social scientific approach are discussed. In Section 6.5 we summarise the empirical evidence of the extent and nature of gender discrimination in European labour markets and we also briefly summarise some of the results of investigations of racial discrimination. This is followed by an introductory review of potential equal opportunity policy instruments. The impact of the policies actually adopted by European governments is then assessed and the chapter ends with a summary of the key findings and a guide to further reading.

6.1   The current economic status of female workers

Women's status varies considerably across European countries, with a country's relative position changing with alternative measures of status. For example, women in Scandinavian countries have a high relative status in terms of participation and earnings ratio but are ranked less favourably in terms of occupational segregation and incidence of low pay. In order to clarify these differences in status we now outline some of the key characteristics of the labour market experience of European women. As we noted in Chapter 1, women constitute over 40 per cent of the labour force in most European countries. In recent years, countries such as Greece, Italy and Spain which had relatively low female participation rates have had amongst the highest rates of increase leading to a slow convergence towards the EU average, though Table 1.1 showed that female participation rates are high and rapidly rising in the Nordic countries.

Overall, the rise in participation rates primarily reflected an increase in the participation rate of females between 25 and 49 years of age, that is women of child-bearing and child-rearing age. Indeed, in recent years the fastest growth of participation has been amongst women in this age group with young children, though apart from Denmark and the UK marital status has a much greater effect on participation in the EU than having children (European Commission, 1993). Throughout the EU the probability of women participating in the labour force increases with the level of education, with rates for the highly-educated approaching those for males. Women whose partners are unemployed tend to have lower participation rates. Dex *et al.* (1995) show that cross-national differences in these rates can be explained by differences in unemployment benefit régimes. All these findings are consistent with our initial analysis of the causes of rising female participation in Box 2.1. Career interruption of mothers differs between European countries with the differences associated with extent of the provision of publicly subsidised child care provision (Joshi and Davies, 1992) and the generosity of parental leave entitlements (OECD, 1995). The length of career interruptions appears to have been decreasing over time, though in both the UK and France (Dex *et al.* 1993) those taking advantage of maternity leave to remain in full time work tend to be the more highly qualified.

Women are more likely than males to work part-time and to have shorter working-weeks when in full-time employment. Nearly 30 per cent of females work part-time compared with less than 5 per cent of males, though as we noted in Section 1.1.4 there are large differences in the relative importance of part-time working in the EU. Belgium apart, part-time working is most prevalent amongst women aged 50 and over, though across the EU 40 per cent of women with children work part-time compared to 30 per cent of married women without children. Denmark, Portugal and Greece were exceptions to this rule. Women are more likely to be in temporary employment and be unemployed than male workers, though Finland, Germany, Portugal, Sweden and the UK are exceptions to the latter tendency. Unemployment rate differentials by gender narrowed in the 1980s, except in Greece and Spain, though the ratio of female to male unemployment is higher in the EU 12 than in North America, Japan and Oceania (see Table 6.1). All of these findings indicate that the growth of flexible employment and segmentation has had a much greater influence on female workers.

An important determinant of female labour market behaviour is the pattern of household formation, fertility and household dissolution, and there have been radical changes in these patterns in recent decades. Elias and Hogarth (1994) compare trends in France, Germany and the UK and find a similar downward trend in fertility together with a strong increase in the divorce rate and a resulting decline in the average number of persons per household. The decline in marriage rates and rise in cohabitation have made household formation and dissolution rates difficult to measure by traditional proxies, though the latter is thought to have increased. These changes may have large effects on female labour market behaviour. For example, lone parents, overwhelmingly female, are particularly prone to unemployment with rates almost four times greater than those of husbands and twice those of wives. Also of importance in determining women's labour market experience is the division of domestic work among married or cohabiting couples. All time-use studies suggest that women in full-time employment do a larger share of total market and domestic work than do their full-time partners: this has been called the 'dual burden'. In Table

Table 6.1 The 'dual burden', division of work
(Hours per week, couples in German socio-economic panel, 1992)

	Wives			**Husbands**		
	Domestic Work	Paid Work	Total Work	Domestic Work	Paid Work	Total Work
Total population	53	15	68	21	34	55
Both employed	47	33	80	20	48	68
Husband employed wife not	71	0	71	17	48	65

Source: Gershuny (1995), Table 1.

6.1 we report evidence for German married couples in the early 1990s. Employed wives work an average of 12 hours per week more than their husbands and their share of domestic work is only slightly lower than that of wives who do no paid work. Gershuny's (1995) survey concludes that these results are consistent with those found in other single and multinational studies.

In all European economies women receive lower wages than men, but before we examine this gap we must emphasise that the existence of a gender wage gap need not indicate labour market discrimination since women may possess different labour market characteristics or tastes. Data on the gender pay gap in European countries are shown in Figure 6.1. These figures are gross hourly wage ratios for manual workers in manufacturing. It can be seen that the Scandinavian countries appear to have a small gender wage gap and Blau and Kahn (1992) have shown that a major reason for the relatively high status of women in these countries is their more equal overall wage distribution. When comparisons are made for full-time workers the gap has universally narrowed since the 1950s when the gap was around 40 per cent, though the gap remains larger for non-manual workers, and part-timers have not always improved their relative position. The improvement in the relative wage of full-time female employees in recent decades may be due to either a rise in the relative wage of females in a given employment or from favourable changes in either the distribution of female employees across occupations or of occupational wage differentials. We investigate the relative importance of these changes later. A detailed examination of pay gap trends shows that in countries with the highest ratios in 1980, Denmark, Italy and Sweden for example, female employees in industry experienced a decline in their relative earnings in the following decade. As can be seen in Figure 6.1, in most countries the gender pay gap was fairly static in the 1980s. Only in France, Greece and Norway was the gap appreciably closed. In Britain whilst women have improved their relative wages over a long period of time, these improvements have been concentrated into two periods. The first coincided with the implementation of the 1970 Equal Pay Act and the second occurred in the late 1980s.

In general, the gender wage gap is smaller for single women than for married women, smaller at younger ages and larger for those with children. De Luca and Bruni (1993) report that in Italy for equal seniority, males earn some 30 per cent more at the start of their career and about twice as much after 30 years, replicating the flatter age-earnings profiles of female workers in the UK illustrated in Figure 1.1. Not only do women earn less than men, their incomes tend to be more equally distributed. An important consequence of this feature is that women's earnings tend to reduce family income inequality, even though women in low-income households are less likely to work than those in better-off households. In terms of low pay, that is full-time women workers who receive less than 66 per cent of the median weekly wage, Germany and Spain have the highest incidence and France and Portugal the lowest. In Britain, women of ethnic minorities received roughly the same hourly wage rate as white women in 1994, whilst non-white men earned 89 per cent of white men's earnings.

Sex discrimination in the labour market may also be indicated by gender differences in the distribution of employment between industries and occupations. The gender mix of employment by industry is relatively stable, with the overall increase in

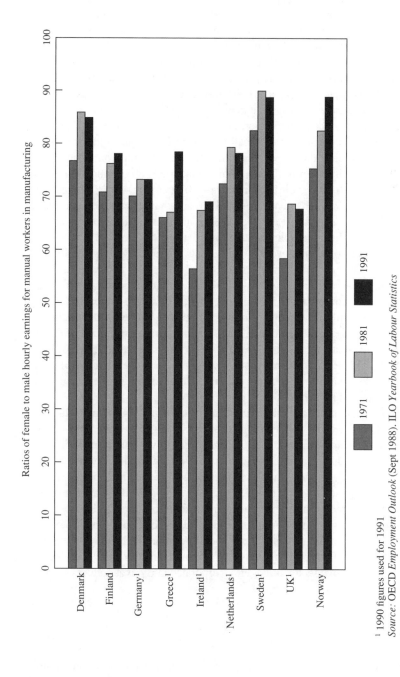

Ratios of female to male hourly earnings for manual workers in manufacturing

1971   1981   1991

[1] 1990 figures used for 1991
Source: OECD *Employment Outlook* (Sept 1988). ILO *Yearbook of Labour Statistics*

Figure 6.1 Gender pay gaps in Europe

female employment being largely caused by the growth of female-intensive industries and the decline of male-intensive manufacturing. Occupational gender mixes have undergone more changes, but women are still over-represented in service, clerical and social work and under-represented in administrative and manufacturing occupations and amongst the self-employed. As indicated in Table 6.2, a half of female workers in the UK are employed in just four occupational groups: clerical, secretarial, personal services and other elementary occupations. Rubery and Fagan (1994) found a similar trend towards a polarisation of female labour markets across all European countries. Whilst women have been increasing their share of higher level occupations, especially in the public sector, they have also been increasing their share of traditional female occupations and overall both occupational and industrial segregation appears to be highly stable over time. Sweden and Denmark have the highest percentages of women in either professional or managerial occupations (41 per cent and 37 per cent respectively) with Luxembourg (14.7 per cent) and Portugal (11.8 per cent) having the lowest. However, Portugal tends to have a low inequality in its gender occupational distribution along with Greece and Italy whilst Norway and the UK on this basis have the greatest amounts of inequality (OECD, 1988).

Around 55 per cent of female workers in the EU are employed in distribution, catering and other services (which includes health and education) compared with just 28 per cent of male workers. This occupational crowding of female workers in the EU prevails across member states regardless of whether activity rates are high or rapidly rising. Even within the female-dominated sectors women are still concentrated in the lower occupations such as clerical and administrative positions, whilst the skilled workers and senior professional, technical and managerial staff are still predominantly male. This tendency is also found within an occupation. In teaching, for example, women dominate pre-school and primary school teaching positions but have a much smaller share of higher education posts.

As a rule women are less likely to be members of trade unions and more likely to work in smaller firms. Green's (1993) analysis for Britain suggests that employers systematically provide less training for their female employees than for their male employees with otherwise identical characteristics. Women's tenure in their current employment is usually below that of males as previously indicated in Table 5.1, France has the highest average tenure for women (9.6 years) and the Netherlands the lowest (4.3 years). This high tenure in France has been attributed to their child care provision, including cheap high-quality pre-primary education child care for the 3–6 year olds (facilities which are also available for after-school and school holidays care). Also in France, rights to flexitime and taking days off when children are ill are provided by law for parents in the public sector and often incorporated into private sector contracts.

6.2 Prospects

Whilst women are set to continue to increase their share of total European employment in the next decade, many of the recent trends in labour market behaviour which

Table 6.2 Occupational segregation in the UK
(Percentage share of total employment, 1991)

	Male	Female	Ratio (Female-Male)
Corporate managers and administrators	11.0	5.9	0.54*
Managers/proprietors in agricultural and services	7.7	4.6	0.60*
Science and engineering professionals	4.2	0.6	0.14*
Health professionals	0.8	0.6	0.75
Teaching professionals	3.4	6.5	1.91
Other professional occupations	3.0	1.8	0.60*
Science and engineering associate professionals	3.1	1.1	0.35*
Health associate professionals	0.6	5.5	9.17
Other associate professional occupations	4.7	3.7	0.78
Clerical occupations	6.8	18.2	2.68
Secretarial occupations	0.3	9.6	32.00
Skilled construction trades	4.4	0.1	0.02*
Skilled engineering trades	7.7	0.2	0.03*
Other skilled trades	10.9	2.8	0.26*
Protective service occupations	1.8	0.4	0.22*
Personal service occupations	2.5	11.0	4.40
Buyers, brokers and sales representatives	2.8	1.1	0.39*
Other sales occupations	2.1	9.8	4.66
Industrial plant operatives	8.1	4.1	0.51*
Drivers and mobile machine operatives	5.6	0.4	0.07*
Other occupations in agriculture etc.	1.0	0.4	0.40*
Other elementary	7.4	11.7	1.58
Total	**100.0**	**100.0**	**1.00**

Source: Lindley and Wilson (1993).
* Indicates that they are significantly under-represented (a ratio < 0.67).

we identified in Chapter 1 may worsen the relative position of female and racial minority workers in Europe. Increasing flexibility is likely to reduce employment security still further for many of these workers. Part-time working in Britain has been found to be associated with not only low pay but also low status and occupational downgrading (Dex, 1992), though in France part-time work may be more frequently used to retain women who start families. Trends towards the decentralisation of bargaining and individualisation of employment contracts encourage the reintroduction of discrimination as managerial discretion is enhanced, whilst at the same time they threaten the consensus which has generated low gender wage gaps in Scandinavian countries. In addition the prospect of increasing wage inequality threatens to reproduce American experience, where gains generated by improvements in the work-related characteristics of female and black workers were offset by unfavourable changes in the pattern of pay.

These changes are influencing the labour market at a time when the prevailing political philosophy has been re-discovering the virtues of *laissez-faire* and popularist politicians have focused their attacks upon political correctness and championed 'traditional' values and social customs. Add to these ingredients historically high unemployment rates and increases in the fragmentation of society then we appear to have a particularly hostile environment for further improvements in the relative position of women and racial minorities. Forecasts of the occupational distribution of employment, such as those for Britain reported in Wilson (1994) and for other countries summarised in OECD (1994), suggest a strong tendency towards polarisation within the female labour market. Women with good educational qualifications and with continuity of employment are likely to increase the desegregation of high-ranking occupations, while those with lower qualifications and with intermittent participation and/or part-time working will further increase segregation in the occupations where women are already over-represented (Rubery and Fagan, 1994).

One consequence of the decline in the national institutional framework for pay determination has been the greater use of European law to mount campaigns about specific de-regulatory proposals of national governments. Thus, for example, British legislation which weakened unfair dismissal rights for short-tenured employees was successfully challenged in British courts on the basis of indirect discrimination effects, since female workers were less likely to secure the newly restricted employment protection.

6.3   Discrimination

6.3.1   *Defining labour market discrimination*

We have seen that a comparison of the average gross hourly wage rates of workers in Europe indicates that women receive about three-quarters of male earnings. Competitive theory developed in Chapter 2 would interpret this differential as indicating that females face a lower demand curve than males and/or have a lower supply curve. These possibilities are illustrated in Figure 6.2 which concentrates solely upon differences in wage rates. Wage rates for females, w_f, may lie below that for males, w_m, if women face a lower demand curve due to perceived or actual productivity differences or have a lower supply curve due to differences in investments in human capital or tastes.

Discrimination only occurs when some superficial personal characteristic is used in an attempt to restrict an individual's opportunity for economic or social advancement. To assume that the earnings difference, $w_m - w_f$, is solely attributable to discrimination would require that male and female workers are alike in every respect apart from gender. Differences in earnings which reflect differences in tastes or education and training, may not be discriminatory if such tastes reflect unconstrained choice and if equal opportunity for, and rewards from, educational investments exist. Earnings differentials may be broken down into a wage gap and productivity gap, with typically

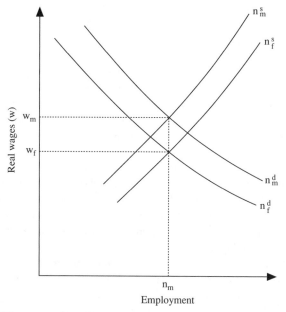

Figure 6.2 Possible causes of gender wage gaps

the former being utilised as an indicator of the size of labour market discrimination. Thus if women anticipate less attachment to the work-force then it may be optimal, given the arguments developed in Chapter 4, for them to invest less in education and training than males. An earnings gap would then be observable even for those with *ex post* equivalent tenure and experience. Similarly our analysis of search theory developed in Chapter 5, suggests that less attachment to the work-force may lower the reservation wage of women searchers relative to that of males since they anticipate wage gains from further search to be discounted over a shorter period. According to such human capital and search interpretations the existence of male-female wage differentials may be consistent with economic efficiency.

The human capital approach has been augmented by Becker (1985) who argued that the lower earnings of married women can also be attributed to the consequences of specialisation within family units. In this case even having the same participation rates would not eliminate male-female earnings differentials. Becker argues that given the existence of increasing returns from specialisation, families allocate time and labour market investments on the basis of comparative advantage. As we have seen, the division of household production between partners remains one in which women specialise in child care and housework, which are more effort intensive than leisure and other household activities, though households can alter the absolute effort-level of those tasks by purchases of durable goods like freezers and microwave ovens or arranging child-care. According to Becker, to adjust to their household specialisation women spend less effort on each hour of market work than do male partners working the same number of hours. The consequence of women seeking less demanding jobs than their partners is that they experience lower hourly earnings.

171

The traditional division of family labour may not reflect present comparative advantage, and if overall there is the same distribution of talents between sexes then ultimately the traditional divisions should break down in the face of economic inefficiency. Ultimately in half of the families males should specialise in household production and females in the others, yet we have seen that the evidence indicates only a weak trend towards less inequality in family specialisation. However, social customs are likely to interact with economic forces to perpetuate wage differentials; since women specialise in home production, families bias investment in human capital towards husbands and sons. Hence the comparative advantage of husbands in labour market production is transmitted to the next generation. Both the human capital and family specialisation approaches suggest that women are paid less because they are worth less. Their lack of human capital and desire for less demanding jobs makes their supply curve lower than that for males, and since they are less valuable to employers they receive lower wages. Any discrimination precedes employment in the labour market, as long as these differences in tastes and time allocation are not themselves a reaction to labour market discrimination.

It may be helpful to relate these arguments to our diagrammatic representation of human capital theory developed in Chapter 4. If women had the same tastes, family roles and faced the same labour market opportunities as men, then their supply and demand functions for investment in human capital would be identical to those of men and optimal investments would not differ. However, if role specialisation causes women to have less attachment to the labour market then they face lower rates of return on their investments as the benefits accrue over a shorter period and, as discussed in Chapter 5, their investment in labour market search is lower. Additionally depreciation of capital is faster off-the-job and career interruptions will therefore be associated with 'human capital atrophy'. On the supply side this difference may make financial institutions less likely to lend to female investors and/or induce firms to ask female trainees for a larger share of training costs. This raises the rate of interest which females have to pay for a given investment in human capital: the supply curve for females, S_f, lies above that for males, S_m. This situation is shown in Figure 6.3, and the optimal investment for female workers is accordingly at I^*_f which is a lower level than the optimum investment for males, I^*_m. Alternatively, labour market discrimination may cause women to receive lower returns on their investments. In this case D_f lies below D_m, women accordingly invest less and this causes relative female earnings to be even lower as a consequence. Here human capital effects reinforce labour market discrimination.

Differences in characteristics, motivations and tastes between different groups of workers make defining labour market discrimination extremely problematic. A conventional definition is unequal treatment in terms and conditions of employment for groups of equal productivity (Sloane, 1985), though such a definition requires discrimination to reflect forces on the demand side of the market only. Here, employers must exhibit a preference for one group of workers over another group with identical supply characteristics. Such employer preference may reflect their own prejudice or that of their existing workers, consumers or even government. However, such direct discrimination is likely to affect the investment decisions of those suffering discrimination.

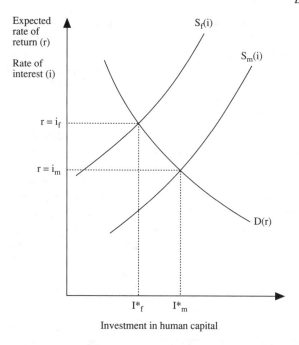

Figure 6.3 Differences in optimal investments in human capital

Figure 6.3 Differences in optimal investments in human capital

Discriminatory differences in earnings are in this case reinforced by supply-side adjustments to that discrimination, this is sometimes termed secondary or indirect discrimination. Here, the labour market discrimination experienced by women further lowers their expected rate of return on human capital investments. In terms of Figure 6.3, now females' demand curve for human capital investments lies below that of males, causing I^*_f to be even further below the optimal investment for males.

6.3.2 *Types of labour market discrimination*

When examining the economic status of different groups of workers it is initially helpful to identify three possible sources of discrimination:

  (i) differences in access to productivity-augmenting or screening investments, such as schooling;

 (ii) differences in occupational attainment for a given set of characteristics and tastes;

(iii) differences in pay and non-pecuniary benefits for given employment.

These three possible sources of discriminatory differentials are usually termed, respectively: pre-entry discrimination, employment or occupational discrimination and wage discrimination. Economists initially concentrated their analysis on wage discrimination, but if the major source of discrimination is due to experience before entering the labour market or to the crowding of particular groups into a small range

173

of occupations, then such analysis may have little policy relevance. Our concern with labour market discrimination means that we shall concentrate upon the last two forms of discrimination but we precede our review of the economic theory of post-entry discrimination with a brief discussion of pre-entry discrimination.

6.3.3   *Pre-entry discrimination*

If the source of the gender wage gap and occupational crowding of female workers is differences in tastes between male and female workers then Lazear (1991a) argued that there is neither a problem nor a remedy. However, tastes are not wholly innate and may reflect pre-labour market conditioning. Psychologists have established the gender differences in tastes and personality traits which socialisation induces and the potential importance of these differences in causing labour market inequality means that we can no longer treat preferences as exogenous. The gender differences in the distribution of domestic work may not only limit women's pre-entry investments in education but also affect their post-education human capital formation and further contribute to their lower occupational attainment.

Unequal provision of public funds may cause differences in the quality and quantity of schooling available to different groups, whilst different expected returns to investments, attitude to risk-taking, tastes or access to capital markets may cause differences in the demand. The extension of voting rights to women eventually ensured similar access to education, though non-market skills were often emphasised rather than vocational ones (domestic science instead of technical drawing). Table 6.3 shows educational statistics for European countries indicating that women are more likely to have attained only primary and lower secondary qualifications and are less likely to be university graduates, Belgium, Germany and the UK having particularly low female graduation rates. These differences are much larger among older age groups; among women aged 25 to 34 in many European countries the traditional gender differences have been reversed. Such comparisons may conceal gender differences in the quality of attainment and in the fields of study. For example, in the UK although current female school-leavers are significantly more likely to obtain high secondary education qualifications than males, they are less likely to have passes in mathematics and science. Bennett *et al.* (1992) found that female schooling behaviour in the UK did not correspond with the predictions of human capital theory, with too few staying-on in full-time schooling even though expected rates of returns were high. The OECD statistics show that in Europe women are less likely to graduate in science, engineering, law and business but more likely in medical and human sciences. Such striking differences are usually interpreted as reflecting predominantly sex-role socialisation rather than educational provisions, though evidence is lacking on the relative importance of these and other factors.

It was suggested earlier that women may demand a smaller quantity of schooling or prefer less vocational schooling because of differences in their life-cycle labour force participation. Role specialisation, both institutionally and biologically determined, may dissuade investments due to an expected accelerated depreciation of human capital. Women who expect to be absent from the labour force for long or frequent periods will choose occupations in which the costs of intermittent participation are

Table 6.3 Gender differences in educational attainment
(Proportion of women in total population, aged 25 to 64 years of age, having attained a specific level of education, 1992)

	Early childhood, primary and lower secondary	Upper secondary	Non-university tertiary	University
Austria	65	43		43
Belgium	51	47	60	34
Denmark	55	43	57	47
Finland	49	52	52	42
France	55	46	56	46
Germany	68	49	35	35
Greece[1]	52	53	40	40
Ireland	47	58	54	41
Italy	52	48		43
Netherlands	56	45		42
Portugal[1]	52	46	74	48
Spain	53	46	34	48
Sweden	47	50	54	46
UK	59	46	34	36
Norway	51	50	51	40

[1] 1991 data.
Source: OECD: *Education at a Glance* (1995a) Table C02.

lowest, typically those occupations with little on-the-job training. This human capital approach suggests that women will be under-represented in professional jobs partly as a consequence of their optimal investment strategy. Both this human capital approach and Becker's allocation of time model suggest that there will be marked differences in occupational attainment between married and single women without dependants. Such differences would reflect different investments in education and training and also different family care commitments, rather than be wholly attributable to discrimination in the labour market. However, different expected returns for different groups from the same investments may reflect anticipated occupational and wage discrimination and thus any attempt to estimate the relative importance of pre-entry discrimination is problematic.

6.4 Theories of labour market discrimination

6.4.1 *Taste/prejudice models*

Modern economic analysis of discrimination is usually assumed to start with Becker's study (1957) which utilised the tools of competitive economic analysis we developed in Chapter 2. He assumed that employers have a 'taste' or preference for discrimination and are prepared to sacrifice profits to exercise this taste. Employers, or more precisely managers, may therefore refuse to hire black or female workers in competitive markets, even where the value of their marginal product exceeds the marginal costs of hiring them. As a consequence white males and other favoured groups of workers receive higher wages than in a non-discriminatory market, since competing labour supply has been restricted. Black or female workers receive lower wages because they are viewed as inferior substitutes for white male workers of the same quality, and wage reductions are required to induce their employment.

If there is a dispersion of discrimination tastes between employers and identical production functions, employers who discriminate the least will have lower labour costs and therefore under competitive conditions should be able to eliminate more discriminatory firms from their market. Ultimately only non-discriminatory employers should survive; persisting discrimination is therefore indicative of non-competitive markets or severe transaction costs, reflecting the influence of government, trade unions or monopolists. In general, the same conclusions follow if it is employees or consumers, not employers, who exhibit a taste for discrimination. In this case assuming different groups are perfect substitutes for each other, competition should eliminate wage discrimination but the end result would be segregated workplaces. The Becker approach assumes that the taste for discrimination is independent of any benefits obtained from discrimination. Women or black workers are excluded because of the supposed deterioration in the work environment their presence creates, not because of any financial benefits from the restriction on the supply of labour. The source of this taste remains problematic and the Becker approach whilst providing a model of the effects of discrimination has nothing to say about the causes of discrimination.

A major problem for neoclassical analysis is that discrimination is a social not an individual phenomenon, it is a dominant group which discriminates against a minority group. Yet for discrimination to persist in competitive markets there needs to be some kind of group pressure which restricts the behaviour of employers. Explanations for such group pressures are generally inconsistent with a neoclassical framework, with its emphasis on an individualist choice-theoretic approach. Akerlof (1976) assumed that individual utility depends upon prestige as well as consumption levels, and that prestige depends in part upon compliance with social customs. Believing that others are racialists and male chauvinists in his model can make it rational for an individual worker or firm without such tastes to comply with such labour market behaviour. Alternatively since discrimination is always practised against minorities, the taste for discrimination may in fact be a taste for dominance and power which directly yields utility.

6.4.2   *Imperfect information/statistical theories*

An alternative approach to the analysis of discrimination, still within the framework of competitive analysis, is to consider the consequences of employers having imperfect information about an applicant's potential productivity. The increased use of line managers in the recruitment and selection of employees in European companies makes the possibility an important one. Arrow (1972) and Phelps (1972) consider cases where it is costly to acquire such information; in these markets employers will wish to find a proxy to predict the employability of particular applicants. Race and sex being easily observable characteristics, applicants may be considered to have the mean productivity of previous workers hired with these characteristics. If firms, for example, have in the past observed that on average white males had the highest productivity or have subjective beliefs to that effect, statistical discrimination can occur against the higher productivity female or black applicants. Figure 6.4 illustrates this situation; employers believe that the mean, realised productivity of male applicants, P_m, lies above that of female applicants, P_f. Accordingly the employer prefers male applicants where possible and the shaded area represents low-productivity male workers who may experience positive discrimination and high-productivity female workers who suffer negative discrimination.

Employers may react to the anticipated lower productivity of women or black workers by offering employment only at a lower wage. Where there are restrictions on the payment of lower wages then such applicants may be screened-out completely. Statistical discrimination against women may also exist if employers view pregnancy, childbirth and child-rearing as imposing direct and indirect costs upon themselves. Women may be viewed as less productive during pregnancy and discontinuities may occur with mothers having to be replaced during maternity leave. Even if such beliefs are warranted then discrimination occurs against women employees who do not have children since they are unable to signal this characteristic to their employers. Black or women workers will only be hired on equal terms to white males in industries and occupations where their 'inferior' characteristics are unimportant to productivity. This leads to occupational crowding in employments with low on-the-job training and to a further depressing of the relative wages in those occupations.

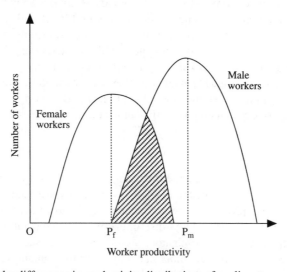

Figure 6.4 Gender differences in productivity distributions of applicants

If the stereotype is accurate, such as a belief that women live longer, then there need be no inter-group discrimination in aggregate. Initially economists believed that this form of statistical discrimination was efficient, since employers were making use of a low cost proxy to aid decision-making in a world of imperfect and costly information. If such behaviour is efficient then any attempt to eliminate statistical discrimination by legislation would reduce national output. However, when supply-side responses, both in participation and human capital investments, to this form of screening are considered it is no longer clear that the use of the screen, even when it is based upon accurate stereotypes, is welfare improving. Favoured groups will supply too much labour and invest above their socially optimal level whilst disfavoured groups under-invest and their lifetime labour supply may be below their optimal level.

We have so far assumed that the stereotypes utilised by employers are accurate and continually updated, but where labour markets are experiencing rapid changes stereotypes may become outdated and erroneous discrimination can occur. For example, employers may not distinguish between immigrant workers and those born locally. If the observed low productivity of immigrants was due to the limitations of their native country's educational or training system, then race is no longer an appropriate stereotype when workers are predominantly locally educated and trained. Such prejudice or erroneous discrimination should not persist in the long run in competitive markets, as firms with accurate stereotypes will have a competitive advantage and displace those with obsolete stereotypes. Tight labour markets which force employers to experiment with groups not normally hired for particular occupations would increase the speed of adjustment of stereotypes.

'True' stereotypes while reflecting employers' previous experience are also likely in practice to reflect and perpetuate self-fulfilling expectations. If employers only hire female or black workers for dead-end jobs believing them to have high turnover rates, then the behaviour induced by such tasks will conform to that anticipated by employers. Hence where productivity is job-based, stereotypes may be self-perpetuating. Alternatively because potential employers find it difficult to ascertain the quality of minority workers, current employers may be reluctant to promote them since to do so provides a signal to competitors. Milgrom and Oster (1987) argue that talented women and black workers may therefore get hidden by their employers, receiving lower pay and status than other workers of similar ability. In this case competition fails to eliminate discrimination, but unlike the Becker model the process is costly to society as job-matching is inefficient for these 'invisibles'.

6.4.3 *Monopsony*

So far we have failed within a competitive framework to provide an explanation for the persistence of inter-group discrimination. It may be that we need to introduce elements of monopoly in product markets or monopsony in labour markets. Monopolists are not threatened by lower cost non-discriminatory firms penetrating their markets and therefore can exercise discriminatory prejudices without such a restraint. It has also been argued that women are more likely to suffer from monopsony than males. Gender earnings gaps suggest that the male partner's work location dominates locational decisions and that women with male partners will therefore tend to be less geographically mobile and to search and commute over smaller distances. Particularly in less urban areas, many women will face a small number of potential employers who can therefore exercise their monopsony powers to reduce wage offers to this group. Where racial minorities are heavily concentrated in specific locations then monopsony may also reduce their relative earnings. As discussed in the previous chapter, women and racial minorities may also face higher search costs since they have poorer contacts with the informal networks providing labour market information. This results in a greater immobility and makes their labour supply more inelastic, the profit-maximising monopsonistic firm will therefore offer them lower wage rates than those offered to white male workers.

6.4.4 *Non-competitive approaches*

The models discussed provide little insight into either the origins of labour market discrimination or its persistence; some would argue that this failure reflects the need to integrate sociological and psychological elements into models of discrimination. Alternative economic approaches start from the weaknesses of competitive forces, presuming that firms' employment policies are largely independent of market conditions: 'insiders' can resist competition for good jobs by 'outsiders'. Wage discrimination will therefore be a feature of firms with structured internal labour markets since competitive forces are unable to undermine discriminatory labour market practices in primary labour markets. Discrimination in the primary labour market will reflect managers' own social attitudes and an awareness that their present employees would resent and resist any changes in the customary divisions of jobs. In such conditions childhood socialisation, sex specific schooling or biological and anthropological differences give rise to a socially-dominant division of market/non-market work between the sexes. Employers, in allocating applicants between and within primary and secondary labour markets, merely reflect such social customs.

In this framework, employers with established internal labour markets hire workers on the basis of future productivity. Employers reflecting social custom may assume that female entrants to the labour market have a lower long-term commitment to the labour force or that black workers have higher turnover rates and therefore exclude both groups from the structured internal labour market. Alternatively firms may hire on the basis of performance in tests, and these tests may be gender or culturally biased, leading to black or female applicants being screened out. Statistical discrimination or subjective judgements by personnel staff also prevent entrance to primary sector jobs by minority applicants. Because of vertically structured internal labour markets in this sector, there is low mobility between the primary and secondary sectors of the economy. Thus black entrants unable to initially gain a 'good' job enter the secondary sector where they experience high job turnover, frequent unemployment and experience little on-the-job training. Their work record accumulated in the secondary sector will prevent their transfer to 'good' jobs, the stereotype is confirmed and discrimination is perpetuated. Given that firms rarely hire large quantities of new workers and are usually making marginal adjustments to their work-force, the preferences of their existing employees will also influence hiring decisions. Where employees are unwilling to work with black or women workers, employers wishing to reduce turnover or x-inefficiency, may acquiesce and the workplace remains segregated. Segregation in the primary labour market may also result from the use by employers of their current work-force for recruitment. Hiring from amongst the friends and relatives of existing workers often sustains the existing racial and gender composition of the work-force.

A more radical version of this approach attributes this segmentation of the labour market to employers' desire to fragment their work-force and so reduce their bargaining power. In contrast to the work of Becker, now employers' tastes for discrimination are induced by the expectations that such tastes are profitable. Managers may wish to integrate the workplace, whilst segregating by occupation. The resulting tension between majority and minority employees will reduce their cohesiveness and therefore their bargaining power. This 'divide and rule' strategy will tend to lower wages of both groups, again benefiting profitability. If white or male workers interpret the low wage as reflecting the competition from black or female employees then divisions amongst the work-force may continue to grow. Unions may become the agents of the majority workers and in alliance with employers strengthen employment and wage discrimination against minority workers. This approach views discrimination as just one feature of the inherent conflict between capital and labour, elimination of discrimination requiring fundamental reforms or replacement of the capitalist system.

6.5 Measuring labour market discrimination

6.5.1 *Empirical studies of gender discrimination*

Most researchers have estimated wage discrimination as a residual, rather than directly testing a specific model of discrimination. Whilst this may be understandable given the weaknesses of conventional economic models of discrimination it represents an unusual methodology in economics and means that most empirical studies provide, at best, indications of the size of discrimination rather than the underlying causes. Most attempts to measure the extent of discrimination start from the Mincer earnings function introduced in Chapter 4. This is estimated by means of a cross section regression on data for individual workers. Separate regressions are then estimated for each group, so allowing discrimination to affect both the intercept of the earnings equation and also the coefficients on personal work-related characteristics. It is possible to break down earnings differentials between groups into three sources: differentials resulting from different personal characteristics; different coefficients on those characteristics, and different intercept terms. The latter two terms are often taken as the appropriate measure of discrimination, Appendix 6.1 outlines the conventional methodology.

An introductory review of the many problems with such estimation methods can be found in Sloane (1985). The reliance on applying earnings functions to cross-sectional data has led to a tendency to concentrate upon the average discrimination faced by a particular group. The most recent work suggests that there are large differences in the discrimination faced by individual members of groups and that more disaggregated studies are required even when we are only concerned with providing an overall measure of the effects of discrimination. Economists have also generally avoided the issue of the efficiency losses resulting from discrimination, implicitly assuming that their estimates of the private costs of discrimination proxy social costs.

Most of the early studies were American and they suggested that at least half of the actual earnings gap in the US could not be attributed to differences in work-related characteristics. Estimates of the extent of discrimination were much lower when actual rather than potential labour market experience was included for female workers and adjustments made for gender differences in occupational structures. Recently, O'Neill and Polachek (1993) attribute up to a half of the narrowing of the US gender gap in the 1980s to improvements in women's work-related characteristics and the remainder to increases in the returns to women's experience and the decline in blue-collar workers' wages and other influences. British estimates of sex discrimination from earnings functions have usually produced broadly similar results. Their findings are often interpreted as indicating that female wages could be about 10 per cent higher if discrimination was eliminated. The range of estimates provided by British studies is still fairly wide. In part this reflects two particular problems faced by empirical work: selectivity bias and intermittent participation. Selectivity bias follows if employed women in the chosen sample possess some unobserved characteristic which makes work especially remunerative to them. In this case the sample selected are a biased sample of the female population as a whole and the analysis will underestimate discrimination faced by the average woman. Intermittent participation is an important characteristic of the female labour supply; compared to a representative woman without children, a mother of two children would on average lose about eight years of employment in Britain, ten years in Germany, two in Sweden and none in France (Joshi and Davies, 1992). The higher incidence of part-time working amongst mothers increases these differences in terms of full-time equivalent years of employment. These differences suggest that using a conventional imputed work experience proxy might lead to an overestimation of discrimination. Wright and Ermisch (1991) utilise corrections for both sample selection bias and actual experience in their study of the UK wage gap. They conclude that about 17 per cent of the 1980 gender wage gap can be explained by the inferior labour market characteristics of females and a further 25–30 per cent by intermittent participation (home time). This leaves around half of the wage gap which could be attributed to direct discrimination, equivalent to about one-fifth of women's wages. Callan and Wren (1994) report broadly similar results for married women in Ireland, with about half of the total wage gap of 20 per cent being unexplained by differences in productivity-related characteristics, whilst in Britain the average gender wage gap appears to have significantly closed during the late 1980s. This seems to have been due to changes in the characteristics of female workers, while increasing wage inequality has restricted the improvement in women's relative earnings.

The asymmetric effects of marriage on male and female earnings is well established empirically (Sloane, 1994). Whether the boost to male earnings which marriage appears to provide is a reflection of specialisation or discrimination against single men remains to be resolved. For females more recent work suggests that the source of adverse effect of marriage on earnings appears to be linked to the presence of children. Waldfogel (1995), in her study of young British workers, finds that mothers' gender wage gaps are over two and a half times greater than those of non-mothers. She favours an interpretation of this family gap which emphasises human capital and work–family conflicts. Dolton and Makepeace (1987) find that although participation falls with marriage, earnings are not separately influenced in the absence of children. Their study of the graduate labour market finds a range of estimates for residual earnings differential of between 4 and 25 per cent between the sexes. Such a wide range suggests another reason why it is unwise to select a single estimate of discrimination: such estimates are not only highly sensitive to specification but also to sample selection.

Terrell (1992) concluded that in most countries it was the difference in the return to an additional year of schooling or experience rather than differences in their levels which explained the majority of the gender earnings gap. While the use of earnings functions can give some insights into the size of discrimination, studies utilising this technique tell us little about the nature of that discrimination. Non-competitive approaches emphasise the importance of persistent gender segregation and more work has been undertaken in this area in recent years. Miller (1987) using very broad occupational groups found that the presence of occupational segregation contributed little to the size of the gender wage gap in Britain. Other studies have not always supported this conclusion; Terrell (1992) concludes that there is now much agreement internationally that much of women's inferior position is due to occupational crowding. For example, Dolton *et al.* (1989) found that far fewer female graduates entered business than would be expected from the application of the male occupational choice model with more entering public administration. Whether such segmentation reflects employment discrimination or taste differences cannot be considered by aggregate studies, though longitudinal studies such as Watts and Rich (1993) suggest that the pattern and extent of industrial and occupational segregation in the UK have been remarkably stable over time.

For occupational crowding to be a significant cause of earnings differentials, predominantly female jobs must either be under-valued by the labour market or female workers are under-employed in those jobs. Few disaggregated studies of discrimination are available though Jenkins (1994) suggests that discrimination in Britain varies significantly with the level of education and between regions. Jones and Makepeace (1994) found in their study of an internal labour market that women had to meet more stringent requirements to gain promotion to a specific grade than did men. Millward and Woodland (1995) utilising the 1990 Workplace Industrial Relations Survey concluded that high female concentration, both within occupational groups and within workplaces, depresses wage levels in those jobs substantially. Controlling for a wide range of explanatory factors they find that in establishments where the unskilled workers are largely men, they earn nearly 30 per cent more than they would if they were mostly female. Dolton and Kidd (1994) found that the gender wage gap of 23 per cent for their sample of graduates was mostly due to intra-occupational wage differences which could not be explained by differences in observed characteristics, with only a quarter of the gap being due to inter-occupation effects. There now seems general agreement that differentials within occupations are more important than differentials between occupations, suggesting that discrimination in occupational recruitment may be more important than occupational crowding and other types of discrimination (Sloane, 1994). Conflicting results can be partly explained by the sensitivity of the relative importance of intra and inter-occupational effects to the level of occupational aggregation.

Non-participation appears to account for a major part of the gender differences in wage levels and employment structure. It is married women who experience much less upward mobility and have tended to move into the low status, and often part-time, occupations left by more upwardly mobile groups (Greenhalgh and Stewart 1985). Only about half of women returning to the labour force after child-rearing retained their previous occupational status, such downwards mobility being more common in Britain than in the US. Wright and Ermisch (1991) estimated that each year at home lowered the wages of women when they returned to work by between 1 and 1.5 per cent, whilst Rekko *et al.* (1993) produced very similar results for German women workers, though Sprague (1994) found larger returns to actual labour market experience.

Our review of empirical evidence suggests that significant gender discrimination can still be found at the beginning of the 1990s, twenty years after the passing of equal pay legislation. Segregation seems to be a key element in the explanation for such differentials, particularly inter-establishment segregation, whilst intermittent participation seems to be important in determining low incomes of mothers. Our survey has been heavily dependent upon British sources and there is some limited evidence of important differences between European countries with Rekko *et al.* (1993) finding that the rate of return to education is much higher for German women than for Dutch women, whilst the effect of potential experience is much greater for Dutch women. Blau and Kahn (1992a) conclude that labour market institutions, particularly the degree of centralisation of wage-bargaining, are an important determinant of international gender wage gaps, and recent increases in the gender gap in Denmark and Italy have been attributed to more decentralised bargaining (Smith, 1992 and Bettio and Villa, 1993).

6.5.2   *Empirical studies of racial discrimination*

American studies indicate that once productivity characteristics have been adjusted for, the residual discrimination against black males is of the same dimensions as that against females. Dickens and Lang (1987) found that a substantial proportion of this differential was explained by the concentration of black workers in secondary sector employment with the differential disappearing in the primary sector. Because racial minorities account for only a small proportion of the economically active population in European countries, less than 6 per cent in Britain for example, aggregation of different groups into a non-white group is usually necessary with existing data sources.

Most early British studies used data in which first generation immigrant workers dominated and education and training dissimilarities between their country of birth and Britain may have distorted the earnings functions. Gazioglu and Sloane (1994) found some evidence that sons of immigrants were treated more favourably by the labour market than their fathers. The diversity of the non-white population causes further problems in empirical work. In the UK, for example, the unemployment rate amongst workers from a Pakistani and Bangladeshi background is double that for those from an Indian background and there are as large differences in the pattern of female employment between minority ethnic groups as there are between minority and majority ethnic groups (Bruegel, 1994).

Niesing *et al.* (1994) consider the lower probability of ethnic minorities being employed in the Netherlands. They estimate that only about half of the difference between their probability and that of the indigenous Dutch can be explained by differences in work-related characteristics. Estimates of discriminatory earnings differentials of around 10 per cent have been common in British studies of racial discrimination, though some of this differential may reflect inferior quality or inappropriate education received in the country of birth. Kee (1995) concluded that the wage gap between natives and immigrants in the Netherlands was largely due to differences in schooling acquired in the Netherlands, rather than discrimination. Stewart (1983) concluded that the main source of discrimination against ethnic workers was in their lower level of occupational attainment for any specified education and experience. There is evidence that low occupational attainment is now a smaller source of discrimination for young ethnic workers in Britain than it was in the early 1980s (Evans and McCormick (1995)). Blackaby *et al.* (1994) examine the increase in the racial earnings gap in the 1980s and conclude that it was predominantly due to an increase in the higher returns which whites received on their work-related characteristics. As in the US the increase in wage inequality also tended to worsen black inequality, though additionally Britain's higher levels of unemployment disproportionately affected black workers.

6.6 Policy implications

On the basis of economic efficiency considerations it may appear that the target of equal opportunities policies should be to produce a gender wage gap and an occupational distribution of employment by gender which reflects the distribution of skills and experience across male and female workers. However, for this to be an appropriate target the distribution of skills and experience should reflect the choice of workers unconstrained by discriminatory behaviour of employers and other workers. In addition, how far we may wish to promote policies which compensate women for the constraints on their labour market behaviour generated by their current role in social reproduction remains a matter dependent upon value judgements.

The conventional case for specific equal opportunity, as opposed to anti-poverty, policies in the labour market rests upon the belief that earnings differentials between groups in society do not exclusively reflect differences in productivity-influencing characteristics or innate tastes. It presupposes that different groups within the labour market experience different treatment purely because of their membership of that group, a presupposition in favour of which we have found strong evidence. Whether such discrimination is inefficient remains problematic to competitive theorists. The disfavoured group are under-employed and the favoured group over-employed as a consequence of discrimination, and potential output is therefore reduced. However, neoclassical economics takes tastes as given, hence if tastes (prejudices) are a fundamental cause of discrimination then inefficiency cannot be assumed. Since conventional economic analysis does not distinguish between the ethical merits of different tastes then neoclassical economics provides no clear support for anti-discriminatory policy.

If equal opportunity policies are desired in European labour markets then there remains the issue of the appropriate level at which those policies should be implemented. The diversity of national wage determination systems, work organisation and payment practices in Europe outlined in Chapter 1 would seem to preclude on subsidiarity grounds reliance upon pan-European policies. Two examples may help to illustrate this argument. Firstly, Denmark, Greece and Portugal have a wage-fixing system where occupational bargaining dominates and in which comparisons between occupations in a firm or industry are not directly made. Hence a policy designed to reduce the gender earnings gap in these countries would require a different format to those designed for other EU countries where bargaining is at the firm or industry level. Secondly, Rubery and Fagan (1994a) report that whilst seniority pay appears to have narrowed gender pay differentials in Italy, such payments in Germany and the UK have had the opposite effect due to the greater importance of career interruptions in these two countries. We conclude that the diversity of payment structures and systems in Europe means that the form which discrimination takes differs between countries, thus necessitating the design of detailed policies at the national or subnational level. Though social cohesion objectives may require member states' legislation to adopt a uniform objective.

Our earlier discussion indicates that the targets of equality of opportunity and equality of outcome are only tenuously linked in the labour market. Policies aimed at establishing equality of opportunity whilst maintaining current family structures and division of labour patterns will not achieve equality of outcome. There are several possible causes and forms of discriminatory behaviour, and if it is desired to reduce such behaviour then the appropriate policy response should be determined by the relative importance of the contributory causes and the specific market and institutional environment. A particular policy measure which is an appropriate response to one type of discrimination may only reinforce discrimination when additional causal factors are in operation. For example, if measures are introduced to eliminate pay discrimination within occupations, this will tend to cause additional employment discrimination as more employers introduce discriminatory hiring practices to segregate their work-force. What is required is a 'policy mix', where complementary policies are combined in a manner which reflects the relative importance of the various sources of discriminatory behaviour. In this section the most common policy responses are introduced and related to the causes of discrimination. We organise this discussion around five types of policies: increased competition; compensatory public finance; statutory maternity and parental leave; intervention into wage-fixing and intervention into hiring decisions.

6.6.1 *Increased competition*

The taste and statistical theories of discrimination suggest that inter-group discrimination should be undermined in the long run by competitive forces in the labour market. As Polachek and Siebert (1993) state in 'an economy devoted to free enterprise the problem of unequal opportunity cannot exist' (page 171). According to this general approach anti-discriminatory policies require the strengthening of competitive forces in the product, labour and capital markets. Market forces should force discriminating employers out of the market, and monopoly and restrictive practices legislation and the de-regulation of capital markets all should assist this process. In addition any policy which increases labour mobility should reduce the extent of occupational crowding and monopsony in the market and therefore reduce the potential for discrimination. Measures to reduce restrictive practices of employers and trade unions, to reform housing markets and reduce commuting costs will also assist the undermining of discriminatory labour market practices.

From this viewpoint much of the existing equal opportunity legislation is ineffective and inefficient. Equal employment opportunities policies are superfluous if competitive markets have been established. Policies which penalise employers on the basis of their inequality of treatment of different groups of workers are misplaced, since competitive firms only respond to differences in productivity or tastes amongst their work-force. Inequalities of outcome in this competitive framework only reflect differences in worker tastes, reflecting innate and socially-conditioned preferences. Only in the public-sector and amongst not-for-profit organisations can direct anti-discriminatory measures be countenanced, in these sectors competitive forces cannot provide the necessary constraint on discriminatory behaviour.

Whilst increased competition should increase the costs of acting on prejudice or on incorrect information, it is not clear that even within the neoclassical approach this tackles the underlying cause. If there exists a preference for discrimination which results from a lack of contact between groups, increased competition may not reduce segregation significantly, similarly increased competition is also unlikely to break down discrimination resulting from social custom. Non-competitive approaches suggest that given the ability of internal labour markets to isolate themselves from external market forces, the effects of policies designed solely to increase competition are likely to be small (even in the long run). Though within the general competitive philosophy there are two further policies which may overcome some of these problems: common systems of grading and the extension of analytical job evaluation techniques. A national system of job grading may provide specific groups of workers with some protection against arbitrary grading by employers and also assist in the elimination of inaccurate stereotypes. In Germany, grading is often based upon vocational qualifications whilst in Belgium grading schemes are more usually based upon

186

levels of education. France and Italy have integrated grading schemes in many sectors which prevents some of the diversity of gradings for similar workers which can be found in countries such as the UK where no widespread system exists. Formal job evaluation schemes, particularly analytical ones, might be an effective way of speeding up the process by which competition eliminates discriminatory behaviour. Ghobadian and White (1987) found some evidence that the utilisation of such schemes reduced the extent of gender bias in the setting of pay in Britain.

6.6.2 *Compensatory public finance*

As discussed in Chapter 3, in certain situations it may be efficient for the government to directly finance and/or produce goods and services that the market fails to provide. In Chapter 4 we presented the argument that where poverty, imperfect capital markets or false discounting of expected returns have caused certain groups to under-invest in human capital accumulation, then government could provide training opportunities. Where social customs dictate a division of labour in which women are largely responsible for child care, one response could be for governments to provide day-care facilities or, as in the US, provide tax concessions for child care expenses when both parents are working. Such policies would tend to raise the relative income of mothers, but are not necessarily anti-discriminatory unless we argue that there are market failures in the provision of child care facilities or that re-entrants are penalised by income losses which are excessive in comparison to their lower on-the-job training and depreciated human capital. The specific form of any tax concession is important since tax allowances for child care tend to give the greatest support to those on the highest incomes, whilst the British policy of stimulating child care provisions by tax concessions for employer-based schemes distorts both the labour and child care markets.

Joshi and Davies (1992) and Gustafsson and Stafford (1994) conclude that differences in child care policies seem to be a major determinant of the international differences in the labour supply of women with young children. Whilst in Sweden and Denmark there is little difference in women's employment rates regardless of the number and age of any children they have responsibility for. In Britain, Germany and the Netherlands mothers with young children have much lower activity rates. In Ireland and Spain all mothers with children of school-age have much lower employment rates. Joshi and Davies (1992) estimated that a British women would forgo 57 per cent of her potential earnings after age 25 by embarking upon the employment and earnings profile associated with a two-child family. Their corresponding estimates for Germany, Sweden and France were 49, 16 and 1 per cent respectively. Whilst the short school day in Germany and Britain restricts the labour supply of mothers, child care provision appears more important in the explanation of these differences. The extensive French system of support to families with children is designed to promote the work effort of mothers by switching support to subsidised child care when the youngest child reaches 3 years of age. Hanratty (1994) finds that this policy produces a powerful incentive for women to enter or remain in the labour force. Changing public attitudes to single parents has focused attention in North America and Europe on policy initiatives aimed at increasing labour market participation of this group. Since for most single mothers child care costs are relatively high compared to potential income, proposals have concentrated upon introducing child care assistance programmes as part of a poverty reduction programme. Kimmel (1995) in her study of American single mothers found that assistance with child care expenses was highly effective in encouraging their welfare-to-work transition. Tax and benefit systems may themselves sustain social customs which encourage the intermittent participation of mothers with partners. Together they may produce a high marginal tax rate on mother's income and therefore distort household's allocation of time between market work, non-market work, leisure and search. Empirical evidence suggests that the substitution effect of a rise in married women's wages dominates the income effect, accordingly any alteration in their marginal tax rates is likely to have a large impact on their supply of labour.

Becker's taste model of discrimination provides a rationale for a tax-grant policy to influence wage-fixing and hiring decisions. A tax on employing members of favoured groups could provide revenue to subsidise employment of discriminated workers, similar policies have been designed to favour the long-term unemployed and are discussed in Chapter 7. In Norway employment subsidies of 25 per cent of wage costs for up to six months are available for employers taking on women (or men) in non-traditional jobs, in Spain also subsidies are available for hiring women in occupations where they are under-represented. A danger with such policies is that they may most benefit employers who previously discriminated. This can be avoided if the grant is only paid to those employing targeted groups above some norm ratio.

The government is a major purchaser of goods and services in all European economies. As such it has the power to reduce discrimination directly through its own behaviour as a purchaser. The survey of American evidence by Gottschalk (1990) concluded that making public contracts dependent upon non-discriminatory behaviour or even affirmative action can have a major impact on eliminating such practices in the labour market. In addition, the government is also a major employer, Rees and Shah (1995) suggest that adjusted wage differentials in the UK are negative for males in the public sector but high and positive for females. Public sector employment may have been particularly important in both Sweden and the UK in improving the labour market status of women.

6.6.3 *Statutory maternity and parental leave*

Empirical work already surveyed suggests that career interruptions were very expensive for female workers. Indeed the most important single factor in explaining the wage gap of women workers is their smaller amount of labour market experience. Given this situation the gender wage gap may be reduced by policies which encourage mothers to remain in employment, though such policies need not necessarily reduce discrimination. Whilst statutory maternity leave is well-established, parental leave legislation was first introduced in Sweden in 1974, with Austria and the Netherlands following in the 1990s. The OECD (1995) and Blau and Kahn (1992) provide summaries of statutory provisions in European countries. Parental leave is only available as an extended maternity leave in the UK, whereas in Belgium and Denmark parental leave has now been merged into broader systems of career breaks. France, Germany and the other Scandinavian countries also have extensive and flexible provisions.

A priori the effects of maternity and parental leave policies are unclear. Whilst they may encourage some mothers to retain existing employment ties, others who would have taken no leave may increase the incidence and duration of their interruptions. If women's attachment to the labour market is enhanced there are likely to be further favourable effects on women's pay through the stimulation of the demand for, and supply of training. Adverse selection problems and externalities may prevent competitive markets from providing leave entitlements in the absence of statutory provisions. If employees fully value the benefit then the costs to employers of such legislation will be passed on in the form of lower wages of women of child-bearing age. Gruber (1994) finds evidence of this in the US for maternity leave. Where this is prevented by wage-fixing institutions or legislation the policies may lead to greater hiring discrimination against women.

6.6.4   *Wage-fixing legislation*

One of the most frequently advocated anti-discriminatory measures is intervention directly into the wage determination process. Wage equalisation policies attempt directly to ban wage discrimination and in a number of European countries equality of treatment between men and women is specified in their constitution. For example, in Spain Article 35.1 of the 1978 Constitution states that 'All Spanish citizens are entitled to adequate remuneration . . . with the total exclusion of discrimination on grounds of sex'. The mildest form of intervention into wage-fixing is a universal minimum wage law which seeks to protect workers in all sectors and occupations against low pay. The advantages of such laws for females and racial minority workers is that it reduces the impact of occupational and industrial segregation. Female dominated sectors are not free to set lower minimum wages than male-dominated ones. Additionally, any tendency for the growth of flexible employment, such as temporary employment or sub-contracting, to decrease relative wages at the lower end of the distribution can be avoided and the possible harmful consequences of women's low unionisation rate and lack of coverage by collective agreements avoided. We have discussed minimum wage laws in some detail in Chapter 3 and we noted that competitive theory, believing in the underlying efficiency of competitive wage-fixing, views such interference with market forces as harmful and counter-productive. If black and white workers, or female and male workers are in fact close substitutes for each other, then enforcing higher wages for the group discriminated against must reduce their employment opportunities.

Broadly the same arguments apply to more specific policies aimed at reducing pay gaps by regulating wages. If firms can define equal pay narrowly then segregation by specific work task will occur to avoid the undesirable consequences of the legislation for their wage bill. Hence proponents of intervening into wage-fixing argue not for 'equal pay for equal work' but for 'equal pay for work of equal value'. Proponents of comparable worth take this further, arguing that jobs within a firm can be valued in terms of inputs of effort, skill and responsibility. Their arguments and the debate which they have generated are discussed in Box 6.1. It follows that policies aimed at producing equal pay need first to identify what is to be equalised. The original 1970 Equal Pay Act in the UK restricted comparisons to identical jobs or jobs previously graded as equivalent. These restrictions encourage employers to further segregate their work-force to avoid liability, and to comply with EC legislation the UK in 1983 adopted the Equal Pay (Amendment) Regulations which extended the comparison to jobs of equal value within the same employing agency. This extension leaves unresolved the criteria for assessing the value of particular occupations, in particular whether such an assessment should be based upon work content, market value or the value produced by the workers. In both the Dutch and UK legislation we find explicit reference to job evaluation schemes, though the subjectivity of the relative assessment of, say, strength compared with dexterity has led to Italian unions rejecting such schemes and in Sweden the law requires the schemes to be negotiated (Eyraud, 1993). An OECD report (1991a) suggested that in addition to the comparability question

---

Box 6.1: Comparable worth: pros and cons

What is it?
Comparable worth policies involve an extension of equal pay to cover jobs which are comparable in terms of skill, effort and responsibility. Comparable worth therefore implies some sort of implicit or explicit application of job evaluation techniques.

Arguments against
Comparable worth will raise the costs most of those firms who employ a high proportion of female workers and therefore favour the most discriminatory employers. Similarly, if female dominated occupations have their relative wage raised then employment will decline in those occupations, and employment is redistributed to where relative wages have fallen, i.e. the male dominated ones. If in comparison with men, women supply their labour more cheaply to occupations like nursing, it is often because they receive a higher psychic return from employment which involves 'caring'. Since 'caring' involves no investment by workers, it yields no wage differential; the greater the preference for caring employment, the lower the relative wage in those occupations. Attempts to replace this logic of the market by raising the premium of jobs involving caring will distort resource allocation and lower social welfare. In addition, since job evaluation schemes are less likely in small and non-unionised firms, female workers displaced by comparable worth will compete down wages in these sectors and female wage inequality may increase.

Arguments for
Conventional criticisms reflect a static competitive model of the labour market which has little relevance to the reality of labour market behaviour in European labour markets. Equal pay legislation has shown that female relative wages can be raised significantly without harmful employment effects. However, occupational segregation limits the effectiveness of these traditional policies. Whilst there may be some short-run efficiency losses, equity considerations are also important, indeed a more equitable wage distribution may increase social welfare directly and over time raise output through increased worker motivation.

there were two other important dimensions of equal pay legislation. The first of these concerns the extent to which the legislation covered non-wage remuneration, such as allowances and pensions. The other dimension concerns whether the legislation incorporates proactive measures such as an enforcement agency or reporting requirements on employers.

Where equal wage laws only apply to certain labour markets then occupational crowding is likely to occur in those markets not covered putting further downward pressure on wages in these markets. With statistical discrimination, equal wage legislation will tend to cause differences in unemployment rates to emerge instead of wage discrimination. As fewer members of the disfavoured group are hired there is a slower dissemination of information regarding the correct distributions of productivity and inaccurate stereotypes persist longer. Where discrimination arises from monopsony, wage equalisation can eliminate wage differences and, depending on relative elasticities, actually increase employment opportunities for the discriminated against group. Wage equalisation legislation can also be beneficial where social customs are preventing economic forces from eliminating discrimination.

6.6.5   *Positive discrimination and affirmative action*

If the major cause of earnings differentials between groups is believed to be occupational crowding, not reflecting qualifications and taste differences, then alternative policies to comparable worth are available. European companies appear to be devolving more responsibility for recruitment and training to line managers and the fear remains that discrimination is more likely to occur in the absence of specialist personnel staff. Potentially effective in such situations are either positive discrimination, the establishment of job quotas for certain groups, or affirmative action policies which give encouragement to the employment and promotion of specified groups. Positive discrimination can take various forms, such as specifying quotas for schooling, training, occupations or individual employers. Quotas are effective in eliminating discrimination due to employer or employee prejudice or social custom, since better information produced by greater contacts creates more accurate stereotypes of the discriminated group. Where labour markets are segmented, this elimination of discrimination based on prejudice will also result in a reduction of both earnings and unemployment differences between groups. Quotas may also be effective in combating discrimination occurring prior to entry into the labour market or in offsetting the consequences of discrimination against previous generations. In the latter case 'inferior' applicants from discriminated groups may be favoured over applicants from advantaged groups in the short term. This is based upon a belief that qualifications or performances in hiring tests may be biased indicators of ability and employability for members of groups who have suffered historically from discrimination. This may reflect the influence of environment on human capital decisions, imperfections in the capital market which constrain the investment decisions of those with low family incomes and wealth, or the result of tests which are culturally or socially biased. Such policies are advocated by those who believe that competitive forces are unable by themselves to eliminate discrimination. The break up of segregated workplaces and the reduction of occupational crowding are assumed by advocates to produce efficiency gains greater than any losses resulting from interference with firms' hiring decisions.

The belief that positive discrimination may conflict with other objectives in society such as freedom of contract and individual justice has led many to only advocate such policies in extreme situations. For some reason positive discrimination is typically tolerated more commonly in the elimination of employment discrimination against disabled workers than in the case of racial or sexual discrimination. Linking government contracts to the implementation of internal policies to eliminate discriminatory behaviour and targeting government training and other manpower policies has been widely adopted in the US, but is rare elsewhere.

In some of the theories of discrimination previously considered, majority groups may benefit directly from discrimination by receiving higher wages and better non-pecuniary returns from work such as status and power. The elimination of discrimination is therefore likely to be resisted and widespread evasion poses a threat to the effectiveness of policies. Governments have therefore stressed the moral, social and political dimensions of equal opportunities legislation and minimised the impact which their policies have had on the long-term economic well-being of the majority group. Compliance with legislation will reflect the costs of conforming relative to the expected costs of violating the law. The former will reflect how successfully the measure has defined and targeted discrimination. Where targeted groups are a small proportion of the total work-force resistance is likely to be small. High prevailing levels of aggregate demand are also likely to facilitate the introduction, implementation and acceptance of legislation by lowering the costs of conforming. Affirmative action policies are therefore much easier to conduct where employment opportunities for white males are plentiful. Compliance will also reflect the penalties imposed for violating the law, adjusted for the probability of the violation being detected and the penalty enforced.

6.7 The impact of current policies

The United States is usually identified as the innovator in equal opportunities legislation, although France and some other countries could claim precedence since it was not until 1963 that the Federal Equal Pay Act was finally passed. Gottschalk's 1990 review of the effectiveness of these and associated policies in the US concluded that they had been successful in raising the average income of women and black workers but they had been less successful at improving the position of the most disadvantaged. Whilst Italy rapidly followed the US legislation, Germany (1980), Spain (1980) and Greece (1984) were much later in enacting equal pay legislation. In 1975 the European Commission issued a directive based upon Article 119 of the Treaty of Rome requiring member states to introduce into their national legislation measures to implement the principle of equal pay for women based upon the principle of equal pay for work of equal value. This directive was assured of implementation following the European Court's ruling in 1976 that Article 119 had 'direct effect' on member countries irrespective of whether national governments had incorporated equal pay laws into their national law. Also in 1976 the Equal Treatment Directive was adopted which targeted sex discrimination at the point of entry into the labour market, in vocational training, promotion and working conditions. Mazey (1988) provides a summary of the development of EC policy in this area, a summary we partially update in our discussion of the Social Charter and the European Union Treaty in our final chapter.

Dex and Sewell (1995) have attempted a cross-national approach to the assessment of the impact of equal opportunities policies on the status of women workers. Their tentative conclusions in this ambitious paper are that the duration of time since equal pay legislation was enacted is associated with improvements in occupational segregation, occupational status and the incidence of women's low pay though not the gender earnings gap itself. Studies in the UK have largely concluded that the Equal Pay Act of 1970 did improve women's relative pay. Snell *et al.* (1981) reported that employers often minimised their obligation under the Act by moving workers and changing job content, during the transition period. The impact effects of the Equal Pay Act may therefore have been to worsen occupational segregation. The requirement that women covered by collective agreements, employer's pay structures or Wages Council's orders be paid at or above the lowest male rate did appear to eliminate much pay discrimination in non-segregated firms and occupations, even amongst the smaller companies. Their survey of employers also concluded that although the Sex Discrimination Act had eliminated overtly discriminatory hiring and promotion practices, it had not significantly altered firms' actual labour market behaviour. Rather than adopt this workplace study of the impact of the measures, most other investigations have adopted an aggregate econometric approach, and these are now considered.

Relative female earnings rose rapidly in Britain between 1970 and 1980 and it is difficult to resist the temptation to link this rise in female relative earnings directly with the introduction of equal opportunities legislation in Britain. However, alternative explanations of this rise have been advanced. The occupational crowding of female workers means that structural changes in the economy, such as deindustrialisation, can cause changes in relative pay (Borooah and Lee, 1988). The general level of economic activity, the incidence of flat-rate incomes policies and declining skill differentials at that time, may also have caused the rise given the concentration of women workers in jobs with low pay and training. Whether the rise in female relative earnings reflects reduced discrimination remains an empirical issue. Zabalza and Tzannatos (1985) found that the change in the distribution of female workers and changes in the industrial wage differentials had little impact on the overall movement of female relative wages. The improvement in relative female earnings was due largely to a reduction in wage differentials within industrial sectors. On inspection they concluded that anti-discriminatory legislation appeared to have a large positive effect on relative female earnings and relative employment. The impact had been to shift the demand curve for female labour, and depending upon whether one views the depressed earning capacity of non-participants as discriminatory, Zabalza and Arrufat (1985) estimated that the Acts reduced discrimination by between 30 and 50 per cent.

193

The failure of female employment to fall in the face of the large change in female relative wages has invoked interest, as this behaviour appears incompatible with conventional models of the labour market unless an upward shift in the demand for female labour occurred at the same time. Manning (1993) rejects the various explanations for such an upward shift in demand and instead interprets this behaviour as evidence that the female labour market is monopsonistic. Sloane and Theodossiou (1994) discover that the upward movement in female relative earnings was not uniform across the earnings distribution, with a relative deterioration in female-concentrated occupations in the early 1970s as, perhaps, employers sought to evade the measure. The pattern of changes in the distribution was broadly consistent with both the impact of the legislation and a change in relative demand for female workers, throwing further doubt on the accuracy of earlier estimates of the impact of the legislation on discrimination.

In 1960 the Swedish trade union and employers' confederations reached agreement on the abolition of separate wages for women over a five year period, although legislation did not follow until 1980. Gustafsson and Lofstrom (1991) in their study concluded that about half of the increase in the relative wage of female blue-collar workers in Sweden between 1960 and 1985 could be attributed to the elimination of night-working restrictions and the introduction of equal pay for work of equal value. We have so far ignored the issue of compliance and the effectiveness of any policy will be dependent upon the effectiveness of enforcement. In the Netherlands in 1985 only 6 complaints reached the enforcement committee, although a survey conducted by the investigating agency in the same year found that about 29 per cent of enterprises were contravening the equal pay principle (Asscher-Vonk, 1993). This discrepancy has been explained by lack of information about legal rights and the imprecise formulation of the equal pay provision in the Netherlands. Pérez del Rio (1993) similarly argues that the ineffectiveness of Spanish equal pay legislation reflects inadequate procedures which prevent social groups initiating action, give inadequate protection against victimisation and prevent rulings from being applied to groups outside the initial action by way of requiring that discriminatory practices are discontinued. Similar comments are made by McCrudden (1993) in his assessment of equal pay legislation in the UK, where delays and the costs of actions have also become significant barriers to justice for many applicants. Overall, Eyraud (1993a) concludes that whilst equal pay legislation has been successful in eliminating direct and flagrant discrimination, it has been less successful at combating the indirect discrimination inherent in many day-to-day company practices.

In 1990 the European Commission initially submitted a draft directive of the pregnant workers directive under the safety and health framework. The directive originally proposed paid maternity leave on normal earnings, though eventually it was reduced to the amount which workers would receive under statutory sick pay schemes. As Addison and Siebert (1994a) explain, this was a consequence of British hostility to the cost of the original directive to employers and tax-payers, though the new eligibility requirement substantially increased the coverage of mandated maternity benefits in the UK. The impact of statutory maternity benefits and parental leave provisions on the career development of female workers has yet to be fully evaluated. The OECD

(1995) reports that take-up rates of all but the initial leave period are often low and few fathers have taken advantage of parental leave apart from in Sweden. The growth of atypical employment may be partly responsible for this low take-up as eligibility is often on the basis of continuous employment. Sundstrom and Stafford (1992) and Gustafsson and Stafford (1994) report that the extension of Swedish parental leave policies and provision of public child care on a needs-based payment scale, has been associated with women having a longer period of employment prior to the birth of their child and high participation rates for mothers of older pre-school children. In contrast, the Dutch system encourages mothers to stay at home with their children, providing little public day-care and few financial incentives to re-enter the labour market. As a consequence, Blank (1994a) points out that the participation rate of mothers of young children in the Netherlands is a quarter of the Swedish rate. While parental leave provisions may increase female attachment to the labour market they appear to have had little impact on the unequal division of child care responsibilities between parents or on occupational segregation.

6.8   Conclusions

Discussions of discrimination in the labour market often treat the existence of gender pay gaps as indicating the presence of discrimination. We have seen that defining discrimination operationally is extremely difficult. The main problem is that since males and females receive different returns to their job-related characteristics, it is not possible to identify the extent to which their characteristics would be different in the absence of discrimination. The presence of direct discrimination distorts the preferences, investment and participation decisions of both female and male workers and the resulting indirect discrimination cannot be readily identified separately. This results in a necessarily unsatisfactory methodology for breaking down the gender wage gap. The almost arbitrary measures of discrimination which result mean that it is still possible to sustain very different views about the extent and sources of discrimination in European labour markets. At the same time conventional economic theory provides no explanation of the origins or the persistence of discriminatory wage differentials and occupational segregation. These weaknesses prevent the normal methodological approaches of the discipline from being applied to empirical work in this area and result in measurement without theory.

Discussion of equal opportunities policies does not always clearly distinguish between the objective of reducing discrimination and that of reducing the gender earnings gap. Policies aimed at the latter objective need not necessarily attain the former. In the present environment there is pressure on governments to move away from targets measured in terms of average gender gaps to ones related to the distribution of female earnings. The plight of lone mothers arouses much concern from both sides of the political spectrum. Such a reorientation would not only reflect structural changes in society and the labour market but also respond to the possibility that policies implemented in the 1970s may themselves have contributed to a polarisation of women's status in the labour market. It may be that this outcome is itself the result of the conflict between equity and the other goals of public policy.

The persistence of occupational crowding means that women and men are largely working in different jobs and, in the main, 'feminised' jobs have lower wages for a given set of characteristics. As a consequence the 'equal value' clause of equal pay legislation is of paramount importance in reducing gender pay gaps. Policies to reduce occupational segregation and inequalities in occupational attainment need to target inequalities in access to education and training and reduce tax and benefit regulations which discourage a more equal division of non-market production within families. Overall, future policy may have to move away from its traditional concern with discriminatory practices in the workplace to confront inequalities in the distribution of domestic responsibilities between partners.

Guide to further reading

Blau (1990) remains a good place to start a study of discrimination against women, though the treatment concentrates upon US experience. European Commission (1993) provides a survey of the pattern of employment of women workers in Europe. Callan and Wren (1994) introduce international evidence on wage gaps and introduce the key policy issues. MacEwen Scott (1994) contains a wide-ranging empirical investigation of gender differences in six local labour markets in the UK. Eyraud (1993a) provides the most detailed description of the operation of equal pay legislation in Europe. Perlman and Pike (1994) and Rhoads (1993) provide very different assessments of the merits of comparable worth.

Appendix 6.1: Estimating discrimination

The most popular way of decomposing wage differentials into productivity and discrimination components is developed from work by Oaxaca (1973):

Let

$$y_m = g_m(x_m) \qquad\qquad [6.1]$$

and

$$y_f = g_f(x_f) \qquad\qquad [6.2]$$

where y_m and y_f are mean male and female earnings
 g_m and g_f are the male and female earnings functions of the type introduced in Chapter 4.

Then the mean earnings of females if they had male characteristics is:

$$y_{fm} = g_f(x_m) \qquad\qquad [6.3]$$

It follows that $(y_{fm} - y_f)$ is the difference in mean earnings explained by differences in measured productivity-related characteristics. Thus the portion of the wage gap explained by differences in characteristics is:

$$c = \frac{\left(y_{fm} - y_f\right)}{\left(y_m - y_f\right)} \qquad\qquad [6.4]$$

Hence one measure of discrimination is:

$$d = 1 - c \qquad\qquad [6.5]$$

Such an approach ignores pre-entry discrimination and assumes that different returns to attributes are not reflecting autonomous tastes. Oaxaca and Ransom (1994) examine the variety of measures derived from this approach which have been utilised in research. They show that the utilisation of different measures of discrimination can produce radically different results from the same data. Polachek and Kim (1994) point out that differences in lifetime work patterns between men and women may affect work motivations and that research should allow the slopes of earnings functions to vary as well as intercepts, since men will invest more and therefore have steeper age-earnings profiles.

7   Unemployment

The return of mass unemployment to Europe at the end of the 1970s has led to exten-sive debates about its origins and appropriate policy responses. Recently this debate has focused on the persistence of high unemployment in Europe, with the European Commission (1994b) and the OECD (1994a) both arguing the need to make labour markets more flexible. In this chapter an examination of the ability of different economic approaches to explain European experience will enable us to assess this proposal together with the Swedish Government's proposal for a full employment commitment to be added to the Maastricht treaty. Strangely, whilst there is no con-sensus regarding the relative importance of particular causes of high European unemployment there has been a convergence of policy, with successful policies in one country being imitated in other European countries. Specifically, the 1990s have seen a gradual movement away from a largely passive policy response towards an active stance, with governments targeting their expenditure to create employment or improve the speed of job-matching.

Explanations of the causes of unemployment can still be broadly divided between neoclassical and Keynesian approaches, though this distinction has become more blurred since the development of disequilibrium models. Neoclassical analysis explains the rise in unemployment and its persistence in terms of institutional restric-tions on the operation of labour markets. The operation of trade unions and unemployment insurance and social support schemes largely distort the supply side of the labour market, causing the equilibrium rate of unemployment to rise. Accordingly, since unemployment reflects the weakness of competitive forces in the labour markets, it is a microeconomic problem requiring a microeconomic policy response concentrating upon the supply side. Since the 1970s new classical econom-ics has attempted to refine these arguments within a framework of rational, forward-looking decision-makers in which exogenous shocks can cause inter-tempo-ral substitutions between work and leisure. In contrast, conventional Keynesian analysis has argued that unemployment is inevitable in unregulated competitive mar-kets, concluding that governments may have to use macroeconomic policies to adjust levels of aggregate demand, if acceptable levels of employment are to be sustained. Recently, New Keynesian analysis seeks to provide a rigorous explanation for quan-tity-adjusting in competitive markets, and now provides a rationale for government intervention at the micro level. In simple terms, the neoclassical explanation provides the rationale for the right-wing view that unemployment is predominantly voluntary and that government policy may have to reduce the attractiveness of being unem-ployed. The Keynesian explanation produces the left-wing view that unemployment is predominantly involuntary and governments should consider policies which directly stimulate job creation.

We do not seek to provide a complete review of theoretical and empirical work on European unemployment, the guide to further reading at the end of this chapter suggests suitable sources for those requiring such a review. Instead, we wish to concentrate upon an assessment of the role of government policy. To understand and assess the variety of current policy responses we will first define our terms carefully, and identify the costs of unemployment in European economies. This is followed by a review of the stylised facts of unemployment and a summary of the present level and composition of European unemployment. Next, we review current explanations of the causes of unemployment, initially concentrating upon the natural rate of unemployment and theories of wage rigidity. We then utilise these theories to examine the rise of unemployment in Europe in the 1970s and its persistence since that time. The differing policy perspectives of these theories are then summarised, preceding a review and analysis of existing policies within the EU. The recent calls by the European Commission and the OECD for the creation of a more flexible European labour market are then assessed and the chapter concludes with a consideration of alternative policy prescriptions for the creation of a high employment-high productivity European economy.

7.1 Unemployment: methodology and evidence

7.1.1 *Measuring unemployment*

The term 'unemployment' is used ambiguously in the literature and the definitions underlying the measurement of unemployment may not be consistent over time or between countries. In some usage unemployment refers to a measure of the under-utilisation of the potential work-force, including those who in certain situations would enter the labour market. Here the extent of under-employment of workers may be as significant as the number without any employment. For many economists, unemployment usually refers to a measure of immediately available, non-employed workers willing to accept market-clearing wages. It is this usage which approximates to the International Labour Organisation (ILO) definition of unemployment adopted by the Labour Force Survey. The ILO definition relates to those people without a paid job who were available to start a job in the four weeks prior to the interview or who were waiting to start a job they had already obtained. In Britain, the most common official measure of unemployment in the mid-1990s was of registrants for, or claimants of, unemployment and social security benefit. As such the total can be adjusted by altering incentives to register or benefit eligibility regulations. Indeed, since 1979 there have been thirty changes in the way the British figures are calculated. The claimant measure will overestimate the ILO measure of unemployment to the extent to which some claimants are non-active searchers or are fraudulently making claims. On the other hand it excludes certain groups who would be included in the ILO definition, such as searchers not entitled to benefits, particularly amongst the re-entrants. Both measures exclude groups who some may consider to be unemployed such as: the economically inactive (predominantly the long-term sick, discouraged searchers, premature retirees and those who would work if adequate child care was available), those in part-time work seeking full-time employment, and those who continue in full-time education because employment is unavailable.

The last twenty years have seen the proportion of the population of working age who are economically inactive rise rapidly in all OECD countries, quadrupling in Britain to around 12 per cent of males in that age group. Elmeskov and Pichelmann (1993) analyse this interaction between unemployment and labour force participation in OECD countries, assessing the appropriateness of measured unemployment as a social and economic indicator. The OECD (1995) has begun to complement ILO measures of unemployment with measures including discouraged workers and involuntary part-time workers, they estimate that these two groups add another 50 per cent to the unemployment stock. For example, in Sweden the number of involuntary part-time workers exceeds the number officially unemployed. Such augmented measures of unemployment when combined with figures for the non-employment rate amongst prime age adults give a more complete picture of the under-utilisation of labour and the degree of social hardship (Martin, 1994).

It follows from our discussion that debates about the 'true' level of unemployment are usually futile, since the number of unemployed will depend upon which definition is adopted. Which is the most appropriate definition of unemployment will depend upon one's belief about how labour markets operate. For example, neoclassical analysis views labour markets as price-adjusting and unemployment should measure the difference between the supply and demand for labour, the emphasis here being on active searchers and unfilled vacancies. However, supply of labour is dependent on the real wage rate, non-labour market earnings and non-market work and leisure opportunities. Accordingly, the level of unemployment will change as any of these variables change or when the demand curve shifts due to changes in firms' environment.

Once it is recognised that the appropriate definition of unemployment will depend upon the theoretical framework adopted and upon the particular issue of concern, then consistency of measurement becomes the real issue. Care needs to be taken in any historical or international comparison to ensure that the data are consistently defined. In the following pages the unemployment data we consider are measured according to the ILO definition which assists us in making international comparisons.

7.1.2 Assessing the costs of unemployment

Unemployment is a major economic problem because it is costly, both to individuals who experience it and to society as a whole. Firstly, unemployment imposes costs upon society; labour is perishable and labour that is not utilised for production causes a permanent loss of output and therefore consumption. Secondly, unemployment imposes suffering upon individuals, not just in terms of forgone consumption. The associated low self-esteem often results in behavioural and physical health problems and family/marital instability.

In an average recession in a European economy gross national product will fall below potential by about 5 per cent for around two years. In crude numbers this is equivalent to a loss of around £2,000 per worker in British terms. On average, disposable income will only change by about half this level, as the tax and benefit system initially absorbs some of this change. Estimates of the output costs of unemployment are often much lower, Matthews and Minford (1987) estimated annual losses of only about 1 per cent of British GDP. Their low figure reflects the concentration of unemployment amongst low-productivity workers and off-setting gains in the form of increased leisure and non-market production. The main way in which society shares the cost of unemployment is through changes in government spending and tax receipts. The European Commission estimated in 1993 that the total costs of unemployment in the EU were some 210,000 million ECU, including benefits, lost tax revenue, increased social service costs, increased health costs and increased crime (European Commission, 1993c). This figure is broadly compatible with Layard and Philpott's (1991) calculation that each unemployed person in the UK cost the Exchequer just over £8,000 a year. The rise in unemployment in Europe has occurred at a time of important demographic changes which have increased the burden of unemployment. Taking the Netherlands as an example, the ratio of economically inactive persons to economically active ones was 0.44 in 1970, 0.66 in 1980 and 0.82 in 1990 and currently stands at around 0.86. This doubling of the ratio at a time of relatively slow productivity growth implies a dramatically increased burden on the economically active.

For unemployed individuals the pecuniary costs of unemployment will depend on the income lost, offset by the receipt of unemployment benefits and increases in leisure and search time. The earlier view that unemployment spells caused transitory changes in income has now been supplanted, following evidence which suggests that job loss results in substantial, often permanent, reductions in earning power (Topel, 1993). Costs to the individual are likely to rise with the duration of unemployment since the long-term unemployed receive lower income from the state and may also experience a diminishing marginal utility of leisure. The effects of falling reservation wage, adverse selection and obsolete firm-specific human capital all contribute to the downwards occupational mobility suffered by many re-employed workers.

The above calculations of the exchequer and individual costs of unemployment are poor proxies for the total costs to society of unemployment. The earlier estimates ignore the external costs of unemployment upon employed workers' productivity: high unemployment reduces on-the-job search and depresses reservation wages, causing workers to tolerate jobs which under-utilise their abilities. In addition, crime levels, sickness, premature death and social disruptions all appear to be positively related to the level of unemployment, though the magnitude and direction of causation have been difficult to establish as Pyle and Deadman (1994) explain for the case of crime. Clark and Oswald (1994) analysed data from the 1991 British General Health Questionnaire and concluded that unemployed workers had much lower levels of mental well-being than those in work. Being unemployed seemed to reduce well-being more than divorce or marital separation. Distress from unemployment was lower amongst the young, the less educated, the long-term unemployed and those living in high unemployment regions.

In a growing economy some unemployment is a natural and desirable consequence of the structural changes we identified in Chapter 1, and our discussion of the job-matching process in Chapter 5 suggested a positive role for unemployment in certain situations. Whilst the socially optimal level of unemployment is greater than zero, the arguments above suggest that the net costs of current levels of unemployment in Europe are often large, and tend to increase with the level and duration of unemployment. Evidence in the next section suggests that unemployment is highly concentrated amongst certain groups, accordingly the bulk of these costs are born by a relatively small proportion of the total population. In a democracy, because unemployment costs are borne by a minority, the political tolerance of unemployment may be high. It follows that efficiency and equity objectives may require governments to pursue policies which aim to alter the distribution, as well as the level, of unemployment.

7.1.3 Some 'stylised facts' of OECD unemployment

The unemployment rate in the then European Community increased from under 4 per cent in the 1960s and early 1970s to over 10 per cent in the mid-1980s. Although the unemployment rate fell at the end of that decade, it has since returned to fluctuate around one in ten of the work-force being unemployed. As Figure 7.1 indicates, the behaviour of the unemployment rate in the US, Japan, Sweden and the EU has been very different over the last thirty years. Before we investigate the nature of these differences and the extent of the similarities within the EU, it will be helpful to establish some of the 'stylized facts' concerning the behaviour of unemployment in developed economies which have been established in recent work (for example, Layard *et al.*, 1991 and OECD, 1994a).

1. *Unemployment fluctuates over the business cycle and between cycles, but over the very long run it is untrended.* For most developed countries, and especially in Europe, unemployment varies more between cycles than within cycles. Particularly over the last 25 years, unemployment in Europe has varied less between the peak and trough of business cycles than it has between the same stage of different business cycles. Unemployment was relatively low throughout the cycles of the 1960s and high during those of the late 1970s and 80s. Conventional business cycles by themselves explain little of the behaviour of unemployment over time, indicating that simple cyclical theories of unemployment are of little relevance to our search for explanations of European unemployment. Layard *et al.* (1991) interpret the dominance of long-run fluctuations as indicating the importance of changes in social institutions, benefit and wage determination systems, together with the long-lasting effects of major shocks such as wars and oil price rises.

   The absence of any trend in unemployment over the very long run indicates that, contrary to widely held beliefs, population growth and productivity growth, together with any associated technological unemployment, are relatively unimportant in determining the aggregate rate of unemployment over time. It also

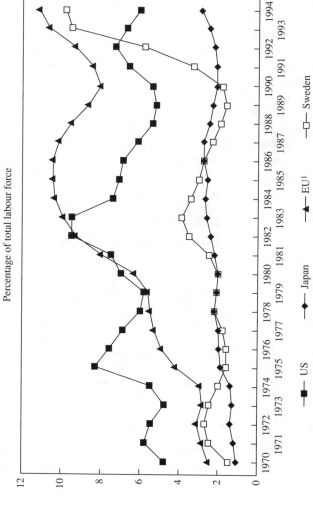

Percentage of total labour force

■— US   ◆— Japan   ▲— EU[1]   □— Sweden

[1] EU Countries shown are Belgium, Finland, France, Germany, Ireland, Italy, Netherlands, Portugal, Spain, Sweden and UK.
Source: OECD *Quarterly Labour Statistics 1995*, no. 3

Figure 7.1   Unemployment rates 1970 to 1994

suggests that there are adjustment mechanisms at work in the long run which cause the number of jobs to respond to large changes in the numbers wishing to work.

2. *Unemployment changes by small amounts most of the time; unemployment rates display a high degree of positive serial correlation.* High unemployment today is associated with high unemployment in the future. Whilst unemployment can at times change rapidly, most changes are relatively small. Where contractionary shocks to the labour market have large effects they are not easily reversed, even when economic activity and employment pick up again. These persistence effects are more pronounced in Europe and Oceania than in the US.

3. *Unemployment rates differ greatly between countries.* Over the 1950s and 1960s the average unemployment rate in Europe was significantly lower than in the US. Since the mid-1970s the average unemployment rate in Europe and Oceania has been much higher than that in the US. In general, countries with corporatist (Austria and the Nordic countries) and highly co-ordinated (Japan) wage-fixing systems have experienced much lower post-war unemployment rates, as have countries with a short entitlement to unemployment benefits (US). We explore the economic performance of the corporatist economies in more detail in the following chapter. There is some evidence (Martin, 1994) that making adjustments to the ILO definition measures of unemployment to include discouraged workers and involuntary part-time workers narrows the dispersion of labour market slack across OECD countries. Similarly, measures of non employment amongst prime age males show more convergence than do those for unemployment rates alone, although Japan remains an outlier.

4. *The profile of the duration of unemployment varies widely between developed economies.* Over the past two decades, unemployment duration has been much longer in the EU than in the US and Japan. These differences remain even after adjusting for differences in unemployment rates, with the burden of unemployment being more unevenly distributed in Europe. Large increases in the stock of unemployment are usually associated with changes in the duration of unemployment, normally with the shorter spells of unemployment becoming longer.

In order to clarify the importance of duration consider the following identity which links the stock of unemployment to the underlying flows:

change in the stock of unemployment $\equiv$ (inflow − outflow)

As we discovered in Chapter 5 these flows in most national labour markets are large. Changes in the number of unemployed can be caused by changes in the number becoming unemployed or changes in the numbers leaving unemployment. Alternatively, if we assume a constant stock of unemployment, then:

unemployment = inflow rate x average completed duration of an unemployment spell

Thus, the same unemployment rate could be associated with high inflow-rates and relatively short duration in one country whilst another could have the opposite pattern. Inflow rates are relatively high in North America, Austria, Denmark and

Finland when compared with those in the other EU countries and Japan. These other EU countries also tend to have a low outflow from unemployment, and taken together the consequence is a much higher share of the long-term unemployed in the EU. The reason why these differences in the distribution of unemployment are particularly important is negative duration dependence: the longer people are unemployed the lower are their chances of leaving unemployment. Whether this represents genuine duration dependence or is the result of heterogeneity amongst those entering unemployment remains unresolved (Pedersen and Westergård-Nielsen, 1993).

5. *Unemployment rates vary widely between age-groups, skill-groups, regions and races.* Unemployment rates amongst those under 25 years of age have exceeded 30 per cent in Finland, Italy and Spain, though those countries with a strong apprenticeship system, Austria, Germany and Switzerland, have managed to maintain rates of around 5 per cent. The young are more likely to be unemployed than older people, largely because they suffer from a high probability of becoming unemployed, though between 40 and 60 per cent of the young unemployed in Belgium, Ireland, Italy and Spain had been unemployed for over a year in the early 1990s. For older workers, although the incidence of unemployment is relatively low, those becoming unemployed have a much greater probability of suffering long term unemployment. In some countries social security systems (Austria, Belgium, Denmark, Finland, France, Germany, Italy and Norway) and collective bargaining (the Netherlands and Sweden) have encouraged older workers to leave the work-force.

Low-skilled manual workers have an unemployment rate up to five times greater than that for professional and managerial workers. In most economies manual workers account for three-quarters of male unemployment; the reasons for this preponderance are related to our discussion of the impact of the decline in the relative demand for low-skilled workers on wage inequality in Chapter 1. Interestingly, the 1990s recession may have been biased against skilled workers (Nickell and Bell, 1995) and the service sector has played less of a cushioning role. The potential earnings of the unemployed are much lower than those in employment, predominantly due to their less favourable characteristics. Regional imbalances have already been discussed in Chapter 5 and gender and racial differences in Chapter 6. Amongst other groups, lone parents tend to have above average unemployment rates, usually at least twice the rate for husbands and wives, and overall, between a third and a half of the unemployed in OECD countries live in households where no other person has a job. This latter proportion has been increasing, particularly amongst the long-term unemployed (OECD, 1995), causing a further concentration of unemployment and a weakening of the unemployeds' contacts with the world of work.

7.1.4 *Key characteristics of European unemployment*

We now concentrate on identifying and ultimately explaining the characteristics of European unemployment. This requires us to refine the stylised facts previously outlined. Table 7.1 contains recent unemployment rate data for the major European economies, the US and Japan. The figures confirm the higher rates of unemployment in the EU and the different incidence amongst entrants and female workers. The high rate in Finland follows a rapid rise in unemployment since the collapse of trade with the Soviet Union. Spain's high rate is the subject of later discussion. Unlike the experience of the US, Japan, Norway and Sweden, Nickell and Bell (1995) show that a significant part of the increase in 1980s EC unemployment was amongst skilled workers in Germany, Netherlands, Spain and the UK. Another feature of European unemployment much discussed is the rise in the rate of unemployment associated with a given vacancy rate. Elmeskov and MacFarlan (1993) illustrate these shifts in the Beveridge curve or UV curve, the usual interpretation being that vacant jobs are less easily filled than previously. The most striking difference between Europe and other countries is the relative importance of long-term unemployment.

Table 7.1 Unemployment in the major OECD countries[1]

	Unemployment rates (percentage)			
	All persons 1994	Youths (15–24) 1994	Women 1994	Long-term unemployed[2] as a share of total unemployment (1993)
Austria	4.3[3]	4.7[3]	4.9	16.9[4]
Belgium	9.7	18.4[3]	10.8[3]	52.9
Denmark	10.3[3]	14.6[3]	11.1[3]	25.2
Finland	18.2	30.9	16.7	30.6
France	12.3	27.5	14.3	38.3[5]
Germany	8.8[3]	8.2[3]	10.4[3]	40.3
Greece	9.4[3]	28.8[3]	15.0[3]	50.9
Ireland	15.7[3]	25.1[3]	15.9[3]	59.1
Italy	11.0	32.4	15.7	57.7
Luxembourg	2.3[3]	4.4[3]	3.1[3]	32.4
Netherlands	7.2	10.2	8.1	52.3
Portugal	5.4[3]	12.0[3]	6.5[3]	43.4
Spain	23.8	42.8	31.4	56.1[5]
Sweden	9.8	16.6[4]	6.7	17.3
United Kingdom	9.5	16.2[4]	7.5[3]	42.5
Norway	5.4	12.6[4]	4.9	28.9[5]
United States	6.1	12.5[4]	6.0	12.2[5]
Japan	2.9	5.5	3.0	17.5

[1] OECD unemployment rates (national estimates for Austria).
[2] The long-term unemployed refers to all persons unemployed continuously for one year and over.
[3] Figures refer to 1993.
[4] Ages 16–24.
[5] Figures refer to 1994.
Source: OECD (1995a) Tables B,P and Q, OECD: *Labour Force Statistics 1973–93.*

Notwithstanding the alphabet of schemes targeting the long-term unemployed in Europe, their share of total unemployment is around three to four times greater than their share of unemployment in North America and Japan. As we shall see, the rise in European unemployment has largely been due to increases in the spell length, rather than to higher inflows into unemployment. In many European economies two out of every three unemployed older workers (aged 55 and over) have been out of work for over a year.

Some potential contributory factors to high rates of European unemployment can easily be eliminated. Labour supply, for instance, has not risen faster in Europe in recent years than elsewhere. Labour productivity growth has declined as much as output growth, this being inconsistent with the argument that technology has been destroying jobs at a faster rate in Europe. Restrictive monetary and fiscal policies whilst important in the process which generated higher unemployment in the 1970s and early 1980s, do not appear to be a significant direct cause of the persistence of high unemployment given that inflation rates have been broadly stable in recent years. Finally, the service sector has been creating jobs in Europe at about the same rate as in the US (Glyn, 1995).

To begin our search for contributory factors we will analyse the flows into and out of unemployment. The OECD (1993) has shown that monthly outflows from unemployment expressed as a percentage of the stock of unemployment at the beginning of the 1990s ranged from over 37 per cent in the US and 30 per cent in Sweden to around 5 per cent and below in Belgium, France, Greece, Ireland, Italy, the Netherlands, Portugal and Spain. In addition, in many of these countries with low outflows, the increased duration of unemployment since the late 1970s resulted from a relative decline in outflows from unemployment. This has led to researchers concentrating upon employers' hiring rate and the search behaviour of the unemployed in Europe, rather than the inflow to the stock of unemployment. Spain appears to be an exception: the CEPR (1995) calculate that Spanish unemployment would be close to zero if the separation rate had remained at its 1973 level. While the probability of an employed worker becoming unemployed is not particularly high in the EU, once unemployed a person in the EU has relatively little chance of quickly finding another job.

The view that Europe has a hiring problem has been reinforced by the relatively slow growth of employment in the EU. The real GDP of the EU 12 grew at an average annual rate of just over 3 per cent between 1961 and 1993, a rate slightly faster than that achieved in the US. However, whilst employment grew at an annual average rate of 1.8 per cent in the US, it only grew by just 0.25 per cent annually in the EC, and until the mid-1980s much of this growth was in the public sector. Even during 1983–89, a time when the GDP growth in the Community was over twice that of the US, employment growth only achieved a quarter of the American rate. In the United States, labour and product markets tend to move together, with employment and production being positively related. This tendency is much less pronounced in Europe.

Some commentators have related this to the strength of employment protection legislation in Europe and the high social charges on employers, whilst others note that real wage rigidity appears to be relatively high in most member countries of the EU. Those seeking institutional sources of this rigidity have also pointed out the extensive minimum wage legislation in most EU countries and the associated low dispersion of wage rates of production workers in the EU. We discuss all of these possibilities later in this chapter, but first we develop a theoretical framework within which we can examine the determinants of unemployment.

7.2 Theories of unemployment

7.2.1 Introduction

Consider the model of the labour market developed in Chapter 2 and illustrated in Figure 7.2. Initially the labour market is in equilibrium at E, with a real wage of w^* and employment level of n^*. Let us subject this market to a contractionary shock so that the demand for labour contracts to n^d_1, at every real wage employers now wish to hire less labour. If neoclassical economics is right and labour markets are best described as auction markets, wages rapidly adjust to clear the market and a new equilibrium occurs at A where real wages and employment are lower at w^*_1 and n^*_1. At A, demand matches the supply of labour so the lower employment level does not cause any unemployment.

Another possibility is that real wages remain at w^* after the demand shock and now desired employment shrinks to n_c, we have moved from A to B on Figure 7.2. A wage gap now exists and the difference between n^*_1 and n_c has been termed 'classical

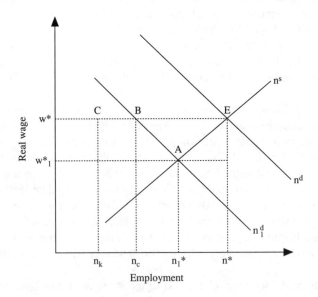

Figure 7.2 Theories of unemployment

unemployment'. Alternatively, many Keynesians have argued that firms may be demand-constrained following a contractionary shock, so that demand for labour is constrained to C which represents an 'off the demand curve' position. The resulting additional unemployment, $n_c - n_k$, can be termed 'Keynesian unemployment'. Whilst not all economists would accept the appropriateness or exclusivity of these distinctions, we will find them useful in developing our survey.

7.2.2 *Keynesian theories*

Keynes's argument is nowadays usually interpreted as being that money wages cannot be relied upon to fall in the face of unemployed workers, and that any movement towards lower wages may not be effective anyway in clearing the labour market. As such his argument encapsulates both of the classical and Keynesian categories of unemployment of the previous section. Though the downwards rigidity of wages is a crucial element in traditional Keynesian analysis, only in the last twenty years has there been much activity in explaining the causes of such rigidity. Indeed, there was much disagreement on whether it was the rigidity of real or money wages that was being asserted in the proposition that labour markets failed to clear. Keynesians championed the use of expansionary demand-management policies to tackle any widespread unemployment, since firms would be encouraged to expand output, and therefore employment. Such policies were not costless as prices also would be adjusted upwards. The Phillips' Curve was originally thought to present the policy 'menu' which governments faced. Policy-makers decided the socially-optimal combination of inflation and unemployment, adjusting aggregate demand to achieve that combination. Lags and forecasting errors meant that disturbances from desired output levels still occurred, but the weakness of the self-correcting mechanism of price adjustment favoured the adoption of counter-cyclical demand-management policies. The presumption that a trade-off existed between the inflation rate and unemployment rate caused the term 'full-employment' to gradually disappear from the literature, just as in the neoclassical model, there was a range of possible employment levels rather than a unique level which corresponds to an unambiguous socially optimal level.

Within this tradition some economists have queried whether the above emphasis on wage rigidity is appropriate and instead concentrated on another element of Keynes's analysis of unemployment, co-ordination or communication failure. Benassi *et al.*, 1994) survey these models. Originally the emphasis was upon the possibility of false trading and the 'disequilibrium' co-ordination problem, with recent developments concentrating upon the idea that trading is more costly in a thin market. The lower the level of activity on one side of the market the higher the search costs on the other side, an argument we first developed in Chapter 5. Expectations can be self-fulfilling, in which case expectation of low economic activity discourages people from trading and therefore generates low activity. Howitt and McAfee (1987) provide an example of such a model displaying multiple equilibria, both high and low unemployment outcomes can result at the same real wage rate, due to these externalities in the search process.

7.2.3   *The natural rate of unemployment*

Beginning in the late 1950s the neoclassical counter-revolution gradually undermined Keynesian arguments for demand management policies. New theories of aggregate consumption expenditure, of crowding-out, of the demand for money, and above all, the re-interpretation of the simple Phillips' curve, weakened the case for policies aimed at stabilising employment levels. Keynesian economics had become focused upon the manipulation of aggregate demand to the exclusion of other issues. The inappropriateness of such manipulations in the face of stagflation gave added impetus to the monetarist critique. According to the Phelps-Friedman, expectations-augmented Phillips' curve, governments could no longer manipulate employment by macroeconomic policies. The tendency of the labour market to clear was reasserted, but equilibrium was now consistent with a positive, 'natural' level of unemployment reflecting imperfections in the labour market. A major weakness of the Phelps-Friedman approach was that decision-makers could be repeatedly fooled in the short run, even by systematic policies. The new classical approach is to maintain the market clearing assumptions of the Friedman-Phelps approach but to assume that expectations are formed rationally. In such a model anticipated changes in fiscal and monetary policy can have no impact on real variables, since decision-makers merely revise their expectations of the future price level. Systematic macroeconomic policy is now impotent with respect to the level of unemployment: no trade-off between unemployment and inflation exists even in the short run. In the long run, and when expectations are correct in the short run, unemployment will be at the natural rate. If the natural rate does not change much through time, the actual rate of unemployment in the economy will tend to move randomly around it, reflecting unexpected shocks which cause expectational errors and hence deviations from the natural rate. In order to explain the cyclical pattern of unemployment, real business cycle theories have been developed which utilise technological shocks and inter-temporal substitution between work and leisure to explain the observed serial correlation of unemployment. New classical economics and real business cycle theory thus provide a final eclipse of Keynesian policy prescriptions: any attempts to reduce unemployment by expanding aggregate demand merely cause rapid upwards adjustments of prices: cyclical unemployment is an optimal response to unfavourable technology shocks.

The size of this natural rate was dependent upon the extent of imperfections in the labour market, what had previously been termed frictional and structural unemployment. Occupational and locational immobilities, imperfect information, union and government interference could all give rise to unemployed workers and unfilled vacancies, although there is an overall balance between the demand and supply of labour in the market. In Figure 7.3 we provide a diagrammatic representation of the natural rate of unemployment; the demand side of the labour market is defined to exclude vacancies and we distinguish between the total supply of labour, n_t, and the amount of workers willing to accept offered jobs, n^A. At w^* the number of workers willing to accept offered jobs equals existing employment, also the number of existing vacancies does not induce any change in the real wage to alter the flow of applications. The difference between n_1 and n^* measures the difference between the

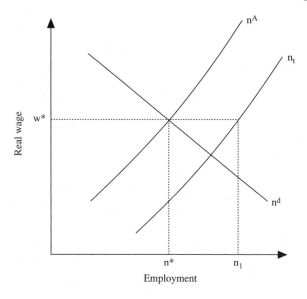

Figure 7.3 The natural rate of unemployment

total supply of labour and the amount of employment offered and accepted and hence represents the natural rate of unemployment. Factors which cause the total labour supply to diverge from the number of workers willing to accept offered jobs cause the natural rate of unemployment to increase. Thus increased mismatch shifts the n^A curve to the left and increases the natural rate since vacancies and searching workers are becoming less compatible. The term natural rate of unemployment does not imply an optimal level of unemployment in the economy, since in part it reflects avoidable inefficiencies. However, attempts by government to reduce unemployment below this natural rate by Keynesian-style expansionary macro policies would cause excess demand and lead to accelerating inflation.

Less restrictive models of labour market behaviour utilise a slightly different concept of the equilibrium rate of unemployment: the non-accelerating inflation rate of unemployment, or the NAIRU. We will use this term to also encompass the OECD's preferred non-accelerating rate of wage inflation rate of unemployment (NAWRU). The most popular model of the NAIRU, or sustainable unemployment rate, is currently that originally developed by Layard and Nickell. Essentially their approach provides a generalisation of the competitive model developed in Chapter 2, allowing for imperfections to product and labour markets. Appendix 7.1 provides a formal summary of Layard *et al.*'s (1991) basic model. Within a bargaining framework the NAIRU is where the 'feasible' real wage implied by the pricing behaviour of firms equates the 'target' real wage implied by the behaviour of wage-bargainers. If we assume that a firm's mark-up on wages rises with output and employment is positively related to output, then it follows that since the real wage is the reciprocal of the mark-up, the real wage falls as the employment rate rises. This is the price-setting curve, shown as PS in Figure 7.4; it can be thought of as representing the feasible wage since it is the real wage that price-setters are willing to concede in any bargain. With competitive product markets this would correspond to the labour demand curve of Chapter 2. The positively sloped wage-setting curve, WS in Figure 7.4, describes how wages are set and derives from the argument that wages are set as a mark-up on expected prices and that this mark-up increases with the employment rate. Phelps (1994) calls this a surrogate labour supply curve. WS represents the target real wage which wage-setters intend. If we make the simplifying assumption that aggregate labour market participation is perfectly wage inelastic we can represent the labour supply, LS, as vertical. The NAIRU is therefore the difference between labour supply and equilibrium employment, the latter occurring where the wage-setting and price-setting curves intersect and the target wage equals the feasible real wage, w*. In Figure 7.4 the sustainable rate of unemployment or the NAIRU is therefore 1−e*. The NAIRU can increase either because the feasible real wage which the economy can sustain at a given employment rate has fallen or wage fixers' target wage has risen relative to that feasible wage at a given employment rate.

Theoretical and empirical studies utilising this framework have concentrated upon structural factors which influence the position and slope of the wage-setting curve, such as the operation of the benefit system, the degree of mismatch in the labour market and the pressure on wages from trade union militancy. In this type of model any increase in wage-push pressure as a consequence of changes in these structural factors, shifts the wage-setting curve leftwards and real demand has to be reduced to stabilise inflation. The new equilibrium position has higher real wages and a lower employment rate and hence greater NAIRU. Demand has to be low compared to

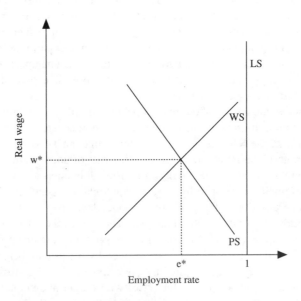

Figure 7.4 The Layard and Nickell model of the NAIRU

potential output, and unemployment high, in order to induce bargainers to settle at the feasible real wage. In the short term unemployment can diverge from the NAIRU due to demand and supply shocks but in the medium term the economy returns to the NAIRU as the inflation rate stabilises. Unemployment is hence determined only by long-run supply factors in the long run and by the interaction of aggregate demand and aggregate short-run supply in the short run.

The previous argument is what Blinder (1994) has called 'the approximate dichotomy'. In the short run changes in aggregate demand can change the unemployment rate by about 2–3 per cent, the sort of changes observed over the typical European business cycle. Whereas in the long run, the unemployment rate converges on the NAIRU regardless of macroeconomic policy, since in the long run only microeconomic policies which influence the efficiency of labour markets can affect the rate of unemployment. It is this 'approximate dichotomy' which represents current economic orthodoxy in North America and most parts of Europe.

7.2.4 *Summary*

Since the mid-1970s both Keynesians and neoclassical economists have belatedly turned their attention to the issue of how labour markets adjust to shocks. Neoclassical economists still largely see high unemployment as reflecting a high NAIRU, itself largely the consequence of institutional interference with the market mechanism. Keynesians, on the other hand, still view unemployment as a consequence of the inherent weakness of adjustment mechanisms in the labour market, with contractionary shocks causing long-term, perhaps even permanent, deviations from the NAIRU. Traditionally this division has also been interpreted as reflecting Keynesian stress on involuntary unemployment and neoclassical on voluntary unemployment. Keynesians believing that workers are supply constrained in the labour market, whilst in some versions of the neoclassical approach unemployment is either efficient off-the-job search, discussed in Chapter 5, or a rational response to low labour market productivity and relatively high unemployment insurance benefits. Thus Lucas writes, 'To explain why people allocate time to ... unemployment we need to know why they prefer it to all other activities' (1986, p. 38). The distinction between voluntary and involuntary unemployment has always been problematic, particularly if one tries to apply the distinction in practice. A redundant teacher could deliver newspapers. If she chooses not to when such jobs are available, is she voluntarily or involuntarily unemployed? In some recent models any distinction breaks down as, say, a workforce in aggregate may prefer unemployment as a response to demand reductions, but the specific individuals who actually lose their job do so unwillingly. Our earlier finding that the unemployed in general suffered distress and dissatisfaction gives further incentive for us to resist using this distinction in the remainder of this chapter.

We have introduced the basis of contemporary analysis of unemployment and we now need to concentrate upon analysis specifically related to European unemployment. Since the European experience of unemployment has been so different to that of North America we should not be too surprised to learn that analysis of unemployment has also become differentiated. In the late 1980s much attention was devoted to the supposed inflexibility of wages in European labour markets: greater inflexibility of wages implying more adjustments to shocks being required in the form of employment changes. It is this proposition to which we now turn, initially reviewing the empirical evidence and then appropriate theory.

7.3 Wage rigidity in Europe: theory and evidence

7.3.1 *Evidence for European economies*

The debate about the degree of flexibility of wages in the economy is not directly about the variability of wages, but about how responsive wages are to disequilibrium pressures in the labour market. In other words, the key question concerns how effective wages are in clearing the labour market rather than how stable they are. In terms of Figure 7.4 we can think of real wage rigidity as causing the wage-setting curve to become flatter, hence any shock which causes a shift in one of these curves will lead to a larger employment change than in a more price-adjusting world.

Empirical studies, reviewed in Bean (1994) and the OECD (1994a), suggest that if anything, Europe has a relatively low degree of nominal wage inertia, and differences in the adjustments of nominal wages have largely been dismissed as an explanation of the distinctive unemployment experience of Europe. Since the early 1980s real wage rigidity has been advanced as an explanation for the European unemployment problem. Studies by amongst others Alogoskoufis and Manning (1988) have concluded that the responsiveness of real wages to unemployment was much lower in the EC and the US than in Japan, Austria, Switzerland and the Nordic countries.

In the traditional analysis of competitive labour markets any change in market conditions produces a speedy adjustment of wage levels ensuring that labour demand and supply are balanced. In this model unemployment is only a temporary disequilibrium phenomenon. Explanations of why firms and/or workers may prefer to adjust to contractions of demand for output by reducing employment rather than wages have become something of a growth industry over the last twenty years. The growth of theoretical work on wage rigidity can be attributed to several convergent forces. The observation that contemporary employment spells were much longer than previously assumed, stimulated interest in how strongly attached workers and firms would adjust to temporary changes in demand. The disappearance of a strong negative relationship between inflation and unemployment, and the development of expectations-based models of inflation also aroused interest in the origins of long-term contracts between workers and firms, and the influence of unions in the form and content of those contracts. We have already discussed many of the arguments briefly in Chapter 2, and we now concentrate upon three: efficiency wages, insider-outsider and union bargaining models.

7.3.2 *Efficiency wage arguments*

Efficiency wage theory builds upon models of internal labour markets developed in Chapter 2, in which employers need to ensure that workers supply acceptable levels of effort for agreed wages. Efficiency wage theory rejects the version of neo-classical theory which views production as determined by a purely technical relationship between inputs and outputs. Firms may be reluctant to lower real wages in the face of excess supply of labour because productivity may fall even faster or non-wage costs of employing labour rise, increasing labour costs per unit of output. As a consequence the unemployed are unable to find jobs by offering to work for less than the prevailing real wage, since it is not in the firms' interest for the wage to fall.

The earliest versions of this positive relation between productivity and wages can be found in Marx, where because the industrial reserve army, the unemployed, acted as a discipline device, employers had an incentive to fix wages at a level which produced an excess supply of labour. Later economists emphasised costly turnover and imperfect information as the source of firms offering real wages above market clearing levels; Benassi *et al.* (1994) provide a review of these models. Perhaps the most popular version stresses the consequences of the high costs of monitoring workers. Discipline in the firm requires that workers are rewarded for 'good behaviour' and penalised for shirking. By paying workers above the rate paid in alternative employments, firms encourage workers to protect their 'rents' by adopting acceptable patterns of behaviour. It is not clear that these theories always produce wage rigidity, other possible strategies include payment by seniority or a 'good-behaviour' bond being required of entrants. As yet there is little direct empirical evidence of the importance of efficiency wage considerations in European labour markets, though Konings and Walsh (1994) find supporting evidence from a sample of UK firms with low unionisation rates. A major problem with these models is their inability to explain the differing experience of unemployment between countries except by relying upon differences in monitoring or information costs which have yet to be observed in practice.

7.3.3 *Insider–outsider models*

Whilst efficiency wage theories are built upon the assumption of firms' imperfect information of employees' productivity, insider–outsider or membership models start by arguing that existing employees have market power due to costly turnover. Existing employees, insiders, when they bargain for wages do not care about the welfare of outsiders, the unemployed or employees not protected by high turnover costs. Outsiders find it difficult to price themselves into good jobs since their productivity is lower. In addition, they may face harassment and a lack of co-operation from insiders, who realise that their rents are threatened. Blanchard and Summers (1986) developed a popular variant of this approach in which the evolution of wages and employment depends critically upon whether an insider who becomes unemployed retains membership of the insider group.

We illustrate the consequences of an adverse shock within this framework in Figure 7.5. Consider a bargaining framework in which the original position is A on the demand for labour curve D_0. A contractionary shock now shifts the demand for labour to D_1 and our new equilibrium position is, say, B. If we assume that the employees who lose their jobs immediately become outsiders then at our new equilibrium, B, we have a kinked indifference curve (UIC_1) representing the union's (insiders) preferences. This curve shows the combination of wages and employment which generates a given level of union welfare, B is the point of tangency between the demand curve and the indifference curve and is therefore where union welfare is maximised. Since insiders gain no utility from an expansion of employment the indifference curve is horizontal to the right of B, whilst at lower levels of employment than n_1 the curve is steeply sloped, reflecting an assumption that risk averse employees require substantial increases in real wages to compensate for higher risks of redundancy. Crucially, any anticipated recovery in the demand for labour, to D_0, will not return employment and real wages to A, insiders prefer higher real wages, w_2, and bargain for C. The only way that employment can return to A, n_0, is through a positive shock to labour demand causing new workers to be hired or through government action, such as wage controls, which produce a similar effect. In this version of the insider-outsider model wages are inversely related to lagged employment and employment becomes a random walk with drift.

In Chapter 2 we reported that studies have established the importance of firm-specific factors in wage determination, however there has been little support for the importance of lagged employment in wage determination as predicted by the model. Blanchard and Summers (1986) and Alogoskoufis and Manning (1988a) have attempted to test versions of the insider–outsider model. The results suggest that

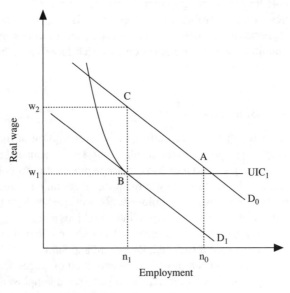

Figure 7.5   The insider–outsider model and unemployment

European countries may have a problem in the persistence of real wage aspirations, rather than a persistence problem stemming from insider membership. The lack of any strong supporting evidence for the insider–outsider model has not stopped the model becoming widely used in explaining unemployment persistence and in the design of, and justification for, policy.

7.3.4   *Union bargaining behaviour*

The analysis discussed so far cannot explain why explicit contracts between firms and unions traditionally specify wages and allow employers to choose employment levels unilaterally. The mutual interest in, and acceptance of redundancy or lay-offs by reverse seniority (Last In First Out, hence LIFO), means that senior workers need not fear displacement, except in the case of complete plant or firm closure. Whilst flexible wages may help the job security of junior employees, they represent unwanted income fluctuations for senior ones. Where union decision-making reflects the interests and votes of senior or median members, they will favour downwards wage rigidity. Alternatively if laid-off workers leave unions, or members are risk neutral and the low probability of unemployment is offset by the higher rewards from work, downwards wage rigidity will still be specified in collectively bargained contracts. Given that unions and employers anticipate a long term bargaining relationship, and that strikes are expensive for both sides, optimal bargaining strategies may favour wage rigidity. In summary, this approach suggests that flexible wages are absent from collectively bargained agreements because unions do not wish them.

Whilst LIFO rules are common, they usually only operate within skill levels and within individual plants. Firms will try to disguise which plants or offices will be closed in the event of contractions in order to reduce median voter pressure for higher real wages. In such situations then we can maintain the assumption of the probability of redundancies influencing wage demands and the union indifference curve used in Figure 7.5 is still appropriate. Lindbeck and Snower (1989) provide union versions of the insider–outsider model.

7.3.5   *Summary*

These theories of real wage rigidity can explain many of the previously puzzling features of unemployment in western economies: unemployed workers cannot price themselves into internal labour markets; existing employees will not in aggregate accept lower wages in preference to lay-offs; work-sharing is not a viable alternative (this would imply senior workers subsidising junior ones). Most of these models suggest that unexpected downturns in aggregate demand will produce increases in unemployment above the NAIRU, as firms initially adjust employment rather than wages. The response of wages to fluctuations in demand is asymmetrical. Whilst wages are slow to fall as demand contracts, these models generally suggest that firms, employees and unions all favour price adjustments to expansions of demand. Any expansionary policies implemented by governments to reduce unemployment may thus risk stimulating inflation, which will be compounded by expectations' adjustment.

217

Hence the interest of many economists who have developed these models in designing expansionary packages which minimise inflationary consequences.

The attention we have given to examining relative wage rigidity in Europe may need reconsideration following the work of Blanchflower and Oswald (1994) who conclude that the degree of wage flexibility across countries may be more similar than previously believed. Their study of regions over time suggests a downward sloping curve between wages and local unemployment rates: the wage curve. The negative relationship between unemployment rates and pay applies to regions, industries and nations and appears identical for the USA, Japan, Austria, Germany, Ireland, Italy, the Netherlands, Norway, Sweden and the UK. In these countries, with the exception of Ireland, the unemployment elasticity of pay is approximately -0.1, a doubling of the unemployment rate being associated with a 10 per cent fall in pay. Whilst these findings are consistent with the bargaining and efficiency wage models, they cannot easily be reconciled with the simple competitive model of the labour market.

7.4   Explaining European unemployment

7.4.1   *Explaining the rise in European unemployment*

The rise in European unemployment which began in 1979 is usually attributed to a combination of disinflationary macroeconomic policies, adverse shocks and increasingly inefficient labour and product markets. Economists differ over the relative importance to be attached to each of these factors, though there is general agreement that some explanations popular with non-specialists are unimportant. We have already dismissed labour supply growth and electronic technical revolution arguments. To be taken more seriously is the proposition that the slowdown of labour productivity growth in the 1970s implied a slowdown in the growth of the feasible real wage (for a given unemployment rate). If there was no similar slowdown in the growth of wage aspirations then rising unemployment could result. The absence of suitable variables to proxy wage aspirations makes investigation of this proposition difficult. As yet no recent work has attributed more than a modest role to the slowdown.

The disinflationary period in Europe at the end of the 1970s and early 1980s could have caused a rise in unemployment above the NAIRU to the extent that these policies were unanticipated or there was nominal inertia in the product and goods markets (Barrell *et al.*, 1994). We have discussed the latter possibility earlier and the former also seems likely. Most commentators, Lindbeck (1995) for example, conclude that restrictive monetary policy made a significant contribution to the severity of the cyclical downturns of 1974 and 1980 in Europe. The strengthening of anti-inflationary policy may be interpreted as unanticipated, since the full-employment guarantees of western European governments in the 1960s and early 1970s led decision-makers to assume governments would always accommodate inflationary pressures. It follows that the abandonment of such policies for monetarist ones would be expected to increase unemployment initially. Many researchers have linked this policy develop-ment with the deterioration of European terms of trade following OPEC-I and OPEC-II. In the context of our NAIRU framework, a deterioration in the terms of trade can cause a wedge between the real wage aspirations of workers and the firms' ability to meet them. Standard analysis treats oil and raw material price increases as operating like productivity reductions. As less value added is available for domestic factors of production, stable employment requires a reduction in the real wage paid by firms, the real product wage rate. In practice, the real product wage did not fall in Western Europe. Indeed, between 1973–1979 it rose at a rate of 4 per cent per annum. In comparison, the real product wage in the US was roughly constant during this time, though between 1979 and 1985 it increased more rapidly than in western Europe. The slower unemployment growth in the US since 1979 is consistent with the more slug-gish growth of the real wage, stimulating labour-intensive production. Hence the faster employment growth in the US since 1979 and the faster growth of productivity in Western Europe, where labour-intensive production did not receive the same rela-tive price stimulus.

The sharp downturn in output growth in Europe in the early 1990s is usually attrib-uted to German economic policies being transmitted to the rest of Europe through the Exchange Rate Mechanism (ERM) of the European Monetary System. Reunification in Germany brought about budget deficits and high domestic interest rates and upwards pressure on other European interest rates resulted in demand deflation in the rest of Europe. This contractionary shock threatened another widespread jump in European unemployment before the effective collapse of the ERM in summer, 1993.

7.4.2   *Explaining the persistence of high European unemployment*

It is the persistence, rather than the origins, of high unemployment in Europe which is generally thought to pose the greater problem for the models of unemployment out-lined earlier. As we have seen, the standard macroeconomic models can all explain why adverse shocks cause temporary rises of unemployment above the normal sus-tainable level. The persistence of high unemployment in Western Europe, according to those models, should indicate structural factors which have caused an increase in the sustainable rate of unemployment. In the absence of such changes we need to make a fundamental re-assessment of the appropriateness of models based upon a unique long-run equilibrium rate of unemployment and rapid adjustment to that rate. We initially concentrate upon structural factors which could have raised the target real wage, relative to the feasible wage rate, at a given employment rate, in European labour markets. In terms of Figure 7.4, we are looking for structural factors which have shifted either the wage-setting or the price-setting curves leftwards, and hence reduced the equilibrium level of employment. A number of possibilities have been considered: trade union bargaining behaviour; unemployment benefits; mismatch and inflexibility resulting from wage controls and employment protection legislation. Anderton and Mayhew (1994), Elmeskov and MacFarlan (1993) and Bean (1994) provide more detailed analysis, the first concentrating upon the relative experience of the UK.

Trade unions

An increase in trade union bargaining power, or a willingness to use that power, would shift the wage-setting curve leftwards and thence, *ceteris paribus*, raise the sustainable rate of unemployment. The main problem in trying to establish the empirical importance of such factors is the inability to directly measure bargaining power or trade union militancy. A common proxy used is trade union density, the proportion of the work-force which is unionised. In most EU countries union density was rising in the 1970s, but in the 1980s a time of high unemployment, densities were generally falling in Europe, Sweden excepted. We discussed some of the reasons for these trends in Chapter 1. Alternative proxies to union density have been utilised in empirical work, such as the number or severity of industrial conflicts and union mark-ups. Layard *et al.* (1991) utilise both union density and measures of strike frequency in their study of post-war unemployment in the OECD, but find no statistically significant effects.

Such results should not lead to an outright rejection of the importance of changes in bargaining power in the determination of unemployment. As we noted in Chapter 1, in most European economies the proportion of employees covered by collective contracts is around twice the union density, and this coverage rate did not appear to fall in the 1980s (OECD, 1994a). In addition, it may not be bargaining power itself which is crucial in the behaviour of the wage-setting curve but the level at which that bargaining takes place. It may be that a high degree of unionisation increases the potential for co-ordinated wage bargaining and for internalising some of the inflation externalities of individual wage bargains. This argument is examined in the following chapter where the potential benefits of centralisation and corporatism are discussed.

Unemployment and other non-employment benefits

As explained in Chapter 5, the level and duration of unemployment benefits may influence the wage-setting curve through the effect on the reservation wage of unemployed job-searchers. In about half of European economies there are more people in receipt of early retirement and invalidity benefits than are in receipt of unemployment benefits and we therefore need to include these benefits in our discussion. The total benefit entitlement of a worker (or family) out of work, compared to total net income in work, is termed the replacement ratio. The replacement ratio may be high for a particular worker because the social security payments are high in comparison to available gross labour market earnings or because tax and national insurance contributions are high at low wage levels. A high replacement ratio may produce a moral hazard problem, by inducing workers to reduce search intensity and raise their reservation wage so that low wage offers are rejected. The consequences of such widespread behaviour, which reduces effective labour supply, must be to increase relative wages and reduce employment at the bottom end of the market. As individual workers face different replacement ratios dependent upon their potential net labour market earnings and entitlement to benefits, it follows that if jobs are rationed in the labour market the replacement ratio will affect the distribution of unemployment, rather than the level. The stock of unemployed workers will in this case contain a disproportionate number of workers with high replacement ratios. In addition to the impact of benefits on the reservation wage of the unemployed, the duration of benefits and the likelihood of disqualification from those benefits will also influence the sustainable rate of unemployment.

Our discussion has already indicated that it would be difficult to provide simple comparisons of replacement rates for different countries and time-periods; Reissert and Schmid (1994) outline the variety of unemployment compensation systems within the EU. The OECD *Jobs Study* provides a careful explanation of the problems of comparing replacement rates, in Table 7.2 we provide a comparison of benefit entitlements in European countries in 1991. These statistics compare benefit entitlement for a 40 year old worker, assumed to have no assets or unearned income. The different duration categories indicate the importance of the variation in unemployment insurance benefits and their relative size compared to unemployment assistance benefits. Since the 1970s there has been a strong upward trend in the ratio in Finland, Norway, Portugal, Spain and Sweden. Britain and Belgium were the only European countries who succeeded in reducing this ratio in the 1980s. Once insurance entitlements have

Table 7.2 Unemployment benefit entitlements[1] in Europe, 1991

Duration categories	First year			Second and third year			
Family Circumstances	Single	With dependent spouse	With spouse in work	Single	With dependent spouse	With spouse in work	Overall average (includes fourth and fifth year)
Austria	42	45	25	40	43	0	26
Belgium	52	52	47	36	52	30	43
Denmark	73	74	72	61	67	54	52
Finland	58	58	56	44	44	27	38
France	58	58	58	37	37	30	37
Germany	37	41	37	33	36	0	28
Greece	44	53	44	4	4	4	17
Ireland	38	52	38	26	41	5	29
Italy	7	8	7	0	0	0	3
Netherlands	70	70	70	56	56	56	51
Portugal	65	65	65	37	40	37	34
Spain	70	70	70	30	30	30	33
Sweden	80	80	80	6	6	6	29
United Kingdom	19	31	19	17	27	0	18
Norway	62	62	62	41	41	41	39
United States	24	26	21	5	10	0	11

[1] Benefit entitlement before tax as a percentage of previous earnings before tax. Data shown are average over replacement rates at two earnings levels (average earnings and two-thirds of average earnings). Ignores housing benefits for unemployed and certain other benefits. In Denmark, Norway and Sweden the guarantee of a place on an active labour market programme for the long-term unemployed makes it possible for the unemployed to receive benefits almost indefinitely.
Source: OECD *Jobs Study* (1994a).

been exhausted or where insurance is unavailable, there are different systems of unemployment assistance and social welfare payments, which can be thought of as establishing a floor for wages. The flat-rate benefit figures in Table 7.2 indicate that, as a proportion of average production worker earnings, benefits are relatively low in Denmark, Portugal and the United Kingdom and much higher in the Netherlands and Finland.

Whilst simple cross-country correlations indicate a strong relationship between benefit generosity and unemployment, econometric studies of the impact of differences in the replacement ratio on the behaviour of unemployment have produced a wide range of results. Layard *et al.* (1991) find that the level and duration of benefits have an important effect on the impact of unemployment on wages in OECD countries. They conclude that shocks appear to be more easily absorbed in countries where the benefit system discourages long-term unemployment by restricting the duration of benefit payment. The OECD Jobs Study suggested that replacement rates and duration of benefits may affect unemployment rates with an elasticity of around 1, much larger than the estimates found in single-country studies. Microeconometric studies provide a wide range of results, perhaps not surprisingly if we re-consider the relationship between benefits and job search. Our discussion has so far ignored the possibility that unemployment benefits may not only affect the reservation wage but also finance job-search activities and, as discussed in Chapter 5, therefore increase the productivity of such search. Wadsworth (1991), using the 1984 UK Labour Force Survey, concludes that benefit claimants search more extensively than non-claimants, thereby increasing the rate of job offers. Recent surveys for the UK (Atkinson, 1993) and West Germany (Zimmermann, 1993) indicate that there is little evidence that benefits represent a major discouragement to returning to work, whilst for Denmark (Pedersen, 1993), Spain (Ahn and Ugidos-Olazabal, 1995) and Sweden (Gustafsson and Klevmarken, 1993) there are stronger indications that unemployment insurance positively affects the duration of unemployment. These conclusions must still be treated with caution, since Pedersen and Westergård-Nielsen (1993) surveying the same studies concluded that US and UK studies showed significant effects of replacement on the escape from unemployment, whilst studies of the more generous continental European systems found little evidence of disincentive effects. In Britain there have been both large and frequent changes in the operation of the social security system since 1979 and Arulampalam and Stewart (1995) find that the effect of income whilst unemployed on the probability of leaving unemployment was much lower in 1987 than in 1978, and the effect disappears after three months. The conclusion of Arulampalam and Stewart is that the effect of benefits on unemployment duration has become much less important whilst demand constraints, as measured by the local unemployment rate, have an increased importance in times of high unemployment. Hunt (1995) in an experimental approach utilising changes in the German benefit system found evidence of significant disincentive effects.

Blöndal and Pearson (1995) include other non-employment benefits in their study; whilst they find some evidence that the generosity of unemployment benefits influenced recorded unemployment, they found similar positive effects on labour-force participation. Overall, in net terms, higher benefits were not associated with lower employment rates, whereas high sickness and invalidity benefits tended to reduce labour force participation. These results suggest that the overall structure of state benefits, not just unemployment benefits, is an important determinant of the relative size of the various non-employed categories.

If job offers are rarely rejected by the unemployed and the arrival rate of job offers is independent of their search behaviour then much of the above discussion is misplaced and our attention should focus on the demand side. The survey of panel data studies by Pedersen and Westergård-Nielsen (1993) cites both UK and Dutch data which suggest that virtually all job offers were accepted by the unemployed, but little research work has been carried out on the determinants of the arrival rate of job offers.

Wage controls and employment protection legislation
It may not be just the benefit/income ratio which has set too high a floor to wage levels in European labour markets; governments' direct or indirect adjustments of minimum wage levels may also be shifting the wage-setting curve leftwards. We have already discussed the operation of minimum wage laws in EU countries in Chapter 3 and concluded that currently the evidence suggests little impact of such policies on unemployment.

Mandated severance pay and the length of notice of termination specified in employment contracts tends to be greater in Europe than in the US. The NAIRU may be increased by employment protection which imposes higher fixed labour costs on employers, altering the desired division of labour input between number of workers and hours per worker. If firms are reluctant to hire new workers because of high firing costs then although their total labour input may not change, an increase in hours worked per worker may cause measured unemployment to rise. Firms may also be less willing to fire workers as a consequence of such regulations since they may be required to make redundancy payments. The short-run net effect on measured unemployment is therefore not clear: job-security legislation will tend to reduce inflow into unemployment whilst also reducing the outflow back into jobs. The study by Burgess (1994) of net job generation in the US and Europe highlights the potential importance of hiring costs. At a disaggregated level, whilst the two economies perform similarly when employment is falling, in upswings employment rises in the US more rapidly and frequently and overall employment growth in US industries is much more diverse than in Europe. Work by Lazear (1990) utilised a reduced form cross-country analysis of OECD countries and found evidence that severance pay reduces employment and increases unemployment. Especially large effects were found for France and Italy. However, Denmark, Ireland and the UK had relatively weak regulations in the time period we are considering and Lazear's results are inconsistent with Bentolila and Bertola (1990) who found that higher firing costs increased long-run average employment levels due to the reduced rate of separations.

Mismatch
Another determinant of the wage-setting curve in Figure 7.4 will be the extent to which the unemployed are suitable for the available vacancies: the degree of mismatch in the

labour market. Mismatch due to the inefficiency of the job-matching process and locational immobility has already been discussed in Chapter 5, in addition mismatch due to changes in the composition of production affecting the skill structure has been considered in Chapter 4. In the US the concentration of unemployment amongst the unskilled and in regions where heavy industry has been in decline has encouraged some economists (Lilien, 1982) to emphasize the importance of sectoral shifts in driving aggregate unemployment. Jackman and Roper (1987) calculate a mismatch index for both occupational and regional groupings and find little evidence of an increase of mismatch in the 1970s and early 1980s. Jackman *et al.* (1991), using an unemployment measure, find no evidence of increasing mismatch in Europe, apart from Sweden. They conclude that mismatch cannot explain the outwards shift in the UV curve in Europe.

The concentration of European unemployment amongst the low-skilled and less-educated has tempted some economists to emphasise the importance of shifts in the demand for labour. As we discussed in Chapter 1, changes in the relative size of different sectors and the impact of electronic, and especially information, technology have reduced the relative demand for unskilled labour. Whilst in the US their 'flexible' labour market has responded to this process by producing a dramatic fall in the relative wage of low-skill workers, in many European countries wage inequality has not increased due to a variety of institutional forces. Jackman (1995) combines this structural shift with the union, benefits and regulation arguments outlined previously, the latter create real wage rigidity at the bottom end of the labour market and thus in combination with the demand shift provide an explanation for high European unemployment. Alternatively, in Minford's model (1995) it is the low-wage competition from 'emerging-market' economies which is at the heart of the structural shift, with the generous welfare state in Europe causing the shift to be reflected in higher unemployment. However, these arguments are challenged by Nickell and Bell (1995) who find that about 80 per cent of the increase in unemployment in the 1980s was due to neutral shocks across skill groups, rather than to a fall in the relative demand for unskilled workers.

Summary

Overall, the discussion of these supply-side factors seems to imply that there should have been a reversal in the upward trend in the European NAIRU in recent years. However, Barrell *et al.* (1994) find that of the big four EU economies only Italy, following the relaxation of wage indexing, had a lower estimated NAIRU in the 1990s. Similarly, the OECD (1994) finds no evidence of a falling NAIRU in the EU in recent years, indeed their data, as summarised in Table 7.3, indicate that the only recent major change has been for the NAIRU to rise in, what was then, non-EC Europe. This latter change is another illustration of the NAIRU tending to follow the trend in the actual unemployment rate. As Blanchard and Jimeno (1995) point out the 'increase in European unemployment over the last two decades has made clear that the natural rate of unemployment is all but natural, and all but constant' (page 212). Elmeskov and MacFarlan (1993) report a positive relationship between the year-to-year volatility of the unemployment rate and the trend rise in unemployment. Countries with the

Table 7.3 Unemployment: actual and estimated NAIRU's

	1973–9		1980–9		1990–3		1994	
	Actual	NAIRU	Actual	NAIRU	Actual	NAIRU	Actual	NAIRU
Non-Europe	4.6[1]	4.8[1]	5.9	5.8	5.6	5.4	5.7	5.5
Big Four								
Europe	4.3	4.3	8.7	8.4	8.8	9.0	10.2	9.4
Smaller EC	4.7	4.6	13.4	12.5	12.9	14.1	16.7	15.0
Other Europe	1.3	1.3	2.1	2.1	3.8	3.5	5.8	5.1

[1] 1970–9.
Source: OECD *Economic Outlook* (1994), Table 12.

greatest variability of unemployment, such as Ireland and Spain, have experienced the largest increases in unemployment rates. Together these observations have led to an interest in models of unemployment hysteresis to which we now turn.

7.4.3   *Hysteresis*

The difficulty in identifying factors which across all European labour markets could have caused a permanent rise in equilibrium unemployment since the 1970s, has led some economists to reject the simple NAIRU approach we have so far adopted. Rather than view the equilibrium unemployment rate as dependent upon the current values of its structural determinants, models of unemployment hysteresis emphasise the slow adjustment of the labour market to shocks. Shocks which cause a rise in unemployment may cause the equilibrium unemployment rate to rise for a considerable time, hence the idea of hysteresis: unemployment breeds unemployment. One of the attractions of this approach is that it can explain the different experience of unemployment in the Nordic countries. Even given their relatively generous benefits, high firing and hiring costs and rigid relative wages, these countries managed to maintain high employment rates until hit by large macroeconomic shocks. These occurred in Denmark in the early 1980s, Norway in the late 1980s, and Sweden and Finland in the early 1990s. Once unemployment rose in these countries they experienced similar persistence problems to those in the rest of western Europe.

Appendix 7.1 explains how hysteresis effects may be included in Layard *et al.*'s formal model. Following Elmeskov and MacFarlan (1993) we can illustrate the argument in Figure 7.6 which utilises the NAIRU model earlier illustrated in Figure 7.4. Starting from A, suppose a temporary demand shock, such as an unexpected tightening of monetary policy, shifts the price-setting curve to the left (PS_2), and the short-run equilibrium is now B with the employment rate falling to e_2 and the unemployment rate rising to $1-e_2$. With full hysteresis this position also represents long-run equilibrium, the wage-setting curve can now be thought of as a vertical line through e_2 and any anticipated recovery back to PS_1 leads only to higher wages and the economy moves to C not to A. Only unanticipated changes can shift employment from e_2.

With partial hysteresis, or slow adjustment, wage-setting behaviour does respond

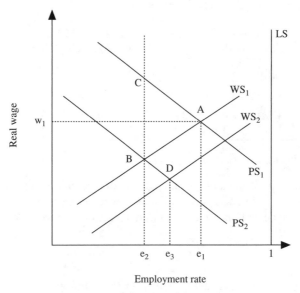

Figure 7.6   Unemployment hysteresis: full and partial

over time to the increase in unemployment. If this adjustment is only partial then gradually the wage-setting curve will shift towards, say WS_2, and eventually we get an equilibrium at D, where the unemployment rate has recovered to $1-e_3$. On the demand-side the presence of high hiring and firing costs in Europe, discussed earlier, could explain why employment only gradually moves to e_3. We will now briefly review alternative explanations of why increases in unemployment may be difficult to reverse; Arestis and Biefang-Frisancho Mariscal (1991) and Wyplosz (1994) provide more detailed surveys.

Capital shortage
In the late 1970s and early 1980s the major European economies all experienced a fall in profitability and in the share of investment in output. Bean (1994) calculated that by 1987, in comparison with a simple extrapolation of the 1960–74 trend, there was an apparent capital shortfall of 14 per cent in France, 21 per cent in the UK and 34 per cent in Germany. This capital shortage could cause a demand shock to have the permanent effect on the price-setting curve already analysed. If we combine this shock with the argument that substitution towards more labour-intensive production is very limited in practice, then hysteresis effects are possible. However, Drèze and Bean (1990) provide a variety of studies for European countries, indicating that in the 1980s only a small proportion of firms were capacity constrained and that in the medium term the labour-intensity of production is sensitive to relative factor price changes. In addition, the tendency of vacancies to have risen relative to unemployment in most European economies is inconsistent with the capital shortage argument and has led to the popularity of alternative hysteresis models based on the behaviour of the wage-setting curve.

Duration theories

It has been suggested that the long-term unemployed (LTU) exert less downward pressure on the wage bargain than those who have recently lost their job, hence the simple NAIRU model is misspecified and the composition of unemployment, as well as its level, become important. We have already noted the relative increase in long-term unemployment in Europe, and it has been suggested that a reason for their inability to influence wage bargains is that their skills and motivation may deteriorate as duration increases. By itself such deterioration need not cause unemployment persistence since relative real wages could fall to still make such labour attractive to employers, a response which appears to happen in the US. However, if the productivity of the LTU falls below their reservation wage, or if the forces of wage rigidity discussed above prevent the fall in their relative wages, then as LTU increases the 'effective' labour force contracts and the equilibrium rate of unemployment will increase. This response is consistent with the observed shift in the UV curve in most European economies and the inability of outsiders to restrain insider bargaining power. Evidence supporting the key propositions that skills and motivation deteriorate amongst the LTU is far from overwhelming, however Hughes and McCormick (1989) using individual data do show that the number of employers contacted declines rapidly after a year of unemployment. Measuring the motivation of the unemployed is problematic and little evidence is available on this proposition and we already know that the LTU are predominantly low-skilled and therefore any skill deterioration can only be of basic work skills.

Another version of the duration dependence model concentrates upon the behaviour of employers. With asymmetric information problems and recruitment costs, firms are always looking for cheap screens to help reduce their formal screening costs. Given the absence of wage flexibility in many internal labour markets as analysed in Chapter 2, firms do not adjust wage offers on the basis of the potential productivity of recruits. Hence, if they wish to screen-out low productivity applicants and assume that other employers are pursuing similar recruitment strategies, then firms will favour applicants who have been unemployed for only a short time. This is what Blanchard and Diamond (1994) have called 'ranking'. Here, a contractionary shock initially reduces hiring and raises the average duration of unemployment spells. Given the duration dependence of hiring probabilities, those who were already unemployed at the time of the shock become the LTU. As Pissarides (1992) argues, if employers believe that the average skill-level of the unemployed has deteriorated then they may react by reducing planned employment growth, causing unemployment persistence long after the initial shock occurred.

Empirical studies suggest that in Britain (Layard and Nickell, 1987) and Germany (Franz, 1987) as the share of the LTU in total unemployment increases, aggregate wages become less sensitive to unemployment, though Coe (1988) only finds supportive evidence for the UK and Andrés (1990) finds no such effects for Spain. At a disaggregated level, Blanchflower and Oswald (1990) also have difficulty in establishing any significant effects of the share of the LTU in unemployment. More recently the whole proposition of negative duration dependence has been questioned. Van den Berg and van Ours (1994) attempt to distinguish between the effects of duration dependence

227

and unobserved heterogeneity on the exit rate out of unemployment. They conclude that whilst in the UK there is evidence of genuine negative duration dependence, in France there are no such effects in the first year whilst in the Netherlands there is an inverse u-shaped duration dependence over the first three quarters of unemployment. The survey by Pedersen and Westergård-Nielsen (1993) shows that in panel studies which do take into account unobserved heterogeneity there is no longer consistent support for negative duration dependence.

Insider membership models

We have already outlined in section 7.3.3 the insider–outsider model of hysteresis. If insiders lose membership after lay-offs, then contractionary shocks can permanently reduce the level of employment. Insiders in their bargaining strategy ignore the interests of workers who lost their jobs when employers adjusted to the shock, and any anticipated increase in demand encourages employed workers to bargain for wage, not employment, increases, generating our vertical wage-setting curve of Figure 7.6. Both the capital shortage and the duration versions of hysteresis may be viewed as complementary to the insider–outsider approach. The former can explain why outsiders may be only slowly absorbed into employment and the latter provides a further explanation of why the unemployed cannot price themselves into insiders' jobs. Bentolila and Dolado (1994) find some evidence for the importance of insider membership effects in Spain. However, our earlier discussion of the microeconometric evidence suggested that a 'wage curve' existed in most labour markets, relative wages are affected by local unemployment rates, which indicates that pure hysteresis effects are not present in most markets.

Summary

The empirical results suggesting a weak effect of long-term unemployment on wage bargaining are inconsistent with full hysteresis. Whilst the short-term variations in unemployment and the degree of real-wage rigidity are similar to those in the US, increases in unemployment are much more persistent in Europe. Our survey of explanations of unemployment persistence provides a surplus of explanations for the high rate of unemployment in Europe based upon partial hysteresis. Persistence mechanisms in Europe may be stronger because unemployment benefit systems promote long spells of unemployment; and unions and job security legislation promote insider-power. Blanchard and Jimeno (1995) provide some support from their consideration of the unemployment experience of Portugal and Spain. The countries have similar histories but their unemployment record has diverged dramatically since 1978 and now Spain has the highest rate in the EU whereas Portugal has one of the lowest rates. Labour market institutions and rules appear to be very similar in the two countries, though eligibility rules for unemployment benefits are slightly tougher in Portugal, and until recently her replacement rates were lower. Blanchard and Jimeno argue that these differences in benefits led to greater unemployment costs of disinflation in Spain in the 1970s and caused higher persistence of unemployment since. They conclude that not only are persistence effects important but in addition differences in the timing of shocks may be an important cause of divergences in unemployment experience.

Phelps (1994) has recently revised the NAIRU model to produce a convergence with models of partial hysteresis. In his model it is the persistence of the underlying forces, particularly real interest rates, driving the NAIRU that accounts for unemployment persistence. With this potential coming together of the Keynesian and neoclassical traditions it is now time to turn from our review of theory and evidence to consider their implications for designing policies to reduce unemployment in Europe.

7.5 Policy implications

7.5.1 *Laissez-faire*

For those economists who view unemployment as predominantly the result of optimizing decisions by workers and firms within efficient markets, there is no obvious role for active government employment policy. Currently the most popular form of this approach is real business cycle theory; this views cyclical unemployment as an inevitable and optimal consequence of negative technological shocks which have temporarily reduced real wages. In such a situation the rational response of optimising decision-makers is to substitute leisure for work, government intervention can only serve to distort market forces and increase equilibrium unemployment. As this approach is concerned with cyclical fluctuations of employment it is unsuited to explaining the persistence of European unemployment and we turn to a consideration of alternative policy stances.

7.5.2 *Demand management*

One of the features of modern theory and policy is the neglect of macroeconomic issues, in the OECD Jobs Study out of a total of fifty-nine recommendations only two concern macroeconomic policy issues (Box 7.2 provides a summary). The first of these is that governments should maintain demand at a level consistent with non-inflationary growth, and the second that they should maintain sound public finances. The origin of this neglect is in the dominance of the natural rate approach, which when combined with rational expectations implies that systematic macroeconomic policy has no effects on employment. Expansionary macro policies have no role to play where the cause of high unemployment is an increasing NAIRU. Within this framework demand management policies need to be targeted at inflation and need to be predictable, hence the OECD proposals earlier. Unpredictable macro policies will cause actual inflation to diverge from expected inflation and decision-makers will make sub-optimal decisions causing unemployment to temporarily deviate from the natural rate. We have argued that this approach provides an insight into the growth of European unemployment in the 1970s and early 1980s, but cannot explain unemployment persistence with broadly stable inflation.

There is now general agreement that demand management policies should be predictable and that when unemployment is above the medium term natural rate policy can be moderately expansionary, but economists who reject the simplest natural rate arguments argue for a more pro-active role for macroeconomic policies. Where labour market adjustments to contractionary shocks are slow and partial, Keynesian-style expansionary policies may be effective at promoting employment in the short run. If prices are sluggish, raising product demand through tax cuts will induce firms to expand output and employment, and the resulting increase in consumer demand reinforces the expansionary stimulus. Whether this multiplier process only affects output and employment depends crucially on the period over which prices and wages are sticky. Apart from inflation, modern theory also recognises that such policies may be constrained by balance of payments/exchange rate and public debt considerations.

Such short-run, counter-cyclical arguments for demand management imply much stronger links between product and labour markets than those we have found in Europe in the 1980s. Whilst in most European economies demand was recovering by the end of 1982, employment did not recover until 1986 in the UK and even later in most other EU countries. Expansionary policy may need to be combined with supply-side and institutional reforms if employment is to be significantly stimulated in the short run. However, unemployment persistence in Europe does reinforce the importance of moderating contractionary shocks, and therefore makes the case for contingent policy rules, which automatically off-set shocks.

For most European countries periods of expansion generate labour productivity growth of the order of 1.5 to 2.5 per cent per annum. Thus maintaining a 4 per cent growth rate of output generates an annual growth rate of employment of around 1.5 to 2.5 per cent. Recently, Snower (1995a) has emphasised the longer-term effects of demand management on employment. Consider Figure 7.4. An increase in product demand can in principle stimulate employment by shifting either the price-setting or wage-setting curves to the right. Since real wages do not move counter-cyclically, we need to explain why the price-setting curve should shift rightwards. Possibilities relevant to the role of demand management include expansionary monetary policy reducing the real interest rate and stimulating the demand for capital and therefore labour. Alternatively, expansionary policies may increase capacity utilisation rates or induce the entry of new firms. However, in the face of hysteresis effects such policies are largely inflationary and economists favouring a more expansionary policy stance have to explain how these effects are to be targeted. Concentrating expenditure on infrastructure and job creation for the long-term unemployed are two favoured policies. The former since it may directly stimulate private sector productivity, the latter since increasing the employability of the LTU increases the effective labour supply and brings downwards pressure on wage inflation.

7.5.3 Supply-side policies

Our outline of theoretical developments explains why there has been much discussion in recent years of policies designed to influence the structural determinants of the equilibrium or sustainable unemployment rate. We can divide them into policies which seek to influence directly the productivity of workers, here termed supply-side policies, and those which seek to change the institutional determinants of employment, these latter institutional policies we discuss in the following section. In many cases supply-side or institutional policies which are effective in reducing the NAIRU are likely to be also effective at tackling full and partial hysteresis. Amongst our supply-side policies are those aimed at reducing skill and informational mismatch: policies we have discussed at length in previous chapters. Whilst we have rejected structural change and a general increase in informational mismatch as significant causes of European unemployment persistence, a combination of the decline in the relative demand for unskilled manual labour and training market failures cannot be so easily dismissed.

In countries with bargaining at the firm and/or plant level, insider-power becomes an issue and whilst supply-side policies can empower outsiders by improving their relative productivity, other measures are likely to be necessary. The most efficient way of reducing the distortionary effects of rent-sharing behaviour may be to remove the ability of producers to earn rents. Tough enforcement of competition legislation, and de-regulation to eliminate entry-barriers and public subsidies of producers, when combined with increased economic integration are likely to assist this process.

7.5.4 *Institutional policies*

We have already touched on a wide variety of arguments which relate to the institutional determinants of European unemployment. Whether one believes in the importance of wage rigidity or increasing NAIRU or hysteresis, reform of European labour market institutions represents a common conclusion. As we shall see, on closer examination this consensus disappears as specific institutions and proposed reforms are examined. The following discussion concentrates upon labour market institutions, ignoring those in product and capital markets and therefore we ignore industrial and competition policies.

Trade union reform was one of the earliest and most repeated of the anti-inflation/ employment policies introduced in Britain by the Thatcher government. The apparent reduction of union bargaining power in Europe in the 1980s at a time of rising and persisting unemployment led us to reject the simplest versions of the rationale for such policies. The championing of local bargaining has often been linked with policies aimed at reducing trade union power. Bargaining at the plant or firm level is supposed to increase the sensitivity of wages to local labour market conditions and therefore promote market clearing. Others have argued the benefits of centralised bargaining and we defer this particular discussion to the next chapter.

In many theoretical frameworks unemployment and associated benefits can compress wage distributions at the lower end and contribute to duration dependence amongst the unemployed. Our previous survey suggested that the extent to which European benefit systems contribute to unemployment persistence is not yet clear, and conflicts between efficiency and equity considerations have restricted reform in practice. For example, whilst amongst economists it has become popular to advocate a limit on the duration of benefit payments, such arguments ignore the political realities faced by European governments. Many European countries, France, Germany, Greece, Ireland and the Netherlands for example, have some limited-duration unemployment insurance, followed by unemployment assistance benefits which are, often, of infinite duration. Merely shortening the period of insurance entitlement, without a more pro-active policy for those on assistance, seems unlikely to make any significant contribution to labour market efficiency. Hence the more radical suggestions of tighter monitoring of job search by benefit recipients and discretionary-only assistance, what Minford (1995) calls the 'Victorian' model.

Complementary to policies to stimulate the unemployed to increase search efforts are policies which directly aim to increase incentives for employers to recruit workers. With employers facing social security charges equivalent to 40 per cent of wage costs in Belgium, France and Italy, it is not surprising that the OECD's Job Study emphasised the need to lower non-wage labour costs in Europe. However, reducing payroll taxes is not the same as reducing unit labour costs, and as Nickell and Bell (1995) point out, in the long run payroll taxes tend to be shifted to employees. Kaldor (1936) was one of the first economists to advocate general wage subsidies to encourage more labour intensive production and in recent years there has been renewed interest in such policies. Phelps (1994a) argues that payroll taxes impact disproportionately on disadvantaged workers, whose relative wages are also depressed by their social security payments and by the impact of globalisation and skill-biased technological change. Given this scenario Phelps argues for a low-wage employment subsidy, payable to firms on the basis of the number of low-wage workers employed. Stimulation of demand for low-wage workers is also advocated by Pencavel (1994), who argues that such a subsidy is in essence an income maintenance scheme, without many of the labour supply distortions produced by traditional benefit systems. Drèze and Malinvaud (1994) have argued the merits of such policies in Europe, producing simulations which suggest that a cut in payroll taxes on low-wage workers financed by a rise in VAT (or a CO_2 tax) would stimulate employment significantly. Begg and Portes (1993) have utilised similar arguments in their proposal for wage subsidies to reduce the economic costs of German reunification. The Phelps and Pencavel arguments in part reflect the greater degree of wage inequality in the US and the recent rapid changes in that wage distribution. Their arguments are also a reflection of the smaller redistributive role of taxes and benefits in the US compared to the EU norm. In the EU employment inequality has remained a bigger issue than wage inequality and therefore the emphasis has usually been on marginal subsidies for the long-term unemployed. General subsidies are likely to produce large secondary effects and favour labour-intensive production and may be self-defeating if not only payroll taxes, but also income and expenditure taxes are borne by employees. More effective are wage subsidies or reductions in pay-roll taxes at the bottom end of the labour market where wages are inflexible due to the operation of minimum wage laws or the benefit system.

The marginal employment subsidy argument originally put forward by Layard in 1976 formed the basis for a small firms subsidy introduced in the UK in the late 1970s. The arguments for a counter-cyclical policy developed in Layard and Nickell (1980) pay particular attention to the UK macroeconomic environment of the 1970s:

chronic inflation and balance of payments problems. At the macroeconomic level, Layard and Nickell argued that subsidies had only a small effect on domestic demand, since the price cannot fall below the average cost of the marginal firm and the price elasticity of aggregate domestic demand is low. However, in the tradable goods and services sectors export sales would expand rapidly when marginal costs fall since many firms are price-takers. Hence a marginal employment subsidy can produce a large employment effect whilst also relieving the balance of payments constraint and in the short term exerting downward pressure on the inflation rate. To maximise the employment effects Layard and Nickell proposed a scheme of limited life with a flat-rate subsidy per additional worker, which declines with tenure. The subsidy was to be equivalent to one-third of average weekly earnings, payable on a firm, rather than establishment, basis to avoid job transfers between plants. Whilst general subsidy proponents tend to emphasize the importance of the substitution effect, Layard and Nickell emphasize the output effects of a marginal subsidy in the tradable goods and services sector. Their argument is for a small open economy and their 'beggar thy neighbour' policy would not only increase the market share of world trade for a country introducing the subsidy but also increase their labour intensity of exports and reduce that of their imports. This essentially neo-mercantilist/labour theory of value proposal was rejected by Whitley and Wilson (1983), who questioned the appropriateness of the assumption that export prices respond to lower marginal labour costs. A later version (Layard *et al.*, 1991) restates the argument in terms of the NAIRU model previously outlined. Here since the firm sets prices as a mark-up on marginal costs, a marginal wage subsidy reduces prices relative to wages and therefore increases the feasible real wage. It follows that the employment rate consistent with stable inflation increases.

The original Layard-Nickell approach generated hybrid proposals closer to the Kaldor-Phelps scheme. Jackman *et al.* (1986) argued that restructuring existing taxes on jobs could alter the trade-off between wage and employment levels. Such a policy increases the demand for labour in low-wage markets at the expense of reductions in the demand for higher paid workers and overall can raise levels of employment. A self-financing tax/subsidy system was also suggested where firms pay a wage-bill tax and receive a fixed per-worker subsidy. This generates a net subsidy for low-paid workers producing supposedly beneficial demand and supply-side responses. To complement the tax-subsidy changes, employers' social insurance contributions could be made more progressive. Such a scheme had a close relationship to tax-based incomes policies also popular amongst some economists at this time. Here a tax on the average wage growth of a firm would also increase the relative demand for low-paid employees. Layard *et al.* (1986) developed a modification aimed explicitly at the LTU, similar to a contemporary Swedish scheme. Employers hiring the long-term unemployed would receive a flat-rate subsidy for up to a year, provided non-subsidised employment did not fall. The proposed subsidy was slightly less than the average benefit received by the LTU to generate a net budgetary saving before secondary effects were considered.

Policies aimed at reducing hiring costs also enjoy a variety of theoretical support. Reducing statutory severance pay or weakening job security legislation may weaken insider-power, and also by reducing turnover costs increase competitiveness in the product as well as the labour market. Relatively high European labour turnover costs can explain both unemployment persistence and the weak link between product and labour markets. During cycles European firms, facing high firing and hiring costs, alter the intensity of use of labour rather than employment levels. In prolonged recessions hoarded labour is finally fired and this employment contraction is not easily reversed in the recovery.

In the early 1980s, Weitzman (1984) generated widespread enthusiasm amongst economists for policies designed to encourage profit-sharing. Profit-sharing was designed to increase wage-flexibility, and by lowering the marginal cost of labour encourage job-creation. Whilst within the insider-outsider framework profit-sharing may present a solution of how to buy-out insider resistance to additional employment, in recent years profit-sharing has been taken less seriously as a cure for unemployment. Apart from some theoretical misgivings, this largely reflects the difficulty of promoting fundamental and widespread changes in the wage-fixing process, since small scale changes appear to have little effect on employment.

We have now linked together our review of the theory of European unemployment with its policy implications. Since policies are in practice implemented by politicians answerable to their party members and supporters in the short term and the electorate in the medium term our discussion so far has only an imprecise relationship to the actual policies pursued by European governments. We shall now critically review recent European experience of employment policy, before discussing alternatives to those policies.

7.6 Current employment policies in Europe

7.6.1 *Expenditure on passive policies*

The OECD has popularised the distinction between active and passive labour market programmes. Passive programmes are defined to include unemployment insurance and assistance, publicly funded redundancy payments and expenditure on early retirement schemes. Grubb (1994) reports that for OECD countries a 1 per cent increase in unemployment between 1985 and 1990 was associated with a more than 1 per cent increase in spending on passive policies in real terms, but a less than 1 per cent rise in expenditure on active policies. Figures reported in Table 1.12 earlier suggest that Belgium, Denmark, France, Greece, Ireland, the Netherlands, Spain and the UK each spend around twice as much on passive measures as on active ones. Indeed between 1985 and 1992 in Ireland, Luxembourg and the UK spending on active policies as a share of GDP actually fell. This distinction is important since we have suggested ways in which passive expenditure may raise unemployment whereas active labour market policies are designed to reduce it. The current tight budgetary position of most EU national governments and the convergence criteria for EMU adopted at the Maastricht conference have further focused attention on the need to reduce the budgetary costs of unemployment in Europe.

7.6.2 *Work-sharing and early retirement*

If we agree that Europe has an employment problem then there are, as Glyn and Rowthorn (1994) point out, essentially three ways in which an economy can generate a rapid increase in total employment. Firstly, it can try to increase job creation in the market economy, requiring output growth to exceed productivity growth. This is the rationale behind the argument for more flexible European labour markets, though the fear remains that, as in the US, it works through lower productivity growth rather than faster output growth. Secondly, it can expand employment in the non-market economy, effectively nationalising the unemployed. Finally, it can, if we measure employment by the number of individual workers, reallocate employment by reducing the average working time or reducing multiple job holding and re-allocating hours to those who were previously not employed.

Our review of recent labour market trends in Chapter 1 indicated a growth of peripheral workers which represents a form of work-sharing, albeit sometimes an involuntary one. Since the war the average working week has been reduced by about 1 per cent per annum; Gregg (1994) points out that this trend seems to have been halted in the 1970s and that policies designed to resurrect this trend could reduce the unemployment rate in the UK by a third. In Britain, a Job Splitting Scheme gave incentives to employers to extend job-sharing and Belgium and France in the 1980s gave subsidies to encourage greater employment flexibility, though the employment creation effects of these schemes were weak (OECD, 1994a). Often the arguments for work-sharing suggest that there is a fixed amount of work to be done in an economy at any moment of time. Such arguments have been termed the 'lump of labour fallacy' and are inconsistent with all of the theoretical frameworks we have discussed. Arguments for work-sharing also assume that the income-sharing linked to the work-sharing prevents wage pressure from rising, since otherwise the NAIRU must rise. The major problem with work-sharing, and early retirement policies discussed later, is that insiders are reluctant to share in the costs of unemployment, hence unit costs rise. Whilst governments can be encouraged to remove obstacles to more flexible working-time arrangements, legislating to restrict working hours or penalising overtime working is unlikely to stimulate employment significantly.

An alternative response to unemployment is to reduce labour supply. Labour force participation rates have been falling for older male workers in recent years and most western European countries have benefit systems which encourage early retirement, especially amongst the long-term unemployed. In Finland, France and the Netherlands high replacement rates for older workers has produced particularly low participation rates. The long-term effects of these schemes must be to reduce the size of the work-force and so permanently lower output. Whilst any short-term re-allocation of unemployment towards a more equitable distribution is desirable, this does not affect the NAIRU. Grubb's (1986) study of OECD labour markets found that a decrease in the size of the labour force generates the same wage pressure as an equal increase in employment. With falling birth rates and consequential declines in the working-age populations it is likely that the labour force will no longer increase after this century, early retirement schemes are therefore unlikely to be financially sustainable in the future.

7.6.3 *Reform of the benefit systems*

Our survey above reported some evidence that high benefit entitlements may not only affect LTU but also may encourage short employment spells, voluntary separations and involuntary part-time unemployment. There have been a number of reforms to benefit systems in Europe which have been designed to reflect the changed employment situation. One of the consequences of a more flexible labour market is that it may increase the disincentive effects of existing benefit systems. Intermittent and part-time work may not be attractive to the unemployed when benefits are reduced pro rata with labour market earnings. Belgium and Norway both have entitlements to unemployment benefits for part-time workers, with around 40 per cent of beneficiaries now in this category. The OECD Jobs Study reports that these policies whilst encouraging the growth of part-time working, did so by discouraging both employers and the unemployed from agreeing full-time contracts. Unlike in the US, employers' unemployment insurance rates are not risk-rated in Europe, thus providing an implicit subsidy to firms competing through more flexible employment strategies. On the other hand, both France and the UK have raised the penalties of disqualification from benefits for voluntary job-quitters, though what constitutes such separations is often arbitrary. Most European countries have reformed their administrative systems to improve detection of fraudulent claimants, whilst France and the UK have tightened-up on evidence required to prove active job-seeking.

7.6.4 *Active labour market policies*

Grubb (1994) classifies active labour market programmes into three broad categories: public employment services, training and job creation schemes, the last category including employment subsidies. Active labour market policies can be viewed as a way of reducing some of the moral hazard problems associated with unemployment benefits, since payment of benefit may be made conditional on participation. As we have seen, active labour market policies may shift the Beveridge/UV curve inwards as the job matching function improves, and by raising the productivity of labour these policies may also shift the price-setting curve of Figure 7.4 to the right, and finally, by empowering outsiders they help to shift the wage-setting curve also to the right. Box 7.1 explains in more detail how active labour market policies operate within the framework of the Layard and Nickell model of Figure 7.4. At the macroeconomic level, the OECD (1993) found some cross-country evidence that expenditure on active labour market policies was positively related to employment growth. Cross-country studies should however be treated with caution, Forslund and Krueger (1994) found a *positive* relationship between unemployment and expenditure on active labour market policies as a per cent of GDP. This reversed the results of Layard *et al.* (1991) for the 1980s, and was a consequence of the growth of unemployment in Nordic countries. Calmfors and Forslund (1991) concluded that some Swedish programmes put upward pressure on wages and thus crowded out regular employment, and similar results have been found for Ireland and Spain, though in most OECD countries a negative relationship has been found (OECD, 1993).

Box 7.1: Active labour market policies and the NAIRU model

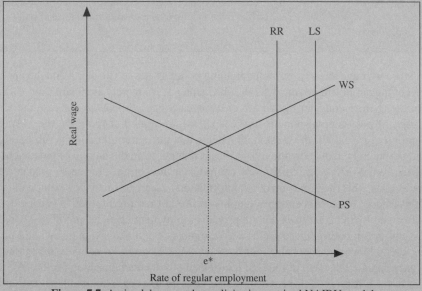

Figure 7.7 Active labour market policies in a revised NAIRU model

Following Calmfors (1994) we can explain the rationale for active labour market policies (ALMPs) in terms of Figure 7.7, which modifies our previous Figure 7.4 by measuring regular employment on the horizontal axis. We can now include participants in training and job creation programmes. They are the difference between the labour supply (LS) and those not on these programmes (RR). The difference between e* and RR measures open unemployment. Increases in numbers on ALMPs, shifts the RR leftwards. In the absence of indirect effects open unemployment falls in line with the expansion of the ALMPs.

Targeting outsiders
By targeting ALMPs on outsiders competition on insiders increases. This shifts the wage-setting curve (WS) downwards, increasing regular employment in equilibrium and causing a further reduction in open unemployment.

Deadweight and substitution effects
If ALMPs provide hiring subsidies to firms employing the unemployed then some sub-sidies will finance hiring which would have happened anyway (deadweight) and some will displace non-subsidised workers (substitution effects). These indirect effects can be represented by a leftward shift in PS, reducing regular employment in equilibrium and off-setting some of the fall in open unemployment.

Reduced welfare losses for the unemployed
If ALMPs make unemployment a less unpleasant experience they may increase the toler-ance of unemployment and reduce incentives for wage restraint. Here the WS curve shifts upwards and the equilibrium level of regular employment again falls.

Box 7.1: *Continued*

Elimination of skill shortages
If ALMPs as well as raising the productivity of participants also eliminate skill shortages, they shift the price-setting curve to the right and increase the equilibrium level of regular employment.

Since we have already examined training policy issues in Chapter 4 and the operation of the public employment service in Chapter 5, we merely summarise our earlier findings before considering the job creation category. Policies to increase the efficiency of public employment services (PES) are aimed at reducing the average duration of vacancies, the presumption being that the current duration is sub-optimal and is able to be reduced without significant reductions in the quality of the matches. Apart from Norway and Spain, few countries at the current time seem prepared to countenance that the provision of job information to searchers may be a natural monopoly. Hence, in most economies employers are not required to notify vacancies to public employment services nor are private employment agencies prohibited. Given this position it is difficult to see how governments can make a significant additional impact on labour market behaviour by extending this group of policies, though both France and the UK have introduced focused employment counselling for the LTU as part of the reform of their benefit systems. The OECD (1995) point out that currently only about 25 per cent of PES staff are engaged in job counselling assistance and to provide just an hour of individual counselling per month to each unemployed requires one qualified counsellor per 100 unemployed. Very few European countries currently get close to this criterion, though Switzerland has adopted this target. Any increased targeting of the LTU by the public employment agency may lead to further growth of private agencies unless this group of searchers is made more attractive to employers, which has been the objective of training policies.

In most EU economies training programmes account for a significantly greater share of public expenditure than employment services. The rationale for such policies rests upon training-market failures. Fears of poaching may constrain the supply of transferable-skill training whilst capital market imperfections may constrain the demand for such training. In addition, wage rigidities may prevent the unemployed from purchasing their training by way of lower wage rates. The co-existence of persistent skill-shortages and mass unemployment has been taken as indicating the strength of training-market imperfections. Training unemployed workers may reduce their probability of both continuing and re-entering unemployment. At the same time training may eliminate skill-bottlenecks and therefore have positive secondary effects on employment. After an evaluation of training programmes, the OECD (1993) concluded that the most closely targeted programmes tended to be the most effective, with Dutch, German, Swedish broadly targeted schemes having no significant positive effects upon the employment prospects of trainees. Pedersen and Westergård-Nielsen (1993) provide a survey of panel data studies which indicates the lack of consensus on the effects of training on the unemployed. This diversity in part reflects the variety of schemes, but it also stems from poor research methodology, in particular inadequate control for selectivity bias and displacement problems. In recent work, Calmfors and Skedinger (1995) reached the conclusion that training programmes in Sweden had more favourable employment effects than job creation schemes, though their results were not robust. The expansion of vocational training programmes in a recession has often been advocated, since the costs of training in a recession are low in both the public and private sector. However, such expansions tend to lead to a rapid decline in post-training placement rates and given that the training offered is usually accelerated, the trainees' skills have often been dissipated by the time an economic upturn appears.

7.6.5 *Direct job creation*

Direct job creation schemes are usually in the public sector and provide periods of employment, normally six months, for targeted groups of the unemployed. Their rationale is usually to increase employability by providing work experience. The inherent contradiction of such programmes is that to ensure 'additionality', that is preventing the displacement of other workers, the work experience is of work that would not normally otherwise be undertaken. Since the early 1980s these types of schemes have been either scaled down or targeted solely at the LTU. This reflects the findings of studies, surveyed in OECD (1993), that there was little evidence of significant effects on the immediate employment prospects of participants.

Most EU countries have also experimented with subsidies for unemployed workers starting their own businesses; in the UK the Enterprise Allowance Scheme peaked at over 105,000 participants and the French scheme at over 70,000. Meager (1994) provides a summary of these programmes and an initial assessment of their impact. In the UK about half of the enterprises survived for two years though the net effect on employment is only around a third of those participants supported. In Europe the client group for this type of subsidy appears to be biased towards males, the middle-aged and well-educated, with the largest schemes only attracting annually between 2 and 4 per cent of the unemployed.

7.6.6 *Employment subsidies*

Job creation subsidies for work in the private sector, if appropriately designed and implemented, appear to have many advantages over the policies previously discussed, not least being their relative cheapness. By their very nature, marginal job-creation subsidies concentrate the subsidy on expanding sectors of the economy. Since only firms that are expanding employment attract the subsidy, they may help offset wage rigidities which constrain sectoral and intra-sectoral adjustments. Whereas general wage subsidies may be expropriated by insiders and thus have little effect on employment, job creation (marginal) subsidies cannot be so easily distorted and may even reduce insider power, especially if training costs are also subsidised. Additionally, for a given exchange rate they improve competitiveness and therefore further aid employment growth. At the same time, wage subsidies for unemployed workers offer the prospects of internalising some of the budgetary externalities of unemployment benefits.

Where financial inducements are given to firms or workers to adopt certain behaviour there are going to be secondary effects which must be examined if the net effects of the policy are to be established. In the case of marginal subsidies firstly, there will be 'deadweight' effects: subsidies paid for hires which would have occurred regardless of the payments. These effects may be partially offset by the squeezing of employment in the hidden economy. Secondly, 'displacement' effects are produced when non-subsidised firms and workers are harmed by competition from subsidised ones. Thus for instance, employment subsidies for the LTU may cause employers to substitute these workers for on-the-job searchers and the short-term unemployed. In addition, certain types of marginal employment subsidies induce employers to substitute extra workers for extra hours per existing worker. This change in the desired combination of workers and hours substitutes under-employment for unemployment, and has ambiguous effects on efficiency and welfare. One further problem with conventional employment subsidies targeted at the LTU is that they will tend to favour labour-intensive, low-tech sectors of the economy. This directly follows from their cheapening of labour in general and unskilled labour in particular. In addition, indirectly subsidies increase the employability of the LTU and therefore increase the supply of unskilled labour and further reduce the relative wage of these workers. The international displacement effect of such subsidies means a further bias in favour of the low-skill low-tech tradable goods and services sectors of the economy. Hence, if employment is further concentrated in sectors with low income elasticities of demand the substitution effects of conventional employment subsidies may in the medium term produce off-setting output effects.

Ireland has had a job creation subsidy since 1977 and Greece since 1982, Gregg (1990) and Employment Policy Institute (1993) provide comprehensive surveys of the development of active labour market policies in the UK whilst de Wachter and Somers (1989) and OECD (1993) provide international surveys. As indicated earlier most economists have concluded that, given the importance of secondary effects, marginal employment subsidies are to be preferred to a blanket subsidy. A non-selective employment subsidy becomes equivalent to a change in employer social insurance contributions or pay-roll tax and fails to target public expenditure on employment expansion. If we accept the efficiency arguments favouring the marginal employment subsidy then it may take the form of either a job-creating subsidy, which pays firms on the basis of additional employees, or a job-preserving subsidy which induces firms to delay redundancies.

Although job-preserving subsidies tend to have a low displacement effect within a national labour market, job-creating subsidies are generally to be preferred. Job-preserving subsidies present severe policing problems, since counting new jobs is much easier than counting jobs not lost. To illustrate, the first and one of the largest Special Employment Measures in the UK was the Temporary Employment Subsidy (TES), a marginal job preservation subsidy scheme introduced in August 1975. At its peak it covered about 200,000 workers, providing employers with a subsidy to defer redundancies. TES was output-augmenting and the strong international displacement effect, especially within the EC, led to the abandonment of TES in 1979 since it was in contravention of the Treaty of Rome. Deakin and Pratten (1982) estimated that TES saved in the short run around 39 per cent net of the jobs covered. TES was replaced by the Temporary Short-Time Working Compensation Scheme, a subsidy aimed at inducing employers to substitute work sharing for redundancies. This essentially subsidised worker leisure and it substituted under-employment for unemployment. It covered nearly a million workers at its peak. Metcalf's (1986) inter-industry study of redundancy rates suggested that this subsidy delayed rather than avoided redundancies. Experience with these schemes indicates the difficulty in distinguishing firms and industries in long-term decline from those who, given short-term assistance, have a 'sound' future. Experience also indicates that governments rarely have the political resolve to support only the latter.

Experience with job creation subsidies in the UK has been more varied, though on a much smaller scale. Various marginal job creation subsidies have been targeted at young entrants and small firms. The New/Young Worker Scheme (YWS) paid employers a subsidy for each youth employed at a 'realistic', i.e. low wage, and covered about 60,000 young workers at the beginning of 1986. These schemes suffered from large deadweight effects, estimates of the net job creation ratio being as low as 16 per cent. Uniquely the British government experimented with a subsidy given to the long-term unemployed themselves, the Jobstart Allowance. This was a six month subsidy for those taking a low-paying job. The scheme never attracted more than 7,000 participants at any time and was rapidly abandoned. In summer 1993 following the arguments of Snower (1994) and others the Workstart scheme was piloted in four locations, funding was only £2.6 million and it was designed to cover 1,000 unemployed. The scheme provided subsidies of £60 per week for employers of the long-term unemployed but contained no anti-displacement restrictions on take-up. Early assessments by the Institute for Employment Studies (1995) suggest that the scheme was effective in changing employers' perceptions of the long-term unemployed, with half claiming that they would not have recruited from the LTU without the subsidy.

Since 1984 Sweden has offered a hiring bonus to employers hiring unemployed workers of at least six months duration. The bonus was substantial, up to 60 per cent of wages for six months. Early subsidy schemes in Australia and Ireland had deadweight effects of up to two-thirds and a Dutch voucher scheme had a three-quarters displacement effect. In Norway wage subsidies up to 50 per cent are available for employers of the LTU and those at risk of so becoming, such as young and older workers. Previous experience was that Norwegian employers were hiring only for the length of subsidy and the scheme has been modified to try to restrict subsidies to permanent jobs. Similar problems occurred in Finland where employers often screened out non-subsidised applicants. The Danish job-offer scheme provides jobs for nine months duration for the LTU. Around 40 per cent of participants were in work one year after finishing the scheme, a half with different employers (European Commission, 1995a). The attractiveness of the scheme to the fiscal authorities will depend upon the duration of the subsidy and regulations covering eligibility. Belgium in the 1980s introduced a scheme where the very long-term unemployed were placed into permanently subsidised jobs. France and Germany also introduced subsidies for the LTU. In France one of the first measures of the Chirac Presidency was a new employment initiative (CIE) in which the subsidies in total reduced employers' labour costs of recruiting a LTU at the minimum wage by 40 per cent. As we have recorded, the Belgian government allowed benefit claimants who found part-time jobs to retain some of their benefits to top-up their earnings. Essentially this was a subsidy for part-time workers and their employers, a similar scheme operates in Norway. Denmark has specifically targeted employment subsidies at the home services sector, arguing that such policies have a particularly large displacement effect on 'hidden economy' employment. In Italy the reluctance of the government to modify the permanent nature of employment contracts induced a massive expansion of subsidised 'temporary' lay-offs in the mid-1980s. The long-duration of these lay-off spells and the low search activity of workers on this scheme led to various policy experiments, including marginal employment subsidies. Subsidies of up to two thirds of annual labour costs were available to employers. Felli and Ichino (1988) concluded that the effects of the policy were to significantly reduce the duration of those on the lay-off subsidy by around half, though the displacement effects on non-subsidised workers was not modelled. In summary, a marginal job-creating subsidy must be designed so that higher labour turnover is not rewarded, only net recruitment should be subsidised with displacement and deadweight effects minimised.

7.6.7 Reforming labour market institutions

We will discuss the extensive programme of labour market reforms pursued by the British government since 1979 later in this chapter, here we consider reforms in other European countries. In Spain in the early 1990s administrative approval was required for collective dismissals of more than 10 per cent of the work-force and severance pay of at least 20 days per year of service was required. Such high firing costs boost insider power which could be exercised in a Spanish bargaining system in which collective agreements provided a floor for firm level bargaining. In 1984 the Spanish government allowed firms to hire workers on fixed-term contracts, with temporary contracts having a minimum duration of six months and being renewable for up to three years. Nearly 40 per cent of Spanish employees were on various forms of fixed-term contracts by the early 1990s, and male long-term unemployment fell in relative and absolute terms. However, Bentolila and Dolado (1994) argue that by creating a buffer of flexible employment at the margin, the policy further reduced the lay-off probability of permanent workers and therefore further increased insider-power. Indeed, they find that wage growth is positively related to the proportion of fixed-term employment. Milner *et al.* (1995) argue that the failure of deregulation in Spain is also due to the pervasive role of labour ordinances and a worker representation system which in practice leads to the permanent contract workers dominating wage bargaining decision-making. More recent reforms have limited temporary contracts to apprentices. France too experimented with legalising temporary contracts in the 1980s, which again led to around half of new jobs being on temporary contracts. While temporary contracts were successful in reducing long-term unemployment in these cases, as we recorded in Chapter 1 many European economies already have employment legislation in this area which is permissive.

7.7 Increasing flexibility of EU labour markets

The *White Paper on Growth, Competitiveness and Employment* which was presented to the European Council of Heads of State in Brussels in 1993 shifted the focus of EC policy from reducing unemployment to increasing employment. It also represented a change towards supply-side policies, arguing the need for a reform of impediments to job creation, specifically labour market, taxation and social security systems and institutions (European Commission, 1994b). This recognition of the virtues of flexible labour markets represents a movement towards the US and post-Thatcher UK labour market policies and in the following section we assess the effects of the Thatcher reforms on the performance of the British labour market in recent years.

7.7.1 *Increasing labour market flexibility: the British experience*

The Thatcher government elected in 1979 introduced a wide range of reforms aimed at improving the relative performance of the UK labour market. Initially the focus was on reducing trade union power, and Employment Acts of 1980, 1982, 1984 and 1988 reduced union immunities, regulated strike actions and curtailed closed shops. Government regulation of the labour market was also reduced as the selective minimum wage controls (Wages Councils) were abolished, employment protection legislation weakened and private pensions encouraged. At the same time the direct role of the government in the labour market was reduced as state-owned industries were privatised, compulsory competitive tendering enforced on local government and local bargaining and performance-related pay encouraged for those workers remaining in the public sector. Work incentives were targeted by policies which reduced the replacement rate for unemployed workers and reduced benefit entitlement for diverse groups. Finally, the 'enterprise culture' was encouraged by various initiatives in the education and training areas, and taxation and benefit systems were redesigned to favour the self-employed. Overall, these policies were designed to create a flexible labour market in which market forces were strengthened and wages were made more responsive to local conditions. The result was to move towards a decentralised US-style labour market and away from the regulated and institutionally structured labour markets which were the norm in the EU.

We have identified some of the consequences of these reforms in Chapter 1. The reforms contributed to the large fall in trade union density (Metcalf, 1994) and strikes per worker fell more rapidly than in other countries. Productivity growth was now faster in union firms compared with non-union ones (Gregg *et al.*, 1993), as management reasserted control and restrictive practices were reduced, though overall there was only a small fall in union wage differentials for manual workers (Stewart, 1995). On the benefit side, the Social Security Act (no. 2) 1980 abolished the earnings related supplement of unemployment benefits and Britain became the only member of the EU without a link between unemployment benefits and past earnings. Overall, the various changes detailed in Atkinson and Micklewright (1989) reduced replacement rates by around a quarter by the early 1990s for those still entitled to benefits. More stringent administration of benefits was reflected in the introduction of the Restart scheme in 1987. There is some evidence that the Restart Programme put downward pressure on manual wages and Lehmann (1993) estimated that the programme accounted for around 35 per cent of the fall in LTU between 1984–90, although a strong substitution effect on the short-term unemployed was in evidence.

Blanchflower and Freeman (1994) have tried to estimate the overall impact of these measures on the performance of the UK labour market. They eliminated the impact of the poor macroeconomic performance by taking a low unemployment year (1990), and concentrating upon a low unemployment region (the South East region). They conclude that in comparison with other OECD countries the UK's relative performance improved in terms of inflation and growth, but deteriorated in terms of unemployment and employment rates. On a disaggregated basis they find that the transition from unemployment to employment worsened overall in the 1980s, reflected in a rise in LTU. Although the policies had made work more attractive, for unemployed males they did not improve their flow into employment. Blanchflower and Freeman find some evidence that employment flexibility increased and that wages became slightly more responsive to market conditions, including local unemployment rates. We have already discussed in Chapter 1 the growth of wage inequality in the UK since 1979, and Blanchflower and Freeman suggest that the reduction in institutional constraints had the perverse effect of increasing labour market segmentation and contributing to an increase in wage inequality for workers of similar skills, an increase inconsistent with improving market efficiency. Coulton and Crumb (1994) find that most studies suggest that the UK's NAIRU declined significantly in the second half of the 1980s, though changes in the terms of trade and other forces external to the labour market may have been largely responsible for this change whilst hysteresis effects made the reduction less significant in efficiency terms.

Although there is some evidence that the British labour market became more efficient in the 1980s, the evidence is weak and the persistence of unemployment and growth of '-inefficient' wage inequality make it difficult to conclude that the overall effects were beneficial. A more generous interpretation is that the reforms may have more beneficial effects in the longer run, or that increased labour market flexibility can only produce the anticipated gains when tight labour market conditions are sustained by appropriate macroeconomic policies. Regardless of which interpretation is preferred the conclusions reached by Bertola and Ichino (1995) in their study of labour market reforms in the EU are pertinent. They concluded that the social cost of reforms is likely to be smallest if the policies to be implemented are credible and speedily implemented.

7.7.2 *Some problems with increasing labour market flexibility*

The British experience suggests that we should be cautious in implementing the European Commission's and the OECD's Job Study recommendations (see Box 7.2)

Box 7.2: The OECD Jobs Study: policy recommendations

1. Set appropriate macroeconomic policy
   - Interpreted as limiting cyclical fluctuations and providing price stability and sound public finances.
2. Enhance the creation and diffusion of technological know-how
3. Increase working-time flexibility
   - Encourage voluntary part-time working and more flexible retirement.
4. Nurture an entrepreneurial climate
   - Encourage new firm start-ups and the growth of existing small businesses
5. Increase wage and labour cost flexibility
   - Weaken minimum wage legislation and reduce non-wage labour costs
6. Reform employment security provisions
   - Permit fixed-term contracts and allow dismissals on economic grounds
7. Expand and enhance active labour market policies
   - Target long-term unemployed
8. Improve labour force skills and competencies
9. Reform unemployment and related benefit systems
   - Limit disincentive effects by restricting entitlements, lowering high replacement rates and reducing duration

in a period of depressed economic activity. The benefits of a flexible labour market can also be questioned by a more detailed consideration of the supposed achievements of the US economy. We have already noted the superior job creation performance of the US, the employment to population rate is currently 10 percentage points higher in the US than in Europe and the higher annual working hours in the US make for an even larger difference in labour utilisation. However, the US has achieved a slower growth of productivity and the consequence of its higher wage flexibility has been the huge rise in wage inequality noted in Chapter 1. As Freeman (1995) points out, this wage flexibility did not help to increase the employment of less-skilled workers in the US, and whilst it has no long-term unemployment problem the US does imprison the equivalent of 2 per cent of the labour force! In total nearly 7 per cent of the American male labour force is in prison or under supervision of the criminal justice system, whereas imprisonment in Europe is only around a tenth of the US rate. Greater wage flexibility may therefore create or exacerbate severe social problems without solving the employment problems of less-skilled workers.

If Freeman is correct, then the attempt to reproduce US-style wage flexibility in Europe by relaxing minimum wage laws and reducing other forms of labour market regulation may well increase wage inequality without solving Europe's employment inequality problem. Hence, we consider alternative policy proposals which may achieve the reduction of unemployment without contributing to an increase in poverty amongst the less-skilled sectors of the work-force.

245

7.8 Policies for a high employment/high productivity Europe

Currently 70 per cent of EU member states' expenditure on labour market policies is directed towards unemployment benefits and early retirement pensions. The rise in unemployment since 1990 has thwarted most attempts to switch expenditure towards more active programmes. We now concentrate upon policies which promote high employment **and** high levels of productivity in the EU. The importance of spillover effects, particularly trade distortion, of such policies, suggests the need for an EU-level initiative.

7.8.1 *Macroeconomic policies*

Between 1987 and 1990 real GDP increased by around 13 per cent and employment by 5.5 per cent for the EU-12. This average output growth rate of 3.4 per cent generated a fall in the unemployment rate from 10.7 per cent in 1986 to 8.3 per cent in 1990. However, the associated acceleration of inflation together with the failure of public deficits to improve meant that the recessionary phase beginning in 1990 was severe. Very different lessons have been learned from this experience. Some economists have re-affirmed the need to pursue conservative fiscal and monetary strategies whilst others point to the potential for Keynesian-style reflationary policies.

The first policy recommendation of the OECD Jobs Study was that 'policy should focus on assisting recovery through faster non inflationary growth of domestic demand where there is substantial economic slack, while policies should be adjusted promptly to avoid a rekindling of inflation when recovery is well under way'. The OECD's emphasis upon supply-side and institutional policy responses has led to the need for accommodating macroeconomic policy being neglected. Given current labour market trends, reducing European unemployment rates to around 6 per cent within 6 years suggests an annual growth rate of the order of 4 per cent. Such a growth rate is unlikely to be maintained without some relaxation of current inflation targets, and as Bean (1994a) argues, a relaxation may have other beneficial effects. Most of the supply-side/institutional policies discussed by the OECD/European Commission have the intention of shifting the wage-setting curve in Figure 7.4 to the right. As can be seen, the resulting higher equilibrium employment rate requires a fall in real wages, and an inflationary surprise may be advantageous to this process.

If the short-run real wage elasticity of demand is around unity in Europe then in order to generate a 5 per cent increase in employment the real wage would need to fall by 5 per cent relative to its otherwise level. For a given money wage this requires an unexpected rise in inflation of 5 per cent, since any beneficial effects of the supply-side policies are likely to be slow and if the change of employment is over say, five years, inflation need only rise by 1 per cent a year to bring about this adjustment. Bean (1994a) points out that a 5 per cent increase in employment with unchanged real interest rates implies, with a capital-output ratio of around 4, a total increase in the capital stock of 20 per cent of one year's output. Bean concludes that an investment-led recovery is therefore possible and that fiscal policy may need to supply only a temporary stimulus. In the EU 12 the share of public investment in GDP fell from 3.9 per cent in the early 1970s to around 2.8 per cent since the mid-1980s. Given the present emphasis upon the importance of infrastructure in the new growth theory, a return of public investment to its previous share may be self-financing in the medium-term. Drèze and Malinvaud (1994) argue this case and present priorities such as low-cost housing and urban transportation schemes which would be labour-intensive examples of direct job creation but on schemes with a high social priority.

7.8.2 *Targeting the long-term unemployed*

Our arguments could be re-interpreted as arguing the need for Europe to find a more efficient way of subsidising unskilled male workers. Supporting these workers through unemployment benefits is inefficient and becoming increasing costly. Whilst there are some grounds for financing their re-training or providing paid workfare, our reading of the present evidence is that such schemes are expensive and only marginally effective. Notwithstanding the above interpretation of US experience, wage flexibility may stimulate overall employment and increased investments in human capital. Reductions in unit labour costs by reductions in pay-roll taxes or selective employment subsidies may be an effective way of targeting job creation measures. Our previous arguments indicate that such subsidies should be targeted on the LTU. As discussed previously, the probability of males leaving unemployment declines rapidly as the duration of unemployment increases. Unemployment hysteresis effects derive from this, since the LTU are not part of the effective labour supply and they play no role in reducing inflationary pressures. Hence, where subsidies for the long-term unemployed cause a more even incidence of unemployment duration, this 'churning' or 'queue-shuffling' increases the effective labour supply which produces the normal market adjustment of lower wage pressure and a lower NAIRU. In contrast Calmfors and Forslund (1991), assessing Swedish experience, found that non-targeted wage subsidies weakened wage moderation, presumably since they lower the unemployment costs of displaced workers. It follows, as argued by Calmfors and Lang (1995), that targeting on the LTU is crucial in determining the effects on wage inflation of active labour market programmes.

Targeting the subsidy on a duration basis also creates an additional built-in-stabiliser for governments since unemployment duration tends to vary more than unemployment inflow over the cycle. Sloan (1993) argues that targeting the subsidies on the LTU offsets employers' higher screening costs for such applicants and therefore can reduce statistical discrimination against these applicants. A social externalities rationale for targeting disadvantaged workers is provided by Phelps (1994a). He argues not only on equity grounds but also on benefit externalities and the harmful community effects of LTU in terms of crime and alienation.

One note of caution is necessary given recent empirical work on duration dependence referred to earlier. Whilst most panel data studies find negative duration dependence, the survey by Pedersen and Westergård-Nielsen (1993) finds that no duration dependence is a common result in those studies which attempt to adjust for unobserved heterogeneity. If the latter result is more generally correct then rather than targeting the LTU, policy should target those groups entering unemployment with low, duration independent, escape rates. In other words, policies need to be targeted at the LTU and the potential LTU.

7.8.3 *Labour market policies*

Given the conclusion that active labour market policies need to be targeted on the LTU, Drèze and Malinvaud (1994) have argued for the need to eliminate the wedge between the private cost to employers and the real opportunity cost of hiring unskilled labour in the EU. In Chapter 1 we noted that in Europe the social insurance contributions and income taxes account for around 40 per cent of employers' labour costs, and Drèze and Malinvaud argue for the elimination of this distortion in periods of high unemployment by exempting employers from social insurance contributions for workers employed at minimum wage levels. They argue that this would reduce the attractiveness of hidden economy employment and enable Europe to create the unskilled jobs as in the US, but without the US-style rise in poverty. They estimate the gross cost of this proposal to be around 1.5 per cent of EU12 GDP, but their simulated employment gains indicate no net budgetary costs. The French new employment initiative (CIE) referred to earlier reflects this argument, though this type of policy will have little impact on countries where employers' social insurance contributions are zero (Denmark) or low (Ireland, the Netherlands and the UK).

Whilst many of the arguments for exemptions and subsidies recognise the possibility of increasing fiscal returns, Snower's (1994, 1995b) championing of a benefit transfer programme (BTP) makes them a central feature. Snower propounds the benefits of a voucher system where categories of the unemployed, particularly the LTU, are given the opportunity of using part of their benefits to subsidise their wage costs to firms who hire them. Wage subsidies and social insurance exemptions for employers appear to be in direct conflict with the concern to create 'good' jobs and avoid increases in the (unskilled) labour-intensity of production. The novelty of the Snower proposal is that the value of the voucher depends positively upon both unemployment duration and the training content of employment but declines with tenure in the subsidised employment. The BTP possesses all of the advantages of a marginal employment subsidy but in addition it assists in combating some of the training market failures we identified in Chapter 4. The long-term unemployed are often credit constrained in the human capital market and poaching fears reduce the training opportunities offered by potential employers. Insufficient training may also reflect two externalities, what Snower (1995) has called the 'vacancy supply externality' and the 'training supply externality'. The former arises because the expansion of skilled employment by firms raises the expected returns from training for workers, whilst the latter follows from increases in the number of skilled workers raising the returns to firms who are creating additional 'good' jobs. In both cases private returns fall below social returns and too little training is undertaken and too few 'good' jobs created. By providing a financial incentive to employers the Snower scheme helps to increase on-the-job training opportunities for the LTU and hence improve their prospects of retaining employment. Since the scheme is voluntary both employers and employees have an incentive to produce work-related training, incentives not always generated on government sponsored training schemes. Like most employment subsidy proposals the BTP requires a two-tier wage structure to be generated. Insiders are assumed to tolerate the scheme since employers do not attempt to use the threat of selective recruitment to undercut existing workers. Snower argues that the size of the voucher should depend inversely on the size of the deadweight and displacement effects. These effects are reduced by concentrating the vouchers on the long-term unemployed and restricting payment to firms who are increasing net employment.

Many discussions of wage subsidies adopt a static framework, primarily analysing their substitution effects on employment. A more relevant approach is one which also considers medium-term output effects and recognises the importance of policy objectives in addition to that of short-term reductions in the stock of unemployment. Given the current EU labour market problems identified earlier and the lessons we have learnt from previous policy experience, we find both the Kaldor/Phelps/Drèze and Malinvaud and the Snower proposals attractive. The former tackle the issue of increasing wage and employment inequality whilst the latter in addition addresses the issue of long-term international competitiveness. A concern with the former is its impact upon productivity growth whilst the latter offers few incentives to those LTU unable or unwilling, due to age for example, to enter employment which is training intensive.

An amalgamation of the two approaches may be proposed: a straight job creation wage subsidy to promote more labour-intensive production in the non-tradable goods and services sector and a wage/training subsidy for the tradable sector. This proposal presupposes mass unemployment and initially limits subsidies to the long-term unemployed. Subsidising labour in the non-tradable sector will increase output in this sector as well as increasing the labour intensity of production. As long as the additional employment has a net positive productivity this must be socially beneficial even in a static framework. The limited size of the subsidy payable to the employer together with the self-financing aspects of the BTP to the Treasury, may cause a concentration of employment creation in the public sector. Administering this component of the scheme through local government and training bodies may increase the sensitivity of the subsidy to the local influences which has been advantageous to the operation of other countries' schemes (Grubb, 1994). Given mass unemployment, productivity growth should not be an issue in the non-tradable goods and services sector at the present time. However, in the tradable goods sector our previous arguments imply that replicating the same wage subsidy would be counter-productive in the medium term. Straight wage subsidies produce both output and substitution effects, the latter would provide a competitive boost to the most labour-intensive plants and firms in any sector and distort the movement towards more technologically sophisticated production. These dynamic considerations, together with the training market failures discussed earlier, dictate that in this sector subsidies should only be available where significant training is provided. This requirement generates the additional advantage, discussed earlier, of reducing insider power since the employer's cost of hiring entrants is reduced. In support, empirical work suggests that factor prices influence the demand for labour in the UK largely through competitiveness (Barrell *et al.*, 1994a). Both theoretical and empirical arguments indicate that particularly generous funding should be available for these marginal job-creation subsidies for the private sector. As we reported in Chapter 4, Snower (1995) has argued that the training market failures may cause sectors to be locked into a low-skill, bad-job stable equilibrium, and large subsidies may be required to shift the sector toward a high-skill, good-job equilibrium.

Such proposals encourage firms in the tradable goods sector to adopt more skill-intensive methods of production, extending their flexible manufacturing practices and exploiting the economies of scope we identified in Box 1.2. This process should increase the income elasticity of demand for exports whilst reducing the income elasticity of demand for imports and the growth rate consistent with balance of payments equilibrium should therefore increase. We therefore reject the argument of Glyn and Rowthorn (1994) that a Snower-type wage subsidy is bound to worsen the balance of payments. Their conclusion relied upon their assumption that aggregate domestic consumption expenditure would increase significantly in the case of a subsidy. This need not occur when the subsidy is financed from reduced unemployment benefits. Their conclusion that a wage subsidy is inferior to an expansion of public expenditure programmes as an anti-unemployment policy appears untenable when the favourable long-run output effects of the subsidy are included. Whilst 'beggar thy neighbour' objections are still pertinent, the advantages of our proposal, as with most BTP schemes, is that they lower traded goods and services prices without raising world interest rates. Hence in aggregate they must produce a positive net output effect in the global economy.

7.9 Conclusions

Fashions change in economic policy-making and the 1990s have seen governments move away from large-scale general training and public work schemes for the unemployed. In part this reflects the disappointing results of these programmes, but this change also reflects a philosophical shift away from interventionist and regulatory policies. The present popularity of flexible labour market policies lacks substantial empirical justification and often reflects concerns about public finances rather than any great faith in the merits of extending the Reagan/Thatcher policies to European labour markets.

Policies of supply-side and institutional reform are unlikely to be successful in a depressed labour market. This suggests that macroeconomic policy should not be neglected and that relaxation of monetary policy in the short run may be a necessary part of an effective active labour market policy package. In addition, the major restructuring of some national social welfare systems will be politically impossible to sustain unless macroeconomic policies are able to generate sustained economic growth. To avoid merely redistributing unemployment in the EU, macroeconomic and instituted policies need to be co-ordinated at the EU level.

Guide to further reading

The CEPR study *Unemployment: choices for Europe* (1995) provides an excellent introduction to the topic. Layard *et al.* (1991) still provides a rigorous and internally consistent analysis of unemployment. Bean (1994) provides a complementary survey of empirical research into the causes of high European unemployment. The OECD Jobs Study (1994a) provides a monumental analysis of unemployment in the OECD, though its comprehensiveness is not always matched by coherence or consistency. Start with *The OECD Jobs Study: Facts, Analysis, Strategies* which is the 'executive summary' and then sample the two volumes of *Evidence and Explanations*. As alternative starting place try Symes (1995) who provides an interesting study of five major European cities with high levels of unemployment. De la Dehesa and Snower (1996) contains a collection of papers covering many of the policy topics we have covered. Bertola and Ichino (1995) provide an assessment of labour market reforms in the EU.

Appendix 7.1: A simple model of the NAIRU

In the following analysis we follow the base model developed in Layard *et al.* (1991) outlined verbally in Section 7.2.3. Consider first of all the price-setting behaviour, prices are set as a mark-up on expected wages. The mark-up is assumed to rise with the level of employment, where this effect is non-existent ($\beta_1 = 0$) then we have 'normal cost' pricing. Thus, the real wage that is intended by price-setting, the 'feasible' real wage is given by:

$$p - w^e = \beta_0 - \beta_1 u \qquad (\beta_1 \geq 0) \qquad (7.1)$$

where p is log prices, w^e log expected wages and u is the unemployment rate, (7.1) is represented by the PS curve in Figure 7.4.

Wages are set as a mark-up on expected prices, again the mark-up is assumed to rise with the level of economic activity. Thus, the real wage that is intended by wage-setting, the 'target' real wage is given by:

$$w - p^e = \gamma_0 - \gamma_1 u \qquad (\gamma_1 \geq 0) \qquad (7.2)$$

This is a version of our WS curve in Figure 7.4. When actual wages and prices are at their expected levels ($p = p^e$ and $w = w^e$) then the equilibrium unemployment rate is given by (7.1) and (7.2):

$$u^* = \frac{\beta_0 + \gamma_0}{\beta_1 + \gamma_1} \qquad (7.3)$$

Where u^* is represented in Figure 7.4 by $(1 - e^*)$, that is where WS and PS intersect. Exogenous increases in price and wage push increase β_0 and γ_0 respectively and increase u^*. Any factor which reduces price and wage flexibility, reduces β_1 and γ_1 respectively, again increasing u^*.

In the long run unemployment will be at the NAIRU, u^*, and be determined by long-run supply factors. However, in the short run unemployment can deviate from u^* in response to demand and supply-side shocks. Short-run aggregate supply in Layard *et al.*'s model is given by :

$$\Delta p - \Delta p_{-1} = -\theta_1 (u - u^*) \qquad (7.4)$$

and aggregate demand is given by:

$$u = \frac{-1}{\lambda}(m - p) \qquad (7.5)$$

where m is the log of nominal GDP, adjusted for trend real growth. This implies that:

$$\Delta p = \Delta m + \lambda \ (u - u_{-1}) \tag{7.6}$$

Thus an expansionary demand shock which increases Δm causes a rise in inflation and a fall in unemployment, while a supply shock which increases u* will raise both inflation and unemployment. Combining (7.4) and (7.6) gives us a general expression for the level of unemployment:

$$u = \frac{1}{\theta_1 + \lambda} [\theta_1 \ u* + \lambda \ u_{-1} - (\Delta m - \Delta p_{-1})] \tag{7.7}$$

It follows that if Δm is constant long enough and u* is constant, then Δp_{-1} converges on Δm and unemployment converges on u*.

Within this framework Layard *et al.* introduce unemployment hysteresis, section 7.4.3, by modifying the short-run aggregate supply curve (7.4). If wage and price behaviour depends upon the change in unemployment as well as its level then we can re-write (7.4) as:

$$\Delta p = \Delta p_{-1} - \theta_1 \ (u - u*) - \theta_{11} \ (u - u_{-1}) \tag{7.8}$$

and the short-run NAIRU $u*_s$ now becomes:

$$u*_s = \frac{\theta_1 \ u*}{\theta_1 + \theta_{11}} - \frac{\theta_{11} \ u_{-1}}{\theta_1 + \theta_{11}} \tag{7.9}$$

The short-run NAIRU now lies between last period's unemployment rate and the long-run NAIRU, with the relative size of θ_1 and θ_{11} determining the position of $u*_s$ within this range.

8 European Union: some policy issues

So far in this book we have considered labour market behaviour and policy issues from the perspective of individual European economies, it is now time to concentrate specifically on the EU and to discuss the policy issues which arise from the increase in European economic integration. We specialise in topics which have assumed importance in the EU in the mid-1990s and which are likely to retain that importance in the new millennium. The chapter starts with a description of the development of social policy in the EU, explaining its origins and the problems of agreeing a common policy given the diversity of labour market behaviour, institutions and policies between individual member states which we have discovered in the previous chapters. We then consider whether increased economic integration in Europe and the gradual elimination of unfair trading practices and policies in goods and capital markets, inevitably forces member states to pursue similar labour market policies. This analysis of the rationale for a common EU social policy leads to a consideration of a topic which has proved to have the potential for generating much debate and division in the EU: social dumping. The origins of the social dumping argument are examined and the evidence concerning the importance of such effects is assessed.

Our discussion of whether increased European economic integration necessitates the convergence of labour market behaviour and institutions leads to a consideration of the importance of the wage-fixing institutions in determining relative economic performance. The purported relatively successful economic performance of the corporatist economies in Europe in the 1970s and 1980s aroused much interest as to whether their institutions and performance could be reproduced in the less successful, less centralised European economies. We analyse the relative merits of corporatist economic systems and consider whether such systems are sustainable in an integrated European economy.

We follow this topic with one which has virtually disappeared from the Anglo-American policy agenda but which is treated much more seriously in continental Europe: worker participation. The success of the German economy in the post-war period generated research into the contribution which worker participation made to this success. The adoption of the European Works Council directive and the entry of the Nordic countries has given new impetus to this topic. We use the term 'worker participation' to include both policies designed to increase information flows between employers and employees and those which seek to increase the influence of employee interests in the decision-making process of corporate capitalism. In this section we briefly review European practice and current EU policy and then consider the arguments for and against mandatory worker participation.

In this book we have followed common usage in using the term 'European' to cover Northern and Western Europe and the Mediterranean members of the EU. Our discussion has completely ignored any detailed consideration of Central and Eastern Europe and the problems which transition has generated for labour market behaviour and regulation. In this chapter we make a single exception to this neglect by briefly considering some of the labour market implications of any future enlargement of the EU to include these economies.

We end this chapter and the book by returning to the issue of flexible labour markets, a theme which has dominated much of our previous discussion. Here, we seek to consolidate our earlier discussion by concentrating on the link between flexibility and competitiveness. This enables us to address the key policy issue of whether a Delors-style package of policies aimed at raising labour standards in the EU or a Thatcher-style deregulation of European labour markets is best suited to improving the overall performance of EU labour markets.

8.1   The evolution of EU social policy

The use of the term 'social policy' within the EU has been the cause of some confusion. The major use of this term has been to identify areas of economic policy which relate to human resources, such as the Social Charter, the Social Chapter of the Treaty on European Union (the 'Maastricht Treaty') and the Social Protocol subsequently accepted by 11 of the, then, 12 member states. Social policy has also been utilised to describe regional policy, including not only training and other human resource issues but also infrastructure and industrial development. We adopt the former usage in this chapter. The social provisions of the Treaty of Rome were relatively limited and scattered throughout its various parts. As we noted in Chapter 6 a key rationale for the inclusion of social policy in that treaty was to avoid the possibility that increased economic integration, with its stimulation of greater product market competition, would favour cost-cutting policies in the labour market rather than stimulate improvements in the quality and technological sophistication of output. The fear that increased product market competition would spill over into the labour market, driving down the level of social protection is at the heart of the concern to maintain 'social cohesion' within the EU. The need for social cohesion has become a recurrent theme in the publications and pronouncements of the Commission over the last twenty-five years. Without this social cohesion there was the fear that the EU would fail to attract popular support, and social policy was thus targeted at offering some tangible benefits to ordinary EU citizens. Opposed to this view, and repeated by most British governments also over the last twenty-five years, is the argument that EU social policy has reduced the competitiveness of European industry and therefore worsened the economic status of those groups of workers it was originally designed to favour.

Within post-war Western Europe, comparative social policy theorists have identified four types of social policy regimes, a classification which complements those we made of legal frameworks in Chapter 1 and of economic policy in Chapter 3. The

255

traditional-rudimentary model was where the state did little to regulate labour market behaviour or redistribute income and wealth. Religion and local loyalties dictated prevailing social and political customs and restrained the operation of market forces. Agricultural production dominated and the extended family internalised child care and provisions for the elderly. Greece, Portugal, Southern Italy and Spain up until the 1960s and 1970s are often cited as exhibiting behaviour approximating to this model. The *liberal-individualist* model is where market forces dominate labour market behaviour, with *laissez-faire* policies resolving social welfare problems for all but the non-participants. Safety nets are provided for such groups but these are means-tested and provide minimum support. The predominance of economic liberalism saw the adoption of this model of social policy in Anglo-American countries, with its latest form extolling the virtues of the deregulated, flexible labour market. Whilst this variant emphasises the importance of the freedom of contract it otherwise prefers a voluntarist approach to labour market regulation, whilst the *conservative-corporatist* model is willing to constrain market forces by establishing legal rights for workers and citizens. Such rights are designed to prevent class conflicts and establish limited political influence for workers. The development of social insurance is favoured as a means of providing a safety net without requiring a significant redistribution of income and wealth. This model is associated with Catholic social thought and usually associated with the development of modern Germany and the Roman-Germanic labour law system. Finally, in the *social democratic* model the state becomes the vehicle for breaking the constraints which market forces impose upon workers' social, economic and political behaviour. Social insurance is universal with elements of redistribution and relies upon full employment to provide relatively generous support for the disadvantaged. This requirement leads to tri-partite decision-making in the labour market where bargaining becomes centralised and active manpower policies are pursued to encourage bargainers to internalise inflation and employment externalities into their wage-fixing. The corporatist policies pursued by the Nordic countries in the 1970s and 1980s are the usual example given of this variant.

These differences in social policy regimes in member states, when combined with the differences in labour market behaviour which we discussed in Chapter 1, can explain the problems of reaching agreement on an EU-wide social policy. Articles 117 and 118 of the Treaty of Rome seek to promote improved working conditions and charge the Commission with promoting co-operation among member states in social policy, whereas Articles 119–22 establish the objective of equal pay for equal work and link to provisions to promote internal migration in the EU. The principle agency responsible for formulating and implementing social policy is the Commission's Directorate-General (DG) V which deals with Employment, Social Affairs and Education. Whilst the Commission proposes legislation and the European Parliament has a consultative role, power remains with the Council of Ministers. Articles 123–28 establish the European Social Fund with the objectives of promoting employment opportunities via training and other labour mobility programmes. Whilst the operation of this fund has changed over the years its size has remained relatively small, notwithstanding a threefold increase since 1988.

The limited role envisaged for social policy in the Treaty of Rome reflected the original, largely customs union, objectives of the EC. With the advent of the Single European Market initiatives in the mid-1980s social policy entered a new phase. Although the emphasis remained on employment-related objectives, the 1986 Single European Act committed member states to improving and harmonising health and safety standards, implemented in a number of directives between 1989 and 1992. In addition, the Commission received responsibility for promoting a social dialogue between management and labour, the 'social partners', at European level. The introduction of qualified majority voting in the Council of Ministers enabled some progress towards a community-wide social policy, especially in health and safety, although all other issues related to the rights and interests of employees remained subject to the unanimity rule and could still be blocked by a single member state.

This new emphasis placed on social policy in the Commission was reflected in the adoption, with the dissent of the UK, at the 1989 Strasbourg Summit of the Community Charter of Fundamental Rights, the 'Social Charter'. Whilst the Charter was largely symbolic, it assumed importance as a statement of legislative intent and because of its emphasis upon employee rights. The adoption of rights, such as freedom of movement and of association and collective bargaining, reflected the dominance of the social democratic/conservative-corporatist philosophies within the EU. The UK, often with the assistance of Denmark, managed to hold up progress on parts of the Social Action Programme which sought to implement the Charter, especially those concerned with the rights of part-time and temporary workers and proposals for transnational works councils. Though working time and maternity leave directives were approved under the guise of health and safety measures, where qualified majority voting applied, Addison and Siebert (1991, 1992, 1993 and 1994a) provide a critical summary of the rise and progress of the Social Action Programme. The Social Charter formed the basis of the Social Chapter of the Maastricht Treaty ratified by all Member States in 1993. The UK insisted that the Social Chapter was formally excluded from the Treaty, though a protocol was signed by the other 11 countries agreeing to comply with the terms of the omitted Social Chapter (see Box 8.1). Whilst the new subsidiarity article now required EU action only when this was appropriate, new objectives were added on social protection, social dialogue and the development of human resources. Qualified majority voting now applies not only to health and safety issues but also working conditions and sex equality at work, but issues concerning industrial democracy, social security and redundancy still require unanimity. The consequence of the Maastricht Summit has been to increase the authority of the Commission in pursuing its social policy objectives and also to create an enhanced role for the Union of Industrial and Employers' Confederations (UNICE), European Centre of Public Enterprise (CEEP) and the European Trade Union Confederation (ETUC), the 'social partners', in the formulation of social policy.

The general inability of EC social policy directives and regulations in the 1970s and early 1980s to exert a significant influence on labour market behaviour within national economies has led to a different policy of harmonisation being attempted. Rather than a convergence of national systems being encouraged and gradually being required, the Social Chapter formulates a general norm of minimum social policy, which can still accommodate institutional differences and economic disparities

---

Box 8.1: The British opt-out: who loses?

The British opt-out from the Social Chapter of the Maastricht Treaty represented a rejection of the Roman-Germanic system of labour market regulation; a system in which the state guarantees fundamental worker rights and regulates to ensure minimum acceptable standards for remuneration, working conditions and participation. Since for most member states the Social Chapter largely duplicated their existing policies, the British hostility to this and earlier EU measures aroused surprise. Different political and economic philosophies underlie the British tradition of labour market regulation. It relies upon a statutory framework establishing freedom of contract, and ensuring that firms and workers can then reach mutually beneficial bargains with the minimum of regulatory constraint. These differences in regulatory frameworks have themselves contributed to differences in the structure of employment and labour market behaviour, with Britain having more atypical workers and relying on more decentralised bargaining.

These differences explain the origins of the British '*Non*', but a more interesting question concerns its consequences. The signatories to the social policy Protocol and Agreement fear that the opt-out gives British firms an 'unfair' competitive advantage and will lead to Britain increasing its share of foreign direct investment. It is too soon to assess this fear, though a study utilising the 1990 Workplace Industrial Relations Survey found little evidence that multinationals had exploited the differences in regulatory environments (OECD, 1994a). In Britain, multinationals offered similar working conditions to those in more regulated European countries. Multinationals also offered their British work-force more stable employment and higher wages than firms only producing in the UK. These findings are consistent with our conclusion that the social dumping argument places too much emphasis upon differences in the costs of employing labour and too little on the determinants of competitiveness. The UK's opt-out may increase the dispersion of the structure of labour costs in the EU but it is unlikely to significantly alter relative unit labour costs.

A more lasting consequence of Britain's opt-out is likely to be that if the UK decides to opt in to the Protocol and Agreement, it will be faced with implementing directives which have not been designed to reflect the peculiarities of its labour market.

---

between the member states. Commentators differ over whether this represents a process of 'negative co-ordination' or a re-regulation of European labour markets. Opinions also differ about the extent to which the Commission's White Paper on *Growth, Competitiveness and Employment* (1993) with its championing of a flexible labour market, represents a change in the Commission's priorities or a failure to acknowledge the inconsistency between its social and competition policy stances. The 1994 White Paper, *European Social Policy : The Way Forward* represented a slowdown in the pace and volume of European directives, making implementation of the Social Action Programme and the passing of held-up directives, particularly employment rights for atypical workers, a priority. It contained a commitment only to two new directives, both concerning issues related to occupational pensions.

The Commission's first report on the operation of the Treaty on European Union, *Preparing Europe for the 21st Century* (1995) confronted the consequences of the UK's opt-out from the social policy Protocol and Agreement appended to the Treaty.

Whilst the Commission accepted that some member states require longer than others to adjust to certain policies, they reasserted that this must be done within a single institutional framework. The Commission commented that permanent exemptions 'have the effect of creating an *à la carte* Europe . . . allowing each country the freedom to pick and choose the policies it takes part in would inevitably lead to a negation of Europe'. Indeed, it can be argued that the switching of dead-locked proposals on atypical workers and parental leave to the social policy Agreement track has reinforced this '*à la carte* Europe' process.

Box 8.2: TUPE or not TUPE?

The 1977 directive on the safeguarding of employees' rights in the event of transfers of undertakings, businesses and parts of businesses was until recently seen as a relatively modest contribution to the regulatory framework. Market failures may result from unexpected changes of firm ownership in the form of sub-optimal investment in firm-specific training and labour market search. Establishing legal safeguards for workers faced with changes in ownership simplifies contractual bargaining and eliminates some of the potential for opportunistic bargaining resulting from asymmetric information regarding risk of transfers. The initial lack of controversy regarding this expansion of worker rights was indicated by the British government enacting the Transfer of Undertakings (Protection of Employment) Regulations (TUPE) in 1981 implementing fully the 1977 directive.

It was the imposition of widespread compulsory competitive tendering (CCT) on local government and the public-sector health service in the late 1980s and 1990s which suddenly made TUPE an important issue. The British government's economic liberal philosophy dictated that the absence of the discipline of market forces must produce bureaucracy and inefficiency in the public sector. Although parts of the public sector could be directly exposed to market forces through privatisation, other parts such as defence and law and order could not be satisfactorily produced by the private sector, whilst still others, such as education and health, lacked a political consensus for such a fundamental change. The introduction of CCT was an attempt to open up some of the remaining public sector services to the discipline of market forces.

Since the public services targeted for CCT, such as cleaning and school meal services, were largely labour-intensive with little prospect of significant factor substitution, any benefits from tendering were likely to be at the cost of the quality of service provided or the remuneration and/or working conditions of the workers currently employed. Walsh and Davis (1993) found evidence of such consequences with the average savings of around 12 per cent in service costs, largely financed through a deterioration in wage and non-wage benefits and alterations in the pattern of working. However, to the surprise of the British government, in 1994 the Court of Appeal's decision in the Dines case (Adnett *et al.* 1995) made it clear that contracting out a service following competitive tendering would normally be covered by TUPE. Mrs. Dines was made redundant following the failure of her employer to retain a hospital cleaning contract, to be immediately re-employed by the successful contractor on inferior terms and conditions. The decision that contracting-out was normally covered by TUPE threatened to halt further extensions of competitive tendering and led to a fierce and prolonged debate in the EU over the Commission's proposed revisions to the 1977 directive.

The medium-term social action programme submitted by the Commission in April 1995 established the principle of retrenchment for EU social policy for the next three years. The new emphasis is on linking social policy with job creation and competitiveness, a link we critically examine at the end of this chapter. However, the impact of 'social Europe' on national labour market behaviour depends not only on the measures agreed by the Council of Ministers but also on the speed with which these directives are implemented in national legislation and the degree to which they are enforced. Perversely, the British government have been amongst the speediest in implementing the directives and, they argue, are amongst the countries with the highest compliance rates. Though as Box 8.2 illustrates their interpretation of implementation has not always accorded with that of the Law Courts.

8.2 Do we need an EU social policy?

8.2.1 *The case against EU social policy*

In the next few sections we address aspects of current debates concerning the role of social policy in the EU, concentrating in this first section on the arguments against centralisation. Addison and Siebert (1993) and Deakin and Wilkinson (1994) provide more comprehensive, but very different, reviews of this topic. The criticisms which British governments and economic liberals have made of the Commission's attempts to extend 'social Europe' have been extensive, though they can be summarised into four main areas. Firstly, a natural convergence of social policies will emerge as economic integration proceeds, it follows that centralisation is either not necessary or counter-productive. Secondly, a more sophisticated variant of the former argument is that rather than impose a centralised system of regulation and entitlements, institutional competition should be encouraged and that would ensure that the most efficient national social policy automatically prevails. Thirdly, and in direct contradiction to the first two, we have the argument that the principle of subsidiarity should apply and that the diverse labour market behaviour within the EU necessitates systems of regulation which are country-specific. Finally, we have the argument that whilst there is nothing inherently wrong with a centralised policy, the one currently favoured by the majority is neo-corporatist and at odds with the principles of economic liberalism. Much confusion stems from the failure to identify the differences and contradictions between these individual arguments and we now seek to examine their substance in more detail.

Some commentators, such as Britton (1994), have argued that there is likely to be a spontaneous convergence of practice regarding social policy in member states, regardless of national government or EU policy. This process will be led by the multi-national firms, who, reflecting the increasing integration of national economies, will adopt common human resource management policies. Rules will gradually evolve on the basis of successful experimentation, and the similarity of employment environments within the EU will cause these rules to be applied across national boundaries. The OECD (1994a) found limited evidence of a convergence towards more flexible rules and arrangements governing labour market behaviour in Europe. According to this viewpoint any tendency towards the least regulated national labour market increasing their share of employment will be limited. Relative wage movements will offset some of the differences in non-wage labour costs, but most of the costs of regulations will fall on capital rather than on labour in the short run. Given free mobility of capital then governments will be forced to harmonise non-wage costs rather than allow the outflow of capital to reduce domestic employment and their tax base. Hence, as long as product and capital markets are competitive convergence will occur and centralisation is irrelevant. Perversely, this argument bears a striking resemblance to the original social dumping argument used by German employers and unions to support the levelling-up of social standards in the EU!

A more sophisticated and formalised variant of the previous argument has been developed by Siebert and Koop (1993) in their discussion of institutional competition. The origin of their argument lies in the notion of competing governments and jurisdictions introduced by Tiebout (1956). Assume that an objective of national governments is to provide a regulatory framework which attracts mobile factors of production. The inflow of capital and firms is required in order to generate new and better jobs and, if achieved, the resulting higher incomes cause voters to re-elect the government. Governments who have a regulatory framework which generates an outflow of capital and firms are therefore forced to modify their policy or face electoral defeat. The alternative to this process of institutional competition is *ex ante* harmonisation: where national laws are replaced by an agreed set of rules covering the whole EU. Siebert and Koop attribute the standstill of the European integration in the 1960s and 1970s to the impractical nature of the bargaining process necessary for such agreements. They argue that only with the introduction of majority voting and the mutual recognition of national regulations, in a 1979 ruling of the European Court of Justice, was the integration process revitalised.

Institutional competition allows governments to react individually to changes in their own environment, encouraging innovation and reducing the costs of failure. Since it requires less centralised decision-making it will be less bureaucratic and more flexible. The essential prerequisite for institutional competition is the mobility of residents and resources: the model assuming that rational optimising agents operate in competitive markets which internalise externalities and where natural monopolies are absent. Within this framework, a country which improved their social policies would face a trade-off between benefits and costs. Firstly, if human capital investments increased or absenteeism and industrial conflicts fell as a consequence of the new policies, then the resulting improvement in productivity would encourage an inflow of capital and firms. Secondly, and working in the opposite direction, the higher expenditure on social policies would increase unit labour costs, as domestic firms suffered some of the burden of higher taxes and social insurance contributions. More expensive labour will change the optimal production technologies, with the production of labour-intensive goods switching to countries with lower labour costs. Overall these countervailing forces ensure that any changes to social policy are subject to the discipline of the market. Since the demand for social policies has a high income elasticity of demand, this process will tend not only to lead to the reduction of international income differentials but also to a convergence of social policies. Though differences in national preferences, customs and histories will prevent a complete convergence of social policies.

Our third argument against centralisation was the principle of subsidiarity, an argument we introduced in Chapter 3. Subsidiarity allows national governments to take action in all areas that do not fall within the exclusive competence of the EU and where EU level decision-making would not achieve significantly better outcomes. In the case of social policy, critics would argue that much of the Social Action Programme concerned measures which were not appropriate for harmonisation. Thus, the Young Workers Directive sought to curtail paid work by school children, threatening traditional British services, such as newspaper deliveries, without any impact upon cross-national competition. From this viewpoint only national social policies which are designed to distort trade flows need harmonisation, such as health and safety regulations. Ermisch (1991) provides a formal version of this argument, in his analysis capital mobility ensures the equalisation of after-tax returns on capital across the EU. Hence, regulations which raise the cost of labour have effects which depend upon the mobility of labour. With perfect capital mobility and zero labour mobility, regulations have no effect on a firm's location, since the resulting fall in the demand for labour causes the market clearing wage to fall; there being no emigration to offset this fall. In this situation workers pay the full costs of any regulation, either by lower wages or where there are wage rigidities it is their employment probability which falls. Since intra-EU labour mobility is low, as we have seen in Chapter 5, Ermisch concludes that the Social Charter violates the principle of subsidiarity in that the optimal level of social protection is a matter for national decision-making given that the spill-over effects of such policies are minimal.

Our final category of criticism reflects the fundamental dislike of regulations by economic liberals, as such it lies behind all of the arguments we have discussed so far. We have covered much of the general argument against regulations in our initial discussion of labour market policy in Chapter 3 and here we concentrate upon regulations specified in recent proposed directives. The mandatory admission of part-time and temporary workers to occupational pension, sick-pay and holiday pay schemes would produce benefits for these workers in Britain of about 5 per cent of their total wage bill (Department of Employment, 1992). To the extent that these costs are borne by employers then employment opportunities for these workers must decline, with inequality of employment opportunities replacing inequalities in working conditions. The Working Time Directive which initially sought to restrict maximum working hours to 48 a week over a 4 month reference period, was likely to affect around 3 per cent of the total hours worked in Britain and a further 0.4 per cent would have contravened the proposed minimum rest period regulations. However, competitive theory suggests that freedom of contract prevents workers from having to accept unfavourable contracts offered by prospective employers. It follows that mandated benefits can only increase social welfare if the freely negotiated contracts are inefficient and if wages adjust to reflect the costs of the increased benefits (Addison and Siebert, 1994a). Where mandates do not correct a market failure the cost to the firm of complying will exceed the benefits received by workers, and firms and workers both suffer as a result. Firms may not be able to adjust wages, for example to 'pay' for maternity benefits, if such adjustments are incompatible with equal pay or minimum wage legislation or where insider power is sufficient to resist. In these cases since wages cannot adjust, employers reduce employment opportunities for these groups, hence mandatory maternity benefits reduce female employment.

8.2.2 *The case for an EU social policy*

We have so far concentrated upon the arguments against the centralisation and harmonisation of social policy in the EU, it is now time to consider the opposing view. Once again there are a variety of arguments to consider, often mutually contradictory. We again concentrate on areas which have appeared in recent directives, though we ignore discussion of health and safety measures already discussed at length in Chapter 3, and defer the social dumping argument to the following section. We start by re-stating the general rationale for regulating labour market behaviour developed in Chapter 3. As we noted in the previous paragraph, intervention requires that market failures distort freely negotiated contracts and make 'employment at will' policies sub-optimal. For example, regulations may be supported where asymmetric information prevents efficient contracts and leads to market failures. Firms do not have the information to finance maternity benefits and sickness benefits through risk-rated premiums. If only some firms offered such benefits adverse selection would make such schemes progressively more expensive as, for instance, women not likely to become pregnant switch to firms offering no maternity benefits but higher basic pay. The introduction of minimum mandatory maternity benefits eliminates the problem of adverse selection, potentially increasing social welfare above the level achieved through freely negotiated contracts. Such policies are also likely to redistribute wealth towards those claiming the benefit. Indeed, many policies aimed at improving labour market efficiency are also likely to influence the distribution of income and wealth and therefore have equity considerations.

The presence of asymmetric information may also form the rationale for establishing rights of consultation and advance notice of redundancies. Houseman (1990) has argued that where firms have informational advantages over workers about the long-term employment prospects, workers may invest in sub-optimal amounts of search and firm-specific training. In addition, firms may withhold information about forthcoming redundancies to avoid premature turnover and losses of morale. Early notification of plant closures may also help to offset some of the consequences of the locational and contractual rigidities and again encourage efficient search and investment strategies. These problems of asymmetric information and the associated possibilities for opportunistic behaviour complicate the bargaining process and together with the problems associated with the enforcement of the, usually, implicit contract provide a possibility that regulations may improve labour market efficiency. Regulation of hours of work may seem unnecessary where compensating wage differentials are present, but externalities may not be internalised into contracts. Where, for example, accidents are a function of the hours worked and length of shifts, then where accident costs are not born solely by the firms and workers concerned, the accident risk will exceed the socially optimal level, and regulations can promote efficiency.

While we have now restated some of the arguments for regulations and mandatory benefits, we have yet to address the issue of the appropriate level at which policy should be designed and implemented. If we assume democratic decision-making and market failures which are idiosyncratic to national labour markets, then the principle of subsidiarity would seem to imply that social policy should be decided at national or sub-national level. However, increased economic integration together with the European Monetary System and the single market legislation have increased the attractions to national governments of manipulating labour costs via social policies. Abraham (1993) points out that this leads to a prisoner's dilemma problem: every country would be better-off by not lowering social protection, yet no country has a unilateral incentive to abstain from such policies. The centralisation of regulations and mandatory benefits may therefore be preferred on second-best grounds, since as Van Rompuy *et al.* (1991) have also argued, they prevent national governments from pursuing policies which distort competition.

8.2.3   Social dumping

Our discussion of the arguments which favour a centralised social policy in the EU has so far ignored the fear of social dumping; a fear that lay behind the inclusion of social policy in the Treaty of Rome. Social dumping refers to the belief that employers and workers in high social charge economies with extensive systems of social protection will lose market share to firms in economies with lower social charges and less protection as economic integration continues. The increased competition faced by firms in high social charge economies will encourage them to consider relocating in economies with lower social charges, the threat of such relocation putting pressure on the firm's existing workers to make bargaining concessions. In addition, workers may emigrate to the high social protection economies, increasing their labour force and putting further pressure on their existing workers to make concessions over pay and conditions. Over time, even in the absence of governments pursuing 'beggar-thy-neighbour' social policies, these processes lead to social protection being competed down to the lowest levels in the EU. The fear of such a process lay behind the policy of levelling-up, or upward harmonisation, of labour standards and social policies adopted in the Social Chapter.

Social dumping has become an important global issue with the establishment of a World Trade Organisation and demands for the inclusion of social clauses in international trade agreements. Conventions adopted by the International Labour Organisation (ILO) have established international labour standards encompassing areas such as trade union and equal pay rights, employment security and working conditions. Conventions have to be ratified by ILO member states before they come into operation and although most European countries have ratified a large number, global coverage is patchy. From the viewpoint of developing countries labour standards and social clauses represent a new form of protectionism, with the developed economies seeking to impose their value judgements and tastes upon trading partners. Adamy (1994) and Grossman and Koopmann (1994) provide different views on the desirability of such clauses. A study by the OECD (1994a) concluded that there was no compelling evidence that social dumping had so far occurred in OECD countries and we now concentrate upon the European dimensions of this issue.

Proponents of free trade view the social dumping argument as yet another example of special pleading for protection on the fictitious grounds of 'unfair competition'. Given that the demand for social protection is highly income elastic, high social protection is usually an indicator of high income per capita, which itself reflects high productivity and usually superior infrastructure and other competitive advantages. Indeed, the OECD (1994a) has shown that there is a strong relationship between the cost of labour and GDP per capita in European economies. Their study concluded that cross-country differences in labour standards do not fundamentally alter the operation of market forces. That is, by themselves high social charges do not indicate high unit labour costs, and it is the latter which drives competitiveness. It follows that requiring low income and low productivity economies to level-up their social protection distorts the economic forces which help to produce economic convergence. Workers in low wage economies are forced to consume too much social protection, as the increase in their wages is artificially dampened by the increases in the level of social protection. Harmonising labour market regulations and mandatory benefits is therefore not the same as harmonising unit labour costs.

The large differences in the level and composition of employers' labour costs in the different member states of the EU, shown in Table 1.4 do not by themselves indicate a potential for social dumping. Lange (1992) points out that the large differences in social costs within the EU do not appear to cause similar differences in product competitiveness. The reason why high wage-high social cost countries remain competitive seems to be that their firms employ different factor mixes and have access to better skilled labour and infrastructure. Adnett (1995) has pointed out that the differences in employers' social charges in the EU have been sustained over long periods, often re-enforced rather than offset by exchange rate movements, without any significant social dumping effects being observed. Erickson and Kuruvilla (1994) in their analysis of unit labour costs in 1980 find that the large differences in compensation within the EU are not entirely offset by productivity differences and that unit labour costs did not appear to have been converging in the 1980s. Erickson and Kuruvilla find little evidence that the lower unit labour costs in the less-developed countries in the EU have stimulated an inflow of capital from higher cost countries. Abraham (1993) reaches broadly similar conclusions and finds that, except in the most competitive product markets, the benefits of a member country unilaterally cutting labour costs are relatively small. Although the OECD (1994a) provides some evidence that inflows of foreign direct investment have been larger in European economies where labour standards are lower, overall our conclusion is that currently the weight of evidence is against the social dumping argument. Though the reduction of barriers to capital mobility within the EU, together with the maintenance of fixed exchange rates, may yet be shown to strengthen the adjustment process underlying the social dumping argument.

A critical weakness of the social dumping argument is its over-reliance on labour costs in the locational decisions of firms. Not only are unit labour costs the more appropriate measure for locational decision-making, but it may be that commercial strategy may be dominated by market considerations. Where cost factors do dominate then transportation and energy cost together with taxation considerations may dominate labour cost differences. Vaughan-Whitehead's 1992 survey of locational decisions in the EU reaches this conclusion, with the social dumping hypothesis only being applicable to the most labour-intensive sectors, such as textiles and footwear.

8.2.4 *Economic convergence in the EU and social policy*

There is one other area which we must consider before reaching any conclusion concerning EU social policy: economic convergence. For political as well as economic reasons a sustainable economic union requires a convergence in the economic performance of member states. As we discussed in Chapter 5, regional and social policy in the EU have been directed at assisting this process of convergence. Competitive theory assumes that the removal of trade restrictions and the adoption of policies which produce free mobility of capital and labour will foster rapid economic convergence within an economic union. Part of this process will be the equalisation of wages for workers of similar skills across countries. Our previous discussions, and those earlier in this book, have questioned whether this process describes actual EU experience. In this section we briefly consider arguments concerning the convergence of labour market behaviour in the EU before concentrating upon whether an EU social policy may assist or prevent such convergence.

Factor mobility plays a key role in the convergence mechanism, with labour moving to high-wage economies and capital to low-wage ones. We have already discussed the low intra-EU mobility of labour in Chapter 5 and Flanagan (1993) concludes that labour markets in the EU have proved to be a weak engine of economic equality. Convergence may also be hindered by the diversity of labour market institutions, particularly those associated with the wage-fixing process. Indeed, convergence may not occur when we have imperfectly competitive goods and labour markets combined with national differences in technological development and stocks of human capital. New Trade Theory and endogenous growth theory have together provided an alternative story to that of the competitive convergence model. As Dollar and Wolff (1993) point out, trade is increasingly concentrated in high-technology areas in which research and development is important. They argue that economies of scale in the production of new technology lead to nations specialising in different sub-industries and product lines. Whilst these leading firms produce in a variety of countries they tend to reserve their research activities and production of their most advanced products for their home country, making that country the productivity leader in that sub-industry. Thus, the process of convergence in nations' productivity levels is one where productivity growth has been concentrated in different industries in different countries. Dollar and Wolff show that Germany has had particularly rapid productivity growth in transport equipment and machinery, whilst France and Italy have done well in textiles, clothing and leather products. If leading sectors differ between countries on the basis of national technological superiority, then the process of convergence is more complex than initially assumed in the competitive model. It is possible for some countries to lag behind, such as the UK, even with economic integration and mobile resources; adjustment in this case coming through a decline in that economy's exchange rate and relative real wages.

Some non-mainstream economists have also considered the possibility that economic performance within the EU may diverge, with some economies suffering from persistent slow growth. Finegold and Soskice (1988) and Steedman and Wagner (1987) have suggested that producers of low quality, technologically unsophisticated goods in less-developed member states may be prevented from moving up-market. Their inability to finance more sophisticated production techniques may not be compensated for by incoming foreign firms, if skilled labour or infrastructure constraints prevent those firms from attaining their 'home' productivity levels. Economies can therefore get stuck in low-productivity production, producing a slow-growth environment. Amable (1993) provides a model which allows sociological and institutional factors to also contribute to this process, generating a diversity of national growth performances following economic integration.

The increase in European economic integration, interdependency and policy co-ordination have made country-specific shocks less frequent. If monetary union is achieved then asymmetrical shocks will become even less important and national economies in the EU will normally face symmetrical shocks. The inability to adjust exchange rates together with a reduced national sovereignty over monetary and fiscal policies, implies that any required adjustment to shocks will increasingly rely upon labour market adjustments. Differences in national labour market structures and institutions means that even symmetrical shocks may produce asymmetrical responses in the EU, posing problems for authorities committed to convergence and policy co-ordination. Anderton and Barrell (1995) find evidence that the ERM may have provided some pressure for more symmetric labour market responses to shocks, though they conclude that the changes have not been great. Adnett (1993) argued that convergence of social policies and labour market institutions in the EU can assist the objective of producing more symmetrical labour market responses to EU-wide shocks.

8.2.5   *EU social policy: an assessment*

It should be of no surprise after reading the previous chapters, to learn that the debate about European social policy is fundamentally based upon different perceptions of the operation of market forces in product and labour markets. If one believes that labour markets can rapidly adjust to changes in regulations and market conditions then institutional competition would seem a logical policy choice. For those who believe in widespread market failures in European labour markets, that markets adjust only slowly to change, and that governments seek to gain competitive advantages through competitive devaluations of social policy; then centralisation appears an effective policy response. The recognition that arguments for EU social policy also stem from the need to produce 'social cohesion' and may be motivated by a desire to promote redistribution of income, both between and within member states, further complicates the debate.

While our discussion has often emphasised the diversity of European labour markets and institutions, we should not ignore the important similarities which assist harmonisation. As Mitchell and Rojot (1993) show, European countries have almost uniformly tended towards public provision of health insurance, leaving a much smaller role for employers than is found in North America. In retirement pensions provision there is again a major role played by state benefits in Europe, though here there is much more variation in the importance of the employer's role. If more flexible labour markets and the associated increasing mobility of labour, increases the desirability of having benefit structures external to the firm, then Europe will find it easier to make such changes than would the US.

The central issue which we have been discussing in this section, concerns whether increased European economic integration means that member states must adopt the same labour market regulations and level of social protection. As both Ehrenberg (1994) and Freeman (1994) have pointed out, employees in different developed economies work under very different rules. We have questioned the extent to which these differences are reflected in differences in unit labour costs between European economies. Where exchange rate movements are still possible some of the costs of different labour standards will be shifted to the whole population through devaluation. Many of the costs of social policies which are nominally placed on employers will be shifted back to workers, whilst some of the nominal costs will be avoided through non-compliance. For example, whilst mandatory employer contributions for employee sickness benefits reduce the demand for labour and therefore lower employment, there are effects on the other side of the labour market. The provision of sickness benefits may make work more attractive, increasing the labour supply and causing workers to share the costs. Ehrenberg (1994) concludes that the evidence suggests that workers pay for at least a good share of their benefits in the form of lower wages. In terms of non-compliance, de la Rica and Lemieux (1994) find that the high payroll tax in Spain which is used to fund national health insurance has led to a large grey sector where firms and workers connive to avoid the tax. From this discussion we draw two major conclusions. Firstly, harmonisation of labour market regulations and social policies is not a precondition for economic integration, though it may promote the stability of an economic and monetary union. Secondly, increased European economic integration will not by itself produce a convergence of social policies.

8.3   Corporatism: achievements and prospects

The diversity of labour market institutions and social policies within the EU increased sharply with the accession of Austria, Finland and Sweden. In the mid-1980s there had been widespread interest in these corporatist economies and particularly in the contribution which their wage-fixing systems had made to their macroeconomic performance. Early empirical work suggested that their employment and inflation performance was superior to that achieved in economies with a more decentralised wage-fixing system. Sweden was often cited as an example of a successful corporatist economy in which unions and employers bargained at the national level, with government utilising macroeconomic and active labour market policies to maintain stability and eliminate any unemployment consequences of the bargain. One feature of the 'Swedish model' was that the wage was linked to average productivity across the whole bargaining area as opposed to the process in decentralised bargaining where firm-specific productivity dominates wage determination. The resulting egalitarian, 'solidaristic' wage policy was claimed to be the promoter of structural change and productivity growth. The Rehn-Meidner model argued that this promotion of equal wages for equal work, regardless of ability to pay, favoured high productivity, modern plants and hence lowered the operating time of each vintage of capital. While the net effect of such a process on the rate of investment remains uncertain, this 'creative destruction' required government support to increase the mobility of labour by training policies aimed at switching the displaced workers into the expanding firms and sectors. The overall increase in wages was determined in line with the sum of international price inflation and the rate of growth of labour productivity, hence the exposed (tradable goods) sector became the wage leader; this has been termed the Scandinavian inflation model and its link to the Swedish model is more fully examined in Delsen and van Veen (1992).

Amongst the major benefits claimed for the corporatist model are the ability to internalise bargaining externalities, especially inflation. Individual bargainers face a 'prisoner's dilemma': whilst they will benefit by accepting a lower wage in so far as this generates a lower national inflation rate, there is no mechanism which can ensure that their reduced wage increase will be followed by other bargaining groups. In this situation it follows that the inflation externalities will be ignored by every bargaining group. Other disadvantages of the decentralised systems have been identified, including their inability to adjust real wages rapidly to counter adverse shocks. Bhaskar (1990) has shown how in an uncoordinated-bargaining framework asymmetrical responses to relative wage increases and relative wage decreases could lead unions to negotiate a high-wage low-employment bargain. In Layard *et al.*(1991) the internalisation of unemployment and tax externalities encourages unions in centralised bargaining to choose real wages consistent with full-employment. Mulder (1993) also concentrates upon fiscal externalities, arguing that in more centralised bargaining systems the consequences for tax rates of higher public sector pay and unemployment will be taken into consideration in union bargaining behaviour.

It was Calmfors and Driffill (1988) who questioned the conclusion of earlier studies that there was a monotonic relationship between the degree of corporatism and economic performance. They concentrated upon the degree of centralisation in wage-fixing and found, as illustrated in Figure 8.1, that there was a hump-back relationship between the degree of centralisation and unemployment performance. Countries with decentralised bargaining (such as the US), and those with centralised bargaining (such as Sweden), out-performed countries with industry or occupational bargaining (such as the UK). At low levels of centralisation, they argued that the high wage elasticity of demand for labour constrains union bargaining strategy, since high wage increases

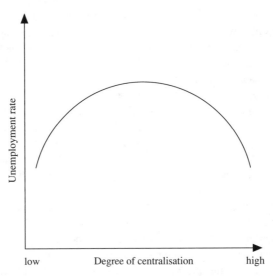

Figure 8.1 The degree of centralisation and the unemployment rate

caused the affected firm to lose market share and employment to fall. Bargaining at the intermediate level, industry-level for example, reduced the size of the substitution effect since all firms' costs were affected and individual firms did not lose market share, though the total market size would be smaller as purchasers switched to alternative goods and services. Bargaining at the national level as well as producing possibilities for internalisation of externalities, also constrains unions by output effects, since a given money supply means that as higher wages raise the price level then real aggregate demand must fall.

The Calmfors and Driffill analysis has been criticised in later studies. Soskice (1990) pointed out that their hump-back relationship is produced by treating Japan and Switzerland as countries with decentralised wage bargaining. In both of these countries there is a high degree of co-ordination of wage-bargaining which may be an effective substitute for centralisation. When these two countries are ignored then the decentralised economies performed relatively poorly compared with the highly-centralised. The rise of insider–outsider models has given further arguments to those who point to the problems of decentralised wage bargaining. The most obvious weakness of the discussion of the benefits of corporatist economies has been the neglect of open economy issues. Where the prices of imports are determined in world markets then any increase in domestic real wages in a small open economy will displace domestic production. In this situation the relative advantages of centralised bargaining and disadvantages of intermediate levels of centralisation are less clear.

In Austria, Finland and Sweden the share of imports in Gross Domestic Product increased by 50 per cent in the twenty years after 1960, and the collapse of the solidaristic wage policy in Sweden is often attributed to the pressures produced by increasing international trade (Ramaswamy, 1994). Whilst the growth of flexible working practices was partly responsible for undermining the solidaristic wage policy, ignoring the dictates of market forces in the wage-fixing process is bound to lead to the possibility of individual unions withdrawing co-operation. This free-rider problem is most severe in labour-scarce sectors, where the interests of both employers and unions are to negotiate outside the national norm. For example, in the mid-1980s in the Swedish metalworking industry both employers and workers preferred decentralised bargaining, the former to enable restructuring to retain competitiveness through higher productivity growth, whilst the unions were seduced by the prevailing high profitability of the industry. As the social and political consensus for corporatism in Sweden declined, the ability of unions to deliver wage moderation also declined, as productivity deals, increased wage drift and profit sharing undermined union solidarity. At the same time the increased openness of the Swedish economy, together with the increased mobility of capital and labour meant that the Government was now less able to deliver its side of the bargain: full employment. Demand shocks were now more likely to be both sector-specific and permanent, whilst demand-management policies were no longer capable of providing a suitable adjustment mechanism (Jackman, 1993). Independent monetary policy was no longer viable in such an environment and fiscal expansions were less effective at stimulating the domestic economy as increased demand spilt over into the economies of trading-partners. At the same time the increased mobility of capital and labour prevented the Government from maintaining a high tax-high public expenditure fiscal policy, high earners and capital preferring low tax regimes.

Following the admission to the EU of Austria, Finland and Sweden attention has turned towards a consideration of the sustainability of corporatism in an integrated Europe. Soskice (1990) amongst others has argued that there are a number of factors which are moving economies towards a more decentralised wage-fixing process. Technology is encouraging more idiosyncratic production, requiring a more individualised rewards system both between and within firms. In addition, the shift in demand towards services both reduces the size of the average unit of production and contributes to a decline in unionisation. Union bargaining power has been further weakened by a number of factors apart from increased economic integration, such as the slow-down of productivity growth and the contraction of public sector employment. These changes together with the recent dominance of right-wing political philosophies have led, in some countries, to deregulation of labour markets and direct attempts to reduce union bargaining-power further by restricting union behaviour or curtailment of trade union legal immunities.

The direct effects of European economic integration on corporatism have recently been examined by Danthine and Hunt (1994) who utilise a model in which unions have significant market power. They point out that integration directly reduces the degree of centralisation of wage-bargaining unless unions merge. More fundamentally, integration makes the domestic aggregate price level less sensitive to domestic wage increases, reflecting the increased importance of imports. Whilst this will tend to reduce union wage moderation in an economy with centralised wage-fixing, working in the opposite direction is the greater wage elasticity of employment due to the increase in international competition. For a low elasticity of substitution between domestic and foreign goods the former effect dominates and the macroeconomic

271

performance of the corporatist economy will deteriorate. In Danthine and Hunt's analysis the hump-back relationship of Figure 8.1 flattens out as integration increases, that is, the degree of centralisation becomes less important in determining economic performance. Tougher product market competition and converging prices reduce the potential for divergent wage policies. However, the common course which tends to be followed in an integrated system resembles the low price-low wage policies of the decentralised structures. Hence it may be difficult for a centralised economy to achieve the necessary adjustments to real wages following entry into an economic union.

The successful corporatist countries have been small and cohesive economies in which full employment helped to create and maintain widespread support for centralised bargaining and solidaristic wage determination. Attempts to follow corporatist policies in larger, more fragmented societies, such as in France, Italy and the UK in the 1960s and 1970s, were rapidly abandoned. Certain aspects of EU policy have already been heavily influenced by Nordic experience; the present popularity of active labour market policies and interest in industrial democracy being two examples. While, for reasons discussed earlier, there is little prospect of a growth of corporatism in the near future, the problems of market economies which corporatism was designed to address have not disappeared. Market economies face the prospects of increased instability, inequality and conflict: it is likely that institutional change will be required to resolve or suppress these problems.

8.4   Worker participation

The European Works Councils Directive was adopted in September 1994, the first under the social policy Protocol and Agreement procedures. This directive requires the 11 signatories and the 3 new member states to implement legislation or otherwise ensure that the social partners establish European Works Councils for the purposes of information and consultation. This directive was the product of a protracted debate within the EU on the desirability of expanding the legal rights to worker participation in management. The debate was heavily influenced by Germany having the dominant national economy and the most developed worker participation arrangement in the EU 12.

The OECD (1994a) provides a survey of the status of employees' representation rights at the beginning of the 1990s and Rogers and Streeck (1994) survey the operation of works councils in European countries. Works councils are representative bodies elected by all workers at a particular plant or workplace, irrespective of union membership, as such they represent a 'second channel' of industrial relations to collective bargaining. Currently in Europe these councils are typically mandatory and institutionalise rights of collective worker participation, including rights to consultation and information. In some European countries health and safety issues are the subject of separate mandatory councils. In Austria, Denmark, Finland, Germany, the Netherlands, Norway and Sweden, works councils enjoy extensive co-determination rights. whilst in Belgium and France legislation has given employees' representatives an important say in working conditions. In Greece, Portugal and Spain the demise of authoritarian regimes led to an extension of workers' rights with mandatory works councils. In general, there has been a tendency for workers' rights to increase in Europe, especially in regard to the introduction of new technology, though in Sweden and the UK rights of unions have been curtailed. We can identify four kinds of worker participation: direct (quality circles and semi-autonomous work groups); profit-sharing; works councils; and company board membership. Direct participation and profit-sharing have usually been employer-led in Europe, as management attempted to imitate Japanese production practices (Turner, 1993). In this section we concentrate upon negotiated worker participation, having briefly considered profit-sharing in the previous chapter.

While the European Commission has often favoured negotiated worker participation in management based upon legal rights, employers and several national governments have favoured voluntary arrangements. Trade unions have been pursuing participation rights at the European level, responding to the consequences of intensified international competition and the decentralisation of bargaining. As we have seen in the mid-1970s a number of directives were approved covering the expansion of workers' rights in health and safety, plant closings, changes of ownership and equal opportunities. At this time worker participation issues were raised as part of the proposed European Company Statute and these proposals, together with those for expanding and harmonising employee information and consultation rights in multinationals, the Vredeling directive, aroused fierce controversy in the early 1980s, the latter being finally withdrawn in 1995. The German system of co-determination involves employee participation on companies' supervisory boards, with elected works councils at the plant and firm level, the rights and obligations of worker representatives and management being established in legislation going back to the early 1950s. Works councils have information and consultation rights prior to the implementation of decisions affecting personnel, with veto rights over limited specified areas. It is often claimed that the German system of co-determination has forced management to use labour efficiently and promote consensus, whilst encouraging worker motivation and promoting co-operative, rather than adversarial, industrial relations. Though Germany has the most developed system of worker participation in the EU, only Britain and Ireland lack mandatory works councils throughout the economy, and only Britain, Ireland, Greece, Italy, Portugal, and Spain lack significant co-determination rights (Rogers and Streeck, 1994). We now assess the theoretical and empirical issues which lie behind the arguments concerning the desirability of statutory rights to worker participation.

Workers' support for works councils may reflect their desire for representation and industrial democracy, while government's support may reflect the role of councils in the enforcement of labour market regulations, such as health and safety issues. Employers will be more concerned with issues concerning productivity and flexibility and we now concentrate upon this economic rationale for works councils. From the perspective of competitive models of labour market behaviour, enforced worker participation must reduce social welfare. Where worker participation would produce mutual benefits it would occur voluntarily through the negotiation of efficient contracts. From this perspective, often referred to as that of property rights theory, enforced worker participation distorts the relationship between risk-bearing and decision-making. This further worsens the agency problems considered in Chapter 2 and leads to unnecessary and inefficient bargaining. From an insider-outsider perspective, mandatory worker participation will worsen insider problems, since improved communication may further raise workers' bargaining power and increase the capital-labour ratio as existing employees seek to maximise their rents. In contrast, the participation theorists argue that the traditional measures of performance used by the property rights school ignore the psychic and other benefits which accrue to management and workers from co-determination. These benefits, such as reduced alienation, are reflected in an increased supply of effort, generating productivity gains whilst at the same time reducing firms' monitoring costs. As we noted in Chapter 1, decentralised decision-making is favoured by modern production technologies, but decentralisation requires mutual trust between workers and managers. Similarly, more idiosyncratic production technologies together with a more competitive market environment generate increased possibilities for opportunistic bargaining behaviour. Mutual trust between employers and employees therefore becomes a more important determinant of individual firm performance. Works councils can provide a vehicle for the development and sustaining of that mutual trust. The resulting long-run increase in net revenue per worker can then be shared by owners, managers and workers and the zero-sum game approach of the competitive model is therefore inappropriate.

Even within an agency framework it is possible to develop a case for participation: where asymmetric information prevails, participation can increase the flow and quality of information between workers and management, thereby improving the quality of decision-making. Indeed, direct participation and profit-sharing have both been advanced as a means of changing the goals of workers so that they may more closely resemble those of the firm, perhaps inducing concessions by workers in difficult trading conditions. Works councils may also act as a vehicle for exerting pressure on management to move 'up-market', since existing employees wish to avoid low productivity solutions to trading problems. While works councils do not bargain over wages, they can exert pressure on firms to extend training opportunities and therefore promote high-wage policies.

Others have questioned whether participation always leads to higher morale and satisfaction in the work-force, and whether any reliable link exists between morale or satisfaction and increased worker productivity. The effect of worker participation is ultimately an empirical question, not one that can be resolved theoretically. Conte and Svejnar (1990) and Levine and Tyson (1990) provide excellent surveys of theoretical and empirical studies of these effects. The diversity of methodologies employed by investigators and the variety of forms that participation may take, make any attempt to reach broad conclusions difficult. However, studies which find that increased participation harmed productivity and firm performance are rare, with the overwhelming majority finding at least short-run productivity gains. Gurdon and Rai (1990) analysed the effects of the 1976 West German Co-determination Law and concluded that increased participation led to increased profitability. In contrast, Addison and Wagner's 1995 survey of German studies reaches less positive conclusions on the effects of works councils on profitability. The absence of large-scale panel data precludes a resolution of these conflicting findings at the present time. Martin and Kersley (1995) analysed data from the 1990 British Workplace Employee Relations Survey and concluded that better worker-firm communication resulted in higher productivity growth, with informal communication through quality circles and the like appearing to have the strongest effects. Fernie and Metcalf (1995) analysed the same data and concluded that workplaces with employee involvement had the best productivity performance, though more authoritarian workplaces had lower quits and a lower rate of absenteeism. Overall, Levine and Tyson conclude that participation is likely to produce a significant and long-lasting increase in productivity when it involves decisions being taken on the shop floor and where it involves substantive rather than consultative arrangements. In addition benefits are greater when profit-sharing and long-term contracts are the norm and where measures are taken to increase worker cohesiveness and guarantee individual rights.

On the issue of profit-sharing earlier positive results have been supported by Bhargava (1994) for the UK and Kruse (1992) for the US. They find evidence that the introduction of profit-sharing produces positive effects upon profitability and productivity respectively, though profit-sharing and employee-share ownership plans may do little to extend industrial democracy (Pendleton *et al.*, 1995). Only Sweden has experimented with wage-earner investment funds with five funds being established in 1984 and abolished in 1991. These funds received contributions from profit and payroll taxes and by 1990 they owned around 5 per cent of the total market value of the Swedish risk-capital market. Whilst the objective of these funds was to increase worker influence in firm decision-making, the policy was also seen to be complementary to that of wage solidarity discussed earlier and to a strengthening of the state pension scheme and Swedish capital formation. George (1993) concludes that the Swedish funds succeeded in meeting these objectives, though their impact upon employee participation in firm decision-making was small.

The results of international studies seem to be broadly supportive of participation measures, though data inadequacies prevent a firm conclusion from being drawn. In most European countries the production-related communication role of consultative councils has now been supplemented by participation rights. Rogers and Streeck (1994) conclude that works councils improve communication and speed up the diffusion of best practices, as well as promoting social consensus and an improved ability to respond to changed economic circumstances. Such a conclusion raises the issue of appropriate policy responses. From the *laissez-faire* perspective such favourable results indicate that workers and firms will voluntarily adopt appropriate participatory measures since there are mutual benefits to be gained. However, this argument requires the absence of significant levels of participation in North America and some parts of Europe to be explained. The attractiveness of participation may be greater in countries with low average unemployment and where capital markets have long-term horizons and close working relationships with the businesses they finance. Externalities may also be important in explaining international differences; Levine and Tyson (1990) argue that firms introducing worker participation will face greater screening and monitoring costs, since other firms rely upon unemployment to prevent shirking. Where the latter is the dominant policy then the resulting social costs of high unemployment are not internalised and we have a sub-optimal level of worker participation. Similarly, firms trying to increase the cohesiveness of their work-force by egalitarian wage policies will find that they lose their best workers to firms with less egalitarian policies. The possibility of multiple equilibria and that the optimal policy may be unstable, can lead to mandatory co-determination regulations increasing social welfare. Such regulations may help shift economies to a superior equilibrium and prevent the unravelling of that high participation equilibrium.

8.5 Enlargement

Since the ending of the Soviet domination of Central and Eastern Europe in 1989 the former socialist countries have increased their economic and political ties with Western Europe. The ultimate objective of these ties for many of these countries is full membership of the EU, a principle which the EU heads of government acknowledged in their 1993 Copenhagen meeting. The consequence of existing agreements is that the Central and Eastern European countries (CEECs) have introduced low-tariff trade policies whilst the EU has reduced their trade barriers, especially in the areas such as agriculture and textiles. The vague conditions set at the Copenhagen Summit for enlargement did not specify a timetable but did recognise the problems which enlargement posed, especially for the EU budget. The large agricultural sectors in most CEECs together with their relatively low income per head means that retention of current EU policy would make huge demands upon the Common Agricultural and Structural and Cohesion Funds.

Of the current member states only Finland (6.9 per cent), Greece (15.8 per cent), Ireland (9.7 per cent) and Portugal (6.3 per cent) have agricultural sectors which contribute significantly over 5 per cent of GDP. Of the CEECs only the Czech Republic and Slovenia have proportions lower than Portugal, while in Latvia, Lithuania and Romania agriculture accounts for over 20 per cent of GDP. These structural differences are linked to the huge difference in living standards between CEECs and existing EU member states. Per capita GDP in most CEECs was at about a tenth of French and German per capita GDP in the early 1990s. Only the Czech Republic, Estonia, Hungary and Slovenia had per capita living standards more than a third of those in Greece and Portugal, the poorest EU member states.

In the context of this book it is the consequences of any enlargement on EU labour markets with which we are concerned. Traditional competitive models of trade would suggest that the up to six fold difference between wage rates in CEECs and those in most existing member states would lead to major shifts in the location of industry and massive migration of labour following enlargement. The CEECs tend to have a comparative advantage in sectors which are already declining in the EU, such as textiles, iron and steel and agriculture. Their full membership would therefore threaten a rapid decline of Western European production in those sectors. However, in 1993 only 4.6 per cent of total extra-EU manufacturing imports came from the Visegrad Countries (Czech Republic, Hungary, Poland and Slovakia) and the trade balance has been continuing in the EU's favour. The composition of the EU's imports from the CEECs is similar to the imports from the Mediterranean countries and some of the growth in imports has been at the expense of the Mediterranean countries (European Commission, 1994d). The growth of intra-industry trade between the CEECs and the EU, has been taken to indicate that their factor endowments are converging with those of the EU. Thus the removal of all manufacturing trade barriers with the CEECs is unlikely to create overwhelming problems for existing member states' economies, though the agricultural sector remains a real problem, especially for Greece and Ireland and parts of Spain and Italy (Rollo and Smith, 1993). Labour migration from East to West has so far been quite small, consistent with what we learnt from our discussion of the history of EU migration in Chapter 5.

Jackman (1995a) points out that the enlargement of the EU to include these economies transforms the problems of unequal development into a problem of regional inequality, a topic we discussed in Chapter 5. It is worth restating the conclusion of that discussion. The low intra-national and intra-EU mobility of labour prevents a rapid convergence of regional income levels. The low migration rate of workers from the Mediterranean countries to the higher-income Northern European member states of the EU should caution against any over-reaction to the possibility of enlargement. Capital mobility may pose a more important problem, with a possible diversion of foreign direct investment from existing low-wage economies to those of the new member states amongst the CEECs. However, weaknesses in the infrastructure of CEECs may limit such diversions to the more labour-intensive and less technologically sophisticated sectors. These conclusions seem to be broadly supported by the recent experience of Austria, an EU country experiencing a disproportionately large growth of trade with these countries. Aiginger *et al.* (1995) concluded that overall trade creation appeared to have a small positive effect on manufacturing employment in Austria, while industrially-mobile workers benefited from higher wage growth. Overall there appears to be no evidence that a further opening of EU markets to the CEECs would have any major impact upon aggregate labour markets in the EU.

8.6 Flexibility and labour market regulation

8.6.1 *EU social policy and labour market flexibility*

A major factor influencing the direction of EU social policy in the mid-1990s has been the increased priority given to job creation and increased European competitiveness. The 'Delors' White Paper, *Growth, Competitiveness and Employment* has resulted in the fight against unemployment taking priority over the establishment of new employment rights (European Commission, 1994e). The extent to which the establishment of employment rights has itself contributed to the rise in European unemployment has been discussed in the previous chapter. We now wish to extend that discussion to a consideration of whether the championing of a 'flexible' labour market must inevitably lead to a dilution of social protection and employment rights in Europe.

In 1980 the Secretary-General of the OECD identified amongst the universal principles of social protection, the role of the state in promoting a more equitable distribution of income and as the main guarantor against social risks, such as unemployment, ill-health, disability and old age (Scherer, 1994). Only the US and the UK have, as yet, repudiated such principles, though fiscal constraints associated with the slowdown of economic growth and demographic, technological (predominantly in health care) and labour market changes have placed severe constraints on the funding of social security schemes throughout Europe. At the same time, as we noted in Section 8.4, the increase in the mobility of capital and, to a lesser extent, of labour have limited the ability of national governments to pursue a high tax-high social protection policy package. As Scherer (1994) records public social protection expenditure as a proportion of GDP ceased to grow after 1983 in OECD countries. However, this stability of the OECD average reflects a variety of levels and trends as we showed in Table 1.11. Scherer reports that variations in public expenditure on health were not the main cause of these differences, with expenditure on the aged and transfers to the non-aged (family allowances, unemployment and disability benefits) being more important. For example, in Greece and Italy the maturation of generous public pension schemes saw a rapid rise in transfers to the aged at the end of the 1980s. Yet in West Germany and Denmark a narrowing in entitlement produced a small fall in this component as a proportion of GDP.

In the previous chapter we noted the tendency in the 1980s to attribute the lengthening of the duration of unemployment spells and poor job creation performance of European economies to the effects of social protection systems and associated labour market regulations. This diagnosis generated policy prescriptions which required lower social benefits to encourage work incentives and reduced employment rights to stimulate job creation. As Blank and Freeman (1994) record these arguments produced widespread policy changes in European labour markets in the 1980s. France, the Netherlands and Spain encouraged decentralised bargaining, Italy abandoned automatic wage-indexing, and the Netherlands, Sweden, West Germany and the UK tightened eligibility requirements for the payment of unemployment benefits. The results of these policies have been disappointing. Aggregate unemployment in Europe has not been significantly reduced, and while US-style wage inequality has generally been avoided, problems of funding the transfers system have intensified as labour market flexibility increased. While it can be argued that this failure resulted from inadequate and patchy reforms, reflecting the failure to generate a political consensus for creating a US-style labour market, this argument is difficult to sustain for the UK and suggests that the original 1980s critique of European labour markets may have been faulty.

The original case against social protection policies was based upon their distortion of labour supply and demand. Unemployment and welfare benefits artificially lower the price of leisure and off-the-job search, whilst low-cost public housing can reduce the geographical mobility of workers. Moral hazard problems in the labour market have also been linked to state sickness and disability benefits. The net result of these policies is to distort individual maximising behaviour in the labour market and hence reduce aggregate social welfare. On the demand side of the labour market, social protection policies generate similar distortions. Employers' social insurance contributions alter optimal capital-labour ratios, whilst mandatory benefits distort the relationship between productivity and wages and therefore reduce the efficiency of the allocative process. On the same basis, minimum wage and equal pay laws merely reduce employment opportunities for the targeted group, and direct taxes and transfers would be a more efficient way of achieving any distributional goals (Saint-Paul, 1994). Overall, these policies are likely to reduce output and reduce competitiveness. In addition, their impact on the distribution of income produces a bias against saving and investment, causing further output losses as economic growth is reduced.

These arguments are all based upon the assumption of the prevalence of competitive markets without significant market failures. They merely identify the costs of distorting individual behaviour without considering the potential benefits of social protection policies. As we noted in Chapter 3, there are likely to be market failures in the provision of sickness and unemployment insurance due to adverse selection and moral hazard problems. In which case social protection policies may correct sub-optimal provision of insurance in the labour market. The arguments against social protection also ignore dynamic consequences of those policies. For example, our discussion in Chapters 4 and 6 indicates that training allowances and maternity leave programmes may encourage a faster growth in the stock of human capital, producing faster productivity growth. Similarly, job security policies may promote investments in job-specific human capital and increase productivity through morale and reduced shirking effects. As this discussion indicates, economic analysis does not provide unequivocal answers to the question of whether social protection policies should be diluted.

Whether specific social protection policies raise social welfare remains therefore an empirical issue, though an implication of the discussion above is that policy initiatives should always be assessed in terms of their static and **dynamic** costs and benefits. As Blank and Freeman (1994) point out, empirical studies have often concentrated upon static efficiency considerations neglecting the impact of social protection policies on labour market adjustments and economic growth. Blank (1994a) summarises existing studies as indicating that the overall effects on labour market flexibility and long-run unemployment are relatively modest, indicating that the efficiency costs of social protection policies are low. To illustrate, we concentrate upon job security legislation, initially considered from a theoretical perspective in Chapter 3 and assessed in relationship to European unemployment in Chapter 7.

In 1988 just as the Worker Adjustment and Retraining Notification Act gave American workers their first notification rights, most Western European countries were weakening their employment protection legislation. In Belgium, France, West Germany and the UK there was a significant weakening of dismissal rights in the 1980s. Table 1.10 provided a ranking of the relative strictness of employment protection legislation in the EU, and Buechtemann (1993) provides a comprehensive review and analysis of these measures. As Lazear (1990) pointed out, in a perfectly functioning market, notification rights and mandatory severance pay will be made superfluous by compensating adjustments in employment contracts. However, as we noted in Chapter 2, the impact of employment protection legislation on labour market efficiency becomes ambiguous, once the existence of externalities and asymmetric information prevent the negotiation of efficient contracts under employment-at-will policies. Circumvention of job security legislation is likely, since if legislation makes new hirings expensive for firms, then substitution will occur in favour of workers not covered by the legislation, such as temporary and part-time workers. As a consequence, legislators may wish to extend the scope of the legislation to include such workers, a process which has occurred in many European economies. Lindbeck (1994) points out that job-security legislation increases the complexity of labour market bargaining, reducing the benefits of intra-firm transactions to managers. Higher transaction costs within firms will then increase the attractiveness to employers of sub-contracting, again undermining the objectives of the legislation. In its turn this further raises pressures on governments to restrict the freedom of firms to employ sub-contractors, a restriction which applied in Sweden up to 1993.

Lazear's empirical results indicated that severance pay tended to reduce employment and increase unemployment rates, though his results were sensitive to model specification. Burgess (1994a) finds some evidence, in his study of industrial data in OECD countries, that employment protection legislation may slow down the reallocation of labour from low to high-productivity sectors. Abraham and Houseman (1994) in their comparison of Belgium, France, Germany and the US find that stronger employment protection in Europe had led to greater adjustments in hours worked, but an overall slower response in labour market adjustment to shocks than in the US. Their results also indicated that the relaxation of employment protection laws in these European economies in the late 1980s did not speed up employment adjustment. Van Audenrode (1994) in his study of OECD countries concludes that those European countries with both restrictions on firings and generous short-time working schemes exhibit the same degree of flexibility of overall labour adjustments as the US. Hence, employment protection legislation need not be incompatible with a flexible labour market, though it changes the type of flexibility with more adjustment through hours and less through employment. One advantage of encouraging adjustment through hours is that the costs of downturns are shared more broadly amongst the work-force.

While there is substantial evidence that social policies affect individual behaviour, remarkably little evidence suggests that they affect labour market flexibility, or at least that part of flexibility which is critical in determining labour market efficiency. Blank (1994) interprets this result as indicating the alternative adjustment mechanisms available to labour markets. As we discovered regulating employment adjustment through job security legislation promotes adjustment of hours, whilst generous public pension schemes promote the exit of older workers from the work-force in times of economic downturn (Rebick, 1994). Our conclusion that European social welfare programmes had only modest effects on labour market adjustment is consistent with the finding that de-regulations of labour markets have little effect on flexibility.

8.6.2   *Flexibility and labour market performance*

So far we have been unable to comment on the desirability of existing European social policies, since we know little about the short and long-term benefits of these programmes. We can merely record that European levels of social protection appear consistent with labour market flexibility. In the previous chapters we have raised the question of whether policies aimed at directly stimulating labour market flexibility may not favour short-run employment growth at a cost of reduced long-run productivity growth and, hence competitiveness. Policy changes which reduce the relative cost of low-skilled workers, such as abolition of minimum wage laws, may merely increase the labour-intensity of production. Such a change may perhaps be desirable in the non-tradable sectors given the present high rates of unemployment, but modern theories of trade and growth suggest that such changes are unlikely to promote long-run improvements in competitiveness in the present global trading climate. Similarly, policies which reduce employers' costs of employing atypical workers may again encourage more labour-intensive, less human and physical capital-intensive production.

Recent data on the pattern of international specialisation suggest that countries whose industrial structures have changed to reflect expanding world markets have been more successful at expanding employment. It is this form of flexibility which appears important when comparing cross-country economic performance and it is this type of flexibility which may be harmed by the de-regulation of European labour markets. Within manufacturing it is only the science-based industries which have been consistently expanding employment internationally since the 1970s, whilst in services it is the knowledge-intensive sectors which have been amongst the most rapidly growing sectors. Studies by the OECD (1995) and the European Commission (1994f) suggest that EU member states had become increasingly specialised in low-wage and low-technology manufacturing industries when compared with the US and Japan. This weakening of the comparative advantage of European countries in the high technology areas has been attributed to their failure to compete effectively in the fast-growing markets for information technology products. Of the 20 products where the annual average percentage growth of imports between 1970 and 1992 exceeded 14 per cent, the EC countries increased their specialisation only in pharmaceutical, aircraft and chemical products. As a consequence whilst Japanese employment in high-tech industries grew at an annual rate of nearly 2 per cent on average between 1970 and 1991, in Germany it grew at just 0.4 per cent, in France and Italy there was no growth and in the Netherlands it declined at 0.5 per cent and in the UK at 1.4 per cent (OECD, 1995).

Our earlier discussion noted that modern theories of trade and economic growth emphasise the importance of the institutional set-up which generates new technology and promotes the supply of highly-skilled workers. In terms of labour market policies this requires support for science and education and intensified efforts in training and retraining. Flexible employment policies are of relevance only in so far as they promote human resource development. Functional mobility is conducive to the development of sustainable employment in high-tech and knowledge-intensive industries, while numerical flexibility may be harmful. Policies which target labour market flexibility by encouraging a fall in the relative wage of unskilled workers are likely to be counter-productive, unless combined with the sort of policies already discussed. We conclude that flexibility is no panacea and the wrong sort of flexibility may merely encourage European labour markets to converge on US, rather than Japanese, behaviour and performance.

8.7 Conclusions

Although European economies are facing pressures which favour decentralised bargaining, there has as yet been little assault on the collective labour market and prevailing institutions. With the exception of the UK, policy-generated pressures encouraging deregulation and decollectivisation have been rare. In most European economies it seems likely that the existing regulatory framework and levels of social protection can be maintained, as more flexible work practices are enhanced and more rapid adjustments made to technological and competitive changes. Sustainable improvements in productivity growth need not be sought at the expense of existing worker rights and levels of social protection. The encouragement of flexible working practices can be made compatible with strong firm-worker attachments which encourage the development of job-specific skills and flexible specialisation in production.

Guide to further reading

Purdy and Devine (1994) provide an interesting introduction to EU social policy. McDonald and Dearden (1994) provide an alternative textbook treatment of many of the issues discussed in this chapter. Freeman (1994) and Schmid (1994) edit collections of papers which provide excellent in-depth review of many of the topics covered here. In particular, Rogers and Streeck (1994) provides a comprehensive and stimulating review of the operation of works councils in Europe and elsewhere. Henley and Tsakalotos (1993), Calmfors (1993) and Walsh (1995) provide accessible surveys of the literature on corporatism. Baldwin (1995) provides an assessment of the overall consequences of enlargement for the EU, and Peters (1995) introduces the labour market consequences of EMU.

References

Abell, P., Khalaf, H. and **Smeaton, D.** (1995) An exploration of entry to and exit from self-employment. Centre for Economic Performance Discussion Paper No. 224. London.

Abraham, F. (1993) The social dimension of an integrated EC-Nordic economic area. In J. Fagerberg and L. Lundberg (eds) *European economic integration: a Nordic perspective.* Avebury, Aldershot. 313–31.

Abraham, K. and **Houseman, S.** (1994) Does employment protection inhibit labor market flexibility? lessons from Germany, France and Belgium. In Blank, R. (ed.) *Social protection versus economic flexibility: is there a trade-off?* University of Chicago Press, Chicago, Ill., 59–94.

Adamy, W. (1994) International trade and social standards. *Intereconomics*, Nov./Dec. 269–77.

Addison, J. and **Siebert, W.** (1991) The social charter of the European community: evolution and controversies. *Industrial and Labor Relations Review*, **44**: 597–625.

Addison, J. and **Siebert, W.** (1992) The social charter: whatever next? *British Journal of Industrial Relations*, **30**: 495–513.

Addison, J. and **Siebert, W.** (1993) The EC social charter: the nature of the beast. *National Westminster Quarterly Review*, February. 13–28.

Addison, J. and **Siebert, W.** (1994) Vocational training and the European Community. *Oxford Economic Papers*, **46**: 696–724.

Addison, J. and **Siebert, W.** (1994a) Recent developments in social policy in the new European union. *Industrial and Labor Relations Review*, **48**: 5–27.

Addison, J. and **Wagner, J.** (1995) On the impact of German works councils: some conjectures and evidence from establishment-level data. *University of Lüneberg, Institute of Economics Arbeitsbericht*, No. 142.

Adnett, N. (1993) The social charter: unnecessary regulation or pre-requisite for convergence? *British Review of Economic Issues*, **36**: 63–80.

Adnett, N. (1995) Social dumping and European economic integration. *Journal of European Social Policy*, **5**:1–12.

Adnett, N., Hardy, S. and **Painter, R.** (1995) Business transfers and contracting-out. *Employee Relations*, **17(8)**: 22–29.

Ahlroth, S., Björklund, A. and **Forslund, A.** (1994) *The output of the Swedish education sector.* National Institute of Economic Research, Stockholm, Working Paper No. 43.

Ahn, N. and **Ugidos-Olazabal, A.** (1995) Duration of unemployment in Spain: relative effects of unemployment benefit and family characteristics. *Oxford Bulletin of Economics and Statistics*, **57**: 249–64.

Aiginger, K., Winter-Ebmer, R. and **Zweimüller, J.** (1995) East European trade and the Austrian labour market. Centre for Economic Policy Research Discussion Paper No. 1168.

Akerlof, G. (1976) The economics of caste and of the rat race and other woeful tales. *Quarterly Journal of Economics*, **90**: 591–617.

References

Akerlof, G. (1981) Jobs as dam sites. *Review of Economic Studies*, **48**: 37–49.

Akerlof, G. (1982) Labor contracts as a partial gift exchange. *Quarterly Journal of Economics*, **97**: 543–70.

Alba-Ramirez, A. (1994) Formal training, temporary contracts, productivity and wages in Spain. *Oxford Bulletin of Economics and Statistics*, **56**: 151–69.

Alogoskoufis, G. and **Manning, A.** (1988) Wage-setting and unemployment persistence in Europe, Japan and the USA. *European Economic Review*, **32**: 698–706.

Alogoskoufis, G. and **Manning, A.** (1988a) On the persistence of unemployment. *Economic Policy*, **7**: 428–69.

Amable, B. (1993) Catch-up and convergence: a model of cumulative growth. *International Review of Applied Economics*, **7**: 1–25.

Anderton, R. and **Barrell, R.** (1995) The ERM and structural change in European labour markets: a study of 10 countries. *Welwirtschaftliches Archiv*, **131**: 44–67.

Anderton, B. and **Mayhew, K.** (1994) A comparative analysis of the UK labour market. In R. Barrell (ed.) *The UK labour market: comparative aspects and institutional developments*. National Institute of Economic and Social Research and Cambridge University Press, 5–50.

Andrés, J. (1990) The influence of demand and capital constraints on Spanish unemployment. In J. Drèze and C. Bean (eds) *Europe's unemployment problem*. MIT Press, Cambridge, Mass., 366–408.

Antolin, P. (1994) Labour mobility, unemployment flows, vacancies, and job search behaviour in the Spanish labour market. Instituto de Analisis Economico, CSIC Barcelona, Working Paper 276.94.

Arestis, P. and **Biefang-Frisancho Mariscal, I.** (1991) Hysteresis and unemployment in wage determination – an overview. *British Review of Economic Issues*, **13**: 1–26.

Armstrong, H. (1994) Regional growth within the European union: a reappraisal of the cross-sectional evidence. University of Lancaster, Management School Working Paper No. EC22/94.

Armstrong, H. and **Taylor, J.** (1993) *Regional economics and policy*. Harvester Wheatsheaf, Hemel Hempstead.

Arrow, K. (1972) Some mathematical models of race in the labor market. In A. Pascal (ed.) *Racial discrimination in economic life*. Lexington Books, Lexington, Mass. 83–102.

Artis, M. and **Lee, N.** (1994) *The economics of the European union*. Oxford University Press, Oxford.

Arulampalam, W. and **Stewart, M.** (1995) The determinants of individual unemployment durations in an era of high unemployment. *Economic Journal*, **105**: 321–32.

Ashenfelter, O. and **Krueger, A.** (1994) Estimates of the economic returns to schooling from a new sample of twins. *American Economic Review*, **84**: 1157–73.

Asscher-Vonk, I. (1993) Equal pay in the Netherlands. In F. Eyraud (ed.) *Equal pay protection in industrialised market economies: in search of greater effectiveness*. International Labour Office, Geneva, 107–23.

Atkinson, A. (1993) Have social security benefits seriously damaged work incentives in Britain? In A. Atkinson and G. Mogensen (eds) *Welfare and work incentives: a North European perspective*. Clarendon Press, Oxford, 161–91.

Atkinson, A. and **Micklewright, J.** (1989) Turning the screw: benefits for the unemployed 1979–1988. In A. Dilnot and I. Walker (eds). *The economics of social security*, Oxford University Press, Oxford.

van Audenrode, M. (1994) Short-time compensation, job security, and employment contracts: evidence from selected OECD countries. *Journal of Political Economy*, **102**: 76–102.

284

Audit Commission (1995) *Making markets: a review of the audits of the client role for contracted services*. HMSO, London.

Auer, P. (1994) Further education and training for the employed. In G. Schmid (ed.) *Labor market institutions in Europe*. M.E. Sharpe, New York.

Averitt, R. (1968) *The Dual Economy*. Norton, New York.

Baker, G. and **Holmstrom, B.** (1995) Internal labour markets: too many theories, too few facts. *American Economic Review*, **85(2)**: 255–9.

Baldwin, R. (1995) The eastern enlargement of the EU. *European Economic Review*, **39**: 474–82.

Barnard, C., Clark, J. and **Lewis, R.** (1995) *The exercise of individual employment rights in the member states of the European community*. Employment Department Research Series No. 49, HMSO, London.

Barr, N. (1993) *The economics of the welfare state*. Stanford University Press, Stanford, Conn.

Barr, N. (1993a) Alternative funding resources for higher education. *Economic Journal*, **103**: 718–28.

Barrell, R., Caporale, G. and **Sefton, J.** (1994) Prospects for European unemployment. In J. Michie and J. Grieve Smith (eds) *Unemployment in Europe*. Academic Press, London, 32–44.

Barrell, R., Pain, N. and **Young, G.** (1994a) Structural differences in European labour markets. In R. Barrell (ed.) *The UK labour market: comparative aspects and institutional developments*. National Institute of Economic and Social Research and Cambridge University Press, 214–57.

Barro, R. and **Lee, W-H.** (1993) International comparisons of educational attainment. *Journal of Monetary Economics*, **32**: 363–94.

Barro, R. and **Sala-i-Martin, X.** (1991) Convergence across states and regions. *Brookings Papers on Economic Activity*, **1**: 107–82.

Barron, J., Bishop, J. and **Dunkelberg, W.** (1985) Employer search – the interviewing and hiring of new employees. *Review of Economics and Statistics*, **67**: 43–52.

Barron, J. and **Gilley, O.** (1981) Job search and vacancy contacts. *American Economic Review*, **71**: 683–91.

Barron, J. and **Hannan, M.** (1994) The impact of economics on contemporary sociology. *Journal of Economic Literature*, **32**: 111–46.

Barron, J. and **Mellor, W.** (1982) Labour contract formation, search requirements and the use of a public employment service. *Economic Inquiry*, **20**: 381–7.

Bazen, S. (1994) Minimum wage protection in industrialized countries: recent experience and issues for the future. *International Journal of Manpower*, **15**: 62–73.

Bean, C. (1994) European unemployment: a survey. *Journal of Economic Literature*, **32**: 573–619.

Bean, C. (1994a) The role of demand management policies in reducing unemployment. In Federal Reserve Bank of Kansas City, *Reducing unemployment: current issues and policy options*, 99–131.

Beatson, M. (1993) Trends in pay flexibility. *Employment Gazette*, September: 405–28.

Beatson, M. (1995) *Labour market flexibility*. Research Series No. 48. Employment Department, Sheffield.

Becker, G. (1957) *The economics of discrimination*. University of Chicago Press, Chicago, Ill.

Becker, G. (1975) *Human capital: a theoretical and empirical analysis*, 2nd edn. National Bureau for Economic Research, New York.

Becker, G. (1985) Human capital, effort and the sexual division of labor. *Journal of Labour Economics*, **3**: S33-S58.

References

Becker, G. (1992) Habits, addictions, and traditions. *Kyklos*, **45**: 327–46.

Begg, D. and **Portes, R.** (1993) Eastern Germany since unification: wage subsidies remain a better way. *Economics of Transition*, **1**: 383–400.

Begg, I. (1995) Factor mobility and regional disparities in the European union. *Oxford Review of Economic Policy*, **11(2)**: 96–113.

Benassi, C., Chirco, A. and **Colombo, C.** (1994) *The new Keynesian economics*. Basil Blackwell, Oxford.

Bendick, M. (1989) Matching workers and job opportunities: what role for the federal-state employment service? In D. Bawden and F. Skidmore (eds) *Rethinking Employment Policy*. The Urban Institute Press, Washington, DC 81–108.

Bennett, R., Glennerster, H. and **Nevison, D.** (1992) Investing in skill: to stay on or not to stay on? *Oxford Review of Economic Policy*, **8**: 130–45.

Bentolila, S. and **Bertola, G.** (1990) Firing costs and labour demand: how bad is Eurosclerosis? *Review of Economic Studies*, **57**: 381–402.

Bentolila, S. and **Blanchard, O.** (1990) Spanish unemployment. *Economic Policy*, **10**: 234–81.

Bentolila, S. and **Dolado, J.** (1994) Spanish labour markets. *Economic Policy*, **14**: 53–99.

van den Berg, G. and **van Ours, J.** (1994) Unemployment dynamics and duration dependence in France, the Netherlands and the United Kingdom. *Economic Journal*, **104**: 432–43.

Bertola, G. and **Ichino, A.** (1995) Crossing the river: a comparative perspective on Italian employment dynamics. *Economic Policy*, **10**: 359–420.

Bettio, F. and **Villa, P.** (1993) *Wage determination and sex segregation in Italy*. Report for the European Commission network on the Situation of Women in the Labour market, Working paper, UMIST, Manchester.

Bewley, T. (1995) A depressed labor market as explained by participants. *American Economic Review*, **85(2)**: 250–4.

Bhargava, S. (1994) Profit sharing and the financial performance of companies: evidence from UK panel data. *Economic Journal*, **104**: 1044–56.

Bhaskar, V. (1990) Wage relativities and the natural rate of unemployment. *Economic Journal*, **100 Supplement**: 60–66.

Bird, D. (1994) International comparisons of labour disputes in 1993. *Employment Gazette*, December: 433–9.

Björklund, A. (1991) *Labour market policy and unemployment insurance*. Clarendon Press, Oxford.

Björklund, A. (1994) Evaluations of labour market policy in Sweden. *International Journal of Manpower*, **15(5)**: 16–31.

Björklund, A. and **Freeman, R.** (1995) Generating equality and eliminating poverty the Swedish way. Centre for Economic Performance Discussion Paper No. 228.

Blackaby, D., Clark, K., Leslie, D. and **Murphy, P.** (1994) *Black-White male earnings and employment prospects in the 1970s and 1980s: evidence for Britain*. Manchester Metropolitan University, Department of Economics and Economic History, Working Paper 94–13.

Blackaby, D. and **Manning, D.** (1990) North-south divide: questions of existence and stability. *Economic Journal*, **100**: 510–27.

Blackburn, M. and **Neumark, D.** (1993) *Are OLS estimates of the returns to schooling biased downwards? another look*. National Bureau of Economic Research Working Papers No. 4259.

Blanchard, O. and **Diamond, P.** (1992) The flow approach to labor markets. *American Economic Review*, **82** (May): 354–59.

Blanchard, O. and Diamond, P. (1994) Ranking, unemployment duration and wages. *Review of Economic Studies*, **61**: 417–34.

Blanchard, O. and Jimeno, J. (1995) Structural unemployment: Spain versus Portugal. *American Economic Review*, **85(2)**: 212–7.

Blanchard, O. and Summers, L. (1986) Hysteresis and the European unemployment problem. *NBER Macroeconomics Annual*, 1986: 15–78.

Blanchflower, D. and Freeman, R. (1994) Did the Thatcher reforms change British labour market performance? In R. Barrell (ed.) *The UK labour market: comparative aspects and institutional developments.* National Institute of Economic and Social Research and Cambridge University Press, 51–92.

Blanchflower, D. and Lynch, L. (1994) Training at work: a comparison of US and British youths. In L. Lynch (ed.) *Training and the private sector: international comparisons.* University of Chicago Press, Chicago, Ill. 233–60.

Blanchflower, D. and Oswald, A. (1990) The wage curve. *Scandinavian Journal of Economics*, **92**: 215–35.

Blanchflower, D. and Oswald, A. (1994) Estimating a wage curve for Britain. *Economic Journal*, **104**: 1025 -43.

Blank, R. (1994) Public sector growth and labor market flexibility: the United States versus the United Kingdom. In R. Blank (ed.) *Social protection versus economic flexibility: is there a trade-off?* University of Chicago Press, Chicago, Ill. 223–264.

Blank, R. (1994a) Does a larger social safety net mean less economic flexibility? In R. Freeman (ed.) *Working under different rules.* Russell Sage Foundation, New York, 157–87.

Blank, R. and Freeman, R. (1994) Evaluating the connection between social protection and economic flexibility. In R. Blank (ed.) *Social protection versus economic flexibility: is there a trade-off?* University of Chicago Press, Chicago, Ill. 21–41.

Blanpain, R. (ed.) (1994) *International Encyclopaedia for Labour Law and Industrial Relations.* Kluwer, Dordrecht, the Netherlands.

Blau, F. (1990) Discrimination against women: theory and evidence. In W. Darity (ed.) *Labour economics: modern views,* Kluwer-Nijhoff, Amsterdam. 53–89.

Blau, F. and Kahn, L. (1992) The gender earnings gap: some international evidence. National Bureau of Economic Research Working Paper No. 4224.

Blau, F. and Kahn, L. (1992a) The gender earnings gap: learning from international comparisons. *American Economic Review*, **82**: 533–8.

Blinder, A. (1994) Overview. In Federal Reserve Bank of Kansas City, *Reducing unemployment: current issues and policy options*, 329 42.

Blöndal, S. and Pearson, M. (1995) Unemployment and other non-employment benefits. *Oxford Review of Economic Policy*, **11**: 136–69.

Blundell, R., Dearden, L. and Meghir, C. (1994) *The determinants and effects of work related training in Britain.* mimeo.

Booth, A. (1991) Job-Related formal training: who receives it and what is it worth? *Oxford Bulletin of Economic Research*, **53**: 281–94.

Booth, A. (1993) Private sector training and graduate earnings. *Review of Economics and Statistics*, **66**: 36–43.

Booth, A. (1995) *The economics of trade unions.* Cambridge University Press, Cambridge.

Booth, A. and Snower, D. (eds) (1995) *Acquiring Skills.* Cambridge University Press.

Booth, A. and Zoega, G. (1995) *Quitting externalities of employment cyclicality and firing costs.* ESRC Research Centre on Micro-social Change, University of Essex, Working Paper 95–9.

Borooah, V. and **Lee, K.** (1988) The effects of changes in Britain's industrial structure on female relative pay and employment. *Economic Journal*, **98**: 818–32.

Bosworth, D. (1993) Skill shortages in Britain. *Scottish Journal of Political Economy*, **40**: 241–270.

Bosworth, D., Dawkins, P. and **Stromback, T.** *The economics of the labour market.* Longman, (forthcoming).

Bosworth, D. and **Simpson, P.** (1995) Skills, training and economic performance. *Economics and Business Education*, **3**(3): 103–9.

Bottani, N. (1995) Comparing educational output. *OECD Observer*, **193**: 6–11.

Bowles, S. and **Gintis, H.** (1976) *Schooling in capitalist America.* Basic Books, New York.

Boyer, R. (1993) Labour institutions and economic growth: a survey and a 'regulationist' approach. *Labour*, **7**(1): 25–72.

Braverman, H. (1974) *Labor and monopoly capital: the degradation of work in the twentieth century.* Monthly Press Review, New York.

Britton, A. (1994) Labour markets in Britain and Continental Europe. *National Institute Economic Review*, **3/94**: 5–7.

Britton, A. (1995) Education and inequality. *National Institute Economic Review*, **1/95**: 6–7.

Bruegel, I. (1994) Labour market prospects for women from ethnic minorities. In R. Lindley (ed.) *Labour market structures and prospects for women.* Equal Opportunities Commission, Manchester.

Buechtemann, C. (ed.) (1993) *Employment security and labor market behaviour: interdisciplinary approaches and international evidence.* ILR Press, Ithaca, New York.

Burda, M. and **Wyplosz, C.** (1994) Gross worker and job flows in Europe. *European Economic Review*, **38**: 1287–1315.

Burgess, S. (1993) A search model with job-changing costs: 'Eurosclerosis' and unemployment. *Oxford Economic Papers*, **44**: 75–88.

Burgess, S. (1994) Where did Europe fail? a disaggregate comparison of net job creation in the USA and Europe. Centre for Economic Performance, Discussion Paper No. 192.

Burgess, S. (1994a) The reallocation of employment and the role of employment protection legislation. Centre for Economic Performance, Discussion Paper No. 193.

Button, K. and **Pentecost, E.** (1993) Short and long-term economic convergence in the European community. Loughborough University, Centre for Research in European Economics and Finance, Research Paper 93/2.

Callan, T. and **Wren, A.** (1994) *Male-Female wage differentials: analysis and policy issues.* Economic and Social Research Institute, Dublin.

Callender, C. and **Toye, J.** (1994) Employers' take-up and usage of NVQ/SVQs. *Employment Gazette*, November: 417–22.

Calmfors, L. (1993) Centralisation of wage bargaining and macroeconomic performance – a survey. *OECD Economic Studies* **21**: 161–91.

Calmfors, L. (1994) Active labour market policy and unemployment: a framework for the analysis of crucial design features. *OECD Economic Studies*, **22**: 7–48.

Calmfors, L. and **Driffill, J.** (1988) Bargaining structure, corporatism and economic performance. *Economic Policy*, **6**: 14–61.

Calmfors, L. and **Forslund, A.** (1991) Real-wage adjustment and labour market policies: the Swedish experience. *Economic Journal*, **101**: 1130–48.

Calmfors, L. and **Lang, H.** (1995) Macroeconomic effects of active labour market programmes in a union wage-setting model. *Economic Journal*, **105**: 601–19.

Calmfors, L. and **Skedinger, P.** (1995) Does active labour-market policy increase employment? theoretical considerations and some empirical evidence from Sweden. *Oxford Review of Economic Policy*, **11**: 91–109.

Card, D. and **Krueger, A.** (1995) *Myth and measurement: the new economics of the minimum wage.* Princeton University Press.

Carmichael, H. (1983) Firm specific human' capital and promotion ladders. *Bell Journal of Economics*, **14**: 251–8.

CBI (1991) *Competing with the World's best.* Confederation of British Industry, London.

Centre for Economic Policy Research (CEPR) (1993) *Making sense of subsidiarity: how much centralization for Europe?* CEPR, London.

Centre for Economic Policy Research (CEPR) (1995) *Unemployment: choices for Europe.* CEPR, London.

Chapman, P. (1993) *The economics of training.* Harvester Wheatsheaf, Hemel Hempstead.

Charney, A. (1993) Migration and the public sector: a survey. *Regional Studies*, **27**: 313–26.

Clark, A. and **Oswald, A.** (1993) *Satisfaction and comparison income.* (mimeo). Centre for Economic Performance, London School of Economics.

Clark, A. and **Oswald, A.** (1994) Unhappiness and Unemployment. *Economic Journal*, **104**: 648–59.

Coase, R. (1960) The problem of social cost. *Journal of Law and Economics*, **3**: 1–44.

Coe, D. (1988) Hysteresis effects in aggregate wage equations. In R. Cross (ed.) *Unemployment hysteresis and the natural rate hypothesis.* Basil Blackwell, Oxford, 284–305.

Coles, M. (1994) Understanding the matching function: the role of newspapers and job agencies. Centre for Economic Policy Research Discussion Paper No. 939.

Collier, J. (1994) Regional disparities, the single market and European monetary union. In J. Michie J. and J. Grieve Smith (eds) *Unemployment in Europe.* Academic Press, London, 145–59.

Conte, M. and **Svejnar J.** (1990) The effects of worker participation in management, profits, and ownership of assets on enterprise performance. In K. Abraham and R. McKersie (eds) *New developments in the labor market: towards a new paradigm.* MIT Press, Cambridge, Mass., 59–84.

Coulton, B. and **Crumb, R.** (1994) The UK NAIRU. H.M. Treasury Working Paper No. 66.

Danthine, J-P. and **Hunt, J.** (1994) Wage bargaining structure, employment and economic integration. *Economic Journal*, **104**: 528–41.

Davies, N. and **Teasdale, P.** (1994) *The costs to the British economy of work accidents and work-related ill health.* Health and Safety Executive, London.

Davis, S., Haltiwanger, J. and **Schuh, S.** (1994) Small business and job creation: dissecting the myth and reassessing the facts. *Business Economist*, **29**(3): 13–21.

Deakin, B. and **Pratten, C.** (1982) *Effects of the Temporary Employment Subsidy.* Cambridge University Press, Cambridge.

Deakin, S. and **Wilkinson, F.** (1994) Rights vs. efficiency? the economic case for transnational labour standards. *Industrial Law Journal*, **23**: 289–310.

de la Dehesa, G. and **Krugman, P.** (1992) EMU and the regions. *Group of Thirty, Occasional Paper* No. 39, Washington DC.

de la Dehesa, G. and **Snower, D.** (eds) (1996) *Unemployment Policy.* Cambridge University Press, Cambridge.

Delsen, L. and **van Veen, T.** (1992) The Swedish model: relevant for other European countries? *British Journal of Industrial Relations*, **30**: 83–105.

Department of Employment (1991) Labour Mobility: evidence from the labour force survey. *Employment Gazette*, August: 437–51.

References

Department of Employment (1992) *Note on the costings exercise for the EC social action programme.* Unpublished paper, DE, London.

Dex, S. (1992) Labour force participation of women in Britain during the 1990s: occupational mobility and part-time employment. In R. Lindley (ed.) *Women's employment: Britain and the single market.* HMSO, London.

Dex, S., Gustafsson, S., Smith, N. and **Callan, T.** (1995) Cross-national comparisons of the labour force participation of women married to unemployed men. *Oxford Economic Papers,,* **47**: 611–35.

Dex, S. and **Sewell, R.** (1995) *Equal opportunities policies and women's labour market status in industrialised countries: a bayesian analysis.* mimeo. Paper presented to the Annual Royal Economic Society Conference, University of Kent.

Dex, S., Walters, P. and **Alden, D.** (1993) *French and British mothers at work.* Macmillan, Basingstoke.

Diamond, P. (1982) Wage determination and efficiency in search equilibrium. *Review of Economic Studies,* **49**: 761–82.

Dickens, R., Gregg, P., Machin, S., Manning, A. and **Wadsworth, J.** (1993) Wages Councils: was there a case for abolition. *British Journal of Industrial Relations,* **31**: 515–30.

Dickens, R., Machin, S. and **Manning, A.** (1994) Minimum wages and employment: a theoretical framework with an application to the UK Wages Councils. *International Journal of Manpower,* **15**: 26–48.

Dickens, W. and **Lang, K.** (1987) Where have all the good jobs gone? Deindustrialization and labour market discrimination. In K. Lang and J. Leonard (eds) *Unemployment and the structure of the labour market.* Basil Blackwell, Oxford, 91–102.

Dickens, W. and **Lang, K.** (1992) Labour market segmentation theory: reconsidering the evidence. *National Bureau of Economic Research Working Paper* No. 4087.

Dignan, T. (1995) Regional disparities and regional policy in the European union. *Oxford Review of Economic Policy,* **11**(2): 64–95.

Dollar, D. and **Wolff, E.** (1993) *Competitiveness, convergence, and international specialization.* MIT Press, Cambridge, Mass.

Dolton, P. (1993) The economics of youth training in Britain. *Economic Journal,* **103**: 1261–78.

Dolton, P. and **Kidd, M.** (1994) Occupational access and wage discrimination. *Oxford Bulletin of Economics and Statistics,* **56**: 457–474.

Dolton, P. and **Makepeace, G.** (1987) Marital status, child rearing and earnings differentials in the graduate labour market. *Economic Journal,* **97**: 897–923.

Dolton, P., Makepeace, G. and **van der Klaauw, W.** (1989) Occupational choice and earnings determination: the role of sample selection and non-pecuniary factors. *Oxford Economic Papers,* **41**: 573–94.

Dolton, P., Makepeace, G. and **Treble, J.** (1994) Public and private sector training of young people in Britain. In L. Lynch (ed.) *Training and the private sector: international comparisons.* University of Chicago Press, Chicago, Ill. 261–81.

Dolton, P., Makepeace, G. and **Treble, J.** (1994a The youth training scheme and the school-to-work transition. *Oxford Economic Papers,* **46**: 629–57.

Drèze, J. and **Bean, C.** (1990) *Europe's unemployment problem.* MIT Press, Cambridge, Mass.

Drèze, J. and **Malinvaud, E.** (1994) Growth and employment: the scope of a European initiative. *European Economic Review,* **38**: 489–504.

Ehrenberg, R. (1989) Workers' rights: rethinking protective labor legislation. In D. Bawden and F. Skidmore (eds) *Rethinking employment policy.* Urban Institute Press, Washington DC.

290

Ehrenberg, R. (1994) *Labor markets and integrating national economies*. The Bookings Institution, Washington DC.

Eichenberger R. (1994) The benefits of federalism and the risk of overcentralization. *Kyklos*, **47**: 403–20.

Eichengreen, B. (1993) Labor markets and European monetary unification. In P. Masson and M. Taylor (ed.) *Policy issues in the operation of currency unions*. Cambridge University Press, 130–62.

Eichengreen, B. (1993a) European monetary unification and regional unemployment. In L. Ulman, B. Eichengreen and W. Dickens (eds) *Labor and an integrated Europe*. The Brookings Institution, Washington DC.

Elias, P. (1994) Job-Related training, trade union membership, and labour mobility: a longitudinal study. *Oxford Economic Papers*, **46**: 563–78.

Elias, P., Hernaes, E. and **Baker, M.** (1994) Vocational education and training in Britain and Norway. In L. Lynch (ed.) *Training and the private sector: international comparisons*. University of Chicago Press, Chicago, Ill. 283–97.

Elias, P. and **Hogarth, T.** (1994) Families, jobs and unemployment: the changing pattern of economic dependency in Britain. In R. Lindley (ed.) *Labour market structures and prospects for women*. Equal Opportunities Commission, Manchester.

Elliott, R. (1991) *Labour Economics*. McGraw-Hill, Maidenhead.

Elmeskov, J. and **MacFarlan, M.** (1993) Unemployment persistence. *OECD Economic Studies*, **21**: 59–88.

Elmeskov, J. and **Pichelmann, K.** (1993) Interpreting unemployment: the role of labour-force participation. *OECD Economic Studies*, **21**: 140–160.

Employment Policy Institute (1993) Making workstart work. *Institute Economic Report*, **7(8)**.

Englander, A. and **Gurney, A.** (1994) Medium-term determinants of OECD Productivity. *OECD Economic Studies*, **22**: 49–109.

Erickson, C. and **Kuruvilla, S.** (1994) Labor costs and the social dumping debate in the European union. *Industrial and Labor Relations*, **48**: 28–47.

Ermisch, J. (1991) European integration and external constraints on social policy: is a social charter really necessary? *National Institute Economic Review*, May: 93–109.

European Commission (1993) *Employment in Europe 1993*. European Commission, Brussels.

European Commission (1993c) Growth, competitiveness, employment, the challenges and ways forward into the 21st century. *Bulletin of the European Communities*, Supplement 6/93.

European Commission (1994) Some economic implications of demographic trends up to 2020. *European Economy*, **56**: 211–225.

European Commission (1994a) *Employment in Europe 1994*. European Commission, Brussels.

European Commission (1994b) *White Paper on Growth, Competitiveness, Employment*. European Commission, Brussels.

European Commission (1994c) *European social policy: the way forward*. European Commission, Brussels.

European Commission (1994d) The economic interpenetration between the European Union and Eastern Europe. *European Economy Reports and Studies* No. 6.

European Commission (1994e) Towards a flexible labour market in the European Community. *European Economy*, **56**, 179–209.

European Commission (1994f) European competitiveness in the Triad. *European Economy*, **56**: 111–36.

References

European Commission (1995) *Preparing Europe for the 21st century.* European Commission, Brussels.

European Commission (1995a) *Employment in Europe 1995.* Office for the Official Publications of the European Communities, Luxembourg.

European Industrial Relations Review (1995) Blue- and white-collar status survey. July: 14–18.

Evans, P. and **McCormick, B.** (1995) *Changes in joblessness and occupational attainment of ethnic males in Britain during the Thatcher era.* mimeo, Department of Economics, University of Southampton.

Eyraud, F. (1993) Equal pay and the value of work in industrialized countries. *International Labour Review*, **132**: 33–48.

Eyraud, F. (1993a) Equal pay: an international overview. In F. Eyraud (ed.) *Equal pay protection in industrialised market economies: in search of greater effectiveness.* International Labour Office, Geneva, 1–21.

Fagerberg, J. (1994) Technology and international differences in growth rates. *Journal of Economic Literature*, **32**: 1147–75.

Felli, L. and **Ichino, A.** (1988) Do marginal employment subsidies increase re-employment probabilities? *Labour*, **2**(3): 63–89.

Fenn, P. and **Veljanovski, C.** (1988) A positive theory of regulatory enforcement. *Economic Journal*, **98**: 1055–70.

Fernie, S. and **Metcalf, D.** (1995) Participation, contingent pay, representation and workplace performance: evidence from Great Britain. Centre for Economic Performance Discussion Paper No. 232.

Finegold, D. and **Soskice, D.** (1988) The failure of training in Britain: analysis and prescription. *Oxford Review of Economic Policy*, **4**(3): 21–53.

Fitoussi, J-P. (1994) Wage distribution and unemployment: the French experience. *American Economic Review*, **84**(2): 59–64.

Flanagan, R. (1993) European wage equalization since the Treaty of Rome. In L. Ulman, B. Eichengreen and W. Dickens (eds) *Labor and an integrated Europe.* Brookings Institution, Washington DC, 167–87.

Forslund, A. and **Krueger, A.** (1994) An evaluation of the Swedish active labour market policy: new and received wisdom. National Bureau of Economic Research Working Paper No. 4082.

Franz, W. (1987) Hysteresis, persistence and the NAIRU: an empirical analysis for the Federal Republic of Germany. In R. Layard and L. Calmfors (eds) *The fight against unemployment.* MIT Press, Cambridge, Mass., 91–122.

Franz, W. and **Smolney, W.** (1993) The measurement and interpretation of vacancy data and the dynamics of the Beveridge curve: the German case. *University of Konstanz CILE Discussion Paper* 4–1993.

Freeman, R. (1986) Demand for education. In O. Ashenfelter and R. Layard (eds) *Handbook of Labor Economics.* North-Holland, Amsterdam, 357–86.

Freeman, R. (1994) How labor fares in advanced economies. In R. Freeman (ed.) *Working under different rules.* Russell Sage Foundation, New York.

Freeman, R. (1994a) Minimum wages – again! *International Journal of Manpower*, **15**(2/3): 8–25.

Freeman, R. (1995) The limits of wage flexibility to curing unemployment. *Oxford Review of Economic Policy*, **11**: 63–72.

de la Fuente, A. and **Vives, X.** (1994) Infrastructure and education as instruments of regional policy: evidence from Spain. *Economic Policy*, **20**: 13–51.

Gazioglu, S. and **Sloane, P.** (1994) Job disamenities, compensating differences and the immigrant worker: an inter-generational analysis. *International Journal of Manpower*, **15**(7): 43–51.

George, D. (1993) The political economy of wage-earner funds: policy debate and Swedish experience. *Review of Political Economy*, **5**: 470–90.

Gershuny, J. (1995) Change in the division of domestic work: micro-sociological evidence. *Deutsches Institut für Wirtschaftsforschung*, Berlin Discussion Paper No. 107.

Ghobadian, A. and **White, M.** (1987) *Job evaluation and equal pay*. Department of Employment, Research Paper No. 58.

Gittleman, M. and **Wolff, E.** (1993) International comparisons of inter-industry wage differentials. *Review of Income and Wealth*, **39**: 295–312.

Glyn, A. (1995) The Assessment: unemployment and inequality. *Oxford Review of Economic Policy*, **11**(1): 1–25.

Glyn, A. and **Miliband, D.** (1994) *Paying for inequality: the economic cost of social injustice*. IPPR/Rivers Oram Press, London.

Glyn, A. and **Rowthorn, R.** (1994) European employment policies. In J. Michie and J. Grieve Smith (eds) *Unemployment in Europe*. Academic Press, London, 188–98.

Gottschalk, P. (1990) Reducing gender and racial inequality-the role of public policy. In K. Abraham and R. McKersie (eds) *New development in the labor market*. MIT Press, Cambridge, Mass., 241–74.

Green, A. and **Steedman, H.** (1993) *Educational provision, educational attainment and the needs of industry; a review of research for Germany, France, Japan, the USA and Britain*. National Institute of Economic and Social research, report series No. 5.

Green, F. (1993) The determinants of training of male and female employees in Britain. *Oxford Bulletin of Economic Research*, **55**: 103–22.

Green, F., Hoskins, M. and **Montgomery, S.** (1994) The effects of training, further education and YTS on the earnings of young employees. University of Leicester Economics Discussion Paper No. 94/10.

Greenhalgh, C. and **Mavrotas, G.** (1994) The role of career aspirations and financial constraints in individual access to vocational training. *Oxford Economic Papers*, **46**: 579–604.

Greenhalgh, C. and **Stewart, M.** (1985) The occupational status and mobility of British men and women. *Oxford Economic Papers*, **37**: 40–71.

Greenhalgh, C. and **Stewart, M.** (1987) The effects and determinants of training. *Oxford Bulletin of Economics and Statistics*, **49**: 171–90.

Gregg, P. (1990) The evolution of the special measures. *National Institute Economic Review*, **132**: 49–58.

Gregg, P. (1994) Share and share alike. *New Economy*, **1**: 13–19.

Gregg, P., Machin, S. and **Metcalf, D.** (1993) Signals and cycles? productivity growth and changes in union status in British companies 1984–89. *Economic Journal*, **103**: 894–907.

Gregg, P. and **Wadsworth, J.** (1994) How effective are state employment agencies? Jobcentre use and job matching in Britain. National Institute of Economic and Social Research Discussion Paper No. 65.

Gregg, P. and **Wadsworth, J.** (1995) A short history of labour turnover, job tenure and job security, 1975–93. *Oxford Review of Economic Policy*, **1**: 73–90.

Gregory, M. and **Sandoval, V.** (1994) Low pay and minimum wage protection in Britain and the EC. In R. Barrell (ed.) *The UK labour market: comparative aspects and institutional developments*. Cambridge University Press, Cambridge.

References

Groot, W., Hartog, J. and **Oosterbeek, H.** (1994) Wage and welfare gains of within company schooling. In L. Lynch (ed.) *Training and the private sector: international comparisons.* University of Chicago Press, Chicago, Ill.

Groot, W. and **Mekkelholt, E.** (1995) The rate of return to investments in on-the-job training. *Applied Economics,* **27**: 173–81.

Grossman, G. and **Helpman, E.** (1991) Trade, knowledge, spillovers and growth. *European Economic Review,* **35**: 517–26.

Großman, H. and **Koopman, G.** (1994) Minimum social standards for international trade? *Intereconomics,* Nov./Dec.: 277–83.

Grubb, D. (1986) Topics in the OECD Phillips curve. *Economic Journal,* **96**: 55–79.

Grubb, D. (1994) Direct and indirect effects of active labour market policies in OECD countries. In R. Barrell (ed.) *The UK labour market: comparative aspects and institutional developments.* National Institute of Economic and Social Research and Cambridge University Press, 183–213.

Grubb, D. and **Wells, W.** (1993) Employment regulation and patterns of work in EC countries. *OECD Economic Studies,* **21**, Winter: 7–59.

Gruber, J. (1994) The incidence of mandated maternity benefits. *American Economic Review,* **84**: 622–41.

Gurdon, M. and **Rai, A.** (1990) Codetermination and enterprise performance: empirical evidence from West Germany. *Journal of Economics and Business,* **42**: 289–302.

Gustafsson, B. and **Klevmarken, N.** (1993) Taxes and transfers in Sweden: incentive effects on labour supply. In A. Atkinson and G. Mogensen (eds) *Welfare and work incentives: a North European perspective.* Clarendon Press, Oxford, 50–134.

Gustafsson, S. and **Lofstrom, A.** (1991) Policy changes and women's wages in Sweden. *International Review of Comparative Public Policy,* **3**: 313–30.

Gustafsson, S. and **Stafford, F.** (1994) Three regimes of child care: the United States, the Netherlands and Sweden. In R. Blank (ed.) *Social protection versus economic flexibility.* University of Chicago Press, Chicago, Ill. 333–362.

Hamermesh, D. and **Biddle, J.** (1994) Beauty and the labour market. *American Economic Review,* **84**:1174–94.

Hanratty, M. (1994) Social welfare programs for women and children: the United States versus France. In R. Blank (ed.) *Social protection versus economic flexibility.* University of Chicago Press, Chicago, Ill. 301–32.

Harmon, C. and **Walker, I.** (1993) Schooling and earnings in the UK – evidence from the ROSLA experiment. *Economic and Social Review,* **25**: 77–93.

Hashimoto, M. (1981) Firm specific human capital as a shared investment. *American Economic Review,* **71**: 475–82.

Haskel, J. and **Martin, C.** (1992) The economic consequences of skill shortages. Queen Mary and Westfield College, University of London, Department of Economics Working Paper No. 250.

Haskel, J. and **Martin, C.** (1993) The causes of skill shortages in Britain. *Oxford Economic Papers,* **45**: 573–88.

Haskel, J. and **Szymanski, S.** (1992) Privatization and the labour market: facts, theory, and evidence. In M. Bishop, J. Kay and D. Thompson (eds) *Privatization and regulation: the UK experience.* 2nd edn, Oxford University Press, Oxford.

Haveman, R. and **Wolfe, B.** (1984) Schooling and economic well-being: the role of non-market effects. *Journal of Human Resources,* **19**: 377–407.

Health and Safety Executive (1991) *Workplace health and safety in Europe.* HSE, London.

Heijke, H. (ed.) (1994) *Forecasting the labour market by occupation and education: the forecasting activities of three European labour market research institutes.* Kluwer Academic, Lancaster.

Henley, A. and **Tsakalotos, E.** (1993) *Corporatism and economic performance: a comparative analysis of market economies.* Edward Elgar, Cheltenham.

Holzer, H. (1987) Informal job search and black youth unemployment. *American Economic Review,* **77**(3): 446–53.

Holzer, H. (1994) Job vacancy rates in the firm: an empirical analysis. *Economica,* **61**: 17–36.

Hosios, A. (1990) On the efficiency of matching and related models of search and unemployment. *Journal of Monetary Economics,* **5**: 153–70.

Houseman, S. (1990) The equity and efficiency of job security: contrasting perspectives on collective dismissal laws in Western Europe. In K. Abraham and R. McKenzie (eds) *New developments in the labor market.* MIT Press., Cambridge, Mass.

Howitt, P. and **McAfee, P.** (1987) Costly search and recruiting. *International Economic Review,* **28**: 89–107.

Hughes, G. and **McCormick, B.** (1989) *Hidden unemployment and suppressed labour mobility in the British labour market.* Mimeo, Southampton University.

Hughes, G. and **McCormick, B.** (1994) Did migration in the 1980s narrow the north-south divide? *Economica,* **61**: 509–27.

Hunt, J. (1995) The effect of unemployment compensation on unemployment duration in Germany. *Journal of Labor Economics,* **13**: 88–120.

Hutchens, R. (1989) Seniority, wages and productivity: a turbulent decade. *Journal of Economic Perspectives,* **3**(4): 49–64.

Institute for Employment Studies (1995) Evaluation of workstart pilots. *IES Report* 279.

1992 Learning mathematics, International Assessment of Educational Progress (IAEP) Educational Testing Service.

International Labour Office (ILO) (annual) *Yearbook of Labour Statistics,* ILO, Geneva.

Jackman, R. (1993) Mass unemployment: international experience and lessons for policy. Centre for Economic Performance Discussion Paper No. 152.

Jackman, R. (1995) What can active labour market policy do? Centre for Economic Performance Discussion Paper No. 226.

Jackman, R. (1995a) Regional policy in an enlarged Europe. *Oxford Review of Economic Policy,* **11**(2): 113–25.

Jackman, R., Layard, R. and **Pissarides, C.** (1986) Policies for reducing the natural rate of unemployment. In J. Butkiewicz, K. Koford and J. Miller (eds) *Keynes' economic legacy.* Praeger, New York.

Jackman, R., Layard, R. and **Savouri, S.** (1991) Mismatch: a framework for thought. In F. Padoa-Schioppa (ed.) *Mismatch and labour mobility.* Cambridge University Press, Cambridge, 44–104.

Jackman, R. and **Roper, S.** (1987) Structural unemployment. *Oxford Bulletin of Economics and Statistics,* **49**: 9–35.

Jarvis, V. (1994) Smoothing the transition to skilled employment: school-based vocational guidance in Britain and Continental Europe. *National Institute Economic Review,* **94**(4): 73–89.

Jenkins, R. (1984) Acceptability, suitability and the search for the habituated worker: how ethnic minorities and women lose out. *International Journal of Social Economics,* **11**: 64–76.

Jenkins, S. (1994) Earnings discrimination measurement: a distributional approach. *Journal of Econometrics,* **61**: 81–102.

References

Johnson, E. and O'Keeffe, D. (1994) From discrimination to obstacles to free movement: recent developments concerning the free movement of workers, 1989–1994. *Common Market Law Review*, **31**: 1313–46.

Johnson, P. and Zimmermann, K (1993) Ageing and the European labour market: public policy issues. In P. Johnson and K. Zimmermann (eds) *Labour markets in an ageing Europe.* Cambridge University Press, Cambridge.

Jones, D. and Makepeace, G. (1994) Equal worth, equal opportunities: pay and promotion in an internal labour market. University of Hull, Department of Economics, Labour Economics Unit Working Paper No. 94/2.

Joshi, H. and Davies, H. (1992) Day care in Europe and mothers' foregone earnings. *International Labour Review*, **132**: 561–79.

Kaldor, N. (1936) Wage subsidies as a remedy for unemployment. *Journal of Political Economy*, **44**. Reprinted in N. Kaldor *Essays on Economic Policy, I*, Duckworth, London.

Katz, E. and Ziderman, A. (1990) Investment in general training: the role of information and labour mobility. *Economic Journal* **100**: 1147–58.

Kee, P. (1995) Native-immigrant wage differentials in the Netherlands: discrimination? *Oxford Economic Papers*, **47**: 302–17.

Keeley, M. and Robins, P. (1985) Government programs, job search requirements and the duration of unemployment. *Journal of Labour Economics*, **3**: 327–62.

Kettunen, J. (1994) The effects of education on the duration of unemployment. *Labour*, **8**: 331–52.

Kimmel, J. (1995) The effectiveness of child-care subsidies in encouraging the welfare-to-work transition of low-income single mothers. *American Economic Review,* **85(2)**: 271–5.

Klette, J. and Mathiassen, A. (1995) *Job creation, job destruction and plant turnover in Norwegian manufacturing.* Statistics Norway Discussion Paper No. 136.

Konings, J. and Walsh, P. (1994) Evidence of efficiency wage payments in UK firm level panel data. *Economic Journal*, **104**: 542–555.

Koutsogeorgopoulou, V. (1994) The impact of minimum wages on industrial wages and employment in Greece. *International Journal of Manpower*, **15**: 86–99.

Kroch, E. and Sjoblom, K. (1994) Schooling as human capital or a signal. *Journal of Human Resources*, **29**: 156–80.

Kruse, D. (1992) Profit-sharing and productivity: microeconomic evidence from the United States. *Economic Journal*, **102**: 24–36.

Lange, P. (1992) The politics of the social dimension. In A. Sbragia (ed.) *Euro-Politics: institutions and policy-making in the new European community.* Brookings Institution, Washington DC, 225–56.

Lansbury, R. (1995) Workplace Europe: new forms of bargaining and participation. *New Technology, Work and Employment*, **10**: 47–55.

Layard, R. (1992) *The training reform act of 1994.* ERSC, Swindon.

Layard, R., Metcalf, D. and O'Brien, R. (1986) A new deal for the long-term unemployed. In P. Hart (ed.) *Unemployment and labour market policies.* Gower, Aldershot. 181–90.

Layard, R. and Nickell, S. (1980) The case for subsidizing extra jobs. *Economic Journal*, **90**: 51–73.

Layard, R. and Nickell, S. (1987) The labour market. In R. Dornbusch and R. Layard (eds) *The performance of the British economy.* Clarendon Press, Oxford, 131–79.

Layard, R., Nickell, S. and Jackman, R. (1991) *Unemployment: macroeconomic performance and the labour market.* Oxford University Press, Oxford.

Layard, R. and **Philpott, J.** (1991) *Stopping unemployment.* Employment Institute, London.

Lazear, E. (1979) Why is there mandatory retirement? *Journal of Political Economy,* **87**: 1261–4.

Lazear, E. (1983) Pensions as severance pay. In Z. Bodie and J. Shoven (eds) *Financial aspects of the US pension system.* University of Chicago Press, Chicago, Ill. 57–85.

Lazear, E. (1989) Pay equality and industrial politics. *Journal of Political Economy,* **97**: 561–80.

Lazear, E. (1990) Job security provisions and employment. *Quarterly Journal of Economics,* **105**: 699–726.

Lazear, E. (1991) Labor economics and the psychology of organizations. *Journal of Economic Perspectives,* **5**(2): 89–110.

Lazear, E. (1991a) Discrimination in labor markets. In E. Hoffman (ed.) *Economics of discrimination.* Upjohn Institute, Kalamazoo, 17–24.

Lazear, E. (1993) The new economics of personnel. *Labour,* **7**(1): 3–23.

Lehmann, H. (1993) The effectiveness of the restart programme and the enterprise allowance scheme. Centre for Economic Performance Working Paper No. 139.

Levine, D. and **Tyson, L.** (1990) Participation, productivity and the firm's environment. In A. Blinder (ed.) *Paying for productivity.* Brookings Institution, Washington DC, 183–243.

Lilien, D. (1982) Sectoral shifts and cyclical unemployment. *Journal of Political Economy,* **90**: 777–93.

Lindbeck, A. (1994) The welfare state and the employment problem. *American Economic Review,* **84**(2): 71–5.

Lindbeck, A. (1995) The unemployment problem. Institute for International Economic Studies, Stockholm (*Foreign Affairs,* forthcoming).

Lindbeck, A. and **Snower, D.** (1989) *The insider-outsider theory of employment and un-employment.* MIT Press, Cambridge, Mass.

Lindeboom, M., van Ours, J. and **Renes, G.** (1994) Matching employers and workers: an empirical analysis of the effectiveness of search. *Oxford Economic Papers,* **46**: 45–67.

Lindley, R. (1994) Policy implications of recent IER assessments of the British labour market. In H. Keijke (ed.) *Forecasting the labour market by occupation and education.* Kluwer Academic, Lancaster.

Lindley, R. and **Wilson, R.** (eds) (1993) Review of the Economy and Employment, 1992–3: Occupational assessment. Institute for Employment Research, University of Warwick.

Lockwood, B. (1986) Transferable skills, job matchings and the inefficiency of the natural rate of unemployment. *Economic Journal,* **96**: 961–74.

London Economics (1992) *Will the single market cause European wage and salary levels to converge?* London Economics (MES).

de Luca, L. and **Bruni, M.** (1993) *Unemployment and labour market flexibility: Italy.* International Labour Office, Geneva.

Lucas, R. (1986) *Models of Business Cycles.* Yrjo Jahnssen Lectures, Helsinki.

Lucifora, C. (1993) Inter-industry and occupational wage differentials in Italy. *Applied Economics,* **25**: 1113–24.

Lynch, L. (1992) Private sector training and the earnings of young workers. *American Economic Review,* **82**: 299–312.

Lynch, L. (1994) Introduction. In L. Lynch (ed.) *Training and the private sector: international comparisons.* University of Chicago Press, Chicago, Ill. 1–24.

Lynch, L. (1994a) Payoffs to alternative training strategies at work. In R. Freeman (ed.) *Working under different rules.* Russell Sage Foundation, New York.

References

MacEwen Scott, A. (ed.) (1994) *Gender segregation and social change*. Oxford University Press, Oxford.

Machin, S. (1995) Changes in the relative demand for skills in the UK labour market. Centre for Economic Performance, Discussion Paper No. 221.

Machin, S. and **Manning, A.** (1994) The effects of minimum wages on wage dispersion and employment: evidence from the UK Wages Councils. *Industrial and Labor Relations Review*, **47**: 319–30.

Maier, F. (1994) Institutional regimes of part-time working. In G. Schmid (ed.) *Labor market institutions in Europe*. M.E. Sharpe, New York, 151–183.

Makepeace, G. (1994) Lifetime earnings and the training decisions of young men in Britain. University of Hull, Department of Economics, Labour Economics Unit, Working Paper 94/1.

Manning, A. (1993) The equal pay act as an experiment to test theories of the labour market. *Centre for Economic Performance*, Discussion Paper No. 153.

Marsden, D. (1986) *The end of economic man?* Harvester Wheatsheaf, Hemel Hempstead.

Marsden, D. (1995) *The impact of industrial relations practices on employment and unemployment*. Centre for Economic Performance Discussion Paper No. 240, London.

Marsden, D. and **Silvestre, J-J.** (1992) Pay and European integration. In D. Marsden (ed.) *Pay and employment in the new Europe*. Edward Elgar, Cheltenham.

Martin, J. (1994) The extent of high unemployment in OECD countries. In Federal Reserve Bank of Kansas City, *Reducing unemployment: current issues and policy options*, 5–40.

Martin, S. and **Kersley, B.** (1995) Should the UK adopt the social charter? Queen Mary and Westfield College, University of London, Economics Department Discussion Paper No. 337.

Marullo, S. (1995) A comparison of regulations on part-time and temporary employment in Europe. Employment Department Research Series No. 52, HMSO, London.

Marx, K. (1970) *Capital*. Volume 1. Lawrence and Wishart, London.

Mason, G. and **van Ark, B.** (1994) Vocational training and productivity performance: an Anglo-Dutch comparison. *International Journal of Manpower*, **15**(5): 55–69.

Mason, G., Prais, S. and **van Ark, B.** (1992) Vocational education and productivity in the Netherlands and Britain. *National Institute Economic Review*, **2/92**: 45–60.

Matthews, K. and **Minford, P.** (1987) Mrs. Thatcher's economic policies. *Economic Policy*, **1**: 57–102.

Mayhew, K. (1994) Labour market woes: deregulation of the labour market has ignored the long-term. *New Economy*, **1**(2): 3–8.

Mazey, S. (1988) European community action on behalf of women: the limits of legislation. *Journal of Common Market Studies*, **27**: 63–84.

McCrudden, C. (1993) Equal pay in the United Kingdom. In F. Eyraud (ed.) *Equal pay protection in industrialised market economies: in search of greater effectiveness*. International Labour Office, Geneva, 141–57.

McDonald, F. and **Dearden, S.** (eds) (1994) *European economic integration*. 2nd ed, Longman, Harlow.

McGregor, A. and **Sproull, A.** (1992) Employers and the flexible work-force. *Employment Gazette*, May: 225–234.

McNabb, R. and **Whitfield, K.** (1994) Market failure, institutional structure and skill-formation. *International Journal of Manpower*, **15**(5): 5–15.

Meager, N. (1994) Self-Employment schemes for the unemployed in the European community: the emergence of a new institution and its evaluation. In G. Schmid (ed.) *Labor market institutions in Europe*. M.E. Sharpe, New York, 183–240.

Metcalf, D. (1986) Employment subsidies and redundancies. In R. Blundell and I.Walker (eds) *Unemployment search and labour supply*. Cambridge University Press, Cambridge, 103–20.

Metcalf, D. (1994) Transformation of British industrial relations? institutions, conduct and outcomes 1980–1990. In R. Barrell (ed.) *The UK labour market: comparative aspects and institutional developments.* Cambridge University Press, Cambridge, 126–57.

Meulders, D. and **Plasman, R.** (1993) Part-Time work in the EEC countries evolution during the 1980s. *Labour,* **7**(3):49–71.

Micklewright, J. (1989) Choice at sixteen. *Economica,* **56**: 23–39.

Milgrom, P. and **Oster, S.** (1987) Job discrimination, market forces and the invisibility hypothesis. *Quarterly Journal of Economics,* **52**: 453–74.

Miller, P. (1987) The wage effect of occupational segregation in Britain. *Economic Journal,* **97**: 885–96.

Millward, N. and **Woodland, S.** (1995) Gender segregation and male/female wage differences. Centre for Economic Performance Discussion Paper No. 220.

Milner, S., Metcalf, D. and **Nombela, G.** (1995) Employment protection legislation and labour market outcomes in Spain. Centre for Economic Performance Working Paper No. 244.

Mincer, J. (1962) On the job training: costs, returns and some implications. *Journal of Political Economy,* Supplement **70**: S50–79.

Mincer, J. and **Higuichi, Y.** (1988) Wage structures and labor turnover in the United States and Japan. *Journal of Japanese and International Economics,* **2**: 97–133.

Minford, P. (1995) Unemployment in the OECD and its remedies. In G. de la Dehesa and D. Snower (eds) *Unemployment Policy.* Cambridge University Press, Cambridge.

Mitchell, D. and **Rojot, J.** (1993) Employee Benefits in the single market. In L. Ulman, B. Eichengreen and W. Dickens (eds) *Labor and an integrated Europe.* The Brookings Institution, Washington DC.

Mookherjee, D. and **Png, I.** (1992) Monitoring *vis-à-vis* investigation in enforcement of law. *American Economic Review,* **82**: 556–65.

Mosley, H. (1994) Employment protection and labor force adjustment in EC countries. In G. Schmid (ed.) *Labor market institutions in Europe.* M.E. Sharpe, New York, 59–81.

Mulder, C. (1993) Wage-Moderating effects of corporatism: decentralized versus centralized wage setting in a union, firm, government context. *Manchester School,* **61**: 287–301.

Muysken, J. (1994) *Measurement and analysis of job vacancies: an international comparison.* Avebury, Aldershot.

Nickell, S. and **Bell, B.** (1995) The collapse in demand for the unskilled and unemployment across the OECD. *Oxford Review of Economic Policy,* **11**: 40–62.

Niesing, W., van Praag, B. and **Veenman, J.** (1994) The unemployment of ethnic minority groups in the Netherlands. *Journal of Econometrics,* **61**: 173–96.

Oaxaca, R. (1973) Male-female wage differentials in urban labour markets. *International Labour Review,* **14**: 693–709.

Oaxaca, R. and **Ransom, M.** (1994) On discrimination and the decomposition of wage differentials. *Journal of Econometrics,* **61**: 5–21.

OECD (1988) *Employment outlook 1988.* OECD, Paris.

OECD (1991) *Employment outlook 1991.* OECD, Paris.

OECD (1991a) Equal pay for work of comparable value: the experience of the industrialised countries. *Labour market and Social Policy Occasional Papers* No. 5. OECD, Paris.

OECD (1992) *Employment outlook 1992.* OECD, Paris.

OECD (1992a) *Economic surveys: Germany.* OECD, Paris.

OECD (1993) *Employment outlook 1993.* OECD, Paris.

OECD (1993a) *The public employment service in Japan, Norway, Spain and the UK.* OECD, Paris.

OECD (1994) *Employment outlook 1994.* OECD, Paris.

OECD (1994a) *The OECD jobs study: evidence and explanations.* 2 Volumes. OECD, Paris.

References

OECD (1995) *Employment outlook 1995*. OECD, Paris.

OECD (1995a) *Education at a glance*. OECD, Paris.

OECD (1995b) *Indicators of education systems: education and employment*. Centre for Educational Research and Innovation, OECD, Paris.

Oliver, J. and **Turton, J.** (1982) Is there a shortage of skilled labour? *British Journal of Industrial Relations*, **20**: 195–200.

O'Mahony, M. (1995) International differences in manufacturing unit labour costs. *National Institute Economic Review*, **4/94**: 85–100.

O'Neill, J. and **Polachek, S.** (1993) Why the gender gap in wages narrowed in the 1980s. *Journal of Labor Economics*, **11**: 205–28.

Oulton, N. (1994) Labour productivity and unit labour costs in manufacturing: the UK and its competitors. *National Institute Economic Review*, May: 49–60.

Oulton, N. (1995) Work-force skills and export competitiveness: an Anglo-German comparison. In A. Booth and D. Snower (eds) *Acquiring skills: market failures, their symptoms and policy responses*. Cambridge University Press, Cambridge.

Oulton, N. and **Steedman, H.** (1994) The British system of youth training: a comparison with Germany. In L. Lynch (ed.) *Training and the private sector: international comparisons*. University of Chicago Press, Chicago, Ill., 61–76.

van Ours, J. (1994) Matching unemployed and vacancies at the public employment office. *Empirical Economics*, **19**: 37–54.

van Ours, J. and **Ridder, G.** (1993) Vacancy durations: search or selection.? *Oxford Economic Papers*, **55(2)**: 187–98.

Paoli, P. (1992) *First European Survey on the Work Environment 1991–1992*. European Foundation for the Improvement of Living and Working Conditions, Dublin.

Parker, D. and **Martin, S.** (1995) The impact of UK privatization on labour and total factor productivity. *Scottish Journal of Political Economy*, **42**: 201–20.

Pedersen, P. (1993) The welfare state and taxation in Denmark. In A. Atkinson and G. Mogensen (eds) *Welfare and work incentives: a North European perspective*. Clarendon Press, Oxford, 241–88.

Pedersen, P. and **Westergård-Nielsen, N.** (1993) Unemployment: a review of evidence from panel data. *OECD Economic Studies*, **20**(Spring): 66–95.

Peltzman, S. (1976) Towards a more general theory of regulation. *Journal of Law and Economics*, **20**: 211–40.

Pencavel, J. (1994) British unemployment: letter from America. *Economic Journal*, **104**: 621–32.

Pendleton, A., McDonald, J., Robinson, A. and **Wilson, N.** (1995) Patterns of employee participation and industrial democracy in UK employee share ownership plans. Centre for Economic Performance Discussion Paper No. 249.

Pérez del Rio, T. (1993) Equal pay in Spain. In F. Eyraud (ed.) *Equal pay protection in industrialised market economies: in search of greater effectiveness*. International Labour Office, Geneva, 125–40.

Perlman, R. and **Pike, M.** (1994) *Sex discrimination in the labour market: the case for comparable worth*. Manchester University Press, Manchester.

Peters, T. (1995) European Monetary Union and labour markets: What to expect? *International Labour Review*, **134**: 315–32.

Phelps, E. (1972) The statistical theory of racism and sexism. *American Economic Review*, **62**: 659–61.

Phelps, E. (1994) *Structural slumps: the modern equilibrium theory of unemployment, interest and assets*. Harvard University Press, Harvard, Mass.

Phelps, E. (1994a Low-wage employment subsidies versus the welfare state. *American Economic Review*, **84**(2): 54–8.

Pissarides, C. (1979) Job matchings with state employment agencies and random search. *Economic Journal*, **89**: 818–33.

Pissarides, C. (1981) Staying on at school in England and Wales. *Economica*, **48**: 345–63.

Pissarides, C. (1982) From school to university: the demand for post-compulsory education in Britain. *Economic Journal*, **92**: 654–67.

Pissarides, C. (1984) Search intensity, job advertising and efficiency. *Journal of Labor Economics*, **2**: 128–43.

Pissarides, C. (1985) Job search and the functioning of labour markets. In D. Carline, C. Pissarides, S. Siebert and P. Sloane (eds) *Labour Economics*, Longman, Harlow, 159–85.

Pissarides, C. (1990) *Equilibrium unemployment theory*. Basil Blackwell, Oxford.

Pissarides, C. (1992) Loss of skill during unemployment and the persistence of unemployment shocks. *Quarterly Journal of Economics*, **107**: 1371–91.

Pissarides, C. and **Wadsworth J.** (1989) Unemployment and the inter-regional mobility of labour. *Economic Journal*, **99**: 739–55.

Polachek, S. and **Hofler, S.** (1991) *Employee ignorance in the labour market.* mimeo, SUNY-Binghamton.

Polachek, S. and **Kim, M-K.** (1994) Panel estimates of the gender earnings gap. *Journal of Econometrics*, **61**: 23–42.

Polachek, S. and **Yoon, B.** (1987) A two-tiered earnings frontier: estimation of employer and employee information in the labour market. *Review of Economics and Statistics*, **69**: 296–302.

Polachek, S. and **Siebert, W.** (1993) *The Economics of Earnings*. Cambridge University Press, Cambridge.

Prais, S. (1993) *Economic performance and education: the nature of Britain's deficiencies*. National Institute of Economic and Social Research, Discussion Paper No. 52.

Psacharopoulos, G. (1985) Returns to education: a further international update and implications. *Journal of Human Resources*, **20**: 583–604.

Purdy, D. and **Devine, P.** (1994) Social policy. In M. Artis and N. Lee (eds) *The economics of the European Union*. Oxford University Press, Oxford, 269–93.

Pyle, D. and **Deadman, D.** (1994) Crime and unemployment in Scotland: some further results. *Scottish Journal of Political Economy*, **41**: 314–24.

Raaum, O., Torp, H. and **Goldstein, H.** (1995) Employment effects of labour market training in Norway. University of Oslo, Department of Economics, Memorandum No. 8.

Rajan Rebitzer, J. (1993) Radical political economy and the economics of labor markets. *Journal of Economic Literature*, **31**: 1394–1434.

Ramaswamy, R. (1994) The structural crises in the Swedish economy. *IMF Staff Papers*, **41**: 367–79.

Rebick, M. (1994) Social security and older workers' labor market responsibilities: the United States, Japan and Sweden. In R. Blank (ed.) *Social Protection versus Economic Flexibility: Is there a Trade-off?* University of Chicago Press, Chicago, Ill. 189–222.

Rebitzer, J. (1993) Radical political economy and the economics of the labour markets. *Journal of Economic Literature*, **31**: 1394–1434.

Rees, H. and **Shah, A.** (1995) Public-Private sector wage differentials in the UK. *Manchester School*, **63**(1): 52–68.

Reissert, B. and **Schmid, G.** (1994) Unemployment compensation and active labour market policy: the impact of unemployment benefits on income security, work incentives and public policy. In G. Schmid (ed.) *Labor Market Institutions in Europe: a socio-economic evaluation of performance*. M.E. Sharpe, New York, 83–118.

References

Rekko, A., Pele, G., Doodeman, J., Schippers, J. and **Siegers J.** (1993) The effects of temporary withdrawals on women's gross wage rates. *Jahrbücher Fur Nationalökonomie Und Statist*, **212**: 105–119.

Rhoads, S. (1993) *Incomparable worth*. Cambridge University Press, Cambridge.

de la Rica, S. and **Lemieux, T.** (1994) Does public health insurance reduce labour market flexibility or encourage the underground economy: evidence from Spain and the US. In R. Blank (ed.) *Social protection vs. economic flexibility: is there a trade-off?* University of Chicago Press, Chicago, Ill. 265–300.

Rice, P. (1987) The demand for post-compulsory education in the UK and the effects of educational maintenance allowances. *Economica*, **54**: 465–75.

Rogers, J. and **Streeck, W.** (1994) Workplace representation overseas: the works councils story. In R. Freeman (ed.) *Working under different rules*. Russell Sage Foundation, New York, 97–156.

Rollo, J. and **Smith, A.** (1993) The political economy of Eastern European trade with the European Community: why so sensitive? *Economic Policy*, **16**.

Romer, P. (1990) Endogenous technical change. *Journal of Political Economy*, **98**: S 71–102.

van Rompuy, P., Abraham, F. and **Heremans, D.** (1991) Economic federalism and EMU. *European Economy* special edition No. 1: 109–35.

Roper, S. (1988) Recruitment methods and vacancy duration. *Scottish Journal of Political Economy*, **35**: 51–64.

Rubery, J. and **Fagan, C.** (1994) Occupational segregation: *plus ça change* … ? In R. Lindley (ed.) *Labour market structures and prospects for women*. Equal Opportunities Commission, Manchester, 29–42.

Rubery, J. and **Fagan, C.** (1994a) Equal pay policy and wage regulation systems in Europe. *Industrial Relations Journal*, **25**(4): 281–92.

Saint-Paul, G. (1994) Do labor market rigidities fulfil distributive objectives? *IMF Staff Papers*, **41**: 624–42.

Salop, S. (1973) Systematic job search and unemployment. *Review of Economic Studies*, **40**: 191–201.

Sapsford, D. and **Tzannatos, Z.** (1993) *The Economics of the Labour Market*. Macmillan, Basingstoke.

Scherer, P. (1994) Trends in social protection programs and expenditure in the 1980s. In R. Blank (ed.) *Social protection versus economic flexibility: is there a trade-off?* University of Chicago Press, Chicago, Ill. 43–58.

Schmid, G. (ed.) (1994) *Labor Market Institutions in Europe: a socioeconomic evaluation of performance*. M.E. Sharpe, Armouk, New York.

Shah, A. (1985) Does education act as a screening device for certain British jobs? *Oxford Economic Papers*, **37**: 118–24.

Siebert, H. and **Koop, M.** (1993) Institutional competition versus centralization: quo vadis Europe? *Oxford Review of Economic Policy*, **9**: 15–30.

Siebert, W. (1985) Developments in the economics of human capital. In D. Carline, C. Pissarides, S. Siebert and P. Sloane (eds) *Labour Economics*. Longman, Harlow, 5–77.

Siebert, W. (1991) The market regulation of industrial safety. In C. Veljanovski (ed.) *Regulators and the market: an assessment of the growth of regulation in the UK*. Institute of Economic Affairs, London.

Siebert, W. and **Addison, J.** (1991) Internal labour markets. *Oxford Review of Economic Policy*, **8**: 76–91.

Sloan, J. (1993) Some policy responses to long-term unemployment. *Australian Economic Review*, (**2**): 35–40.

Sloane, P. (1985) Discrimination in the labour market. In D. Carline, *Labour Economics*, Longman, Harlow, 78–158.

Sloane, P. (1994) The gender wage differential and discrimination in six SCELI local labour markets. In A. MacEwen Scott (ed.) *Gender Segregation and Social Change*. Oxford University Press, Oxford.

Sloane, P. and **Theodossiou, I.** (1994) What really happened to the male-female earnings differential in Britain in the 1970s? *Scottish Journal of Political Economy*, **41**: 464–76.

Smith, N. (1992) Why did the gender pay gap increase in Denmark after the enactment of the Equal Pay Act? University of Aarhus, Centre for Labour Economics, Working Paper No. 92:3.

Smith, S. (1994) *Labour Economics*. Routledge, London.

Snell, M., Glucklich, P. and **Povall, M.** (1981) *Equal pay and opportunity*. Department of Employment Research Paper No. 20.

Snower, D. (1993) The future of the welfare state. *Economic Journal*, **103**: 700–17.

Snower, D. (1994) Converting unemployment benefits into employment subsidies. *American Economic Review*, **84**(2): 65–70.

Snower, D. (1995) The low-skill, bad-job trap. In A. Booth and D. Snower (eds) *Acquiring Skills*. Cambridge University Press, Cambridge.

Snower, D. (1995a) Evaluating unemployment policies: what do the underlying theories tell us? *Oxford Review of Economic Policy*, **11**: 110–35.

Snower, D. The simple economics of benefit transfers. In G. de la Dehesa and D. Snower (eds) (Forthcoming) *Unemployment Policy*. Cambridge University Press, Cambridge.

van Soest, A. (1994) Youth minimum wage rates: the Dutch experience. *International Journal of Manpower*, **15**: 100–17.

Solow, R. (1990) *The Labor Market as a Social Institution*. Basil Blackwell, Oxford.

Sorge, A. and **Streeck, W.** (1988) Industrial relations and technical change: the case for an extended perspective. In R. Hyman and W. Streeck (eds) *New technology and industrial relations*. Basil Blackwell, Oxford.

Soskice, D. (1990) Wage determination: the changing role of institutions in advanced industrialized countries. *Oxford Review of Economic Policy*, **6**(4): 36–61.

Soskice, D. (1993) Social skills from mass higher education: rethinking the company-based initial training paradigm. *Oxford Review of Economic Policy*, **9**(3): 101–13.

Sprague, A. (1994) Work experience, earnings and participation: evidence from the women and employment survey. *Applied Economics*, **26**: 659–667.

Steedman, H. (1993) The economics of youth training in Germany. *Economic Journal*, **103**: 1279–91.

Steedman, H. and **Hawkins, J.** (1994) Shifting foundations: the impact of NVQs on youth training for the building trades. *National Institute Economic Review*, **3/94**: 93–102.

Steedman, H., Mason, G. and **Wagner, K.** (1991) Intermediate skills in the workplace: deployment, standards and supply in France and Germany. *National Institute Economic Review*, **2/91**: 60–76.

Steedman, H. and **Wagner, K.** (1987) A second look at productivity, machinery and skills in Britain and Germany. *National Institute Economic Review*, November: 84–95.

Stevens, M. (1994) A theoretical model of on-the-job training with imperfect competition. *Oxford Economic Papers*, **46**: 537–62.

Stevens, M. (1994a) An investment model for the supply of training by employers. *Economic Journal*, **104**: 556–70.

Stewart, M. (1983) Racial discrimination and occupational attainment in the UK. *Economic Journal*, **93**: 521–41.

References

Stewart, M. (1995) Union wage differentials in an era of declining unionization. *Oxford Bulletin of Economics and Statistics*, **57**:143–165.

Sundstrom, M. and Stafford, F. (1992) Female labor force participation, fertility and public policy in Sweden. *European Journal of Population*, **8**: 199–215.

Symes, V. (1995) *Unemployment in Europe: problems and policies*. Routledge, London.

Terrell, K. (1992) Female-male earnings differentials and occupational structure. *International Labour Review*, **131**: 387–404.

Thaler, R. (1989) Interindustry wage differentials. *Journal of Economic Perspectives*, **3**(2): 181–93.

Thomas, J. (1994) *Public employment agencies and unemployment spells: exploring the relationship*. mimeo, Department of Applied Economics, University of Cambridge, Cambridge.

Tiebout, C. (1956) A pure theory of local expenditures. *Journal of Political Economy*, **64**: 416–24.

Topel, R. (1993) What have we learned from empirical studies of unemployment and turnover? *American Economic Review*, **83**(2): 110–15.

Turner, L. (1993) Prospects for worker participation in management in the single market. In L. Ulman, B. Eichengreen and W. Dickens (eds) *Labor and an integrated Europe*. Brookings Institution, Washington DC, 45–79.

Ulman, L. (1992) Why should human resource managers pay high wages? *British Journal of Industrial Relations*, **30**(2): 177–212.

Vaughan-Whitehead, D. (1992) The internal market and relocation strategies. In D. Marsden (ed.) *Pay and Employment in the New Europe*. Edward Elgar, Cheltenham.

Veljanovski, C. (ed.) (1991) *Regulators and the market: an assessment of the growth of regulation in the UK*. Institute of Economic Affairs, London.

Verdier, E. (1994) Training and enterprise in France. *International Journal of Manpower*, **15**(5): 38–54.

de Wachter, M. and Somers, Y. (1989) Job creation programmes in an international comparison. In J. Muysken and C. de Neuborg (eds) *Unemployment in Europe*. Macmillan, Basingstoke.

Wadsworth, J. (1991) Unemployment benefits and search effort in the UK labour market. *Economica*, **58**: 17–34.

Waldfogel, J. (1995) The price of motherhood: family status and women's pay in a young British cohort. *Oxford Economic Papers*, **47**: 584–610.

Walsh, J. (1995) Convergence or divergence? corporatism and the dynamics of European wage bargaining. *International Review of Applied Economics*, **9**: 168–91.

Walsh, J., Zappala, G. and Brown, W. (1995) European integration and the pay policies of British multinationals. *Industrial Relations Journal*, **26**: 84–96.

Walsh, K. and Davis, H. (1993) *Competition and Service: the impact of the Local Government Act, 1988*. HMSO, London.

Watson, G. (1993) Working time and holidays in the EC: how the UK compares. *Employment Gazette*, September: 395–403.

Watson, G. (1994) The flexible work-force and patterns of working hours in the UK. *Employment Gazette*, July: 239–48.

Watts, M. and Rich, J. (1993) Occupational sex segregation in Britain, 1979–1989: the persistence of sexual stereotyping. *Cambridge Journal of Economics*, **17**: 159–77.

Way, K. (1984) Labour market operation, recruitment strategies and work-force structures. *International Journal of Social Economics*, **11**: 6–31.

Webster, A. (1993) The skill and higher educational content of UK net exports. *Oxford Bulletin of Economics and Statistics*, **55**: 141–60.

Weiss, A. (1995) Human capital vs. signalling explanations of wages. *Journal of Economic Perspectives*, **9(4)**: 133–54.

Weitzman, M. (1984) *The Share Economy*. Harvard University Press, Harvard, Mass.

Whitfield, K. and **Wilson, R.** (1991) Staying on in full-time education: the educational participation rate of 16 year olds. *Economica*, **58**: 391–404.

Whitley, J. and **Wilson, R.** (1983) The macroeconomic merits of a marginal employment subsidy. *Economic Journal*, **93**: 862–80.

Whitting, G., Moore, J. and **Tilson, B.** (1995) Employment policies and practices towards older workers: an international overview. *Employment Gazette*, April: 147–52.

Williamson, O., Wachter, M. and **Harris, J.** (1975) Understanding the employment relation: the analysis of idiosyncratic exchange. *Bell Journal of Economics*, **6**: 250–80.

Wilson, R. (1994) Sectoral and occupational change: prospects for women's employment. In R. Lindley (ed.) *Labour Market Structures and Prospects for Women*. Equal Opportunities Commission, Manchester, 14–28.

Winkelmann, R. (1994) Apprenticeship and after: does it really matter? Centre for Economic Policy Research Discussion Paper No. 1034.

Wood, S. (1985) Recruitment systems and the recession. *British Journal of Industrial Relations*, **23**: 103–20.

Wright, R. and **Ermisch, J.** (1991) Gender discrimination in the British labour market. *Economic Journal*, **101**: 508–22.

Wyplosz, C. (1994) Demand and structural views of Europe's high unemployment trap. *Swedish Economic Policy Review*, **1**.

Zabalza, A. and **Arrufat, J.** (1985) The extent of wage discrimination in Great Britain. In A. Zabalza and Z. Tzannatos (eds) *Women and Equal Pay: the effects of legislation on female employment and wages in Britain*. Cambridge University Press, Cambridge.

Zabalza, A. and **Tzannatos, Z.** (eds) (1985) *Women and Equal Pay: the effects of legislation on female employment and wages in Britain*. Cambridge University Press, Cambridge.

Zimmermann, K. (1993) Labour responses to taxes and benefits in Germany. In A. Atkinson and G. Mogensen (eds) *Welfare and Work Incentives: a North European perspective*. Clarendon Press, Oxford, 192–240.

Zimmermann, K. (1995) Tackling the European migration problem. *Journal of Economic Perspectives*, **9**: 45–62.

Index